India's Foreign Policy

Paradigmatic Shifts in Current Global Scenario

Edited by

Neeta Bora Sharma
Ketki Tara Kumaiyan
Utkersh Bora

ANAMIKA PUBLISHERS & DISTRIBUTORS (P) LTD.
4697/3, 21A, Ansari Road, Daryaganj, New Delhi 110 002
Phones: 011-2328 1655, 011-43708938
E-mail: anamikapublishers@yahoo.co.in

First Published 2022

ISBN 978-93-91524-63-0

PRINTED IN INDIA

Published by Anamika Publishers & Distributors (P) Ltd., 4697/3, 21A, Ansari Road, Daryaganj, New Delhi 110002. Typeset by Shivani Computers, Delhi 110093 and Printed at Vikas Computer & Printers, Tronica City, Ghaziabad

Contents

List of Contributors

1. **Sunanda Singh Bisht:** Advocate High Court, Nainital (Uttarakhand).

   Shuchi Bisht: Professor, Department of Physics, Kumaun University, Nainital.

2. **R.S. Bhakuni:** Associate Professor, Department of Political Science, Govt. Degree College Dosapani, Nainital.

3. **Seema Verma**: Associate Professor and Head, Department of Political Science, Mahila Mahavidyalaya, Kidwai Nagar, Kanpur.

4. **Samardeep Kaur:** Assistant Professor, Govt. Rajindra College, Bathinda.

5. **Manju Chandra:** Assistant Professor, Department of Political Science, Govt. Degree College Guruabanj, Almora.

6. **Sandhyarani Padhy:** Assistant Professor, Department of Political Science, Panchayat Degree College Phiringia, Kandhamal.

7. **Sumit Rana:** Research Scholar, Department of Political Science, Kumaun University, Nainital.

   Pooja: Assistant Professor, Department of Political Science Government Degree College, Raniket.

8. **Shubham:** Dyal Singh College, karnal, Haryana India.

9. **Dhiraj Gurung:** Research Scholar, Department of Political Science, Kumaun University, Nainital.

10. **B.R. Pant:** Professor Dept of Geography, Principal, MBPG College, Haldwani.

11. **Kamna Jain:** Sr. Assistant Professor, Department of Political Science, SSD PC Girls College Roorkee, Haridwar (Uttarakhand).
12. **Priyanka Vishwakarma**: Research Scholar, Department of Political Science, Kumaun University, Nainital.
13. **Manoj Kumar:** Assistant professor, Govt. Degree College Maldhanchaur, Kumaun University, Nainital.
14. **Sanjay Kumar:** Assistant Professor, Govt. Degree College, Amouri.
15. **Amit Kumar Sharma:** Research Scholar, Department of Political Science, Govt Degree College Kashipur, Kumaun University, Nainital.

    Asha Rana: Professor, Radhey Hari Govt. College, Kashipur, Kumaun University, Nainital.
16. **Geeta Tiwari:** Assistant Professor, Department of Political Science, Lal Bahadur Shastri Govt. Degree College, Halduchaur (Nainital).

    Hem Chandra: Assistant Professor, Department of Political Science, Lal Bahadur Shastri Govt. Degree College, Halduchaur (Nainital).

    Girish Chandra Thuwal: B.A. VI Semester Student, Lal Bahadur Shastri Govt. Degree College, Halduchaur (Nainital).
17. **Nusrat:** Research Scholar, Department of Political Science, Kumaun University, Nainital.
18. **Beena Joshi:** Assistant Professor, Department of Political Science, Mahila Degree College, Haldwani
19. **Neema:** Research Scholar, Department of Political Science, Kumaun University, Nainital.
20. **Avinash Jatav**: Research Scholar, Department of Political Science, Kumaun University, Nainital.

Editorial

In the last two decades, India has witnessed a dramatic improvement in socio-economic indicators, buoyant economic growth of 8 per cent per annum and rapid expansion of its foreign policy engagement around the world. Our outreach has not only encompassed the Indian Ocean Region (IOR), South Asia, and ASEAN but also extended to China, Japan, USA, Australia, and Russia. India's foreign policy in 2020 has increasingly become a major determinant of its development, identity, and outlook.

With the advent of Modi government, this complex web of foreign policy is regularly being reviewed to suit the changing dynamics of international system. China's continued expansionism and rise in India's neighborhood, Pakistan's support to jihadi organizations and growing disdain towards India, Japan and South Korea's nuclear caper with North Korea are few among new emerging problems.

What are India's main foreign policy challenges in South Asia? How can they be addressed? Is India's foreign policy isolated from domestic politics and economy of India? How can India balance its political interests, rise as an economic power and maintain a military capable of challenging its neighbors?Foreign policy is one of the most fascinating domains, but at the same time, every country's foreign policy is heavily dependent on domestic politics. This book attempts to analyse India's foreign policy challenges in the 21st Century; why these challenges are there and what

India needs to do in order to tackle these challenges.

The first chapter begins with the research paper by Sunanda Singh Bisht and Shuchi Bisht titled, "The Paradigm Shifts in the Indian Foreign Policy". The paper mainly spots a highlight that how there has been a paradigmatic shift in the Indian Foreign Policy. The paper talks about India as changing military and strategic capabilities and how it shall provide a degree of reassurance against global turbulence and competitive geopolitics.

The edition continues with the second paper by R.S. Bhakuni titled, "Regional Cooperation in South Asian Expectations and Realities". Here the researcher talks about how the South Asian region has come forward for regional integration in respect to security concern, economic cooperation and regional cooperation.

The third paper titled, "2020 As a Challenging Year For Indian Foreign Policy" by SeemaVerma, beautifully highlights that the Indian foreign policy is fundamentally based on the principles of co-existence, friendship and cooperation among all the nation states, how challenging it was for India to maintain her foreign policy during the time of this global pandemic.

The next paper titled, " India and China in South Asia: Challenges and Prospects" by Samardeep Kaur talks about the role of India and China in the South Asian region as both the nations are the dominating nations over the region. The paper focuses on India's foreign policy in the South Asian Region in the light of facing new security and economic challenges.

The fifth paper named, "Indo-US Relations: India's Ever-Changing Foreign Policy", by Manju Chandra talks about the Indo-US relations at present, how it developed through decades as there has been a lot of changes in India's foreign policy according to circumstances.

The next topic titled, "Indo-US Relation, A Zigzag Expedition" by Sandhyarani Padhy showcases how the relation of India and US has taken a zigzag expedition, starting during the Cold War period, post cold war period and recent developments.

The seventh topic titled "Continuity and Change in the Alignment Pattern of Indian Foreign Policy: With Special Reference to Manmohan Singh and Narendra Modi" by SumitRana and Pooja, gives a comparative study and an attempt to examine the changes and continuity in the alignment pattern of India's Foreign Policy under Manmohan Singh and Narendra Modi government. The paper talks about India's relations with other countries in the changing global environment and time demands.

The next paper entitled "Coronary Danger Variables in South West Asia" by Shubham gives an insight about the Coronary danger variables in South West Asia. The paper also talks about the dangers of coronary danger factors, coronary vein ailment (computer aided design) and type 2 diabetes that is similar through South Asia and West Asia that has been a main concern in the Asian continent.

In Chapter 9 B. R. Pant, in his research paper, has studied the geo-political scenario of Uttarakhand in the context of employment of migrants from Uttarakhand on their return to the state due to the lockdown after Covid 19. And what steps have been taken by the government for the migrants who have returned to Uttarakhand, they have been told in the research paper.

In the next chapter, Kamna Jain, "India-China Relations: 1947 to the Present", describes the main issues of conflict in international politics between the two emerging powers in a very precise manner and the current strategy of Prime Minister Modi and Xi Jinping. Explained and also suggested to control China by diplomacy.

Priyanka Vishwakarma has written her research paper with the title 'India-Nepal crisis in the context of current circumstances'. India-Nepal has close relations for centuries - Presented: In the research paper after India's independence, the background of tension between India-Nepal has been analyzed, the real reasons behind it and future solutions, Nepal between China and India. Nepal has also emerged as a buffer state, whose importance is clearly visible on the relations between China and India, after the creation of the constitution in 2015, the tension between the two countries is most visible over the Madheshi officials and the map dispute that arose in 2019 has been described in the present research.

On 'India and SAARC' Manoj Kumar has done a historical and analytical study of aspects related to India and SAARC, in which the origin of SAARC, its objectives, its principles, its structure and financial management have been described. In the research paper, cooperation with other institutions, SAARC funds, trade and marketing cooperation (such as SAPTA and SAFTA) which burns the impact of SAARC and SAARC countries have also been told.

In the next chapter, Sanjay Kumar has written a research paper titled 'Corona Nationalism: The Scenario of India and the Global Order' in view of the current scenario of Corona. Rise up, 'Giving priority to world nationalism, mankind can be freed from Corona. What will be the nature of the world after Corona? What will change in international politics? The fears and possibilities after the corona have been presented in the research paper.

Amit Kumar Sharma and Asha Rana have written a research paper on 'Balance of Power and India' in the current global politics. In the research paper, due to the changes in the balance of power and international politics,

India's central role as a global economic, political and strategic power in the current conditions of world politics, as well as the impact of current conditions on India has been discussed. It also describes the state of balance of power in global politics since the dissolution of the Soviet Union, Russia (in 1991), the relationship between India and the world community, and India's central role in the world.

The research paper 'Role of SAARC as a Regional Organization: An Interpretation' Gita Tiwari, Hem Chandra, Girish Chandra Bhuwal has done an analytical study of the status of SAARC as a regional organization till the present time. The origin of SAARC has been described historically. The research specifically mentioned the achievements of SAARC, in which South Asian Development Fund - 1996, SAARC Development Fund 2010, South Asian Satellite, SAARC COVID-19 Contingency Fund March 2020 are the main ones.

Nusrat has written a research paper titled 'Challenges before India-Russia relations'. In the research paper, India-Russia relations after the dissolution of Soviet Union Russia, the initial challenges of India-Russia relations, treaty of cooperation between the two, India-Russia relations (2007-2010) have been described where on 25-26 January 2007 both The Seventh Summit was held in the countries in which agreements related to nuclear reactors in both countries, agreements related to fifth generation warships took the friendship of both the countries to a new level.

In the next chapter, Bina Joshi's research paper 'India-China Relations Current Perspectives' is based on behavioral political analysis. The research paper has told the challenging history of India-China relations. In which China's negative outlook on China demanding permanent membership in UNSC, India's advice to quit lobbying Japan, China's support to Pakistan on terrorism, India's indirect relationship with Taiwan, China's Maritime Silk Route Project (MSR) etc. The solution to normalization of India-China relations can be found only by resolving the border dispute.

Neema has written the next chapter on 'India-Pakistan relations'. India-Pakistan relations have always been tense due to historical and political issues, mainly due to Kashmir issue, Indus river water dispute, Siachen dispute, Sir Creek dispute and issue of terrorism. The research describes the status of relations between the two countries after the abrogation of Article 370 and 35A and the Uri terror attack. Finally, the ups and downs of relations between the two countries have been told in the context of the Heart of Asia conference, Pathankot terror attack, Pakistan Economic Corridor, VidhiKulbhushanJadhav case political leadership.

Avinash Jatav has written a research paper on 'India and Soft Power in Global Politics'. Soft power is a supplement rather than a substitute for hard power. Post-cold war globalization has increased the importance and utility of soft power due to increase in interdependence among countries. In the present research, the soft power of India has been studied on the basis of historical and contemporary dimensions. In which the philosophical concepts of India, the universality of Hinduism, Indian civilization, Indian culture, Bodh Dharma, classical music and dance, yoga and Ayurveda are embedded in it.

The last chapter by Dhiraj Gurung titled "India's Vaccine Diplomacy" talks about how India played a significant role during the global pandemic. Corona virus has claimed thousands lives thereby creating an atmosphere of threat all over the world. India was successful in making the vaccine or the antidote to fight against the coronavirus. Not only India made the vaccine but distributed it all over the world taking an initiative named 'Vaccine Maitri'. India supplied vaccines to more than 95 countries as well as UN Peacekeepers .The paper talks about the dynamics of India's vaccine diplomacy.

1

The Paradigm Shifts in the Indian Foreign Policy

Sunanda Singh Bisht and Prof. Shuchi Bisht

ABSTRACT

Uncertainty has been looming over the world in almost all sectors of our being, be it economical, political, social or even in the area of international relations. India's foreign policy establishment therefore, is looking to progress along its chosen path bearing in mind the profound and disruptive changes in the international order.

The era of passivity and being averse to risk has receded and India now sees itself as a stabilizing power hoping to build momentum for a multipolar world. This paper aims to discuss India's changing military and strategic capabilities and how it shall provide a degree of reassurance against global turbulence and competitive geopolitics.

Keywords: Foreign Policy, Multi-alignment, Paradigm Shift, Global Powers

INTRODUCTION

India celebrated 74th Independence Day this year, and is looking forward to the important milestone of the 75th year of Independence. We have witnessed many changes in this journey. We are a nation which traversed from consolidating its provinces, rebuilding infrastructure, and combating poverty to stationing its naval ships in some world's most strategically important sea routes. With the changing global economic scenario, and India's ever expanding policies, our economic dominance in near future is not a big surprise. This process of re-establishing India, as a world power is not only a result of progressive domestic policies but also our realigned foreign policy. We have moved on from a defensive perspective to practising an offensive defence. We are no longer a nation following non alignment but a nation practicing multi alignment.

In most democracies, foreign policy tends to stay the course despite partisan changes in leadership. In India's case, such continuities are visible across time and through different governments. For instance, India's attempt to find a permanent seat at the UN Security Council since the early 1990s, its leadership of the developing world in trade negotiations at the WTO, and its refusal to join the Non-proliferation Treaty and the Comprehensive Test Ban Treaty have all remained consistent foreign policy positions despite changes in regime.

THE CHANGING PARADIGM

At the 2019 Raisina Dialogue in January, the then Foreign Secretary, Shri Vijay Gokhale, declared, "India has moved on from its non-aligned past. India is today an aligned state—but based on issues." He specifically emphasized on the role New Delhi must play in the G-20 and the Indo-Pacific, to shape the course of our policies in future which was a hint towards the changing priorities of the Indian foreign policy establishment.

In fact much earlier, in 2015, as then Foreign Secretary Mr. S. Jaishankar delivered the Fullerton lecture at the International Institute for Strategic Studies, he had suggested that today's India "aspire[s] to be a leading power, rather than just a balancing power."

As expected, the government has gradually but decisively been shifting the discourse on Indian foreign policy without many in the country's strategic community even recognizing it. The government now is actively seeking to transform India from being merely an important player in the global order into one that is willing—and able—to define the priorities of the international system. India, from perpetually being a cautious power, is ready to take on a larger global role by being more nimble than ever in playing the great-power game.

The Modi government is redefining strategic autonomy as an objective that is attainable through strengthened partnerships rather than the avoidance of partnerships. By doing so, it is underlining that in today's complex global scene, strategic autonomy should not necessarily be a twin of non-alignment.

INDIA AND GLOBAL POWERS

INDIA AND THE US

Ever since India's independence, ties with the United States have weathered Cold War–era distrust and estrangement over India's nuclear programme. Relations have warmed in recent years but have also borne few bones of contentions.

The Trump administration determined that New Delhi had not provided assurance of providing "equitable and reasonable access" to US markets and terminated India's designation as a beneficiary developing nation under the key Generalized System of Preferences trade programme. India responded by imposing retaliatory tariffs on 28 US products. This came a year after announcing tariffs to counter the US increase in steel and aluminium tariffs and withdrawal of duty-free benefits to Indian exporters.

Nonetheless, Modi visited the United States in September, joining Trump in a joint rally organized by American-Indian groups. The goal was to reduce trade tensions with India's leading export partner. Modi conveyed to Washington that New Delhi is ready to engage with the United States substantively in a spirit of give and take. The visit managed to reverse the relationship's decline. Since then, Trump's rhetoric towards India has softened considerably.

In February 2020, Trump made his First Visit to India and addressed a rally in Ahmedabad with an audience of more than one hundred thousand people. The two leaders announced plans to work together. India agrees to purchase $3 billion in U.S. military equipment, and U.S.-based Oil Company ExxonMobil announces a deal with state-owned Indian Oil Corporation. The officials however did not reach an agreement, with divisions remaining over agricultural products, tariffs, and other trade related issues.

Other major agreements with the US include a foundational military agreement that allows for the sharing of encrypted communications and equipment (COMCASA- Communications Compatibility and Security Agreement) and a change in U.S. export control laws to include India in a privileged category of NATO and non-NATO U.S. allies. A new '2+2' foreign and defence ministers dialogue is also set up. These intense engagements have helped achieve robust support from the US against terrorism which was evident after the Pulwama attack, leading to the designation of Jaish-e-Mohammad Chief Masood Azhar as a global terrorist under UN Security Council Resolution 1967 and also in placing Pakistan on the grey-list of the Financial Action Task Force.

The US under its Pivot to Asia policy views India as an ideal balancer to check the aggressive rise of China. Therefore, the US has formulated the concept of Indo-Pacific to counter China in the South China Sea and the Indian Ocean. The US has designated India as an integral part of the Indo-pacific narrative by the conception of Quad.

In international politics, however, there are no permanent friends and no permanent enemies, only permanent interests. In such a scenario, India must continue to pursue its foreign policy of strategic hedging.

INDIA AND CHINA

Chinese President Xi Jinping visited India for a Second informal Summit with the two leaders engaging in more than five hours of one-on-one talks over two days. The Wuhan Summit in 2018 did reduce tensions after the high-decibel Doklam crisis, steering the China-India relationship from an overtly conflictual stance. The Mamallapuram Summit in October 2019 was another attempt to divert the Sino-Indian conversation away from the immediate differences over Kashmir and Pakistan.

The other side of the coin is that Beijing stood up for Pakistan, otherwise largely isolated, on the issue of Kashmir at the UN Security Council.

In the month of May 2020, Indian and Chinese troops scuffled at Pangong Tso in Ladakh. After the first round of talks on 6th June, 2020, clashes occurred in Galwan Valley (Ladakh) that claimed 20 Indian soldiers' lives and an unknown number of casualties on the Chinese side.

In response, India has moved in additional divisions, tanks and artillery across the LAC to match Chinese deployments. With the push on Atma Nirbhar Bharat and citing the "emergent nature of threats" from mobile applications, including popular ones of Chinese origin government has banned Chinese apps. Further, India's trade deficit with China fell to $48.66 billion in 2019-20 on account of the decline in imports. The trade deficit stood at $53.56 billion in 2018-19 and $63 billion in 2017-18.

For India, the first priority has to be to restore the status quo ante at the border as it existed in April. This will require both a display of military strength at the border by standing up to Chinese aggression, and diplomatic work by making it clear to China that its intervention will lead to heavy costs across all spheres of the relationship.

Talk benefits both sides while confrontation serves neither. Looking into the future of India-China relations, we have to find answers for some important questions. What kind of relationship should we build together in the interests of both countries as well as of the world? Will conflict and confrontation be unavoidable between the two? Can they "decouple" from each other? This is not only a historic challenge to both our countries but also our responsibility to future generations. To return to the tactical issue, besides the boundary conflict, India and China have a lot of points of friction which are sensitive and complicated. We need to find a fair, reasonable and mutually acceptable solution through equal consultation and peaceful negotiation. We need to discuss the issues, but more importantly, we need to understand the whole picture, which is that both countries need a peaceful and stable neighbour policy.

INDIA AND RUSSIA

Modi became the first Indian Prime Minister to visit the Russian Far East Region in September to give "a new direction, new energy and new speed" to relations between the two countries. His presence at the Eastern Economic

Forum was useful at various levels. With the centre of gravity of global economics shifting to Asia, Russia's President Vladimir Putin focuses on the Far East, keen on developing it with the help of Asian powers. Indian investors can also explore investment opportunities in that region and perhaps diversify the one-dimensional nature of Indo-Russian ties, which continue to be driven by defence. Russia has been a long-time friend of India; it not only provided India arms to maintain a formidable military profile but also gave invaluable diplomatic support on a variety of regional issues. Given strategic convergence between Russia and China, it is important that India draw up strategies that protect its national interests, which may include the deepening ties with Russia and leveraging multilateral institutions.

INDIA AND EU

India-EU relations date to the early 1960s, with India being amongst the first countries to establish diplomatic relations with the European Economic Community. The India-European Union 14th Summit was held in New Delhi focused on closer cooperation on counter-terrorism actions; India is one among 10 select countries with whom EU has strategic partnership, launched in 2004. EU constitutes India's largest trading partner, accounting for more than 100 billion Euros, in a balanced trade relationship. India and EU relations have a strong potential to prosper into a strong partnership. Now, India- European Union (EU) plan to hold virtual summit and talk on restarting Free Trade Agreement (FTA) and prepare a roadmap for cooperation, an agreement on research sharing for civil nuclear cooperation and launch a maritime security dialogue as well as negotiations between Europol and the CBI.

INDIA AND JAPAN

The people of India and Japan have engaged in cultural exchanges, primarily as a result of Buddhism, which spread indirectly from India to Japan, via China and Korea. Regular high-level visits and engagements between India-Japan have taken place at G-20 Summit held in Osaka, G-7 Summit in Biarritz (August 2019), and Eastern Economic Forum in Vladivostok (5 September 2019). The India-Japan Comprehensive Economic Partnership Agreement (CEPA), investment of $90 billion Delhi-Mumbai Industrial Corridor, Japanese FDI into India, contribution in operation of Railway Sector Mumbai-Ahmadabad High-Speed Railway (MAHSR), The India-Japan 2+2 dialogues are other examples of this rising relation. Japan wants India in RCEP to more effectively push back against China and is utilizing the 2+2 dialogue to convince India to join RCEP.

INDIA AND OTHER PIVOTAL AREAS

AFRICA

In the last few decades, India is increasingly investing in its relationship with Africa. After Prime Minister Modi's declaration that his government will accord 'top priority' status to Africa in the country's foreign and economic policy, India's long-standing ties with the continent have acquired vibrancy and dynamism, marked by an unprecedented intensification of political engagement. Today, Africa is a continent of limitless possibility, with increasing trade, investments, and a surge in innovation. India's re-engagement with Africa is taking place in a fast-changing and dynamic environment.

WEST ASIA

India maintained a 'non-aligned' presence in West Asia, balancing between the three poles of power—i.e. Israel, Iran and Saudi Arabia. Saudi Arabia hosts more than 2.7 million Indian citizens; the sheer size of this Diaspora makes it a massive responsibility for Indian diplomacy. We have become an economic destination for Saudi petro-dollars, Saudi Oil Co. (ADNOC), has also committed to a new US $50-billion refinery on India's western coast scheduled to start operations by 2025 and designed to be capable of refining upto 1.2 million barrels of oil per day.

India, for a long time, had significantly profited from its close ties with Israel and little was done to acknowledge it. However, after the 2017 visit by Prime Minister Narendra Modi, there is a significant breakthrough in the relationship, enhancing the scope of the ties. Subsequently, India has made significant steps in forging a precarious, yet necessary balance in the Middle East.

CENTRAL ASIA

India has a long history of cultural and commercial relations with Central Asia (CA), facilitated by their geographical proximity and the Silk Route. India's Central Asia Policy received a significant boost in 2018, when New Delhi's diplomatic efforts paid dividends in the form of admission into the Ashgabat Agreement, allowing India to use the existing land connectivity networks to facilitate trade and commercial interaction with both CA and Eurasia, by exploiting the natural resources of the region and exporting products to CA.

INDIA AND THE EAST

Analyst Mishra dubbed "Act East" policy as Modi's biggest foreign policy. "India seems to have regained the opportunity to engage with the region more comprehensively through its Indo-Pacific policy," Mishra said. Analysts say the Act East policy, unlike other diplomatic efforts, gives an equal importance to economic relations and security interests. As a result, India has been more vocal about free maritime navigation and a rules-based order for maritime security, especially in the South China Sea, and has also signed a deal with Indonesia to build the Sabang Port, located in the strategically important Malacca strait.

Success of Act East policy will also define the difference we are able to make to the life and commerce of our people in the north-east because there the connectivity becomes extremely important. We are already doing that but more needs to be done in collaborating with countries in South China Sea. India must continue to focus on further strengthening collaboration with ASEAN nations and others.

India's bureaucratic shift is an important move to articulate its regional policy more cogently, coherently and with a renewed sense of purpose. Partners must work to promote economic revival, seek strategic cooperation to fight terrorism, and enhance maritime security and defence cooperation. Soft power such as Buddhism, tourism, people-to-people contacts, and cultural ties with the region must continue to be harnessed.

1. Beyond, but linked to ASEAN, India must further strengthen strategic and economic ties with the U.S., Japan, Korea, Australia, and also with China.
2. Important sectors like technology transfer, civilian nuclear cooperation, defence and innovation should be given priority
3. Continuous engagement with China too is

necessary to expand cooperation, particularly on the economic front.

INDIA AND PAKISTAN

Pakistan's revanchism and unremitting hostility towards India has reached new heights under the (nominal) leadership of Prime Minister Imran Khan. This will persist regardless of what India does. The present strategy of isolating Pakistan as the principal source of state-sponsored Islamist terror must be maintained, despite Pak efforts to build international pressure against India through false narratives of Muslim persecution. So-called "progressive" elites in the Christian West will readily buy into this propaganda, as will the Islamic countries and the OIC. We will need to create the capacity for sustaining this uncompromising approach towards Pakistan based and sponsored terrorist threats to India's security.

INDIA AND NEPAL

Nepal and India enjoy excellent bilateral ties. Founded on the age-old connection of history, culture, tradition and religion, these relations are close, comprehensive and multidimensional. India should negotiate diplomatically to resolve the boundary dispute with Nepal. In this case Bangladesh-India should serve as a model for this. India should engage more proactively with Nepal in terms of people to people engagement, bureaucratic engagement as well as political interactions.

INDIA AND AFGHANISTAN

India and Afghanistan have always shared warm ties; the Modi and Ashraf Ghani era has been no different. India's development assistance and larges cale infrastructure projects are welcomed in Afghanistan, with New

Delhiconstructing the Parliament building in Kabul and the Afghan-India Friendship Dam in Heart. The signing of the Trilateral Trade and Transit Corridor Agreement between Iran, Afghanistan and India in May 2016 for the development of the Chabahar Port was a major step in expanding the possibilities of trade between New Delhi and Kabul.

INDIA AND BANGLADESH

India's relations with Bangladesh have focused on enhancing trade, and improving connectivity and transit facilities to India's northeastern states.

During Modi's June 2015 visit to Dhaka, India and Bangladesh finally agreed on the implementation of the Land Boundary Agreement, resolving the 41-year old border issue between the two countries. Modi and Bangladesh Prime Minister Sheikh Hasina also inaugurated the 'India-Bangladesh Friendship Pipeline Project'.

INDIA AND BHUTAN

It was Bhutan where Modi made his first state visit as Prime Minister, stating that it was a "natural choice," because of the "unique and special relationship between the two countries". The Prime Minister inaugurated India's assistance projects in the country, including the building of the Supreme Court and laying the foundation stone for the 600-MW Kholongchu hydroelectric project, a joint venture between two countries.

INDIA AND MALDIVES

India's relationship with Maldives severed after President Abdulla Yameen came to power in 2013. Now the new government of Mohamed Ibrahim Solih, has once again led to the warming of ties. During Solih's visit to New Delhi,

India pledged financial assistance of US $1.4 billion for the debt ridden country, and has recently decided to fund the implementation of the Greater Malé Connectivity Project (GMCB) through a $ 100 million grant and a $ 400 million line of credit.

INDIA AND SRI LANKA

The Modi government has moved with speed and intensity to repair India's ties with one of its most important strategic partners. New Delhi and Colombo have intensified their political engagement with a number of mutual visits and projects.

INDIA, MULTILATERAL RELATIONS AND OTHER ORGANIZATIONS

India has been an active participant in mechanisms like the Indian Ocean Rim Association (IORA), the East Asia Summit, Association of Southeast Asian Nations (ASEAN) Defence Ministers Meeting Plus, ASEAN Regional Forum, the Bay of Bengal Initiative for Multi-Sectoral Technical and Economic Cooperation (BIMSTEC), and Mekong Ganga Economic Corridor.

CONCLUSION

A nation that has the aspiration to become a leading power someday cannot continue with unsettled borders, an unintegrated region and under-exploited opportunities. Above all, it cannot be dogmatic in approaching a visibly changing world order. India is friends with everybody but does not ally to any power. New Delhi focuses more on formulating partnerships rather than circumventing them. It works towards maintaining a balance in both the western and the eastern world without leaning majorly to any of these. Critics continue to be sceptical about even the most substantive changes, while the government continued to redefine India's foreign policy priorities, both in substance and style.

REFERENCES

1. Debak Das and Shubha Kamala Prasad, Et Al. "Modi 2.0's Foreign Policy: More Continuity Than Change." *South Asian Voices,* 25 July 2019, Southasianvoices.Org/Modi-2-0-Foreign-Policy-More-Continuity-Than-Changee.
2. 'India Is No Longer 'Non-Aligned', Says Foreign Secretary Vijay Gokhale', January, 2019 https://theprint.in/diplomacy/india-is-no-longer-non-aligned-says-foreign-secretary.
3. IISS Fullerton Lecture by Dr. S. Jaishankar, Foreign Secretary in Singapore, July 20, 2015
4. Harsh, V. Pant and Kabir Taneja, 'Looking Back, Looking Ahead: Foreign Policy In Transition Under Modi', *Observer Research Foundation (ORF).*
5. Harsh, V. Pant, 'Shifting Terrain for India's Foreign Policy', *Observer Research Foundation (ORF)*
6. Amb. Dennis Kux, 'Indo-US Relations: Past, Present and Future': Institute of Peace and Conflict Studies.
7. 'India-China Relations: Looking Forward' august 14, 2020 https://frontline.thehindu.com/cover-story/looking-forward/article32181699.ece
8. The Moscow Reset, https://www.hindustantimes.com/editorials/the-moscow-reset/story-iepz7utux4yblj4kvnj8ti.html
9. Harsh, Pant, Raj Kumar Sharma , *Taking a Far East' turn to deepen a friendship.*
10. https://www.thehindu.com/opinion/op-ed/taking-a-far-east-turn-to-deepen-a-friendship/article29224805.ece
11. No Sign of Eu-india Fta Talks Resuming, *New High-level Trade Dialogue Established* Https://Thewire.in/Diplomacy/India-eu-summit-trade-talks
12. Vikas Dhoot,"An Abe-Modi Plan for Africa," *The Hindu*, 24 May 2017, https://www.thehindu.com/news/national/abe-modi-plan-unveiled/article18572502.ece.

13. Joint Communication: Elements of an EU Strategy on India," *European External Action Service*, 20 November 2018, https://eeas.europa.eu/delegations/india/54057/joint-communication-elements-eu-strategyindia_en
14. "Remarks by External Affairs Minister at the Africa Day Celebrationsat Vibrant Gujarat 2019," Ministry of External Aûairs, Government of India,19 January2019,https://www.mea.gov.in/Speeches-Statements.htm?dtl/30924/Remarks_by_ External_Affairs_Minister_at_the_Africa_Day_Celebrations_at_Vibrant_Guj
15. Elizabeth Roche, "What Mohammed Bin Salman's Visit has Done to Boost Saudi-India Ties," *Livemint*, 11 July 2019, https://www.livemint.com/news/india/what-mbs-s-visit-has-done-to-boost-saudi-indiaties-1550788567619.html.
16. Alexander Cooley, "The New Great Game in Central Asia: Geopolitics in A Post-Western World," *Foreign Affairs*, 2012, https://www.foreignafairs.com/ articles/central-asia/2012-08-07/new-great-game-central-asia.how pm Modi changed the face of Indian foreign policy
17. India's act east policy is slowly becoming act indo-pacific policy under modi governmentPRABIR DEhttps://theprint.in/pageturner/excerpt/india-act-east-policy-is-becoming-act-indo-pacific/389502*Ashok Sajjanhar*India's Act East Policy so far and beyond *https://www.gatewayhouse.in/indias-act-east-policy-far-beyond/*
18. https://www.delhipolicygroup.org/publication/policy-briefs/indias-foreign-policy-agenda-2020.html
19. https://www.thehindu.com/news/national/india-has-never-been-part-of-an-alliance-and-will-never-be-jaishankar/article32142128.ece
20. nishka agrawal'A Shift From The Existing: Indian Foreign Policy Under Pm Modi 19th August 2020Https://Thekootneeti.In/2020/08/19/A-Shift-From-The-Existing-Indian-Foreign-Policy-Under-Pm-Modi.

2

Regional Cooperation in South Asia: Expectations & Realities

R.S. Bhakuni

ABSTRACT

The second half of the 20th century has integrated the world as never before. Despite numerous conflicts and cleavages, flames of war burning in several parts of the world at any given time, there is more cooperation among nations today than any time in the past. With incidents like Cold War, ideologically divided world at horizontal level, economically divided world at vertical level, super-powers trying to woo the poor countries to their respective sides have compelled the nations of the world to interact with the outside world in a cluster. This approach became popular in the form of regional cooperation in the international politics. The states of the South Asian region also tried to be on a common forum known as SAARC to show the world their regional collective efforts. This article is an attempt to analyze this endeavour of this regional entity to work for regional cooperation.

Keywords: India, South Asia, Regional Cooperation, SAARC, SAFTA

INTRODUCTION

One of the fundamental problems of international politics

has been the creation of conditions under which stable, cordial and peaceful relations among the nations could be made possible. The aggravating complex problems of modern states, such as social, economic, technical and political and defence have led these nations and their governments to adopt multi-lateral approach, which has resulted in the growth of various limited and compact regional associations among the nations. This growth of the regional association is so prompt that in the recent years the tendency is looking towards "several worlds, instead of a single world."[1] However, this is not a new aptitude in the field of international politics and it has been in the field of international politics in existence since long time and is known as 'Regionalism'. There may be a lot of differences among the scholars and theoreticians, about the meaning, purpose and the validity of the concept but the fact is that the concept of regionalism is as old as the history of international politics. The South Asian region of the globe couldn't remain untouched by this fever of regional cooperation.

The genesis of regional approach in South Asia is as controversial as the geographical stature of the region. In the foregoing article is an analysis of the efforts for regional cooperation in South Asia and its successes and challenges. Geographically, the South Asian region is confined on the North of the Pamir Knot and the great chain of mountains namely the Himalayas, Karakorum and Hindukush and in the South by the Indian Ocean. But there had been no unanimity about the nation states to be included in this regional entity. It was only during the late 1960s or early 70s or more precisely only during the late emergence of Bangladesh in 1971, there came forth the view that in general South Asia as a region includes Seven nation states, namely; Bangladesh, Bhutan, India, Maldives, Nepal,

Pakistan and Sri Lanka.

It is generally accepted that the call for having a regional approach in South Asia was initiated in 1980. However, history reveals that various leaders of the region in general, and the Indian leaders in particular were quite anxious to develop an identical approach for the solution of common problem and for the realization of mutually shared goals in the reigon.[2] And this desire for an identical approach was inspired by the regional associations like, the formation of EU in Europe, ASEAN in South East Asia, OAS in African continent, OPEC in the Middle East and many more small and large regional organizations across the world. After so many debates, discussions, meetings and dialogues, the leaders of South Asian region came to a point of consensus and on 8th December, 1985, the South Asian Association for Regional Cooperation (SAARC), came into existence with its headquarter in Kathmandu (Nepal).[3]

OBJECTIVES, AIMS AND HIGH HOPES WITH SAARC

In a region, where two wars have already been completed between two major actors of the South Asian region and a new country was formed as a result of these wars, the formation of SAARC welcomed not only by the stakeholder states but also by the nations of the whole world. The institutionalization of SAARC was nothing but an example of the thrust of the leaders of the region for a regional approach in this sub-continent to resolve the regional problems collectively. Since its inception in 1985, SAARC has now achieved a greater degree of stability and maturity with a permanent secretariat and a well-defined institutional arrangement.

The basic principles for cooperation within the framework of the SAARC was supposed to be based on respect for the principles of sovereign equality, territorial integrity, political independence, non-interference in the internal affairs of other states and mutual benefit; based on cooperation that will not be a substitute for bilateral and multilateral cooperation but will complement them; and such cooperation will not be inconsistent with bilateral and multilateral obligations.

Beginning with seven South Asian nations i.e., Bangladesh, Bhutan, India, Maldives, Nepal, Pakistan & Sri Lanka, the eighth member state was included Afghanistan. Moreover, there are currently nine observer states to SAARC, namely: Australia, China, The European Union, Iran, Japan, The Republic of Korea, Mauritius, Myanmar & the USA.

The basic areas of cooperation were identified as Human Resource Development and Tourism; Agriculture and Rural Development; Environment; Natural Disaster and Bio-technology; Economy, Common Trade and Finance; Social Affairs; Information & Poverty Alleviation; Energy & Transport; Science and Technology; Education; Security & Culture etc.[4]

Apart from all this, the basic objective of SAARC was defined as, to promote the welfare of the people of South Asia and to improve their quality of life; to accelerate economic growth, social progress and cultural development in the region and to provide all individuals the opportunity to live in dignity and to realise their full potentials; to promote and strengthen collective self-reliance among the countries of South Asia; to contribute to mutual trust, understanding and appreciation of one another's problems; to promote active collaboration and mutual assistance in the economic, social, cultural, technical and scientific fields' to strengthen cooperation with other developing countries; to strengthen cooperation among themselves in international forums on matters of common interests; and to cooperate with international and regional organizations with similar aims and purposes.

SUCCESSES OF REGIONAL COOPERATION IN SOUTH ASIA

No doubt, the formation of SAARC in 1985 and then sustaining along with a firm institutional framework till now has been one of the classical examples of regional cooperation among South Asian countries. One of the greatest achievements of SAARC is that, for the first time, nations of the sub-continent, who distrust each other the most; which are politically the most explosive and are at different levels of development. The counter reacting forces were prominently controlling the situation, but it was storm desire for collective benefits and acute feeling of coming together that prevailed and SAARC was not only born continue to survive against all odds. And today, SAARC is one of the major regional organizations operating successfully.

SAARC has achieved significant success in economic field and has ventured into vital cooperation in the core sectors of Trade, Commerce, Finance and Money. The most important agreement, SAFTA, has led to abolition of double taxation, free movement of certain commodities across the border and preferential treatment to regional trade than trade outside the region. Most of the member countries have accorded 'Most-favoured Nation' status to each other under the SAFTA. Not to mention Pakistan has not done so in case of India. This will be another side of regional cooperation in South Asia and will be analyzed in the latter part of the article. Despite all ifs and buts, SAFTA can be treated as a positive step to free the regional trade totally and bring about an Economic Union in future. There is extensive collaboration between the stock exchanges and between Chambers of Commerce and Industries.

SAARC has gained a lot of momentum in the fields of Education, Sports, Culture and Media. South Asian University has become fully functional and there are scholarships and fellowships for research in various fields. Cultural exchanges are taking place through film festivals, literary seminars, cultural festivals, media programmes and food festivals etc. Organized tourism of the region is getting boost through VISA exemptions and group tours. Special attention is given to the involvement of youth through Youth Volunteers Programmes, SAARC Youth Award for constructive contribution and Sports Competitions.

In the field of Science and Technology, meaningful and constructive exchanges have taken place in the areas which are relevant to South Asian economy. These include – Solar energy, Bio-fertilizers, Low-cost housing, Prawn Hatcheries, Electronics and Molecular Biology, Bio-Mass Gasification, Recycling of Waste Water and Development of Technologies for Pollution Control, Post Harvest and Food Technology, Renewable Energy Resources, Photovoltaic, Pesticides, Instrumentation, Maintenance and Calibration, Cultivation and Processing of Medicine and Aromatic Plants, Weather Forecasting, Radar Meteorology, Telecommunication and so on.

Apart from all these, SAARC has also ventured into some controversial areas by signing a Convention on Terrorism, Convention on Drug Trafficking and Drug Abuse. These are very serious issues disturbing the sub-continent. SAARC forum created a positive atmosphere to conclude these important treaties.

Health and Population studies have also benefitted through SAARC. Intensive research and exchanges have taken place regarding children, population welfare and policy, maternal and child health, primary health care, disabled and handicapped persons, control and eradication of major diseases in the region such as malaria, leprosy, tuberculosis, diarrhea diseases, rabies, AIDS and iodine deficiency disorder. Special attention is being given to Women and Girl Child and problems of feticide.

However, the areas of Agriculture and Rural Development have received the maximum attention in terms of regional cooperation in South Asia. As it is a well-known fact that these two areas are the backbone of all the South Asian countries, therefore, seminars and training courses covering practically all aspects of rural development including regional planning, poverty focused development, rural energy, design of agricultural projects, local level planning, inter-country comparisons, appropriate technology, disaster management, rural child development, rural sociology, peoples participation, rural water supply, employment generation, social forestry rural communication and development of agriculture markets have been conducted so far. Most important SAARC has created data base that will be useful to all the members.

The regional cooperation in South Asia has also tried to go alongwith such other organizations and bodies at the international level. SAARC has tried to spread wings in Trans South Asian regions also. It has made collaborations with UNCTAD, UNICEF, UNDP, APT, UNDPC, ITU, ESCAP and countries like Japan, Germany. Most of the developed countries of the world have been given the observer's status. This has enabled SAARC to negotiate jointly for sub-continent specific schemes and projects.

CHALLENGES OF REGIONAL COOPERATION IN SOUTH ASIAN REGION

The above discussion of the positive aspects of regional cooperation in South Asia looks like everything is OK in this sub-continent. But one of the most important fact everyone knows that the South Asian region is one of the most untrusting regions of the world. This is the region where two most important neighbouring countries have not only fought two wars but are almost at war like situation every day. And the small countries of the region always feel like not being treated at equal footings. As a result, despite its existence in 1980s, SAARC as a tool of regional cooperation in the South Asian region could not achieve the desired results.

Despite having formed SAFTA, the regional partners have not been able to increase the intra-regional trade to the expected extent. In fact, many of the SAARC members' largest trade partners is not a fellow South Asian nation but the People's Republic of China or some other non-South Asian nation. SAARC has been failed to implement its plans for regional welfare leaving much of the population in adverse socio-economic conditions. The region is home to the world's 415 million poor people, which means nearly 30 percent of the region's population lives below the poverty line. All the SAARC countries have a rather low ranking on the human development index (HDI), which according to the Human Development Report 2016 is: Sri Lanka (73), the Maldives (104), India (130), Bhutan (132), Pakistan (147), Bangladesh (142) and Nepal (145). The HDI ranking is based on the achievements in terms of life expectancy, education and real income. The low HDI ranking reflects that the objective of SAARC to work for the eradication of basic problems of the region could not be materialized the way it was perceived.

One basic problem with SAARC has been despite of an indigenous project of the regional partners and not an outcome of any foreign power or pressure, the South Asian regional cooperation is marred with the concept of hegemony threat perception. Accidently, this hegemony is not external; the bitter reality is that the hegemon is none but India, the chief architect of regional cooperation in the region. India is the largest member of SAARC and dominates the South Asian region due to its size and population. It borders nearly every landed member except for Afghanistan and is the nearest to the island members of the region. This makes India the local hegemon or the 'core state' in the words of Barry Buzan. This fact is more substantiated by recent postponement of Islamabad Summit meeting.

Pakistan being the second most influential nation and unfortunately its tensions with India is another major factor of poor performance of regional cooperation efforts in the South Asian region. The tensions between the two leading powers of South Asia have caused great damage to SAARC. Issues like Kashmir, Sir Creek, mutual mistrust, terrorism, etc. between these two major nations have hampered the efforts for greater regional integration. Though bilateral issues are not a part of SAARC charter, but these issues have a large impact on SAARC proceedings' and functioning.

One of the major objectives of SAARC was focus on socio-economic development of the region. However, the poor trade performance of SAARC member states stands in marked contrast with that of other regional organizations like ASEAN. This is very clear with the fact that the SAARC states comprise almost 23.3 percent of world population with only 3 percent of global GDP in comparison to ASEAN states which comprise 8.4 percent of world population with 7 percent of global GDP. The incapability of SAARC to provide a platform for conflict resolution has become its big weakness. The reason may be non-political issues of the region are often held hostage by high politics of the member states.

Apart from these, the lack of connectivity, low frequency of meetings, various limitations in SAFTA for free trade conditions are the major hindrances in regional cooperation in the South Asian region.[5]

To conclude, it can be argued that while SAARC has had a lot of significance, a variety of internal not external issues have led to an undermining of its effectiveness and performance in regional cooperation in the South Asian region. Still, it is the SAARC that is the only platform where the regional leaders meet and discuss issues of the region and the need of the time is to keep away the high politics for the sake of the socio-economic development of the region as a whole.

REFERENCES

1. Friedman, W., *An Introduction to World Politics*, Macmillan, London, 1956, p. 52
2. Gupta,Bhabani Sen, *South Asian Perspective*, B.R. Publishers, Delhi, 1988, p. 44.
3. http://www.saarc-sec.org/
4. Mansingh, Surjeet, *India's Search for Power*, Sage, New Delhi, 1984, p. 265
5. Vanhanen,T., *Problems of Democracy in Ethnically Divided South Asian Countries*, Paper Presented at the 18th European Conference on Modern South Asian Studies, July, 6-9, 2004.

3

2020 As a Challenging Year For Indian Foreign Policy

Seema Varma

ABSTRACT

Indian Foreign Policy is fundamentally based on the principles of peaceful co-existence, friendship and cooperation among all the countries, irrespective of their political systems. The foreign policy of a country is always shaped keeping it in conformity with its national interest and it is changed occasionally of the national interest.

When India became independent in 1947 there was considerable speculation as to her political alignment. Both U.S.A. and U.S.S.R. were keen to see her tilt the balance in their favour.The credit for formulating a foreign policy keeping in view the national interest of the country goes to our late Prime Minister, Pandit Jawahar Lal Nehru. He was one of the founding father of the policy of Non-alignment in which he was very ably supported by Marshal Tito.

But the year 2020 has proved to be a challenging year for India when it comes to its foreign policy. This paper thus tries to investigate into the causes which have exposed Indian Foreign Policy to testing times.

K*ey-words* : Proliferation, Holocaust, Sino–Indian Conflict, Foreign Policy, McMahon Line.

INTRODUCTION

The world is under the threat of annihilation because of Nuclear Arms proliferation in the world. The nuclear holocaust of 1945 which resulted in the death of millions of people in Hiroshima and Nagasaki is a grim reminder of what a nuclear holocaust looks like. It has become known to man that in the event of a nuclear war, both the vanquished and victor world would be wiped out from the face of the earth.

When India became independent in 1947 there was considerable speculation as to her political alignment. Both U.S.A. and U.S.S.R. were keen to see her tilt the balance of their favour. The Soviet Union kept some distance between herself and the Indian leaders because under the Stalinis tregime the third world countries were dubbed reactionaries.

The credit for formulating a foreign policy keeping in view the national interest of the country goes to our late Prime Minister, Pandit Jawahar Lal Nehru, who steered the country clear of both the blocs and provided us with a new image in the world. Pandit Nehru was one of the founding father of the policy of non-alignment in which he was very ably supported by Marshal Tito who had his own scores to settle with the leaders of the Soviet Union in the aftermath of the World War-II.

The foreign policy of a country is always shaped keeping it in conformity with its national interest and it is changed occasionally if the national interest warrants it. No wonder, a country's foreign policy is dictated by national interest and not by whims and fancies of either an individual or a political party.

However, despite having a strong foreign policy, there has been a marked deterioration in the security environment in the subcontinent as a result of the new tensions in the

Gulf area and S.E. Asia and big power rivalry in the Indian Ocean. India is confronted with a heightened threat from Pakistan with the United States decisions to arm it and the reported Pakistan plan to explode a nuclear device. India is convinced that Pakistan's acquisition of sophisticated arms is out of proportion to its needs.

Further there appears to be sinister designs in the recent maneuvers of practically all of its neighbours. They have been stepping up anti-Indian propaganda at a time when the country is confronted with many domestic problems. Bangladesh keeps on blaming India for the Farakka barrage and is very keen to internationalize the issue of distribution of waters of Eastern India. In Sri Lanka, the Tamil minority is being persecuted and denied basic human rights. The Sri Lanka army has let loose a reign of terror on the helpless Tamil Minorities. In 1966, thousands of Tamil refugees sought shelter in Tamil Nadu. Nepal, one of India's best friends, has of late been embarrassing India by constantly raising the issue of declaring Nepal as a zone of peace.

Further the ugly monster of global terrorism has raised its head in devouring almost the entire world. There are many evidences to prove that Pakistan has been indulging in promoting global terrorism. It is aiding and abetting terrorists to create insurgency in Kashmir Valley. Neighbouring Sri Lanka has also been ripped apart by ethnic violence between the Sinhalese and the Tamilians. The interference of the US in West Asia had to the suppression of the Palestinians.

FOUNDATIONAL PRINCIPLES OF INDIAN FOREIGN POLICY

From the late 1920's, Pt. Jawahar Lal Nehru had a long-standing interest in world affairs among independence leaders and hence formulated the Congress as a platform to raise international issues. Nehru developed from

Buddhist thought: The Panchsheel (as known the five principles of peaceful-coexistence) which included the principles which formed the basis of India's Foreign Policy.

The following are the very foundational principles of Panchsheel:-

1. Mutual Integrity
2. Sovereignty
3. Mutual-non-aggression
4. Mutual-non-interference
5. Equality and Mutuality Benefits

Main Objectives are

1. To protect India from traditional and non-traditional threats.
2. To create a conducive external environment for the inclusive development of India so that benefits of growth can reach the poorest of the poor in the country

FUNDAMENTALS OF INDIA'S FOREIGN POLICY

1. Friendship with all and enmity towards none.
2. Reliance Non-alignment. India has been one of the important leaders of the non-aligned movement which owes its existence to zeal and enthusiasm exhibited by the late Prime Minister Jawahar Lal Nehru.
3. Another corner stone of India's Foreign Policy is to maintain close relations with its neighbours. This policy received special attention of the Janata Government which did everything possible in order to improve its relations with neighbours, especially Nepal, Bangladesh, Sri Lanka, Burma, Pakistan, China and Afghanistan. The Congress (I) Govt. also

showed its commitment to improvement of its relations with Pakistan and China.

4. India has developed a very special relationship with Iran during the reign of former Shah of Iran. The Government established contacts with Ayatollah Khomeini while he was still in Paris and a fruitful relationship between Iran and India exists. The new regime in Iran was very friendly to India and the Indians working in Iran were not harassed during anti-west agitation in Iran.
5. India has emerged as a donor of financial assistance to the countries of the region. Liberal credits have been provided to some of them, especially Sri Lanka, Bangladesh, Indonesia, Mauritius and Mozambique.
6. The cornerstone of India's Foreign Policy is friendship with the Arab World. This friendship goes back to pre-historic times when both the Indians and the Arabs conducted mutual trade and were on very cordial terms who does not know that the muslin which adored the Roman beauties was carried by the Arab Traders from India ? Geopolitical considerations also are responsible for India's very cordial relations with the Arab World. India opposed to the expansionist policy adopted by Israel and favour establishment of a homeland for the Palestinians. India was one of the few countries in the world which advocated the cause of the Palestinians who were victims of Israeli aggression in July-August, 1982.

THE MAJOR CHALLENGE: SINO-INDIAN CONFLICT

China burst into the international scene in 1949, when the troops of Mao triumphed over Chiang Kai Shek. India made a sincere effort to be friend with the new regime and was amongst the first countries to extend its recognition. The late PM Pt. Jawahar Lal Nehru was keen to end China's isolation and to promote a more active role in world politics by the new regime. In order to retain the friendship of a great neighbour, India even surrendered its special rights in Tibet.

So Is Tibet lost forever? No! No! Tibet will not die because there is no death for the human spirit. Tyrannies live and die, but the spirit of man goes on for ever. For Indians the question of Tibet carries great importance. Whether or not Tibetans have a common ancestry, religion and culture have bound them with India long before recorded history. The Tibetan script was born from the Indian Alphabet and two of the most sacred places of Hindus-Kailash and Mansarover, are located in Tibet.

But India failed at a crucial moment and that was a great mistake. The consequences of this biggest mistake not only affected the people of Tibet but also the people of India. This invasion of Tibet which culminated in his holiness Dalai Lama taking refuge in Indian territory. Today all Indian citizens want Tibet to be released from China. The youth considers independence of Tibet as something precious because they have lived in servitude and know the price of freedom

From security point of view, Tibet's independence and neutrality are very vital for India. The real trouble started when, in autumn of 1959, two serious incidents took place on the Himalayan border. China attacked India's border posts killing a few, and capturing others. In spite of this, Pt. J.L. Nehru reaffirmed to 'Panchsheel', showed his willingness to discuss the matter.

A series of meetings were held, but China refused to accept the traditional boundary line which was supported by usage, land revenue record and historical facts and she demanded over 50,000 square miles of Indian Territory, both on eastern and western sectors.

She physically occupied 12,000 square miles of Indian Territory in Ladakh region by construction of Tibet sinkiang highway through Aksai Chin. She occupied post in N.E.F.A. in 1958, and further laid claim to Khinzamane, Shipki, Nilang, Jufhang, Lapthal and Barrahoti (UP). It also claimed a sizeable part of Bhutan, too.

On October 1962, the Chinese army launched a powerful offensive on India's Eastern and Western sectors. From October 28 to November 14, 1962, there was a relative lull on the North-Eastern front through minor skirmishes were occurring every now and then. The Mac Mohan Line drawn up in 1914 on the Eastern Sector running across N.E.F.A. from Bhutan to Burma was repuntiated by China within a year of signing in the Panchsheel agreement in 1955. From 1962, Nov. 14 onward China launched a powerful army in India's Western and Eastern Sectors and occupied Walong. Bomdila fell to the Chinese on Nov. 19, 1962. On the Ladakh front Daulat Beg Oldi, the Indian Fort, fell to the Chinese. Chusual also was threatened, but the Indian troops held on to it.

SIX NATION'S CONFERENCE ON SINO-INDIAN CONFLICT

At the instance of Mrs. Srimavo Bhandarnaike, the Sri Lanka Prime Minister, a conference was held on Dec. 10, 1962, at Colombo to make an effort to resolve the Sino-Indian border dispute.

COLOMBO NATIONS PROPOSALS

1. China should withdraw 20 km on the Western Sector.
2. On the Eastern Sector the line of actual control recognized by both the countries could serve as a

cease-fire line.

3. As regards the middle sector, the problem should be solved peacefully without resort to force.

The first step towards normalization of relationship with China was taken in 1976 when both India and China exchanged ambassadors after a gap of 14 years. The relations of India with China were improved with the installation of Janata Govt. in March 1977.

The former Foreign Minister Mr. Vajpayee, visited China in 1979. The seventh meeting in the series was held in Beijing in July 1986.

In June, 1986, China intruded into Arunanchal Pradesh and India's press note in this regard was rejected.

CHALLENGES FOR INDIA

Root problem of border tension between India and China is poor map making by the British. The British can't escape the blame for India's recent clashes with China in Ladakh, says Kyle J. Gardener, author of the forthcoming book, 'The Frontier Complex: Ceroplastics and the making of the India-China Border, 1846-1962. A non-resident scholar at the Sigur Center for Asian studies at the George Washington University, tells Manimugdha S. Sharma that the terrorist claims of both countries rest on faulty maps'.

India did not inherit a troubled northern border but a border without clear delineation and proper maps, is that assertion correct ? It is fair to say that: India, in the precise sense of 'Border' did not inherit a complete border in North at all. Particularly in terms of Aksai Chin, the series of proposed lines (Johnson and Macartency-MacDonald lines) and borderless maps India inherited from the British reflected limited surveying and a faulty belief that the edge of the Indus Watershed aligned with a clear ring of mountains.

By the early 20th century colonial officials like Henry McMohan (of McMohan line fame) made distinction between "delimiting" and 'demarketing' borders. Delimitation was the general description of the path of the border, usually in writing, and usually following a general border-making principle such as the limit of watershed. Demarcation, in contrast, required a team of surveyors and boundary commissions to go out and actually lay down the border using detailed maps and boundary pillars at specific plotted coordinates, very little demarcation was actually done in what is now known as the western sector.

So has that the lack of clarity in Ladakh manifested itself in India's recent confrontation with China ? Is India suffering because of British Mistakes? Yes, we are seeing this tragic manifestation of the absence of an agreed border. Despite the name, in practice the line of Actual Control has functioned more like a frontier: a vague zone liable to shift depending on the ability of each side to occupy and control it. China has taken advantage of that continued lack of clarity: perhaps India has, too, at other times. But it is fair to say the root problem here the absence of an accepted border-is largely the fault of the British Empire. If the British Empire still existed, it would undoubtedly deserve to be hauled into International court for this and many other reasons.

What do you think about India making its territorial claims today based on colonial surveys done in the 19th century? Many of today's borders around the world are direct or indirect products of colonialism and now defunct empires. That the Republic of India should carry the territorial claims of its political predecessor is not surprising. The People's Republic of China (PRC) is doing the same, insisting as it does on claim (to Tibet for instance) that harkens, back to the Quing Empire. But, unfortunately, the claims to Aksai Chin and the Eastern boundary of Ladakh rest on sketch maps that in some cases depicted geographical features that simply don't exist.

So claiming a territory the shape of which comes, above all, from a solitary 1965 map with vogue and dubious geographical features is bound to produce problems. India does not take it lightly when maps that don't show territories held by Pakistan and China as part of India are published; it calls it, "Cartographic aggression".

Post empires like the British could generally tolerate a degree of ambiguity in the outlines of their territory. But for nations like India, borders have become sacred things worth sacrificing lives for. That said, it may be that Aksai Chin's greatest value to India is cartographic. Nehru was basically right when he said that, "not a blade of grass there". There is a reason no one wants to live there permanently. The winters are brutal, there is little water, and it is mostly above 15,000 feet in elevation. Unlike the eastern sector, the problem of claiming the Aksai Chin was having no one to effectively occupy it. It has no rich resource cases depicted either.

MODI GOVERNMENT ANSWERS THE CHALLENGES

The completion of the first year of the Modi Government's second term in India in office presents a good opportunity to take stock of its success and failures on the foreign policy front. One of the notable successes of this Government has been in its outreach to India's neighbourhood, which began with Modi's visit to the Maldives and Sri Lanka soon after taking office for his second term. The Maldives was very important since it seems to be rearing towards China in the time leading up to the 2018. Modi attended Sanghai Cooperation Organization Summit in Bishkok-Kyragyztan.

Another highlight of the first year of Modi's second

term as a Prime Minister of India, is Modi's highly successful visit to United States in September last year which was followed by a reciprocal visit of U.S. President Donald Trump to India in February 2020 this year.

The recent biggest challenge for the Indian Government has been the outbreak of the Corona Virus - Pandemic. In the light of the pandemic, the Indian Government has launched Vande Bharat Mission, to evacuate Indians stranded in different parts of the world.

Another dispute is the recent Indo-China clash which again was met bravely by India. Indian Defense Minister, Rajnath Singh has sent out a clear message to China while at the clash of LAC and Indian Military between China that India is peace loving country and gave the example of 1993 and 1996. He said that country India is ready to accept challenge of China.

CONCLUSION

India an oasis of religious tolerance and one of the largest democracies of the world but has been bogged down by many social, economic and political problems. She has made rapid strides towards progress but the desired heights have not been attained. But certainly she will emerge as a winner in this millennium.

The new millennium will witness a sea change in political alignments, the word economic structure, the demographic scene and environment. The growing economic and military giant China is likely to challenge American hegemony.

To challenge terrorism and fundamentalism, a new dawn of realization must emerge whereby all nations, big and small must work together to ensure the survival of the world. The world will search for the roots of hidden and lost values to stabilize itself and make for a better future.As

W.H. Longfellow had said, "Look not mournfully to the past it comes not back again, wisely improve the present it is time, go forth to meet the shadowy future without fear and with a manly heart."

REFERENCES

1. Agarwal, M.R. (1987) - *India's Foreign Policy : G.K. Digest*, S. Chand & Co. (Pvt.) Ltd. New Delhi-110055
2. Bohra, R. (2000) - *India's Foreign Policy* (Twitter, N. Modi)
3. Dutt, V.P. (1988) - *India's Foreign Policy: Special Reference to Asia and Pacific*, Google Books.
4. Ganguly, S. (2018) - *India's Foreign Policy,* Amazon
5. Gupta, M.R. (1999-2001) - *Indo-China Tibet*, Udita Coll. Mag. Dehradun, India, p. 129
6. Gardener, K.J. (2020) - Rest Problems of border tension between India and China is poor map making by the British. *In Sunday, Times of India*, Sept. 20, p. 14
7. Jha, N.K. (1988) - *India's Foreign Policy in a Changing World*. Google Books.
8. Kaur, R. (1999-2001) - The Changing Global Scenario in the New Millenium. Udita Coll. Mag. Dehradun, India, p. 165-166.
9. Malone, D.M. & Other, Ed. (2015) - *The Oxford Handbook of Indian Foreign Policy*, Oxford Univ. Press., United Kingdom.
10. Sikri, Rajiv (2009) - Challenges and Rethinking India's Foreign Policy. *Amazon Business and Economics Flipkart.Com*
11. Wikipedia (2019) *History of Indian Relations*.
12. Amar Ujala (2020) - Chin Ke Saath Sandesh, 16 Sept. p. 10.
13. Dainik Jagaran (2020) - Charon or Se Ghir Raha Hai Chin - report. Srivastava, A. 22 Sept. p. 9.

4

India and China in South Asia: Challenges and Prospects

Samardeep Kaur

ABSTRACT

South Asia presents an intense human diversity in all its glory. South Asian countries share history, language, tradition, and even cuisine. No doubt, India dominates the whole South Asian region geographically because India is the only country that shares borders with all the other South Asian countries. None of the other countries of South Asia has common borders. China is not a South Asian country. It belongs to the East Asian region. Nevertheless, China has been playing an important role in the South Asian region. This paper focuses on India and China's present role in this region that needs to study under the new dynamism of the geopolitical environment. So for the purpose of the paper, China's role in South Asia needs deep understanding. The influence of China in South Asia has been increasing rapidly. It has posed many challenges to India's role in South Asia. The methodology that has been used for the study is qualitative in nature and based on secondary data. And descriptive analysis has been used for the analysis part. Therefore, the objective of the paper is trying to present strategic choices of India's foreign policy in this region in the light of facing new security and economic challenges.

Keywords: South Asia, India, China, Neighbours, BRI, BIMSTEC

INTRODUCTION

India occupies a unique position in the South Asian region. By virtue of its size, location and economic potential, India assumes a natural leadership role in the region. But the overbearing presence of a neighbour with aspirations for global leadership has also been a source of apprehensions for the other South Asian countries (Malhotra, 2014). There are ongoing political and military conflicts between the states of this region. Bilateral political relations in this region are defined by suspicion, strife, rivalry and antagonism. Tensions between India and Pakistan on Kashmir and terrorism issues, between India and Nepal on the border issue, between India and Sri Lanka on Tamil Diaspora issue, between India and Bangladesh on River Ganga and refugee issue are some examples of this mistrust and antagonism. The growing nuclear capabilities in the region also result in many complications. India and Pakistan have nuclear weapons and spend an enormous amount on arms and military. Therefore, high expenditure on defence reduces the volume of spending on the social sector. This kind of situation also creates a fear among neighbour nations (Kumar and Sharma, 2015). So the problem is here and China is taking advantage of this. For decades, India was a dominant country in South Asia. China's entry into South Asia is a major new factor. China's alignment with Pakistan and deepening relations with other South Asian countries represent a significant challenge to India's position in the region. China's main interest in South Asia is to expand its power over the Indian Ocean which is concerned as the most significant maritime trade hub. This situation has grown towards a competitive rivalry in the balance of power in South Asia. On one side India is trying to regain its hegemonic role over other South Asian countries. On the other hand, China has built a chain of ports which encircled Indian in India Ocean and those ports are called as "China's String of Pearls". These ports have increased the naval power of China in South Asia (Raja Mohan, 2012).

I have two arguments in this paper. My first argument is that India is not giving proper attention to its neighbours. The reason may be India does not have that kind of ability or capacity to resolve problems of her neighbours neither economically nor strategically. Due to these reasons, other countries in South Asia were tended to move towards China which always forwarded their helpful hands towards them. China had followed a peaceful coexistence policy towards the small countries and tended to grab the South Asian countries and that intention is to some extent successful in recent times. My argument supports Dr. Singh's view of China's Cheque book Diplomacy and Debt Traps. It was during the 1997 world financial crisis, that China came up with the idea of extending its economic and strategic influence overseas through "cheque book" diplomacy, Dr. Singh said (Balachandran, 2018). On the other side, India's foreign policy focusing on strategic autonomy that is the natural external complement to PM Modi's new economic strategy, called "Atmanirbharata" or "Self Reliance"(Raja Mohan, 2020). Therefore, India should look for strong strategic partnerships. My second argument is that as India's strategic autonomy is about coping with Beijing's challenge to its territorial integrity and sovereignty, these strategic partners could be the USA, Japan and Australia.

CHALLENGES

China's engagement with the region is rising day by day as out of the six major projects in China's Belt and Road Initiative (BRI), four are in South Asia. The four specific corridors that constitute major components of the BRI and run through India's South Asian neighbourhood: the CPEC, the BCIM Economic Corridor, the Trans-Himalayan Economic Corridor and the Maritime Silk Road. These four corridors and the infrastructure projects associated with them have been affecting its security interests and strategic environment. They have a direct bearing on India's strategic interests as they run close to India's continental and maritime borders. China's engagement with India's immediate neighbours through these corridors threatens to alter existing power dynamics in the region. India is not opposed to infrastructure development in the region but is concerned about its strategic implications. A primary concern for New Delhi is that Beijing will use its economic presence in the region to advance its strategic interests (Baruah, 2018). Though China has been focusing only on the economic perspective of BRI and denies any geopolitical angle associated with the project, economic influence will certainly spill over to geopolitical influence and unquestionably, BRI has implications far beyond economics (Khan, 2020). One notable example is the strategically located port of Hambantota, which the Sri Lankan government was forced to lease to China for ninety-nine years in 2017. The port was built using Chinese loans but due to the high interest rates, Sri Lanka was unable to repay and suffering debt burden (Schultz, 2017).

China's willingness to play the role of an external balancer against India in South Asia is a serious challenge, and, in some cases, a military threat. China and Pakistan's collaboration has strengthened Pakistan's military capabilities and (at the very least) enhanced Islamabad's nuclear weapons and missile programme. Moreover, the China-Pakistan Economic Corridor worries Indian national security policymakers. One of India's main concerns about the CPEC is a sustained Chinese military presence in Pakistan-occupied Kashmir, which would have serious security implications for India. Going back to history, Beijing and New Delhi went to war in 1962 over a border dispute along the Himalayas in northern and eastern India. So if China were to have a more permanent military presence by way of Pakistan on India's north-western border, that would affect New Delhi's defence and security priorities. At the same time, India already has regular border skirmishes with Chinese troops along its eastern border in Arunachal Pradesh. Moreover, the 2017 standoff between Indian and Chinese troops on the Doklam plateau along the Himalayan border severely tensed Sino-Indian relations (Raja Mohan, 2017). And the recent dispute over Galwan Valley is another example of this.

Aside from Pakistan, China has also been enhancing its relations with some other Indian neighbours—including Bangladesh, the Maldives, Nepal and Sri Lanka. China's great economic power allows it to spread its influence around the world. Therefore Beijing has used its aid and trade policies to promote its interests in the South Asia region itself. For instance, China opened up an alternative trade and connectivity options after the 2015 India-Nepal border blockade: from the highway to Lhasa, cross-border railway lines to the development of dry ports. Chinese goods flooded Nepali markets as Nepal diversified its imports and lessened its dependence on India. China displaced many Indian goods in Bangladesh, offering cheaper Chinese products (especially cotton and other fabrics central to the garment industry) without the visa, transport and customs challenges that had limited trade between India and Bangladesh. Sri Lanka also features prominently in China's Maritime Silk Road project. Another challenge for India is Beijing's focus on deep seaport development. New Delhi's fears of a Chinese "string of pearls" encircling India (Anderson and Ayres, 2015). In Sri Lanka, Bangladesh, the Maldives and Pakistan, China holds strategically, which could also be stimulated militarily in the future. At present, it means China has a stake in the internal politics of those countries. While China's growing presence in infrastructure and connectivity projects has been well-documented, its new interest in internal matters of these countries is a matter of concern. For instance, China stepped in internal matters of Myanmar and Bangladesh over Rohingya refugee issue, by negotiating between Afghanistan and Pakistan's to calm their tensions with the Belt and Road Initiative (BRI) connection between them, and offer to mediate in political matters of Maldives (Haider, 2018).

On its eastern front, India is concerned about China's growing role in a region plagued by insurgencies, narcotics trafficking and other security challenges. China has a record of lending support to Indian insurgencies in north-eastern India. Beijing reportedly supported Naga rebels after the 1962 war on the Tibetan border (Kotwal).

Another challenge for Indian diplomacy lies in convincing its neighbours that India is an opportunity, not a threat. Through it, they can access a vast market and to a productive hinterland that could provide their economies for greater opportunities for growth than if they were to rely on their domestic markets alone. For Bangladesh, greater engagement with India could give way for major economic benefits, as Sri Lanka has already established. But has India done enough to make this option attractive? (Malone, 2011).

PROSPECTS

China's engagement in South Asia questions the existing order and aims to create a structure favourable to its interests. India currently lacks the resources to compete with China in terms of global power ambitions, and this affects New Delhi's strategic and national interests. Given the current geopolitical environment and security concerns, India should find partners in the USA, Japan and other regional powers as there has no competition for dominance between India and these other leading donors in South Asia (Baruah, 2018).

New Delhi must consider prospects for collaboration on projects such as in Myanmar and Bangladesh to promote regional connectivity and boost infrastructure development. India should focus on the Bay of Bengal Initiative for Multi-Sectoral Technical and Economic Cooperation (BIMSTEC). It is a unique collaborative effort to cement sub-regional cooperation, in addition to India; this comprises neighbouring countries like Bangladesh, Bhutan, Myanmar, Nepal, Sri Lanka, and Thailand but does not include China (Baruah, 2018).

India needs to devote more diplomatic and political energy towards tending its relationship with immediate neighbours. Furthermore, to safeguard itself, India has to aim to be strong enough to stand up to China. India will have to devote enormous effort and very substantial resources to lessen the anxieties of its smaller neighbours. India may also need to induce greater complementarities of economic production in its region, as many of the South Asian countries today compete with, rather than complement, each other's exports. Some of the neighbouring countries might develop strategies centered on feeding larger industrial input needs or food requirements in India. South Asia as a whole may have insufficient hydrocarbon energy resources, but it has yet to exploit fully its hydroelectric energy potential available in Nepal and the Indian northeast. There is a very strong case for a pan-South Asian energy grid that can work based on electricity trading—a system that is already in place within India. Greater electricity availability could change the economic face of the whole region. Despite conventional wisdom on the benefits of hard power and realpolitik, India's most potent tool is its soft power. Its successes in Bhutan and Afghanistan, for example, have much more to do with its development assistance than its defence assistance. After the Doklam crisis was defused in 2017, India also moved swiftly to resolve differences with Bhutan on hydropower pricing and announced a tariff hike for energy from Bhutan's Chhukha project, the first in several years. India will need a stronger articulation of its vision for South Asia. Natural ports were cut off from their hinterlands, as Chittagong was from India's northeast and Kolkata from Bangladesh. Twin commercial cities like Mumbai and Karachi have become distant neighbours. The gradual easing of these barriers could produce significant economic (and eventually security) benefits (Malone, 2012).

India must be more active. While China is successfully implementing development projects hundreds of miles from its borders, India is still struggling to design domestic development plans for its border regions. New Delhi intends to prioritize development in its international engagement, but India will have to weave together its ad-hoc initiatives into one coherent road map to regional connectivity and infrastructure construction. Even as India must address infrastructure and development needs at home, it also needs to provide an alternative to China's offerings to the region. To this end, India must not only respond to the changes Chinese engagement is prompting in its neighbourhood but also collaborate with partners to further its vision of regional connectivity, while accounting for its capacity and resource limitations (Baruah, 2018).

India will have to account for its resources and capabilities related to connectivity and infrastructure development. The current government understands the urgency of acting boldly to address the changes in its neighbourhood; its efforts such as burden-sharing will require fresh thinking and new approaches. New Delhi must invest in and develop its strategic assets like the Andaman and Nicobar Islands, for instance, to project power across the Indian Ocean (Baruah, 2018).

India's ongoing response might not be enough to provide neighbours with a viable alternative to Beijing's continental and maritime projects, because of New Delhi's significant resource limitations. Due to India's obligations to develop much-needed infrastructure domestically, the country's ability to act alone in South Asia and the larger Indian Ocean is further limited. New Delhi cannot act alone (Baruah, 2018).

By chance, convergence between the strategic interests of India, the United States and Japan have provided both incentives and opportunities for collaboration. New Delhi must seek help from partners like Japan and the USA, when necessary to build and upgrade its infrastructure and create an alternative to Chinese-led connectivity corridors and infrastructure projects (Baruah, 2016). For instance, US-China trade war was a big opportunity for India to advance its interests. India must have a blueprint to identify specific projects, mechanisms and goals for its connectivity initiatives. Countries like Australia, France, Germany, the UK and the United States are keen to see India play a leading role in the region. These nations have the technical expertise and are already present in the region to some degree. New Delhi must identify the advantages each of these states offer and leverage them to collaborate in areas of common interest and pursue its strategic connectivity goals. Together, India and these countries can coordinate their use of resources to address common goals such as peace and security (Baruah, 2018).

Another choice is instead of opposing every project by China in the region, the government must rethink its approach. As far as possible, India should collaborate with China in the manner it has over the Bangladesh-China-India-Myanmar (BCIM) Economic corridor. No doubt, when it feels a project is a threat to its interests, India should make a counter-offer to the project, if necessary in collaboration with its Quadrilateral partners, Japan, the U.S. and Australia. Therefore, India should coexist with projects that do not necessitate intervention, while formulating a set of South Asian principles for sustainable development assistance that can be used across the region (Haider, 2018).

India must regain its role as a prime mover of the South Asian Association for Regional Cooperation (SAARC), the organization it abandoned over its problems with Pakistan. Despite sneers all around, SAARC has survived three decades despite its biggest challenge, India-Pakistan tensions. New Delhi's cancellation to attend its summit to be held in Pakistan in the wake of the Uri attack is understandable. India has won support from other countries similarly affected by terrorism such as Bangladesh and Afghanistan on this decision. But after four years, the fact that there have been no steps taken to restore the SAARC process is unfortunate. This will hurt the South Asian construct and further loosen the bonds that tie all the countries together, thereby making it easier for China to make inroads (*The Hindu*, August 12, 2017).

Above all, India must recognize that doing better with its neighbours is not about investing more or undue favors. It is about following a policy of mutual interests and of respect, which India is more culturally attuned to than China. Each of India's neighbours shares more than a geographical context with India. They share history, language, tradition and even cuisine (*The Hindu*, August 12, 2017).

CONCLUSION

India and China, both are powerful actors who have rapidly growing economies. Both countries are struggling for power dominance in the South Asian region. China's rise not only introduces a new actor in South Asian dynamics but also highlights the underlying fact that Beijing's influence in the region comes at a cost to India's role and profile as a regional leader. China's engagements in South Asia are a result of its global ambitions to be a great power. No doubt, India dominates the whole South Asian region, geographically, but the new geopolitical dynamism poses several important challenges for India. Because of these challenges, firstly, New Delhi should consider prospects for future collaboration with its small neighbours by way of its development assistance (soft power). Secondly, India should make efforts to collaborate with the USA, Japan and other regional powers. Thirdly, India should build its capacity in kind of self- reliant to advance its strategic autonomy from China in the region. Lastly, India should have to avoid confrontation even with China whereas possible. It should try to cooperate with China for economic development as far as its security interests are not hurting.

REFERENCES

1. Malhotra, Amb (Retd.) Achal (2014), "India's Relationship With Its Neighbours: Conflict and Cooperation", *Distinguished Lectures*.
2. Kumar, Saurabh and Sharma, Aparna (2015), "Regional Cooperation in South Asia Can Prospects Outweigh Problems?" *Discussion Paper*, p. 4.
3. Mohan, C. Raja (2012), *Samudramanthan: Sino-Indian Rivalry in the Indo-Pacific*, Carnegie Endowment for International Peace, Washington.
4. Balachandran, P. K. (December 2018), "Emerging South Asian Scenario: An Indian Viewpoint", *South Asian Journal, http://southasiajournal.net/emerging-south-asian-scenario-an-indian-viewpoint/*
5. Mohan, C. Raja (August 25, 2020), "Reinventing India's Strategic Autonomy", *The Indian Express, https://indianexpress.com/article/opinion/columns/reinventing-india-strategic-autonomy-china-us-6568347/*
6. Baruah, Darshana M. (August 2018), "India's Answer to the Belt and Road: A Roadmap for South Asia",*Carnegie India,https://carnegieindia.org/2018/08/21/india-s-answer-to-belt-and-road-road-map-for-south-asia-pub-77071*
7. Khan, Hamdan (February 2020), "The Other Frontline: South Asia in the Emerging Great Power Competition", *Modern Diplomacy, https://moderndiplomacy.eu/2020/02/28/the-other-frontline-south-asia-in-the-emerging-great-power-competition/*
8. Schultz, Kai (December 2017), "Sri Lanka, Struggling With Debt, Hands a Major Port to China," *New York Times*, December 12, 2017, *https://www.nytimes.com/2017/12/12/world/asia/sri-lanka-china-port.html.*
9. Mohan, C. Raja (December 19, 2017), "Raja Mandala: India and China - Rebuild the Trust," *Indian Express, https://indianexpress.com/article/opinion/columns/india-and-china-rebuild-the-trust-doklam-standoff-4988820/.*
10. Anderson, Ashlyn and Alyssa Ayres (2015), "Economic of Influence: China and India in South Asia", *CFR Project on the New Geopolitics of China, India and Pakistan*.
11. Haider, Suhasini (March 7, 2018), "Making the Neighbourhood First Again", *The Hindu*, */https://www.thehindu.com › Opinion › Lead.*

12. Kotwal, Dinesh, "The Naga Insurgency: The Past and The Future," *Institute for Defense Studies and Analyses, http://www.idsa-india.org/an-jul-700.html.*
13. Malone, David M. (2011), *Does the Elephant Dance? Contemporary Indian Foreign Policy*, Oxford University Press, p. 127.
14. Baruah, Darshana M. (December 2016), "Toward Strategic Economic Cooperation Between India and Japan",*Carnegie India, http://carnegieindia.org/2016/12/01/toward-strategic-economic-cooperation-between-india-and-japan-pub-66326.*
15. Haider, Suhasini(August 12, 2017), "In South Asia, Be The Un - China", *The Hindu, https://www.thehindu.com/opinion/lead/in-south-asia-be-the-un-china/article19476384.ece*

5

Indo-US Relations: India's Ever Changing Foreign Policy

Manju Chandra

ABSTRACT

Indian Foreign Policy has been a subject of constant flux since its inception. One could say that there have been a lot of changes in India's foreign policy according to circumstances. It can be said that most of India's decisions are low-risk ones and with low-risk taking comes limited rewards. To gain benefits, one need to take some risks and this is currently lacking in India. With the coming of Modi government, India has extended its boundaries of initiatives and the same have proven to be quite fruitful. Maintaining relations with other countries across the globe also affects the drafting of foreign policy. The current government has given a lot of attention to the same and this has shown some good results as India's image of being a reluctant power is changing constantly into a powerful one.

India has had good relations with the US for a long time. With the election of Donald Trump, the situation seemed a bit difficult but it has been in India's favour. India and the US support a lot of causes together including human rights, rule of law, etc. India and the US also have mutual interests that include enhancing military, energy resources, trade and improving the economy. There have been agreements between them to enhance the same. They both take a similar stand on a lot of problems that have arisen. An example of the same is their stand on China breaking the rules. In International relations, no one is a permanent friend or enemy. In order to flourish and develop, one has to take into mind the interests of one's country and the other country. India will one day be a developed nation and it's in the right track. However, it is yet to see how this global pandemic affects its path.

Keywords: Indian Foreign Policy, Indo-US Relations, Diplomacy, Global Geopolitics.

INTRODUCTION

To talk about the main topic at hand, one has to first understand the meaning of the term foreign policy. In very simple terms, foreign policy is a framework made by a country envisaging the rules according to which it will conduct its relations with foreigners. Good diplomacy is very essential in order to achieve the objectives of a country. In the modern world, where does India stand? Where does it see itself? And what are the factors that are responsible for this standing? The shift from a traditional approach to a different one had brought in major change in the foreign policy and the same will be analyzed in this paper. There have been a lot of significant changes in India's foreign policy since independence. A majority of these changes have been implemented because of the ever-changing global geopolitical dynamics. Some of these major changes include the rebalancing of the global economy, the rise of technology and trade, and the USA's unilateralism under the first American policy.

After the cold war, India and the US have become strategic partners where they used to be just separate democracies during the war. After Donald Trump promulgated the America First Policy, there have been a lot of changes in trade when the relations with India are taken into consideration. From earlier times, there has been a pragmatic change in the decision-making, predictability, increasing business, etc. The status of India has risen in the global platform in the past few years. This paper seeks to throw light on the changes that have taken place and have led to a paradigm shift in India's foreign policy in the past few years concerning India's relations with the United States of America. The current challenges in this position would also be looked upon and the possible solutions to them would be provided.

INDO –US RELATIONS TILL NOW

There are various reasons because of which there has been constant contact between India and the US. Some major reasons include the rise in India's global economic position, a shift in global relations in the post-cold wartime, a change in the geopolitics, etc. Relations between both countries have flourished as they have a lot of interests in common. They are both committed to democracy, freedom, rule of law, etc. They share interests in trade and connectivity and want to prosper economically. All these shared interests have led them to be strategic partners when they used to be belligerent democracies earlier. The Emergence of China as a possible threat to global security has further strengthened India's relationship with the US ("A Timeline of U.S.-India Relations").

Many US Presidents have visited India in the past decades and we have come a long way ahead by signing agreements, treaties and trade deals. Recently, Donald Trump visited India to further make stronger ties with the country. There were trade deals made which included defence purchases worth $ 3 billion, the building of six nuclear reactors in India, and also involves investment in US gas companies. Both countries are dedicated to have better cooperation in military exercises and technology enhancement (Ahmad et. al., 1999).

The United States looks for an extended exchange relationship with India that is complementary and reasonable. In 2019, by and large, U.S.-India reciprocal exchange products and ventures came to $149 billion. U.S. vitality sends out are a significant territory of development in the exchange relationship. In 2018, India bought 48.2 million barrels of U.S. unrefined petroleum, a huge increment from 9.6 million out of 2017. A year ago, Indian understudies enlisted at U.S. schools and colleges contributed over $8 billion to the U.S. economy (Garekhan, 2020). The all out number of Indian understudies in the United States has dramatically increased in the course of the most recent decade, from 81,000 out of 2008 to a record high of 202,000 out of 2019.

In December 2019, the United States facilitated the second 2+2 Ministerial Dialog in Washington driven by the U.S. Secretaries of State and Defence and their Indian partners, at which the two sides reaffirmed India's status as a Major Defence Partner and developed collaboration on oceanic security, interoperability, and data sharing. While the 2+2 fills in as the chief discourse instrument between the United States and India there are over thirty respective exchanges and working gatherings, which range all parts of human undertaking, from space and health collaboration to vitality and high innovation exchange (Kanth and Kumari, 2003).

Although the relations between the two countries seem to be fine, the same cannot be said about the high import duties that India imposes. In response to the same, Trump terminated India's benefit of having duty free access to over

$5 billion worth of exports to the US. As a reply to the removal of India from the Generalised System of Preferences, India imports heavy tariffs on a lot of products imported from America. US in turn approached the World Trade Organisation regarding this (Kaul, 1974).

There have been other divergences between the two countries due to conflicts in their views. US wanted to expand a lot of its product to India which included dairy and agriculture products, India refused to those terms stating that they want their own domestic products to flourish in their market which acted as a barrier between both the countries and as a result, US walked out of an agreement that they had vested mutual interest (Indo-US Relations, Convergence Of Interests). A difference in the shared interests mentioned in the above paragraph has also started to show up. This is in response to the revocation of section 370, NRC and the citizenship issue arising in India. All these things have started to develop a crack in the values both the countries valued like rule of law, democracy, human rights, freedom, etc. It was argued earlier that these values had a big part to play in the Indo-US relationsand with a change in these principles, it is unlikely that the relations will remain the same. Although the US out front said that these matters are internal to India, the US Congress advised India not to go ahead with the new citizenship law and also gave some advice on India's dealing with Kashmir ("U.S. Relations with India - United States Department of State").

The relations between the two countries are quite strong and mutually beneficial from every aspect and the few discrepancies that have arisen shall be settled down looking at the greater good of both the nations. The Prime Minister, by taking the step of delivering Hydroxychloroquine in the testing times of the pandemic has further shown the US a sign of trust and it is estimated that this will further enhance their relations (Singh). The way forward to their relations is bringing US nuclear energy on Indian land in pursuance to the agreement with Westinghouse and also, both the countries should side together against China on the issue of maritime domain in the Indo-Pacific region as both of them support rule of law (Teja, 2014).

THE PARADIGM SHIFT IN INDIA'S FOREIGN POLICY

India, which was apportioned from British India and accomplished freedom in August 1947, had a few fundamental properties of an ordinary significant power: its history, size and area. India is probably the biggest country as far as the populace and zone. Its region is multiple times greater than that of Japan. It was a significant country, yet its range of authority was basically restricted toward the South Asian district. Given those conditions, India's foreign policy choices have remained rather obliged. To start with, India built up and kept up its supposed non-alignment policy as its essential fundamental of foreign policy between the 1940s and the 1960s under its first Prime Minister, Jawaharlal Nehru (Foreign Policy of India).

Since Independence, India has changed its foreign policy from non-arrangement to partnership with the Soviet Union. For what reason was India constrained to modify its policy? The essential factor would be the deficiency of its public power. The net consequence of India's two foreign arrangements was an insufficient nearness on the universal stage. India's collusion with the Soviet Union was commonly seen to deliver it a reliant entertainer in the predominant worldwide political scene (Dieboldand Paarlberg, 1985). The change of the Indian economy and the accident of the Soviet Union, alongside the changed global structure, have constrained India to update its foreign policy through and through.

In the last few decades, there has been a transformational shift in India's foreign policy due to the paradigm shifts in global geopolitics. The shift now is quiet fierce because of the changes brought by the current Prime Minister, Narendra Modi (Borah, 2020). India has broken new waters because of the bold moves made by the Prime Minister taking the country's relation with the US to the next level and also because of the discontent it has shown over China's actions. To access the shifts in the foreign policy, the points must be identified that made a difference by altering the matrix of global geopolitics. The becoming of Donald Trump as the President of the United States of America is a very major point of inflection as he tends to deviate from the practices that were followed by his predecessors (Dixit, 2020).

A change from the traditional foreign policy to the modern one has been a truly helping point in the rise of the country. To assess the changes in the policy, some major points of reference would be kept in mind. These points will include India's stance on energy security, its commitment to the UN, its stance on climate change and its economic upstanding. Prime Minister Modi has taken a lot of policy initiatives full of innovation and creativity (Hall, 2020).By enhancing India's defence strategies, the country's military strength has become a really significant asset to foreign policy. In addition to this, New Delhi's broad relationship with Washington and Moscow, trailed by "various weapons bargains" has acknowledged Israel as the greatest provider of military innovation to India and the two countries marked joint advancement weapons arrangement of over $2 Billion explicitly focussing on rocket engineering for residential security.

India's foreign policy show slight Nehruvian policy nearness, India's situation at the international level to a great extent relies on the sovereignty and notoriety for common regard. India has endorsed the basic however separated duties and individual capacities (CBDR), making it the auxiliary structure for key arranging focuses during conversation meetings. As per the National Action Plan (NAP), India would follow an eight-step method that explicitly features India's responsibilities to moderate environmental change while satisfying the lack of energy of more than 3 billion masses (Alden, and Brummer, 2019).

India stays a vitality lacking country, particularly in the light of its quickly rising populace and stable economy. To change the equivalent, there was a foundation of a committed Energy Security Division of the Ministry of External Affairs (MEA). Policymakers must comprehend that rich industrialized countries would acquire by drawing in with a rising power, for example, India particularly when the country broadens its innovation on carbon development. India's latest critical commitment to the New Development Bank (NDB) otherwise called BRICS bank grandstands India's dynamic cooperation in the changing worldwide request (Singh, and Sehgal). Built up in participation with Brazil, India, China, Russia and South Africa, the $100 billion BRICS bank is viewed as an option in contrast to the West settled money related establishment, for example, the World Bank and International Monetary Fund (IMF).

India is a country with a lot of uncertainty at the borders and security poses a lot of threat to the development of the country. India's stance against terrorism has yielded a lot of results when we talk about the escalated position of India in the global matrix. India's standing has gone up in the global pedestal (Malhotra). One of the evidence for the same lies in the crisis that Mozambique experienced. The people of Mozambique expected India to come to their aid when the same people expected the US and Japan to be the respondents when they were hit by a Tsunami. India considers itself to be a settling power which discovers advantage in various outer commitments, wanting to gather speed for a multipolar world with a multipolar Asia at its centre. India's adjusting stance and its developing military and vital abilities are believed to give a level of consolation against global disturbance and serious geopolitics. Globally, India needs to stay a significant and affecting power on issues running from atmosphere maintainability to reasonable trade, advanced innovations to the space and digital lodge, through national intrigue based multilateral commitment.

India's foreign policy viewpoint must be set inside a pragmatist comprehension of global logical inconsistencies. India is searching for associations dependent on vital assemblies, not only strategic comfort. The serious issues that India is confronting today incorporate coercive weights from neighbours over disrupted limits and Islamist fanaticism. For the issues with neighbours, India should side up with the US and it is obvious from the past discussion that the US likewise takes a stand against these reasons. The India-U.S. key association is a key part of India's Indo-Pacific vision, given the meeting the test of China's endeavours at territorial predominance. It conveys the capability of giving both common fortification and guaranteeing territorial strength over the Indo-Pacific. For the U.S., India satisfies the requirement for a solid and sound territorial accomplice, which bears its own weight. It is to India's greatest advantage to keep on advancing the financial, guard and key mainstays of the India-U.S. relationship on a bipartisan premise.

CONCLUSION

Prime Minister Modi has very creative strategies with respect to the Indian Foreign Policy. He has taken decisions keeping in mind the need of the hour. His policy of favouring the neighbours has borne fruit and has been a vital asset in regional affairs. By helping the countries in need, he has raised India's position in the global matrix. The image that India carried for a lot of time of being a reluctant power is changing slowly. As discussed before, India has invested and planned to improve its position in the energy, food, defence and economic sector. The same is a good initiative as it is clear that India needs to improve its economic as well as military condition in order to achieve its aim.

India needs to maintain the pace at which it is maintaining relations with countries like France, Japan, Russia, etc. Indian diplomacy cannot be effective without the backing of a good military and economic support. India had a downward pull in its economy recently which makes it a matter of concern but it has invested in military equipment and looking at the disputes arising with its neighbour countries, it is a much needed step. Although the steps taken in the new policy are impressive, they are low-risk steps that only provide limited rewards. To be rewarded heavily, risks have to be taken and it is quite feasible looking at the current decision-making.

Good foreign policy can only be supported by avoiding global contradictions. India's stance on issues regarding Kashmir, the NRC and its regional disputes will affect its reputation on the global level. In global diplomacy, no one is a friend for long and no one is a permanent enemy, everything depends on the mutual interests of countries. As far as India keeps on supporting things that the US stands for and both of them have mutual interests, their relation will keep flourishing which will be beneficial for both the countries and especially for India. The initial terms for the current government were quite eventful but more problems arose with the outbreak of coronavirus which should be taken care of while altering the policy to bearing much better results.

REFERENCES

1. "A Timeline of U.S.-India Relations". *Council on Foreign Relations,* 2020, https://www.cfr.org/timeline/us-india-relations.
2. Ahmad, Eqbal et. al. "India 2020: A Vision forthe New Millennium". *Foreign Policy,* No. 115, 1999, p. 122. *JSTOR,* doi: 10.2307/1149498.
3. Ahmad Nazir, *Contemporary World Politics and Politics in India*, Afzan Publications, Khanyar Srinagar 2011, p. 72.
4. Alden, Chrisand Klaus Brummer. "Foreign Policy Analysis and the Study of Indian Foreign Policy: A Pathway for Theoretical Innovation?" *India Review,* Vol. 18, no. 5, 2019, pp. 471-484. *Informa UK Limited,* doi:10.1080/14736489.2019.1703360.
5. Babu, B. Ramesh, *Domestic and Indo-US Relations Since-1965;* Fulbright House, New Delhi ,1991, p, 35.
6. Borah, Rupakjyoti, "India's Foreign Policy in Modi 2.0's First Year". *The diplomat.Com,* 2020, https://thediplomat.com/2020/06/indias-foreign-policy-in-modi-2-0s-first-year/. Accessed 10 Aug 2020.
7. Diebold, William and Robert L. Paarl berg. "Food Trade and Foreign Policy: India, the Soviet Union, andthe United States". *Foreign Affairs,* Vol. 64, No. 2, 1985, p. 366. *JSTOR,* doi: 10.2307/20042599.
8. Dixit, Rekha, "India's Foreign Policy Underwent Paradigm Shift Under Modi: Jaishankar". *The Week,* 2020, https://www.theweek.in/news/india/2019/04/24/India-foreign-policy-underwent-paradigm-shift-under-Modi-Jaishankar.html. Accessed 19 Aug 2020.
9. *Foreign Policy Of India,* Lok Sabha Secretariat, 1966.
10. Garekhan, C.R., India's Foreign Relations and the Course ofHistory, *The Hindu,* 2020, https://www.thehindu.com/opinion/lead/indias-foreign-relations-and-the-course-of-history/article32006793.ece. Accessed 19 Aug 2020.

11. George Modelski, *A Theory of Foreign Policy*, p. 09.
12. Ghosh, Anjali, *India's Foreign Policy*. Longman, 2009.
13. Hall, Ian, "Author's Response: Foreign Policy, Ideology, and Domestic Politics in Modi's India". *Asia Policy*, Vol. 27, No.2, 2020, pp.184-188. *Project Muse*, doi:10.1353/asp.2020.0017.
14. *Indo-US Relations, Convergence of Interests*. Research and Development Foundation for Integral Humanism, 2002.
15. Kanth, T. Krishna and Lalitha Kumari, "Indo-Us Relations: Emerging Partnership in the New Millennium". *Jadavpur Journal of International Relations*, Vol. 7, No. 1, 2003, pp. 268-275. *SAGE Publications*, doi: 10.1177/0973598403110011.
16. Kaul, T.N., *Indo-US Relations: An Assessment*. India International Centre Quarterly, Vol. 1, no. 1, 1974, Accessed 28 Aug 2020.
17. Khanna, V. N, and Leslie K. Kumar. *Foreign Policy of India*.
18. Malhotra, Achal. "India's Foreign Policy: 2014-19: Landmarks, Achievements And Challenges Ahead". *Mea.Gov.In*, 2020, https://www.mea.gov.in/distinguished-lectures-detail.htm?833 #:~:text=The%20m ain%20and%20first%20a nd,to%20secure%20its %20 nat ional%20interests.& text=India's% 20for eign%20policy's% 20added% 20focus,economic %20diplomacy % 20with%20 political%20diplomacy. Accessed 13 Aug 2020.
19. Memon, S. *India's Foreign policy*, Delhi University, New Delhi, 2009.
20. Singh, Dinesh, *Indo-US Relations. Strategic Analysis*, Vol. 33, no. 6, 2009, pp. 931-937. *Informa UK Limited*, doi: 10.1080/09700160903256010.
21. Singh, Jasjit. *Indo-US Relations in a Changing World*. Lancer Publishers in Association with Institute for Defence Studies and Analyses, 1992.
22. Singh, Hemant and Arjun Sehgal, *Indian Foreign Policy: Assessing the Agenda in 2020. The diplomat.Com*, 2020, https://thediplomat.com/2020/01/indian-foreign-policy-assessing-the-agenda-in-2020/. Accessed 17 Aug 2020.
23. Teja, Jaskaran. "The New India–U.S. Reset". *American Foreign Policy Interests*, Vol. 36, No. 6, 2014, pp. 375-386. *Informa UK Limited*, doi:10.1080/10803920.2014.994418.
24. "U.S. Relations With India - United States Department Of State". *United States Department of State*, 2020, https://www.state.gov/u-s-relations-with-india/. Accessed 12 Aug 2020.

6

Indo-US Relation, A Zigzag Expedition

Sandhyarani Padhy

ABSTRACT

It was due to her attraction towards socialistic ideology and struggle against Western imperialism and colonialism which insisted India to keep peace with Soviet bloc and automatically maintain a distance with US during her early existence in International arena. In addition to this the non-alignment policy made the topic so spicy that for five decades after her Independence U.S. foreign policy for most times become pro-Pakistan instead pro-India amidst giving priority to its own National interest.

United States hardly appreciate India's approach to International Politics and often disgraced by India's non-alignment as well the pro-Soviet Policy. There are a quite good numbers of similarities like both are larger democracies and were with a British colonial rule in their past, both are republics and governed by democratically elected representatives. But at the same time a large number of irritations exists between them like on the question of Kashmir, Arms Aid to Pakistan. Pro-Pak policy of U.S. non-alignment policy of India and of course India's resentment for NPT and CTBT. However with the end of Cold War both countries looking for more cordial relations. An important improvement in this connection is in the field of economic policies. The United States accepted liberalization of Indian Economy and interested to invest more in various Indian industries and projects. Both countries worked to tackle the problem of illegal trafficking of drugs as a serious International problem. Both countries tried to abolish terrorism from world politics.

Key words: Non-alignment, Pro-Pak policy, Pro-Soviet policy, NPT, CTBT

INTRODUCTION

The Second World War gave birth to two powerful blocs like USA and USSR further developing a bipolar power system as both of them had acquired nuclear weapons. Meanwhile India got its Independence amidst the emergence of cold war between the two power bloc rivalries. And while each bloc tried their best to attract all the nations by their side either by giving them military or economic assistance but India at that time decided not to accept permanent alliance of either bloc and tried to maintain friendship with both the super powers including Britain. However somewhere it was found that the early part of India's foreign policy was pro-Soviet against western imperialism and colonialism, which make India detached from the Western bloc. And United States also accepted Pro-Pakistan stand avoiding its cordial relation with India approximately for five decades of her Independence. Both have disputes with regard to the Bangladesh crisis in 1971, the issue of signing NPT since 1968 and the issue of signing CTBT, the question of nuclear weapons and Military alliances like SEATO, the issue of Israel and Palestine etc. However India's assistance to South Korea in favour of UN Security Council was appreciated by U.S.A. Similarly in 1962 during Chinese attack US provided help and support to India.

INDO-U.S. RELATIONS DURING THE COLD WAR PERIOD

After Independence Nehru opted for peaceful co-existence rather to join any super power blocs, keeping a vigilant eye upon the economic growth of India. Nehru adopted the policy of Non-alignment by keeping equi-distance from the super powers and tried to gain a prestigious position in International relationship. However India's non-aligned policy did not coop with her relationship with U.S.A and followed a Zigzag course for approximately 50 years. During this period China, Soviet Union, were the determinants of India's relation with U.S. Though America's stand fully acknowledged by the Indian leaders during her Independence but her policy of non-alignment and denial to join the Military alliances of U.S.A. made it unfriendly towards U.S.A. Further various International issues like Independence of Indonesia and recognition of communist China aggravated the problem more. However India got huge quantities of food grain to meet her food shortage during this period.

Similarly to check communism U.S. started various Military alliances like (SEATO) (South East Asia Treaty Organization, (CENTO) Central Treaty Organization etc. where Pakistan was a Party in opposition to India. At the same time India remained silent in the Soviet intervention of Hungary which strained USA very much. The Goa liberation from Portuguese colonialism also added to American strain as Portugal was a member of NATO.

But the Indo-US relation recognized its raise from Kennedian administration. During the Sino-Indian war in 1962, US supported India unconditionally as Kennedy himself was a supporter of Nehru's policy of non-alignment and peaceful co-existences. The Air Forces of India, Britain, Australia and US carried out joint Air exercises in different parts of India. America signed an agreement to assist 80

Million US Dollars to enable India to set up a Plant for nuclear energy at Tarapur. However the relation again faced a setback during the period of Shastri, as during this period India criticized America's war with Vietnam for which Prime Minister Shastri's visit was avoided by the American President Johnson as "busy schedule".

In the mean time, Pakistan's attack on India with US arms made the relation bitterer. Inspite of India's protest against the use of American arms by Pakistan, America maintained its Pro-Pakistan strategy as usual. During that period six US ships were returned from only 15 kilometers away from Indian coast. While India had acute shortage of food items at that time, the U.S. non-cooperation caused serious hardships of essential goods. However, US maintained neutrality during the preceding stage of Indo-Pak War and also warned China not to intervene directly in this respect. These conflict followed by serious economic crisis, inflation and decrease of foreign currency in India caused its dependence on US.

While the Primeministeriship of Shastri caused a setback in Indo-US relation, Indira Gandhi, his immediate successor tried her best to develop the relation by inviting foreign investments. She drew attention towards China's aggressive policies and moderated India's stand on Vietnam. The new International situation, the US-Soviet detente, the Soviet split, the economic and military assistance of US all compelled India to ensure a long term friendly relation with US. The first formal bilateral talks were held in 1968. However, differences prevailed throughout the periods of Johnson. Johnson was replaced by Nixon in 1969 that stood for assistance to India and tried not to interfere in the bilateral issue of Kashmir question.

However sharp differences remained on US arms

supplies to Pakistan, the West Asian conflicts and the war in Vietnam. The perception of the two countries of their interacts in Asia in particular and International politics in general had been widely divergent. Pakistan's entry into western military alliance and provisions of US military bases in Pakistan confirmed America's support to Pakistan. The strategic interest of US demanded alignment with Pakistan.

The divergence reached at its height during the Bangladesh crisis, as that was the domestic problem of Pakistan which had always been the root cause of Indo-US bitter relationship. After India declined to SEATO, Pakistan was invited to join the Western alliance. As an alliance Pakistan had been receiving military assistance from US since 1954. It became more strong during the 1971 Bangladesh liberation war when Pakistan, China and US alliance made by giving massive military supplies to Pakistan. The Bangladesh crisis created a great division to Indo-US relations. The open American support to Pakistan was highly resented by India. India moved closer towards Soviet Union. And America could not prevent partition of Pakistan. Again in 1974, India had made its first test of nuclear device with clear intention of peaceful purposes however US was highly critical and felt that it might led to nuclear proliferation in South Asia. During the period of Janata government though cooperation in the field of economy grew to some extent but India's refusal to sign the Non-proliferation Treaty again strained Indo-US relation. It was at Cancun meeting where Mrs. Gandhi met President Reagan of US who wanted to re-think about India. However, it can be assumed that India's close relations with communist world made the Indo-US relation more deteriorated.

INDO-US RELATION AFTER THE END OF COLD WAR

The Cold Was came to its end in 1989 immediately followed a spilt to Soviet Union and raised a unipolar world power structure. It became thus essential for almost all countries of the world including India to review their foreign policies, and diplomatic activities. After disintegration, Russia also moved closer to America caused the destruction of Russia's traditional long relationship with India. However, with the end of cold war the United States insisted on the goal of promotion of peace and stability towards South Asia, for which US wanted that both India and Pakistan should sign Nuclear Non-proliferation Treaty. But India argued that depending upon its security and for peaceful purposes India never could suspend, terminates its nuclear programmes. Hence by 1997, India-US differences persisted on the issue of NPT, CTBT, the missiles programme and of course on the everlasting issues of Kashmir and Human Rights. Later it was the Clinton administration which clarified that Kashmir is a bilateral issue and should be solved with the interest of the concerned nations.

INDO-US RELATIONS—RECENT DEVELOPMENTS

Inspite of large ideological gaps, persistence of nuclear issues and pro-Pakistan stand, the ever largest and strongest two democracies of the world have become increasingly close and have exhibited multi-faceted cooperation in areas such as trade, defence, education, science and technology space technology, environment and health. Recently they developed regular contacts at political and official levels with wide-ranging dialogues on bilateral, regional and global issues.

A strategic Dialogue was established in July 2009 during the visit of US Secretary of State Hillary Clinton to India with the objective of strengthening bilateral cooperation across diverse sections. The first round of the strategic Dialogue was held in Washington DC in 2010 followed by the second round in New Delhi in 2011 and third round in Washington in 2012.

A new US Financial and Economic partnership began to strengthen bilateral engagement on macro-economic, financial and investment related issues in New Delhi in 2010. The second such meeting was held in Washington D.C. in 2011. The Indo-US Trade Policy Forum established in 2005 had its last and seventh meeting in Washington D.C. in 2010. An agreement on framework for cooperation on Trade and investment was signed during the visit of Minister of Commerce and Industry of India in 2010. For greater involvement of the private sector, the Indo-US bilateral Forum was reconstituted in 2009.

During the visit of Prime Minister Narendra Modi in 2014, the worldview for both Nations was that they remained silent in various International issues like the situation in Iraq and Syria, cooperation in Afghanistan and Confounding, especially in anti-Islamic, state coalition. On eight issues like energy, health, space, women empowerment, trade, skills, strategy and security dialogues were made between the two Nations after a long gap.

In 2017, US exported 25.7 Billion Dollar worth of goods to India including aircraft, fertilizers, computer hardware, scrap metal and medical equipment and imported 48.6 Billion Dollar worth Indian goods including technology services, textiles, machinery, gems and diamonds, chemicals, iron and steel product, coffee, tea and other edible food products

In 2018, India became the third Asian Nation to be granted strategic Trade Authorization-I status by US, which enables to expert high technical products in civil space and defence from US to India. In 2019, Prime Minister

Narendra Modi visited Houston and addressed a large Indian-American contingent in the Houston NRG stadium. Alongwith President Trump, he reaffirmed India-American ties with an emphasis on increased military cooperation. In 2020, US President Donald Trump visit to India further strengthened the bilateral relations especially in strategic ties and defence.

CONCLUSION

It is observed that entire Cold-war era witnessed a Zigzag relation in between the two countries. Both had divergent views on various global issues. Furthermore both had different views on many regional problems of South Asia, Middle East and South-East Asia. Indo-US relation has always been influenced by India's security concerned and US's geo-strategic interests. The clash of the two countries that began from Second World War continued for 50 years. So many steps were taken to improve the bilateral relationship between the two Nations and it was after the end of Cold-war that eliminating the hesitations of history. India and the US have built a strong and strategic bilateral relationship and continue to contribute to the stability and prosperity of the world. Our first Prime Minister, Jawaharlal Nehru compared American Imperialism to that British and propounded the Non-alignment principle whereby India refused to join either the capitalistic bloc US or the communist Soviet Union.

However, India's Socialistic economic principles tilted her towards USSRwhich deteriorated her relation with US more.With the end of the ideological Cold War and with the development of a unipolar power structure India was forced to look towards West given the paradigm shift in the geopolitics of the world. Today both India and US are amongst the most vibrant strategic partners.

REFERENCES

1. Parthasarathy Sen, Elections in Iran, *The Hindu*, Friday, May 19, 2017, p. 8.
2. Sridhar Krishnaswamy, India-US Sign Framework for Defence Cooperation. *The Hindu*, Thursday June 30, 2015, p. 8.
3. Pant, Harsh V. (Ed), 'Natural Partners; US and India Engaged, No longer estranged', *The Statesman*, Monday July 25, 2005, p. 6.
4. Subasini Haidar and Varghese George, Modi may do a Madison Square in Houston, *The Hindu* Wednesday May-17, 2017, p.11.
5. Mr. Srinivasan (ed.) Ending nuclear dependency The Hindu Friday, May-19, 2017, p.8.
6. Khanna,V.N., *Foreign Policy of India*,Vikas Publishing House Pvt. Ltd.-2017, Noida (U.P.), p. 250.
7. Morgenthau, Hans J & Thompson, Kenneth W., *Politics Among Nations–The Struggle for Power and Peace*, Kalyani Publications , New Delhi-2004.

7

Continuity and Change in the Alignment Pattern of Indian Foreign Policy: With Special Reference to Manmohan Singh and Narendra Modi

Sumit Rana and Pooja

ABSTRACT

This article is an attempt to examine the changes and continuity in the alignment pattern of Indian Foreign Policy under Manmohan Singh and Narendra Modi regime. Indian Foreign Policy has become extremely dynamic in the last six years under Modi's stewardship. The alignment pattern followed after the independence was "non-alignment policy" adopted by Pt. Jawaharlal Nehru to ensure the independence of Indian foreign policy during Cold-war era. But after the disintegration of USSR and changes in the global scenario, there was a need to change the alignment pattern to secure national interest. Consequently, there is a decisive shift towards multi-alignment in recent years. The multi-alignment policy was started by the Vajpayee government as a new strategy called 'strategic partnerships' but its scope was limited. The UPA government led by Manmohan Singh emphasized that the relationship between India and the world will be shaped by its development priorities. For this, Manmohan government greatly engaged in emerging global and regional multi- and mini-lateral institutions and forums. The Modi government continued the policy of multi-alignment showing great interest in multilateral forums in which India can play a role. He made extensive use of strategic partnership agreements that had not been seen before. There is continuity in alignment patterns of Manmohan Singh and Narendra Modi's alignment policy but the strategy used for this purpose has changed.

Keywords: Indian Foreign Policy, Non-alignment, Multi-alignment, Strategic Partnership.

INTRODUCTION

Since independence, India has developed institutions and processes to promote a strong foreign policy. Successive Prime Ministers have directed India's foreign policy in response to the changing international circumstances and the geopolitical dynamics. However, the core values and ideas of Indian history continue to inform foreign policy goals. Foreign policy is generally determined by a number of historical, philosophical, cultural and domestic factors, which shape the objectives of a nation in different areas. Foreign policy is also influenced by geostrategic location, ideology, tradition, military might, economic power and system of government. The basic concern of foreign policy always remains the same which is to protect the national interest of the state but one can witness a paradigm shift in the conduct of foreign policydue to the difference in world view and personality factors of the respective Prime Ministers. In India, the foreign policy is buttressed by the style of Ms. Indira Gandhi, Atal Bihari Vajpayee, I.K. Gujral, Manmohan Singh and recently the stewardship of

Sri Narendra Modi. The chief architect of India's foreign policy is Pt. Jawaharlal Nehru. He emerged as a pre-eminent voice of progressive internationalism and the architect of independent India's foreign policy. His contribution is immense in outlining the broad contours' of the foreign policy. In subsequent years different Prime Ministers have tried to conduct the foreign policy along the principles laid down in the aftermath of the independence.

Dr. Manmohan Singh assumed Prime Ministership in 2004 and the burden of conducting India's foreign policy rested on his shoulders. After the completion of his first tenure, there was no shakeup in India's foreign policy. When Manmohan Singh's second tenure started in 2009, he did not deviate from the Vajpayee pursued-policy of greater engagement concerning the US, China and neighbouring. Manmohan Singh expanded the scope of relations with each of these countries, like India and the US opened a new chapter in their bilateral relations when they signed a landmark civil nuclear deal.

Indian Foreign Policy has become extremely dynamic in the last six years under Modi's stewardship. Narendra Modi is known as a foreign policy Prime Minister as he dedicated his much time and energy to foreign policy. His enthusiastic engagement in global affairs did not allow being revealed Modi's lack of experience on foreign policy. Before taking the helm at the national level, he was Chief Minister of Gujarat state (2001-2014) and never contested Lok Sabha election (lower or popular house of Parliament) before. It is Modi's influence that NDA won with clear majority in the leadership of him which was Modi's first parliamentary election. With a little prior foreign policy experience, Narendra Modi can be said successful in reinventing India's foreign engagement and placed India a prominent actor in International relations. Modi also has been successful in selling Brand India abroad and in leveraging the vast Indian Diaspora to national causes. Modi's ambition towards India's role in global affairs to become a leading player in the international system that shapes global rules and is not merely a rule-taker. In 2015, as then Foreign Secretary, S. Jaishankar had suggested that today's India "aspire(s) to be a leading power, rather than just a balancing power." As a consequence, he said, India was willing "to shoulder greater global responsibilities." He took risks in his foreign policy and more of than not succeeded in converting them into substantive gains for India. To rejuvenate India's foreign policy, the Modi government has taken several initiatives such as the Act East Policy, Neighbourhood First Policy. These initiatives have raised the hope that Indian foreign policy will witness significant changes.

A BRIEF OVERVIEW OF INDIA'S ALIGNMENT PATTERN AFTER INDEPENDENCE

India adopted the policy of non-alignment after independence as the world was divided into two power blocs—the USA and the USSR respectively. Even after the demise of the former Soviet Union and the end of the Cold War, the basic postulates of India's foreign policy remained unchanged. There has been enough discourse regarding the significance of non-alignment as a viable strategic or foreign policy option in the changed international milieu. India never proclaimed to give up non-alignment, rather it sought to justify its continuity as a principle of foreign policy and reiterated that this policy is still relevant even in the post-cold war period, so the principles laid down by the first Prime Minister, Pandit Nehru after getting independence, are by and large still relevant. There is hardly any alteration in the basic principle of foreign policy. However diplomatic style varies due to personality factors as well as individual worldview of Prime Ministers of different periods.

Between 1947 and the mid-2000s, Indian foreign policy passed through three stages. During the first, which lasted from independence to the border war with China in 1962, India's first Prime Minister, Jawaharlal Nehru, pursued 'non-alignment'. Nehru argued that India was too weak to make a meaningful difference in the Cold War and that it could better serve itself and the world by maintaining equidistance from the superpowers, promoting causes such as decolonization and disarmament and seeking to make the internationalist ideal of 'One World' a reality through persuasion rather than coercion. Non-alignment entailed: adherence to the principles of the United Nations; the avoidance of both military alliances and substantive integration into the American-underpinned global market, such as it then was; and active engagement in key normative debates concerning the management of international and intra-state conflict. In the second stage, which lasted from the early 1960s until the end of the Cold War, Nehru's successors set out a more radical agenda for the developing world, rearmed India's armed forces in the face of Chinese and Pakistani threats, and adopted a more assertive stance towards its immediate neighbours and towards the West. It tested a nuclear device in 1974 and embarked on a very slow but determined effort to build a latent deterrent capability, if not fully to develop and deploy it. At the same time, India continued to pursue economic self-reliance and keep its contact with the global market economy to a minimum, to avoid dependence on the West or other emerging economic powers. It maintained an interest in normative issues, but Indian arguments and preoccupations changed, with a marked shift away from causes such as disarmament and towards issues such as economic justice for the developing world. Together, these various moves were intended to boost India's 'strategic autonomy'—essentially it's capacity to pursue its interests with minimal reference to other major powers, especially in South Asia. For Western observers, however, this bid for autonomy was compromised by India's formal alignment with the Soviet Union in 1971, signaled by the conclusion of the Treaty of Peace, Friendship and Co-operation. In the last stage, from 1991 until the mid-2000s, India sought to shore up its deteriorating political and economic positions with a series of new expedients: partially reforming and opening up its economy in 1991 to encourage more foreign trade and inwards investment; introducing the 'Look East' policy in 1994 in the pursuit of partners that might provide finance and know-how, as well as opportunities to boost trade testing five nuclear devices in 1998 and developing a fully-fledged deterrent to address security concerns arising from the rapid economic rise of China and pursuing entente with the US, the dominant state in the post-Cold War order.

INDIA'S ALIGNMENT PATTERN DURING MANMOHAN SINGH'S GOVERNMENT (UPA-I AND II)

The foreign policy of two governments of Manmohan Singh which traditionally called UPA-I, which ran from 2004-2009 and UPA-II from 2009-2014 is too many criticisms, but Manmohan Singh's former Press Secretary ***Sanjay Baru*** said in his memoir, the Prime Minister has especially asserted himself with some success especially in his first term and during his second term Indian foreign Policy underwent significant changes in its driving principles and its practice. Together, these changes shifted India towards multi-alignment. In the first two years of UPA-I, Manmohan Singh outlined a separate foreign policy's Principles. According to ***Baru,*** it had six parts, at first, Manmohan Singh emphasized that the relationship with India and the world will be shaped by its development priorities. Second, Manmohan Singh pushed against many critics of economic globalization in India, arguing that India needs more and more integration, not less. Third, they saw that India's relations with the great powers were growing rapidly shaped by economic factors—especially access to energy resources –and should prioritize its foreign policy on those elements. Fourth, Manmohan Singh argued that deep integration was needed in South-Asia. Fifth, in another departure from traditional knowledge in NewDelhi, he suggested that the progress of India's democratic development model held lessons for others. Finally, Manmohan Singh mentioned that India has the responsibility to help other states in transition to open economic policies and democratic politics.

To put these principles and objectives into practice, Dr. Manmohan Singh continued India-America's engagement began under his predecessor Atal Bihari Vajpayee and maintained the "Look East Policy" initiated by Narasimha Rao, but also in many areas inherited from a series of New Partnerships or further development heritage moving India towards multi-alignment, towards the end of the UPA-II, these ideas were further developed by Congress Politician, writer and then Minister, ***Shashi Tharoor****–pursuing 'strategic autonomy' was, as he put it, 'all very well' but it cannot be the be-all of India's attitude to the world. Today, 'India's sovereignty is no longer under threat' from meddling superpowers in the way it perceived to be during the cold war by the political and strategic elite in New Delhi.* Therefore, India should no longer be reticent about close relations with other states, including large powers and becoming an active member of regional multilateral institutions. It must be enthusiastic because the benefits can be derived from both. For Tharoor: multi-alignment was an immoral strategic' but a potentially effective one seeing:

> ....*India making common cause with liberal democracies when it suited India to do so, and dissenting from them when...... it was expedient for India to preserve relationships that other democracies could be offered to jettism. It is also a promiscuous strategy since it exempts no country from its embrace; China, a potential adversary with which we have a long-standing frontier dispute that occasionally erupts into rhetorical unpleasantness, nonetheless is a crucial partner in several of these configurations.*

As the UPA governments developed it in practice, multi-alignment had three aspects. The first involved an accelerated push for membership and great engagement in emerging global and regional multi- and mini-lateral institutions and forums. India became an inaugural member of the EAS and, in the same year, it was granted observer status at the SCO (Now full Member). In 2006, India joined Brazil China, and Russia in giving diplomatic form to the BRIC grouping, the grouping became the BRICS when South Africa was included in 2010. In 2008, during the financial crisis, India embraced the revamped Group of 20 (G-20), which held its first annual leaders' summit that year. In 2008 too, India held the first meeting of the Indian Ocean Naval Symposium, with 22 members drawn from around the Ocean's littoral. At the same time, India, together with Australia and Indonesia, began to reinvigorate the Indian Ocean Region Association for Regional Cooperation, founded in 1997 and renamed it the Indian Ocean Regional Association in 2013. The second aspect of India's new multi-alignment strategy involved forging a series of 'strategic partnerships' and deepening some existing partnerships agreed under Singh's predecessors. The concept of 'strategic partnership' is relatively new in regional diplomacy, but has become popular in the Asia-Pacific. This distinctive type of bilateral arrangement was first floated by the Soviets at the end of the Cold War as a means of deepening ties between states that would dispense with the need for new alliances or international institutions, but it emerged as a widespread practice in the region only after its adoption by China in the mid- to late-1990s. The People's Republic now has close to 50 such partnerships, with one or more formal bilateral agreements constituting each of them. In general, China's strategic partnerships and those of other regional states involve one or more of six key elements: formalization in written agreements or statements; the creation of formal links or mechanisms at either a government-to-government or a Track II level, involving think-tank professionals, academics and business people; the institutionalization of processes for regular summit meetings or leadership dialogues; the establishment of some form of military-to-military communication; the commitment to improve economic ties; and the initiation or augmentation of bilateral public or cultural diplomacy. Since 1998, India has concluded almost 30 strategic partnership agreements with various states, as well as the European Union. Manmohan Singh's predecessor, Atal Bihari Vajpayee, concluded six of the most important, forming partnerships with France, Germany, Iran, Japan, Russia and the US. Singh's government added 15 more, the majority with significant Asia-Pacific states, including Afghanistan, Australia, China, Indonesia, Malaysia, South Korea and Vietnam, as well as with ASEAN and many others, including Brazil, the EU, Nigeria, Saudi Arabia and three Central Asian republics. These new strategic partnerships reflected Singh's commitment to forging ahead with the 'Look East' policy, deepening engagement with both North-East and South-East Asian states, but also to build better bilateral relations with major trading and investment partners (such as ASEAN and China) and key sources of raw materials, especially oil and gas (such as Brazil, Nigeria, Saudi Arabia and the Central Asian states).

In nutshell, multi-alignment emerged under Manmohan Singh's leadership as a way to maintain and accelerate India's economic development, manage key security challenges, especially those posed by China, provide India with access to regional and global forums at which its voice would be heard and allow it to promote its values without committing to a Western normative agenda. This is not to say, of course, that the UPA governments were always successful in achieving these aims. Under Singh, India was justifiably criticized for failing to provide leadership in the regional institutions and global groupings that it joined, failing to derive full advantage from some of its partnerships and failing to take stands on normative issues when it could and arguably should have done. Despite these shortcomings, it is clear that India's strategy changed during his Prime Ministership, as multi-alignment was employed as a means of giving India new opportunities to achieve its objectives.

INDIA'S ALIGNMENT PATTERN DURING NARENDRA MODI'S GOVERNMENT

Narendra Modi came to power promising major changes in both domestic and foreign policy, but his commitments concerning the latter were somewhat vague, as some analysts observed before and after the 2014 election. Modi largely ignored foreign policy in his campaign speeches, addressing the topic at length in a single talk on 'India and the World', delivered at a book-launch and memorial event in Chennai. The Bharatiya Janata Party (BJP) manifesto devoted just a page and a quarter to foreign policy and one to national security. For these reasons and because of perceived inexperience in foreign affairs, some commentators argued before the election that Modi would take some time before he fully engaged with India's international relations and before he mapped out a foreign policy agenda. As soon as Modi came to office, however, he surprised these and other observers with the energy he committed to the area. Inviting the leaders of the South Asian Association for Regional Cooperation member states to his swearing-in ceremony caught the eye of many in the first few days of his government; the frequency, pace and high profile of Modi's foreign visits in the months that followed also attracted much attention Multi, alignment and Indian Foreign Policy from analysts interest in Modi's leadership were stoked still further by his unprecedented invitation to an American President to attend the Republic Day parade in January 2015 and then by his trip to Chinese President Xi Jinping's home town of Xi'an in mid-May. Similarly eye-catching were Modi's new schemes and slogans, especially about FDI and economic engagement with India—his invitation to foreign firms to 'Make in India', for example, or his concept of 'Digital India', pitched to Silicon Valley entrepreneurs and investors during a typically whirlwind visit in late September 2015. Whether all this frenetic activity signals a significant change in the direction of Indian foreign policy is, however, a moot point. Some—notably the distinguished strategist C. Raja Mohan—argue that Modi 'appears to have many more opportunities ... to engineer a structural transformation in India's international relations' and suggest this transformation is already underway. In a similar vein, the retired diplomat and former Deputy National Security advisor, Satish Chandra, thinks that Modi has 'already left an indelible impress on Indian foreign policy'. But other analysts argue that, despite the hype, Modi's foreign policy is not markedly different in content from those pursued by his two immediate predecessors, Vajpayee and Singh. In terms of overarching foreign policy objectives, it is hard to distinguish between those of Modi's government and those of Vajpayee or Singh. Modi has five aims: first, achieving 'pride of place' in India's neighbourhood; second, 'leveraging the capacities of all countries, particularly major players, for promoting India's development'; third, 'hedging against a rising China'; fourth, 'safeguarding India's national interests'; and fifth, utilizing India's Diaspora to promote those interests. Aside from the first, these differ very little from the objectives of earlier BJP-led or UPA governments.

Like Manmon Singh, Modi has shown great interest in multilateral forums in which India can now play a role, personally attending two BRICS summits, two G-20s and two EAS meetings, as well as the United Nations General Assembly and the Paris Climate Change Summit in December 2015. Under his Prime Ministership, India has also joined the Shanghai Cooperation Organization and like Manmohan Singh and Vajpayee before him, he has made extensive use of strategic partnership agreements, concluding such deals with Canada, Mongolia, Oman, Seychelles, the United Arab Emirates (UAE) and the UK. As under UPA-I and UPA-II, these partnerships fall largely into two categories, one primarily concerned with trade and investment, such as those with Canada, Oman, the

UAE or the UK and those concerned with access to resources, such as those with uranium-rich—and, it should also be noted, geo-strategically significant— Mongolia. The one area in which there may be some change happening under Modi is arguably in India's normative agenda. In his first Independence Day speech, Modi called for 'Mother India' to act as a *Vishwaguru* (or 'world guru') working for the 'welfare of humanity'.

CONCLUSION

The evolution of alignment patterns shows the change in the strategy of Foreign Policy from Nehru to Modi towards playing leading world leaders, role, rather than a mere balancing one, with ambition, energy and confidence. India's policies towards China are growing and their political and economic dominance is becoming geographically overlapping. Under the UPA government, India was not so vocal against China, but the increasing erosion of India's space has made India necessary for assertiveness, as can be seen through the informal grouping of Quad, increasing inclination towards the USA, etc. India's economy and the size of its territory have made India's neighbourhood ideological about India's intentions. The SAARC has been a non-starter due to issues with Pakistan and has made it difficult for India to economically and strategically sustain China's encroachment. The situation has been similar in UPA as well as NDA. However, due to the US dependence on India for the stabilization of Afghanistan, India's Afghanistan policy is currently looking better than the time of Manmohan Singh. Nepal is moving towards China but the recent proposed by China to join India, China +Nepal 2+1 dialogue is a positive step under Modi's government.

During the Manmohan Singh's government, India's

relations with Russia were stronger than today. Also, India's relationship with the United States is stronger than before. The USA made India a 'Major Defence Partner' and at the same time, Russia is conducting a military exercise with Pakistan. Russia's zero-sum approach poses some threat to India's interest in neighbourhood and when it comes to Donald Trump, India's relations with the United States are marked by greater uncertainties. Walking on a tight rope lies ahead. Traditionally, India has taken a firm stand on the issue of Israel-Palestine and during the Manmohan Singh's regime, India-Israel is like weeding in heaven and we have seen India coming out of the closet and having a great relationship with Israel. At the same time, India's relations with Palestine based on its merit, India has effectively balanced its interests with Saudi-Arabia and Iran during Modi's regime. The 'Look East Policy' of India was transformed into 'Act East Policy' during Modi's regime and later on, we saw our partnership deepening, like India's invitation to heads of ASEAN countries on the 2018 Republic Day celebration. During the Manmohan Singh tenure, India's relations with ASEAN remained limited to cultural and trade relations. Under Modi's regime, the government has also integrated with the North East into the development process and added 'Connectivity' and 'Strategic' domains to its policy. India's relations with other countries have been taking shape with the changing global environment and time demands. Such flexibility has enabled us to ensure our national interest and support through the water of international politics.

REFERENCES

1. Dutt, V.P., (2013), *"India's Foreign Policy Since Independence"*, Vikas Publication, New Delhi, pp. 10-43
2. Pande, Aparana, (2017), *"From Chanakya to Modi: The evolution of 2nd*

Foreign Policy" HarperCollins Publications, pp. 56-59

3. Mohan, Raja C., (2015), *"Modi's World"*, Penguin Publication, New Delhi, pp. 56- 60
4. Pant, Harsh (2019), Modi 2.0 Confronts a Challenging Foreign Policy Landscape. Commentaries. https://www.orfonline.org/research/modi-2-0-confronts-a-challenging-foreign-policy-landscape-51229/
5. *ibid.*
6. Sarkar, Badal, (2013), "India's Foreign Policy under Prime Minister Dr. Manmohan Singh" International Journal of Scientific Research. Vol. II. issue XII. pp. 45-56
7. *ibid.*
8. Dutt, V.P, (2016), *"India's Foreign Policy in Changing World"*, V.P. House Publication, New Delhi, pp.10-40
9. Hall, Ian, (2016), *Multi-alignment and Indian Foreign Policy Under Modi and Manmohan Singh*, Vol: 105, Issue 3, pp. 171-186.
10. *ibid.*
11. "The World's Most Powerful People: Manmohan Singh". *Forbes. 3 November 2010.*
12. India's Foreign Policy: With Landmark Deals, Manmohan Singh Government Promised Much, Delivered Little retrieved 10 Sep. 2020.
13. Rajamohan, C., (2005), *"Rethinking India's Grand Strategy"* N.S. Sisodia & Udaya Bhaskar (Ed) *Emerging India: Security and Foreign Policy Perspective*, IDSA and Biography South Asia, New Delhi & Chicago, p.138.
14. C. Raja Mohan, "India's Positive Unilateralism", *The Hindu*, Oct. 26, 2003. p. 4.
15. *ibid.*
16. Rajesh, M. Basrur (14 December 2009). *"The Lessons of Kargil as Learned by India"*. In Peter R. Lavoy (ed.). *Asymmetric Warfare in South Asia: The Causes and Consequences of the Kargil Conflict* (1st Ed.). Cambridge University Press. p. 326.
17. Srivastava, Sanjay (April 2015). "Modi-Masculinity", *Television & New Media*, pp. 331–338.
18. MEA Report on Indo-Sino Bilateral Relations March 2018, pp. 3-4.
19. *ibid.*
20. Mohan, Raja. C., (2015), *Crossing the Rubicon: The Shaping of India's*

New Foreign Policy, Palgrave Macmillan, New Delhi. pp. 348-350.

21. Chaulia, Sreeram, (2016), *Modi Doctrine: The Foreign Policy of India's Prime Minister*, Bloomsbury Publication, New Delhi, pp. 400-410.
22. Vikas Chandra (2017), *Modi's Government and Changing Patterns in Indian Foreign Policy*, Research Article, Source https:doi.org/
23. Rajesh Babrur (2017), *"Modi's Foreign Policy Fundamental: Trajectory Unchanged"*, International Affairs Vol: 93 issues 1.

8

Coronary Danger Variables in South West Asia

Shubham

ABSTRACT

Ongoing investigations demonstrate that wholesome lacks exist together with calculable over nourishment as focal weight and overweight in rising nations, and that one-fourth of the populace is hefty in evolved nations. The creators suggested that overweight starts things out, related to aggravation, hyperinsulinemia, expanded angiotensin movement, vascular changeability issues and focal weight, trailed by glucose bigotry, type 2 diabetes, hypertension, low HDL and hyper triglyceridemia (pre-metabolic disorder metabolic condition). The Worldwide Weight of Sickness Study plainly indicated that the satisfying increases in cardiovascular wellbeing happened in created nations, in relationship with a pestilence of CVD in the creating scene. The dangers of coronary danger factors (CRF), coronary vein ailment (computer aided design) and type 2 diabetes have some similitude all through South Asia and West Asia. In a nutshell, clinical perceptions demonstrate that CVDs and type 2 diabetes mellitus were least regular during the 1950s, when industrialization and monetary advancement were started in the created nations.

Keywords : Cardiovascular, Nourishment, Overweight,

Metabolism, Wellbeing.

INTRODUCTION

The most recent couple of many years of the only remaining century extraordinarily expanded our insight about the worldwide elements of non-transferable sicknesses (NCD), including cardiovascular illnesses (CVDs) [1-3]. Late investigations show that dietary insufficiencies coincide with considerable over nourishment as focal weight and overweight in rising nations and that one-fourth of the populace is corpulent in evolved nations [1-7]. We recommended that overweight starts things out, related to irritation, hyperinsulinemia, expanded angiotensin movement, vascular inconstancy issues and focal corpulence, trailed by glucose bigotry, type 2 diabetes, hypertension, low HDL and hyper triglyceridemia (pre-metabolic disorder metabolic condition). This succession is trailed by computer aided design, gallstones and tumors, lastly dental caries, gastrointestinal maladies, bone and joint illnesses, degenerative sicknesses of the cerebrum and mental issues, during change from destitution to opulence.

As individuals become rich, they start to expand their admission of proinflammatory refined nourishments, wealthy in dietary fat, salt and sugar, as found in handled nourishments, syrups, dairy items and tissue food sources instead of a grain-based eating routine [3-7]. They use autos and stare at the TV more and take an interest less in sports, strolling and moving for entertainment, which likewise upgrades aggravation, dyslipidemia and heftiness. These adjustments in diet and way of life, related to mental strain and increment in tobacco and liquor admission, give off an impression of being essential danger factors in the pathogenesis of irritation and dyslipidemia prompting NCDs.

METHODOLOGY

The Worldwide Weight of Malady Study plainly demonstrated that the satisfying additions in cardiovascular wellbeing happened in created nations, in relationship with a plague of CVD in the creating scene. The dangers of coronary danger factors (CRF), coronary corridor ailment (computer aided design) and type 2 diabetes have some likeness all through South Asia and West Asia.

In South Asians and West Asians, computer aided design happens 10-15 years sooner and the two gatherings have higher commonness of focal weight and type 2 diabetes than the Caucasian populaces [1-5]. The nations of South-West Asia have probably the most noteworthy paces of focal heftiness on the planet, contrasted with many created nations. As indicated by the Establishment for Wellbeing Measurements and Assessment in the US, an expected 66% of men and 60% of ladies in the UAE are overweight or stout [1, 2].

Around 14.2 million individuals between the ages of 30 to 69 pass on rashly every year from way of life infections, including atherosclerosis, coronary illness, stroke, weight, type 2 diabetes and maladies related with smoking and liquor and medication misuse. Diabetes mellitus is depicted as a "tremendous and developing issue" in the Center East and North Africa (MENA) by the Worldwide Diabetes Alliance (IDF), influencing 23.8% of 20 to long term olds in Saudi Arabia, 23.09% in Kuwait, 22.87% in Qatar, 21.84% in Bahrain and 18.98% in the UAE, a year ago [1]. The World Wellbeing Association (WHO) and the IDF consider diabetes the 21st century's driving medical care challenge.

Diabetes confusions and mortality make social and

monetary difficulties that influence people, families, organizations and society overall. Six MENA nations–Bahrain, Egypt, Kuwait, Oman, Saudi Arabia and the Assembled Middle Easterner Emirates (UAE)–are among the world's 10 most elevated for commonness of diabetes and disabled glucose resilience. By 2020, 32% of the grown-up UAE populace (age 20-79) may have diabetes or pre-diabetes, while other information demonstrate that the grown-up UAE populace (ages 18 or more) has just arrived at a diabetes or pre-diabetes pace of 44% [1]. On the off chance that patterns proceed, the IDF extends that by 2030, the quantity of individuals with diabetes in the Center East North Africa (MENA) locale will practically twofold, arriving at 59.7 million.

Weight, hypertension and cardiovascular sicknesses (CVD) are regularly comorbid to diabetes mellitus. Diabetics in the UAE, alongside Qatar, have the most elevated predominance of CVDs among GCC nations.

This is critical on the grounds that co-morbidities muddle treatment and add to death rates. Of grown-up Emiratis, 71% have in any event one danger factor for CVD. In 2005, 31% of all passings in the UAE were because of diabetes and CVD. The danger of a coronary episode is multiple times more prominent and the danger of a stroke is two to multiple times more noteworthy for all people with diabetes, prompting the calming measurement that around half of diabetics inevitably pass on from CVDs including interminable cardiovascular breakdown (CHF). In any case, contemplates have exhibited that compelling anticipation and treatment can prompt over a half decrease in CVDs and cardiovascular breakdown [3-7]. The complete expense of NCDs to the locale could be faltering. Booz and Organization figures that the immediate and roundabout weight in the GCC could hit $68 billion by

2022. As rich ways of life lead to extending midriff lines and an expansion in unfortunate propensities, drug organizations the world over observe extraordinary money related potential in drug advancement to elevate weight reduction and to treat illnesses connected to stoutness.

There was a stamped overabundance of cardiovascular passings in many nations from the area contrasted and information from equivalent western nations (UK, Germany and the US), especially from coronary conduit malady and hypertensive coronary illness. Also, the INTERHEART study (a global case-control investigation of the danger factors for a first myocardial dead tissue led in excess of 15,000 patients giving myocardial localized necrosis in 52 nations) indicated that the middle age at introduction with myocardial dead tissue was 51 years in the Center East; this was lower than the middle age at introduction in nine different areas and was 12 years lower than the middle age at introduction in Western Europe [8]. An extended increment in coronary passings in the Center East of 171% somewhere in the range of 1990 and 2020 was bigger than relating esteems for "set up market economies" (46%), India (127%), China (108%), sub-Saharan Africa (144%), and Latin America (144%). Smoking, stoutness and an absence of activity cause respiratory failures in the UAE 20 years sooner than the overall normal. The 850 respiratory failure patients admitted to Rashid Clinic in Dubai in 2013 were excessively more youthful than such patients somewhere else on the planet. The normal age of the primary cardiovascular failure is 45 years. The worldwide normal is 65 years. Of those 850 patients, 40 percent were diabetic, 40 percent were hypertensive and 25 percent had significant levels of cholesterol. (http://www.thenational.ae/uae/wellbeing/cardiovascular failures strike-20-years-sooner in-the-uae#ixzz3LwN5JbnS) The danger of CVD is changing progressively around the globe. Many created nations, for example, the USA, Canada the UK and Australia have all the earmarks of being reacting to preventive techniques coming about into decreases in CVD dreariness and passings. Different nations and subcontinents like Eastern Europe and Asia are progressively embracing old way of life rehearses which earlier transformed vascular malady into a scourge in the west and in outcome are having a significant development in CV passings. Ongoing evaluations of the WHO, demonstrate that roughly 33% everything being equal (16.7 million of all out 52.2 million) happen due to CVD. Of these passings, computer aided design represented 7.2 million (43%), stroke 5.5 million (33%) and rest were because of provocative or rheumatic coronary illness and so forth. Over 80% of CVD passings happen in low-and center pay nations. Just passings from all irresistible causes surpassed CVD mortality.

There are no accomplice concentrates from South-West Asia to give a proof in regards to relationship of CRF with computer aided design. In a populace review with self-announced pointers, anthropometric measures and blood tests were done to screen 50,138 grown-ups matured 18 years or more seasoned partaking in a populace wide cardiovascular screening programme [9]. Members' mean age was 3682 years (SD = 14.3); 43% were men. Danger factor commonness rates were: stoutness, 35%; overweight, 32%; focal heftiness, 55%; type 2 diabetes mellitus, 18%; pre-diabetes, 27%; dyslipidemia, 44%; and hypertension, 23.1%. Furthermore, 26% of men were smokers, contrasted and 0.8% of ladies. Age-normalized diabetes and pre-diabetes rates were 25% and 30%, individually and age-normalized paces of stoutness and overweight were 41% and 34%. A board of clinical and general wellbeing pros from UAE College and different government wellbeing organizations was appointed to cover the wellbeing status of the UAE populace [10].

They found that: (1) CVDs represented over 25% of passings in 2010; (2) Injury caused 17% of mortality for all age bunches in 2010; (3) Malignancy represented 10% of all passings in 2010 and the frequency of all diseases is extended to twofold by 2020; and 4) Respiratory issues were the second most basic non-deadly condition in 2010. The significant general wellbeing challenges presented by certain individual (e.g., nationality, family ancestry), way of life, word related and ecological components related with the improvement of ceaseless illness are not one of a kind to the UAE; rather, they structure part of a worldwide medical issue, which requires global cooperation and activity. The principle guidance was that future exploration should zero in on populace based general wellbeing intercessions that focus on the components related with the improvement of different interminable illnesses.

Gibson et. al., evaluated the weight of infection owing to six ecological presentation courses: outside air, indoor air, drinking water, seaside water, word related conditions, and environmental change [11]. For each presentation course, we coordinated UAE ecological observing and general wellbeing information in a spatially settled Monte Carlo reproduction model to appraise the yearly sickness trouble inferable from chose toxins [11]. The appraisal incorporated the whole UAE populace (4.5 million for the time of investigation). The investigation found that open air contamination was the main supporter of mortality, with 651 inferable passings (95% certainty stretch [CI] 143-1,440), or 7.3% all things considered. Indoor air contamination and word related presentations were the second and third driving supporters of mortality, with 153

(95% CI 85-216) and 46 inferable passings (95% CI 26-72), individually. The main supporter of medical services office visits was dirtied drinking water, to which 46,600 (95% CI 15,300-61,400) medical care office visits were credited (about 15% of the visits for all the sicknesses considered in this investigation). In view of global correlations, the UAE's natural infection trouble is low for all variables aside from open air contamination. From a general wellbeing point of view, lessening contamination outflows to open air ought to be a high need for the UAE's ecological organizations. Incomprehensibly, CRF and danger variables of type 2 diabetes have all the earmarks of being comparative in all rising economies, yet hazard factors coming from wealth (handled nourishments and stationary amusement advancing weight) seem, by all accounts, to be more noteworthy [4-6, 12-23].

The CVD yearly rate shows that no mainland is excluded from the issue of CVD. In the west, CVD prevails; in the Far East, stroke and cerebrovascular occasions are fundamental; however in South Asians, computer aided design hazard is 40% more noteworthy than in the west [4-7]. The test of CVD in creating economies [50] shows that in 4 of the 5 examination nations (South Africa, Brazil, India and Russia; China excepted), age-explicit CVD passing rates were essentially higher than in the US or Portugal. The pervasiveness of computer aided design in South Asia shifts from at least 7% in Kolkata, East India, to 14% in Trivandrum, South India; dangers of type 2 diabetes and hypertension are comparable [16-23]. In the Five City Study containing 6940 subjects–2002 subjects from Moradabad (North), 1602 from Thiruanantpuram (South), 1542 from Mumbai (West), 900 from Kolkatta (East) and 894 subjects from Nagpur (Focal)–the danger components of CVDs were altogether more prominent in

South India and West India contrasted with East and North India [16-18]. There has been a globalization of riches in the rising nations, absent a lot of progress in wellbeing, inspite of the fact that future has expanded as passings due to under-sustenance diminished [24].

The drug business has reacted by giving admittance to thrombolytics, beta blockers, ACE-Inhibitors, enemies of platelets and statins, all of which have been demonstrated to adjust CVD. Omega-3 unsaturated fat rich nourishments and physical movement are significant progressions in the avoidance and treatment of computer aided design. Be that as it may, these treatment modalities are not successfully applied in light of the fact that doctors are not instructed about chrono-treatment and circadian events of cardiovascular occasions, demonstrating a requirement for more current procedures for anticipation.

MIND-HEART CONNECTIONS

Computer aided design was known to Hippocrates (460 BCE) and Indian specialists Sushrut and Charak (600 BCE) knew about the function of cognizance and hunger in the pathogenesis of sicknesses. These Indian specialists suggested that "gorging, abundance of rest, absence of activity and nervousness may cause narrowing of directs in the body bringing about coronary failure and passing". Notwithstanding, present day doctors overlooked the part of the mind in the pathogenesis of CVDs and other interminable illnesses. Each diet and way of life factor is known to impact thoughtful and parasympathetic exercises, which are significant in the pathogenesis of CVDs and type 2 diabetes [25-28]. There are noteworthy circadian varieties in pulse, cardiovascular yield and blood pressures because of shifting thoughtful and parasympathetic action, demonstrating more prominent pulse, blood weights and contractility in the second quarter of a 24-hour cycle [29-35]. The echocardiographic elements of the heart, influenced by time structure among sound volunteers, are not known. Increments in pulse, blood pressures, supportive of provocative cytokines, blood glucose and oxidative pressure are prompt appearances of expanded thoughtful action which are related with an expansion in catecholamines and cortisol and a diminishing in acetylcholine, because of lower parasympathetic action [33-38]. There is a chance to forestall these issues, if genuine components of the essential danger factors, i.e., unfortunate eating routine, stationary conduct, tobacco utilization and mental burden, can be acquired by a cross-sectional review, since all these eating regimen and way of life variables can improve thoughtful action and diminishing parasympathetic action [24-28]. These social danger factors incline individuals to diabetes mellitus, hypercholesterolemia and hypertension, which are significant danger variables of coronary course infection (computer aided design) and stroke. Heftiness, metabolic disorder and left ventricular hypertrophy (LVH) are likewise connected with autonomic brokenness and are viewed as minor danger elements of CVDs including CHF. Investigation of the relationship of social danger factors with minor danger elements might be valuable in creating avoidance programme for early stage counteraction of CVDs including CHF [24-28]. Populace put together investigations with respect to echocardiographic work are not known; most of the information on echocardiographic capacity, for example, atrial and ventricular weights and discharge portion depend on age and sex coordinated clearly solid subjects, which in genuine sense may not be sound and are available to pre-disposition.

Exploratory examinations show that the favourable to

opio-melanocortin (POMC) pathway is engaged with the guideline of vitality and cardiovascular homeostasis in the nerve center and the mind stem [18]. The intense impacts of POMC-inferred peptides in various mind areas have been explained; the incessant site-explicit impacts of particular peptides, in any case, need further examinations [34-38]. The negative impacts of thoughtful over action and glucocorticoids on long haul cardiovascular wellbeing appear to be progressively clear. Late examinations directed in creature models of CVDs recommend that thoughtful tone to the splanchnic vasculature may assume a significant part in the turn of events and support of these sickness states [24-28]. Halberg's gathering has shown that a similar 2000-calorie feast expended toward the beginning of the day was related with a relative weight reduction, while a similar 2000-calorie supper devoured at night was related with a relative weight gain [39-44]. This methodology ought to be contemplated and applied to help forestall heftiness in the populace.

In short, clinical perceptions demonstrate that CVDs and type 2 diabetes mellitus were least regular during the 1950s, when industrialization and monetary improvement were started in the created nations [45-50]. Urbanization, portrayed with expanded admission of handled, solidified and saved western nourishments, stationary conduct, late night rest and late arousing, tobacco, liquor abuse, psychosocial stress and contamination, might be significant in the pathogenesis of brokenness of the autonomic sensory system, prompting the cutting edge plague of cardio-metabolic danger [40-56]. Since heftiness, type 2 diabetes and CVDs have become an overall general medical issue, contemplating circadian limited taking care of and cerebrum body cooperations, especially regarding PCSK9 levels seems, by all accounts, to be an intriguing methodology for counteraction of this plague [24-28, 39-44, 58]. Considering this survey, there is a requirement for associate examinations with the accompanying destinations with the end goal of avoidance of worldwide weight of sicknesses [57, 58]:

1. Investigation of social danger factors: dietary admissions, stationary conduct, tobacco and liquor consumption, late night rest and late evening eating and psychosocial worry in the populace.
2. Investigation of coronary danger factors: heftiness, focal corpulence, LVH, hypertension, diabetes mellitus, lipids and computer aided design.
3. Echocardiography of populace as a sub-investigation of more youthful versus older subjects, since CHF is multiple times more normal among subjects over 50 years old when contrasted with those under 50 years old.
4. Wandering BP checking and Holter ECG observing for 3-7 days, to decide circulatory strain inconstancy and HRV in a joint effort with the College of Minnesota, Minneapolis, USA and Tokyo Ladies' Clinical College, Tokyo, Japan.
5. Investigation of new danger elements of computer aided design/CHF, cytokines, lipoprotein(a), mRNA, leptin, BDNF, PCSK9, Expert, nitrite, neprilysin, natriuretic peptides.
6. Hereditary polymorphism in different populaces. DNA/chromatid methylation.
7. Autonomic brokenness. HRV, BRS.
8. Partner Study: New imaging methodology to expand affectability and particularity in analysis of intense coronary disorder and various reactions.

CONCLUSION

In 2016, the assessed predominance of CVDs in India was assessed to be 54.5 million. One out of 4 passings in India are currently a direct result of CVDs with ischemic coronary illness and stroke liable for >80% of this weight. CVD is a significant general medical issue in India, regularly affecting the most beneficial long periods of a person's life. The epidemiological progress plays out contrastingly in various areas of India in view of changed monetary turn of events. Dissimilar connections among SES and CVD hazard factors are apparent in districts that are at various phases of epidemiological progress. Nonetheless, tobacco use and hypertension in metropolitan settings are reliably connected with lower levels of training and salary. As the nation advances along the bearing of epidemiological change, other danger components of CVD may later on show comparative social slopes. Assuming responsibility for the CVD plague in India needs all the partners, including the arrangement creators, to recognize and address the social determinants that are firmly connected to CVD hazard factors and to the related grimness and mortality. The rising CVD trouble and the harming results it has on people, families, and populaces require pressing consideration. Inventive techniques are expected to end the movement of the CVD pandemic in asset helpless settings in India. To address the financial differentials in the weight of ailment and medical services needs of Indians, more assets should be coordinated toward applying the current information base to handle the CVD pandemic in strategy, programmes, limit building, and exploration fields.

REFERENCES

1. http://www.middleeasthealthmag.com/cgicontainer/index.cgi?http://www.middleeasthealthmag.com/jan 2013/feature11.htm

2. Van Gaal L.F., Maggioni A.P. *Overweight, Heftiness, and Results: Fat Mass and Past*. The Lancet 2014; 383: 935-6, doi:10.1016/S0140-6736(13)62076-0
3. MacGregor G.A., Hashem K.M. *Activity on Sugar-exercises from UK Salt Decrease Program*. The Lancet 2014; 383: 929-31, doi:10.1016/S0140-6736(14)60200-2
4. Singh R.B., Verma S.P., Niaz Mama. *Social Class and Coronary Vein Ailment in India*. Lancet 1999; 353: 154.
5. Pella D., Thomas N., Tomlinson B., Singh R.B. *Counteraction of Coronary Corridor Sickness: the South Asian Mystery*. Lancet 2003; 361:79-80.
6. Janus E.D., Postiglione A, Singh R.B., Lewis B. *For the Gathering on Arteriosclerosis of the Worldwide Society and League of Cardiology.The Modernization of Asia: Suggestions for Coronary Illness*. Flow 1996; 94: 2671-2673.
7. Singh R.B., Niaz Mama, Ghosh S, Beegum R., Rastogi V., Sharma J.P., Dube G.K.,. Relationship of Trans Unsaturated Fats (Vegetable Ghee) and Explained Margarine (Indian Ghee) Admission with Higher Danger of Coronary Illness in Country and Metropolitan Populaces with low Fat Utilization. *Int. J. Cardiol 1996*; 56: 289-298.
8. Yusuf S., Hawken S., Ounpuu S., et. al. *Impact of Conceivably Modifiable Danger Factors Related with Myocardial Localized Necrosis in 52 nations (the INTERHEART Study): Case-control Study*. Lancet. 2004; 364: 937-952.
9. Hajat C., Harrison O., Al Siksek Z. Weqaya: A Populace Wide Cardiovascular Screening Project in Abu Dhabi, Joined Middle Easterner Emirates. *Am. J. General Wellbeing*. 2012 May; 102(5): 909-914. Distributed online 2012 May. doi: 10.2105/AJPH.2011.300290
10. Loney T., Aw T.C., Handysides, D.G., Ali R. Blair I., Grivna M., Shah S.M., Sheek-Hussein M., El-Sadig M., Sharif A.A., El-Obaid Y. An Investigation of the Wellbeing Status of the Assembled Bedouin Emirates: the 'Enormous 4' General Medical Problems. *Glob Wellbeing Activity*. 2013; 6: 10.3402/gha.v6i0.20100. Distributed online Feb 5, 2013. doi: 10.3402/gha.v6i0.20100
11. MacDonald Gibson J., Thomsen J., Launay F., Harder E., DeFelice N. Passings and Clinical Visits owing to Ecological Contamination in the Unified Bedouin Emirates. PLoS One. 2013;8(3):e57536. doi: 10.1371/

diary .pone.0057536. Epub 2013 Blemish 4.

12. Almahmeed W., Arnaout M.S., Chettaoui R., Ibrahim M., Kurdi MI., Taher Mama, Mancia G. Coronary Vein Ailment in Africa and the Center East. Ther Clin Danger Manag. 2012; 8: 65-72. Distributed online Feb 16, 2012. doi: 10.2147/TCRM.S26414
13. World Wellbeing Association. Information and insights: mortality and Wellbeing Status. [Accessed January 12, 2012]. Accessible from: http://www.who.int/research/en/
14. Okrainec K, Banerjee D.K., Eisenberg M.J. Coronary Vein Ailment in the Creating Scene. Am. Heart J. 2004; 148: 7-15.
15. Singh R.B., Fedacko J., Vargova V., Kumar A, Mohan A., Pella D., De Meester F., Wilson D.W. Singh's Verbal Examination Poll for Appraisal of Reasons for Death, Social Post-mortem, Tobacco Post-mortem and dietary dissection dependent on Clinical Records and Meeting. *Acta Cardiol* 2011; 66: 471-481.
16. Singh R.B., Pella D., Mechirova V., Kumar K. et. al., Predominance of Weight, Physical Latency and Undernutrition, A Triple Weight of Sicknesses During Progress in Creating Nations. The Five City Study Gathering. *Acta Cardiol* 2007; 62: 119-127.
17. Singh R.B., Fedacko J., Pella D., Macejova Z., Ghosh S., Beegom R., Tumbi Z.A., Haque M., Vajpeyee S.K., De Meester F., Sergey C., Agarval R., Muthusamy V.V., Gupta A.A., and the Five City Study Gathering. Pervasiveness and Danger Components of Pre-Hypertension and Hypertension in Five Indian Urban Communities. *Acta Cardiol*. 2011; 66: 29-37.
18. Singh R.B., Sharma J.P., Rasogi V., Niaz Mama, Ghosh S., Beegom R., Janus E.D. Social Class and Coronary Malady in a Country Populace of North India. *Eur Heart J*. 1997:18; 588-95.
19. Singh R.B, Ghosh S., Niaz Mama, Rastogi V. Approval of physical Movement and Financial Poll According to Food Admissions for the Five City Study and a Proposed Grouping for Indians. J. *Assoc Phys. India* 1997; 45: 603-607.
20. Singh R.B., Rastogi S.S., Rastogi V., et. al.. Circulatory strain patterns, Plasma Insulin Levels, and Danger Factors in Provincial and Metropolitan old Populaces of North India. *Coron Corridor Dis*. 1997;8: 463-8.

21. Singh R.B., Beegum R., Ghosh S., Niaz Mama, Rastogi V., Rastogi S.S., Singh N.K. Epidemiologic Investigation of Hypertension and Its Determinants in a Metropolitan Populace of North India. J. Human Hyper 1997; 11: 679-685.
22. Singh R.B., Beegom R., Rastogi V., Rastogi S.S., Madhu V. Clinical Qualities of Hypertension Among Patients of Noninsulin Subordinate Diabetes Mellitus in North and South India. *J. Diab Assoc. India* 1996; 36: 45-50.
23. Singh R.B., Bajaj S., Niaz Mama, Rastogi S.S., Moshiri M. Commonness of Type 2 Diabetes Mellitus and Danger of Hypertension and Coronary Corridor Malady in Country and Metropolitan Populace with Low Paces of Weight. Int. *J Cardiol.* 1998 Sep 1; 66 (1): 65-72.
24. Singh R.B., De Meester F., Wilson D.W. Globalization of Riches Yet not Wellbeing on the Planet. *W.H.J.* 2013 (in press)
25. Pellissier S., Dantzer C., Mondillon L., Trocme C., Gauchez A.S., Ducros V., Mathieu N., Toussaint B., Fournier A., Canini F., et al. Connection between Vagal Tone, Cortisol, TNF-Alpha, Epinephrine and Negative Effects in Crohn's Infection and Fractious Entrail Condition. PLoS One. 2014; 9(9):e105328. Epub 2014 Sep 10.
26. Tran BW1, Papoiu Advertisement, Russoniello C.V., Wang H., Patel T.S., Chan Y.H., Yosipovitch G. Impact of Tingle, Scratching and Mental Weight on Autonomic Sensory System Work in Atopic Dermatitis. *Acta Derm Venereol.* 2010 Jul;90(4):354-61. doi: 10.2340/00015555-0890.
27. Mendonca GV1, Pereira F.D., Fernhall B. Impacts of Cigarette Smoking on Heart Autonomic Capacity During Dynamic Exercise. J Sports Sci. 2011 Jun;29(9):879-86. doi: 10.1080/02640414. 2011.572991.
28. Mischel N.A., Mueller P.J. (In) Activity-subordinate Adjustments in Resting and Reflex Control of Splanchnic Thoughtful Nerve Movement. *J. Appl Physiol* (1985). Dec 2011; 111(6): 1854-1862. Distributed online Oct 6, 2011. doi: 10.1152/japplphysiol.00961.2011
29. Marcheva B., Ramsey K.M., Buhr E.D. et al., Interruption of the Clock Segments CLOCK and BMAL1 Prompts Hypoinsulinaemia and Diabetes. *Nature* 2010; 466: 627-31.
30. Oishi K., Shirai H., and Ishida N. Check is Engaged with the Circadian Transactivation of Peroxisome-proliferator-initiated receptor a (PPAR^a) in mice. *Biochem J.* 2005; 386: 575-81.

31. Turek F.W., Joshu C., Kohsaka An et al. Stoutness and Metabolic Disorder in Circadian clock Freak Pleasant. Science 2005; 308: 1043-1045.
32. Arble D.M., Bass J, Laposky Advertisement, Vitaterna M.H., and Turek F.W. Circadian Planning of Food Admission Adds to Weight Gain. *Stoutness 2009*; 17: 2100-2102.
33. Panda S., Hogenesch J.B., and Kay S.A. Circadian Rhythms from Flies to Human. *Nature 2002*; 417; 329-35.
34. Reppert S.M., Weaver D.R. Coordination of Circadian Planning in Warm Blooded Animals. Nature 2002; 418: 935-941.
35. Singh R.B., Gupta S., Dherange P., De Meester F., Wilczynska An, Alam S.E., Pella D., Wilson DW. Metabolic Condition; a Cerebrum Sickness. *Can J. physiol Pharmacol* 2012; 90: 1171-1183.
36. Singh R.B., Halberg F., Cornelissen G., Siegelova J., Hristova J., Toda E., Takahashi T., Jan Fedacko J., Otsuka K. Customized Circadian Planning of Activity. *World Heart J.* 2013; 5: 79-90.
37. Sherman H., Frumin I., Gutman R. et. al.. Long Haul Limited Taking Care of Modifies Circadian Articulation and Decreases the degree of Fiery and Infection Markers. J. *Cell Molecul Prescription 2011*; 15: 2745-59.
38. Sherman H., Genzer Y., Cohen R., Chapnik N., Madar Z., Froy O. Planned High-fat Eating Regimen Resets Circadian Digestion and Forestalls Heftiness. *FASEB J.* 2012; 26: 3493-502.
39. Singh R.B., Srivastav V., Srivastav S.S.L., Akhilesh J., Cornélissen G., Halberg F. Circadian Variety Under States of Caloric Limitation in North India. Unique 36, Second Global Discussion: Workshop on Chronoastrobiology and Chronotherapy, Tokyo Kasei College, Tokyo, Japan, November 2001, unpaginated (1 p).
40. Halberg F., Sullivan B., Feast Plans and Their Cooperation With the Body's Timetables. *Chronobiologia 1976*; 3: 75-76.
41. Nelson W., Cadotte L., Halberg F., Circadian Planning of Single Every Day "supper" Influences Endurance of Mice. *Proc. Soc. exp. Biol. (NY)* 1973; 144: 766-769.
42. Halberg F., Cornelissen G., Wang Z.R., Wan C., Ulmer W., Katinas G., Singh Ranjana, Singh R.K., Singh Rajesh, Gupta B.D., Singh R.B., Kumar A., Kanabrocki E., Sothern R.B., Rao G., Bhatt M.L.B.D.,

Srivastava M., Rai G., Singh S., Pati A.K., Nath P., Halberg Francine, Halberg J., Schwartzkopff O., Bakken E., Shastri V.K. Chronomics: Circadian and Circaseptan Timing of Radiotherapy, Drugs, Calories, Maybe Nutriceuticals and Past. *J. Exp Therapeutics Oncol.* 2003; 3: 223-260.

43. Cornelissen G. At the Point When You Eat Matters: 60 years of Franz Halberg's Nourishment Chronomics. *The Open Nutr. J.* 2012; 4: 16-44.
44. Singh R.B., Singh A.K., Sharma J.P., Singh R.K., Kumar A., Rastogi S.S., Singh Garima, Kartikey K., Singh S., Fedacko J., Pella D., De Meester F., Wilczynska A., Wilson D.W. Nourishment in Chronocardiology: we are Obligated Teacher Franz Halberg. *The Open Nutra J.* 2012;45-65.
45. Iqbal R., Anand S., Ounpuu S., et. al; INTERHEART Study Examiners. Dietary Examples and the Danger of Intense Myocardial Dead Tissue in 52 Nations: Aftereffects of the INTERHEART Study. Flow. 2008; 118:1929-1937.
46. Teo K., Lear S., Islam S., Mony P., Dehghan M., Li W., Rosengren A., Lopez-Jaramillo P., Diaz R., Oliveira G., Miskan M., Rangarajan S., Iqbal R., Ilow R., Puone T., Bahonar A., Gulec S., Darwish E.A., Lanas F., Vijaykumar K., Rahman O., Chifamba J., Hou Y., Li N., Yusuf S.; in the Interest of the Unadulterated Agents. Commonness of a Sound Way of Life Among People with Cardiovascular Sickness in High-, Center and Low-salary Nations: The Forthcoming Metropolitan Rustic The Study of Disease Transmission (Unadulterated) Study. J.A.M.A. 2013; 309: 1613-1621.
47. Singh R.B., Hristova K., Muthusamy V.V., Basu T.K., Rastogi S.S., Toda E., Takahashi T., Fedacko J., Pella D., Wilson D.W., De Meester F., Mondal R., Ishaq M., Mohideen M.R.. The Unfavorable Impacts of Riches on Cardiovascular Wellbeing: A Logical Articulation of the Worldwide School of Cardiology. *Cardiol Angiol 2013;* 1: 9-22.
48. Singh R.B. and Indian Agreement Gathering. Commonness and Avoidance of Hypertension, Diabetes Mellitus, and Coronary Course ailment in India. A Logical Articulation of the Indian Culture of Hypertension, Global School of Nourishment and Worldwide School of Cardiology. *World Heart J.* 2010; 2: 31-44.
49. Singh R.B., De Meester F., Wilczynszka A., Takahashi T., Juneja L.,

Watson R.R. Could a Changed Food Industry Forestall Cardiovascular Ailments? *World Heart J.* 2013; 5: 1-8.

50. World Wellbeing Association. The 2008-2013 Activity Plan for the Worldwide System for the Counteraction and Control of Non-communicable Maladies (Got to through: http://www.who.int/nmh/Actionplan-PC-NCD-2008.pdf).
51. Shroufi A., Chowdhury R., Anchala R., Stevens S., Blanco P., Han T., Niessen L., Franco Goodness. Savvy Intercessions for the Counteraction of Cardiovascular Ailment in Low and Center Salary Nations: An Orderly Survey. *BMC General Wellbeing 2012*; 13: 285. doi: 10.1186/1471-2458-13-285.
52. Hristova K., Shiue I., Pella D., Singh R.B., Chaves H., Basu T.K., Ozimek L., Rastogi S.S., Takahashi T., Wilson D., DeMeester F., Cheema S., Garg M., Buttar H.S., Milovanovic B., Kumar A., Handjiev S., Cornélissen G., Petrov I. Counteraction Systems for Cardiovascular Ailments and Diabetes Mellitus in Creating Nations: World Congress of Clinical Sustenance 2013. Sustenance 2014; doi: 10.1016/j.nut.2013.12.013.
53. Singh R.B., Takahashi T., Nakaoka T., Otsuka K., Toda E., Shin H.H., Kyu Lee M., Beeharry V., Hristova K., Fedacko J., Pella D., De Meester F., Wilson D.W., Juneja L.R. Sustenance Experiencing Significant Change from *Homo Sapiens* to *Homo Economicus*. *The Open Nutra* J. 2013; 6: 6-17.
54. The "Coronary Illness and Stroke Insights - 2014 Update" Dissemination. 2014; 129: e28-e292. Distributed online before print December 18, 2013, doi: 10.1161/01.cir.0000441139.02102.80
55. Moodie R., Stuckler D., Monteiro C., Sheron N., Neal B., Thamarangsi T., Lincoln P., Casswel S. for the Lancet NCD Gathering. Benefits and pandemics: Counteraction of Unsafe Impacts of Tobacco, Liquor and Super Prepared Food and Drink Enterprises. The Lancet 2013 (doi:10.1016/S0140-6736(12)62089).
56. Bantle J.P. Dietary fructose and Metabolic Condition and Diabetes. J. *Nutr. 2009*; 139, 1263S-1268S.
57. Naghavi M., Wang H., Lozano R., Davis An et. al. Worldwide, Local, and Public Age-sex Explicit All-cause and Cause-Explicit mortality for 240 Reasons for Death, 1990-2013: A Methodical Investigation for the

Worldwide Weight of Infection Study 2013. *The Lancet. 2014* Dec. 17. doi: 10.1016/S0140-6736(14)61682-2

58. Saboo B., Fedacko J., Singh R.B.. Proprotein Convertase Subtilisin/kexin type 9 inhibiters. *World Heart J*. 2015;7: (In Press).

9

India's Vaccine Diplomay

Dhiraj Gurung.

ABSTRACT

The Indian Pharmaceutical companies have been doing well since few decades back, in the times of global health pandemic such as, HIV/AIDS, Tuberculosis (T.V) and Malaria. India has been exporting affordable antiretroviral medicines, thereby making herself as one of the 'Pharmaceutical hub' in the world. With the outbreak of the corona virus, the World Health Organization (WHO) declared it as a global pandemic in March 2020, the virus has claimed 4,197,153 deaths and 196,200,266 cases (29, July,2021). The pandemic has impacted almost every corner of life, causing global economies to stall, and has affected the human lifestyle. All nations around the world have been forced to implement harsh restrictions on human activity to curb the spread of the virus. COVID-19 vaccination is now offering a way to transition out of this phase of the pandemic. Without them, many scientists believe that natural herd immunity would not have been sufficient to restore society to its normal status quo and that it would have resulted in extreme fatality. This is something that has been echoed by many health organizations including the WHO. In a scenario without access to vaccines, strict behavioral measures may have had to remain for the foreseeable future. Fortunately, with the beginning of 2021 saw numerous vaccines given emergency approval and begin their roll out in countries across the world. No country has escaped from this pandemic, thereby creating an environment of global emergency. India reigned its pharmaceutical capability and quickly expanded *"Vaccine Maitri"* to different parts of the world. India has supplied vaccines to more than 95 countries as well as UN Peacekeepers. India has played a major role in fighting this global pandemic by undertaking an initiative *"Vaccine Maitri"* to provide COVID-19 vaccines to countries around the world. Therefore, the main purpose of the study here is to examine the dynamics of India's vaccine diplomacy. The methodology applied for the study here is descriptive and explanatory. Descriptive study in the sense that the main purpose of the research is to describe the situation and events during the time of pandemic. Explanatory in the sense, that the study is to focus the role of India during the global pandemic. The work is largely based on secondary data, as the materials and main sources have been articles, journals and various websites.

Keywords: Vaccine Diplomacy, Vaccine Maitri, COVID-19, Serum Institute of India (SII), Covaxin, Covishield, Sputnik.

INTRODUCTION

Before going to the topic Vaccine Diplomacy, it becomes necessary to understand what actually is vaccine diplomacy? So, vaccine diplomacy can be understood as the branch of global health diplomacy that relies on the use or delivery of vaccines.In other words, vaccine diplomacy refers to vaccine-related diplomatic activities to boost a country's foreign relations and global influence. Today "vaccine diplomacy" is used to describe the global diplomatic efforts to achieve efficient and fair distributions of Covid-19 vaccines around the world, especially to low- and lower-middle -income countries. Diplomacy is conducted to serve a country's national interests. The current wave of "vaccine-diplomacy" in the midst of a global pandemic undoubtedly helps the international community to combat the coronavirus and it is much appreciated. Countries that are willing to help others to control the pandemic are commendable. However, 'vaccine diplomacy', just like other forms of diplomacy, primarily serves a country's own interests. A country may have explicit or implicit goals when carrying out such diplomacy, such as boosting its international status or seeking economic and other opportunities.

India is known as the pharmaceutical hub of the world, as it is the largest producer of generic medicines, accounting for 20% of its global production. It meets 62% of the global demand for vaccines. Since the corona virus pandemic began, the country has been at the forefront of supplying medicines and generic drugs to others. India received requests from more than 100 countries for hydroxychloroquine (oncethought to help treat COVID-19) and paracetamol (a painkiller) and sent supplies to Brazil, the United States, and Israel. By May 2020, India was spending $16million on pharmaceuticals, test kits, and other medical equipment for about 90 countries. India officially started its vaccine diplomacy with the name "Vaccine Maitri" under its Neighborhood First Policy. The vaccine was supplied to the partner countries in a phased manner, keeping in mind the demand. India also helped all the countries in enhancing their cold chain and storage capacities for the delivery of Vaccines. Bhutan, Maldives, Bangladesh, and Nepal were the foremost countries to receive their Covishield vaccines from India.

India continues to cope with the devastating effects of

its second wave of the COVID-19 pandemic, which has taken the lives of thousands of people- the exact number remains uncertain. The unfolding tragedy has also shut the gates of New Delhi vaccine Diplomacy. In January India was not only kicking off its vaccination drive, but also sharing millions of doses with other countries. India was heralded in the news as the nation with the biggest vaccine manufacturing capacity. The country's the then foreign minister was busy tweeting about each shipment of vaccines to another nation. By March, however, that rosy picture gave way to calamity, overshadowing earlier success. Some believe now that India's vaccine diplomacy was a mistake, or at least that it did not yield the desired results. But it resulted too early for that conclusion.

By April it became obvious that India was being hit by a massive wave of COVID-19 infections, and that the spike was not confined to specific states, like Maharashtra, but was quickly on its way to being a national crisis. New Delhi then blocked all exports of vaccines, promising it would be a temporary two-month measure to "prioritize" domestic needs. As Indian hospitals overflowed with patients, many of them with severe symptoms and with thousands dying due to insufficient equipment, the world community started to wend emergency transports of medical aid to India, such as oxygen concentrators. India donated over 10 million doses of vaccines to other countries, while the total number of doses given to its citizens by 26 July stood at around 43 crores. Of these, 33.8 crore were first doses, and 9.2 crore people received both doses.

Besides donations, over 35.7 million doses were sold to other countries and these commercial shipments, presumably, were doses sold by the Serum Institute of India- a private company which has the biggest COVID-19 vaccine producing capacity in the world and which produces AstraZeneca's vaccine on a license. The doses that New Delhi gifted to other countries were also mostly produced by this company, and then purchased by the Indian Government, which decided to donate a part of them to other countries. It is true that the government of India could have halted commercial sales earlier and for longer (it did so briefly in January and in April). Yet, this would have generated legal problems (as the current blocking of exports is doing) and raise moral questions (most of the customers are poorer countries). Moreover, although the number of doses sold was larger than the number of donated doses, and they could have been used to vaccinate millions in India, on a national scale these doses would not have been able to stop the second wave.

The other type of exports were Indian shipments of nearly 20 million doses of vaccines destined to be used by the COVAX facility for poorer countries. This, however, was not just a moral obligation but a formal one-international donors had in fact earlies supplied the Serum Institute of India with funds so that the company could ramp up manufacturing capacity, provided that a part of the vaccine would be later given to COVAX. Indeed, India's Ministry of External Affairs data shows that while the last commercial shipment was on March 29 (and was flown to Palestine), transports for the sake of COVAX continued until mid-April, destined for countries such as Zambia, Mauritania, and Syria.

In an unusual diplomatic initiative, India has donated millions of doses of the British-developed AstraZeneca COVID-19 vaccine being produced in the country to neighboring South Asian nations as mentioned above. The 'vaccine diplomacy' in a way aims to raise New Delhi's global profile and push back against China, which has been expanding its influence in South Asia.

COVAXIN AND COVISHIELD

India succeeded in making two 'Made in India vaccines'- Covishield and Covaxin- against the coronavirus disease and the government declared both vaccines as safe.

Covaxin

India's indigenous COVID-19 vaccine by Bharat Biotech is developed in collaboration with Indian Council of Medical Research (ICMR)- National Institute of Virology (NV). The indigenous vaccine is developed and manufactured in Bharat Biotech's BSL-3 (Bio-Safely Level 3) high containment facility.

The vaccine is developed using Whole-Virion Inactivated Cell derived platform technology. Inactivated vaccines do not replicate and are therefore unlikely to revert and cause pathological effects. They contain dead virus, incapable of infecting people but still able to instruct the immune system to mount a defensive reaction against an infection.

Covishield

Covishield is brand model name of Oxford-AstraZeneca COVID-19 vaccine, also codenamed AZD1222. A viral vector vaccine for prevention of COVID-19, Covishield is developed by Oxford University and AstraZeneca, and is given by intramuscular injection. The vaccine has a good safety profile, with minor side effects such as injection-site pain, headache, and nausea. The vaccine is marketed under the brand name Covishield by the Serum Institute of India (SII).

VACCINE MAITRI

'Vaccine Diplomacy' meaning 'Vaccine Friendship' is a humanitarian and commercial initiative undertaken by the government of India to provide COVID-19 vaccines to different nations. During the time of dire need of the antidote for the corona virus, India produced 60 per cent of all vaccines manufactured in the world. The head of the WHO complained that the developed countries monopolized the Pfizer and Moderna vaccines for their own populations and were not making them available to developing countries.

India, keeping her 'Neighborhood First' Policy at the forefront enunciated by Modi at the beginning of his first term in 2014, Bhutan and Maldives became the first two countries to receive 150,000 and 100,000 vaccines respectively, on January 20,2021. Bangladesh and Nepal received two million and one million doses on January 21. Myanmar received 1.5 million doses, Seychelles 50,000 doses, and Mauritius 100,000 doses on January 22.

The two million doses gifted by India to Bangladesh were the single largest consignment of vaccines provided by India to any country thus far, prompting the Bangladesh Health Minister to comment that India had stood by his country during the Liberation War of 1971 as well as during the pandemic. Bangladesh was supposed to get 110,000 doses of free vaccines from the Chinese form Sinovac Biotech, but its reluctance to contribute towards the development cost of the vaccine, led to a deadlock.

India's vaccine assistance reached Nepal within a week of a request made by Nepalese Foreign Minister during his visit to New Delhi on January 15,2021. India's gesture to Nepal came at a time when its ties have been strained by a territorial dispute as well as concerns over China's expanding political and economic influence in the Himalayan nation. China, which had promised Nepal help to deal with the pandemic, is yet to receive Nepali clearance for its Sinopharm shots.

It is pertinent to flag that there is a huge demand for vaccines in some of the above-mentioned countries who are desperate to revive their tourism-dependent economies. This has provided an important opportunity for the Indian Government to expand and strengthen its outreach.

All the above vaccine supplies by India were made on a gratis basis. Several of these countries are among the reportedly 90 countries including South Africa, Saudi Arabia, UAE and a host of others that have signed commercial agreements with Indian manufacturers, supplies pursuant to which will be made in the coming days. Regulatory approvals by Afghanistan are awaited to effect supplies to it. Shipment of 500,000 doses to Sri Lanka was affected on January 27,2021. India has also conducted training programme for its neighbors to help them in the vacation drive.

Apart from countries in India's immediate and extended neighborhood, Brazil and Morocco, close strategic partners, also got 2 million doses each on January 22. Brazilian President Jair Bolsonaro thanked PM Modi for sending the vaccine supplies and equated the gesture with that of Lord Hanuman bringing the holy 'Sanjeevani'. PM Roosevelt Skerrit of Dominican Republic called for assistance from India 'with great humility and respect... to make our population safe'. The US State Department, the WHO, Bill Gates and several others have spoken warmly and appreciatively of the selfless manner in which India is helping several developing countries with the vaccines.

India's 'Vaccine Maitri' Mission appears to have taken China by surprise and put it on the back foot. Global Times, the mouth piece of the Chinese Communist Party, has started spreading lies and making disparaging remarks about the safety, efficacy and capacity of India to produce vaccines in adequate numbers. This is even as countries like Cambodia, Nepal and Bangladesh have refused to take China's vaccines because of quality concerns or terms of supply. China's 'iron friend' Pakistan, meanwhile, has been informed that it could send its aircraft to Beijing to airlift 500,000 doses of the vaccines. This is in stark contrast to the dispatch effected by India to Nepal and Bangladesh in Air India special flights. Brazil which had also imported Chinese vaccines, is wary of using them because it finds that their efficacy is just around 50 per cent, which is much lower than all other vaccines in use in the world.

Vaccine Maitri Program

- 66 million doses to 95 countries.
- 10 million-grants.
- 20million- as part of global Covax facility.
- 36 million were commercial exports.

SIGNIFICANCE OF VACCINE DIPLOMACY

Strategic Importance: This will give a boost to India's Neighborhood First and Act East Policy. It shows greater coordination between the two countries to save people from the global pandemic of COVID-19. For instance, India is keen on mending its ties with Bangladesh. The citizenship law enacted last year and the news of $40 billion in investment from China to Bangladesh had strained ties between the two nations. The COVID-19 vaccine can let a little slack back in. Similarly, vaccine diplomacy provides an opportunity for India to resolve outstanding issues with Nepal. Relations between the two countries recently hit a new low when they entered into a heated exchange over the Kalapani territorial dispute- an area situated at the strategic China-Nepal-India trijunction.

Tracking Chinese Influence: Vaccine manufacture and distribution is one area where India has some comparative advantage over China, but the competition between the two may still be fierce. China has even explicitly included vaccine distribution in its broader Health Silk Road initiative, which aims to bolster China's international; soft power. In Indian Ocean countries like the Maldives and Mauritius, India's vaccine diplomacy can help foster stronger ties in the region, and offset China's growing influence attribute to its financial investments and social development projects.

INDIA-CHINA VACCINE DIPLOMACY

China was the first major power to practice 'vaccine diplomacy' during the Covid-19 pandemic. In March 2020, President Xi Jimping announced at a World Health Assembly meeting that China considered its Covid-19 vaccines a 'global public good'. China has donated its homemade vaccines to dozens of countries. Often times 'free samples' would result in the recipient country's interest in purchasing the vaccines. China in order to increase its soft power, China has to tie its distribution of vaccines to the advancement of major projects under the Belt and Road Initiative.

In the counterpart, India launched 'Vaccine Maitri' or 'Vaccine Friendship' in early 2021. Vaccine Maitri was instantly designed to repair India's strained relations with South Asian neighbors, where India appeared to be losing pro-eminence to growing Chinese influence. India has leveraged its pharmaceutical power and quickly expanded 'Vaccine Maitri' to different parts of the world. By the beginning of April 2021, India has supplied vaccines to over 95 countries as well as United Nations Peacekeepers. Foreign Minister S Jaishankardeclared that 'Vaccine Maitri', "raised India's standing and generated great international goodwill".

India's vaccine diplomacy has helped soothe some

prickly relationships with neighbors in South Asia, 'where it has been fighting an increasingly sharp diplomatic battle with China'. Even on Chinese borders, Indian shots are showing up. Mongolia's Prime Minister received one of 150,000 free doses delivered by India. On the other hand, Indonesia's Joko Widodo, Turkey's RecepTayyip Erdogan, and the President of Seychelles have taken Chinese vaccines. One place where China's influence still dominates is India's archival Pakistan, recipient of some $70 billion of Chinese financing for infrastructure. China is also having success in Africa and Latin America- major investment regions for Beijing. In China, vaccine development and distribution are a highly state-driven process. All three major Chinese vaccine makers- Sinopharm, Sinovac and CanSino- have been involved in vaccine development and distribution and are playing an active role in China's vaccine diplomacy. And there is coordination between these pharma companies and the Chinese government in the latest round of 'vaccine diplomacy'. For example, Sinopharm has recently partnered with United Arab Emirates to make millions of doses in the United Arab Emirates for local populations, deepening China's engagement with countries in the West Asia. Meanwhile, Sinovac has worked with Brazil and Indonesia to produce tons of millions of doses of its vaccine for local use.

India has supplied vaccines to various countries across the globe. All vaccine distributions are overseen by the Indian government, and vaccines are not yet available on the private market. The Serum Institute of India, the world's biggest producer of vaccines, has partnered with the Indian government. It has been heavily involved in the distribution of vaccines and is the largest supplier to the global vaccine scheme COVAX. The Indian government has purchased vaccines form the Serum Institute and other large pharma companies at low, subsidized rates for both domestic overseas distributions.

Both the countries are keeping a focus on their own self-interest. In case with China, India's vaccine diplomacy serves as an effective tool and instrument of Indian soft-power and influence, serving to deepen ties with other countries. India has been demanding for years a permanent seat on the UN Security Council. India's 'Vaccine Diplomacy' could translate into critical votes at a time when India has secured a non-permanent seat on the UN Security Council and is scheduled to host the G20 summit in 2023. The goodwill India earns through 'Vaccine Maitri' could pay dividends in the future.

India's free-vaccine diplomacy, has been driven by more than altruism. There are geopolitical considerations at play, including building goodwill and influence and countering China's growing strategic footprint in the Indian Ocean region. Supplying free vaccines to combat a raging pandemic also seems a better choice for New Delhi than providing direct and in another form.

In the end, the competition between China and India to provide vaccines, especially to nations where their strategic interests overlap, is likely to help not only those nations but the rest of the world.

SECOND WAVE OF COVID-19 IN INDIA, AND CRITICISM OF INDIA'S VACCINE DIPLOMACY

Pandemic has more power to kill humans without using any weapons as compared to manmade wars, this myth looks true as we see the situation created by the coronavirus pandemic in all over the world. Since the middle of March 2021, the second wave started, and on May 20, the highest number of cases (144,829) was identified in India. The major affected states in the beginning were Maharashtra, Kerala,

Karnataka, Andhra Pradesh, Delhi, Uttar Pradesh, and West Bengal. Despite the high caseload, several national movements such as farmer's movement, election in several states, and pilgrimage tourism was taken place. Those triggered the risk of transmission of COVID-19.

During the 1st wave, the central government imposed a nation-wide lockdown on March 25, 2020. The result revealed a well-controlled infection rate and the Indian policy was appreciated internationally. Although several countries in Europe imposed lockdown in several formats, surprisingly, in the second wave, there appeared a lack of coordination between different health agencies and the government in India.

Nations around the world scrambled to assist India with critical medical supplies and therapeutic/diagnostic equipment. By early May, the country had received some 9,000 oxygen concentrators, over 5,000 oxygen cylinders, 18 oxygen generators, and 3.4 lakh Remdesivir vials. Nearly 40 countries, by mid-May, have offered assistance in varying forms.

While India's 'vaccine diplomacy' had earned, it praises when the case count was low, international publications later criticized the Indian vaccine diplomacy. The nation registered more than 3lakhs cases every day in the second wave, the largest surge in the world is also the country with the largest heart as India: lifted ban of HCQ, send medical teams to neighborhood, and Vaccine Maitri Program.

India's vaccine diplomacy has been criticized on following grounds:

I. For not anticipating the current crisis and sending out the wrong message internationally that India did not need help. On January 29th, in his speech at

Davos Forum, Prime Minister Modi announced that country had won the war against COVID-19 and repeated the same in the Parliament a week later. At that time there were 1100 cases/ day and 1.5 lakh active cases. It later increased to 3 lakhs per day, and 24 lakhs active cases per day were seen during the second wave.

II. Lack of preperation and planning:
Election Campaigns were going on in 5 state and 1 Union Territory, where huge number of public gathering was seen. KumbhMela management and its anticipation as covid hotspot.

III. Not leveraging its strength to ramp up hospital bed strengths, pharma supplies and oxygen production. For not asking for imports and not halting exports like pharma and oxygen that are needed most.

IV. For Vaccine Maitri Program that began as exactly the same time as Domestic Vaccination programme. The government focused more on the export rather than supporting the idea of *'Vaccine Nationalism'* (Vaccine Nationalism: when a country manages to secure doses of vaccines for its own citizens or residents and prioritize its own domestic markets before, they are made available in other countries).

India became from exporter of vaccines to importer of vaccines. (e.g. the government gave emergency approval to Sputnik 5.). Defending this criticism, the government made a statement "India cannot ask the world for help, for vaccine supplies if it is not willing to export its own product to help others". One of the counter arguments for this is, after USA India has highest number of cases; highest number of active cases, highest number of new cases highest number of deaths. India's population is almost 3 billion, i.e. 1/6 of the whole humanity, so if India helps her own citizen, it will take large load of Global Pandemic worry.

CONCLUSION

Each country has its own diplomatic relations with other countries regarding scientific or political aspects. When it comes to the utilization of concepts of science it leads to what is called science-based diplomacy or scientific diplomacy. A subset of this science-based diplomacy or scientific diplomacy is nothing but Vaccine Diplomacy. During an hour of the global pandemic India introduced herself to world as the largest heart giving her helping hand to ensure vaccine supply to the neediest countries. The developed countries on one hand was busy securing vaccines for its own interest and for its citizens, India came forward providing the needy nations the antidote to fight against the global pandemic. It is important to note that India started the mission of exporting the vaccines to the rest of the world at the same time as the domestic vaccination programme was started. This shows the true will of India of giving the world a helping hand during the time of need and a significant step taken to evident its years of heritage and amicable relations with other nations.

The Government came up with a great initiative, Vaccine Maitri, under which vaccines made in collaboration with indigenous are supplied to other nations besides Indians. Though many countries have shown a great interest in so-called vaccine nationalism, our country is keen to put forth its policy of VASUDHAIVA KUTUMBHAKAM, literally saying, the whole world to be our family.

Therefore, India's vaccine diplomacy was not a mistake in the sense that not undertaking it would have stopped the calamity. This is especially true when we conclude that only the 1o million doses donated by new Delhi to other nations can be really counted as vaccine diplomacy (rather than commercial sales or other commitments). Despite till 25th of July just 9.2 crore people had received both doses of a COVID-19 vaccine. There are 94 crore Indians aged 18 years or above. This means that only around 9.8 of the adult population has been fully vaccinated. Given that the vaccination drive has been going on for over six months now, and the fact that over 90% of Indians are yet to be fully vaccinated, this should be a reason for worry. Around 84.8 crore adults still haven't been fully vaccinated. The key problem behind the slow vaccination pace has been the erratic supply of vaccine doses. This is primarily because the central government tool its time to order the doses. Between January and July 16, a total of 41.5 crore doses of vaccines were supplied. Of these 36 crore doses were supplied by the Serum Institute of India (SII), which manufactures Covishield, and 5.5 crore doses were supplied by Covaxin-maker Bharat Biotech. Further, 33 lakh doses of Sputnik V have been imported, taking the total supply to amongst 42 crore doses. India being the pharmacy of the world, she has supplied essential medicines to the needy across the globe in the past and has once again proved the world by providing 60per cent of the world's total vaccine to the needy nations.

India has definitely been successful in promoting the initiative of 'Vaccine Maitri' as with rapidity and selflessness, India rolled out millions of doses and despite the massive requirements of its own vaccination drive. Without keeping in mind, the idea of 'Vaccine Nationalism', India served humanity with her full capacity. At one side, China in the eyes of the world became a threat to humanity, and responsible for the birth of COVID-19, on the other side, contrary to this, India emerged as a savior and an antidote against the ill will of China, by giving her best effort to fight the global pandemic. India's 'Vaccine Maitri' initiative has further strengthened its image as the first responder in emergency situations. This is all more commendable when there are only five countries in the world who have thus far been able to successfully manufacture COVID-19 vaccines.

To conclude, it was the result of the far-sighted vision of the initiative of 'Vaccine Maitri', that helped India to fight against the second-wave of this global pandemic which proved to be more dangerous and disastrous then the first wave.

REFERENCE

1. Iwanek Krzysztof: *Don't Write Off Indian Vaccine Diplomacy Yet*. The Diplomat.
2. Moya A, Holmes EC, Gonzalez-Candelas F: *The population genetics and evolutionary epidemiology of RNA virus.*
3. DharBiswajit: *India's Vaccine Diplomacy*. Global Policy Journal.
4. Frazier W Mark: *How India and China are using Covid-19 'Vaccine Diplomacy' to compete globally*. An interview with Chinese foreign affairs expert Zhiqun Zhu.
5. OjhaSangeeta*: Covishield vs Covaxin: Your vaccine guide to list of possible 'side effects'*. livemint.com.
6. PasrichaAnjana: *India launches 'Neighborly Vaccine Diplomacy'*. voanews.com.
7. SajjanharAshok: *India's 'Vaccine Maitri' Initiative*. Manohar Parrikar Institute for Defense Studies and Analysis.
8. Ghosh Poulomi: *When will 2nd wave of Covid in India be over? Govt's top advisor explains in 4 points.* A report from hindusantimes.com.
9. *COVID-19: From criticism of 'Vaccine Diplomacy' to undercounting of deaths, an overview of global coverage of crisis in India*. Firstpost.com.
10. ParpianiKashish, Bose Sohini, Kapoor Nivedita, Dubey Mrityunjaya, Banerjee Sreeparna, TanejaKabir*: Friendships, Reciprocity, and Diplomacy in the Time of COVID-19: The World Comes to India's Aid.* orfonline.org.

11. Ministry of External Affairs, Government of India, https://mea.gov.in/bilateral-documents.htm? dtl/33853/Joint_statement_on IndiaEU_Leaders_Meeting_May_08_2021.
12. HaidarSuhasini: *What went wrong with India's Vaccine Diplomacy?* thehindu.com.
13. Boehm E, Kronig I, Neher RA, Eckerle I, Vetter P, Kaiser L: *Novel SARS-CoV-2 variants: the pandemics within the pandemic.*https://doi.org/10.1016/.cmi.2021.05.022.
14. Sahoo JP, Mishra AP, Samal KC: Triple mutant Bengal strain (b1.618) of coronavirus and the worst COVID outbreak in India. https://biocainternational.com/ojs/index.php/biorestoday/article/view/837
15. Dyer O: *Covid-19 India sees record deaths as "black fungus" spreads fear.* BMJ, 2021;373n238.
16. Kapoor Mudit, Shamika Ravi: *Making waves in India: Media and the COVID-19 pandemic.* brrokings.edu.
17. *"India's COVID-19 emergency."* The Lancet 397, 1683 (2021). https://www.mohfw.gov.in/.
18. *India's Covid Vaccine Diplomacy-Why it failed? International Relations Current Affairs.* Study IQ education YouTube video. https://bit.ly/2Js0SV.
19. *India's Covid 19 Vaccine Diplomacy-How it will* boost *India's soft power.* Study IQ education YouTube video. https://bit.ly/2Js0SV.
20. *Worldview withSuhasiniHaidar/ what went wrong with India's vaccine diplomacy?* You Tube video. https://www.thehindu.com/news/nationa...

10

उत्तराखंड का भू-राजनीतिक परिदृश्य

बी.आर. पंत

भूमिका

चीन के वुहान प्रांत/शहर से प्रारंभ हुए कोराना वायरस से उत्पन्न बीमारी से आज संपूर्ण विश्व ग्रसित है, लाखों व्यक्तियों की मृत्यु एवं करोड़ो व्यक्तियों को बीमार कर देने वाली लाईलाज संक्रमित को कोविड-19 (COVID-19) से संबोधित किया जा रहा है। वैश्विक स्तर पर इसके प्रभाव को कम करने तथा समुचित एवं प्रभावकारी दवाई को उत्पादित करने के लिए प्रयास किए जा रहे है, जब विश्व के कई विकसित राष्ट्र इस बीमारी से सबसे अधिक प्रभावित हुए है जहां इलाज हेतु अस्पतालों तथा अन्य सुविधाओं की पर्याप्त व्यवस्था है, तो फिर विकासशील देशों में जहां प्रति व्यक्ति अस्पताल एवं सुविधाएं बहुत कम हैं। इस महामारी ने अनेक प्रकार से मनुष्यों के जीवन को प्रभाावित किया है।

भारत में इस महामारी से बचाव के लिए युद्ध स्तर पर मार्च 2020 के दूसरे पखवाड़े से प्रयास किए गए। महामारी से संक्रमित होने के बचाव के लिए 25 मार्च 2020 से लॉकडाउन किया गया। जिसमें अनिवार्य सेवाओं के अलावा सभी सामाजिक, राजनीतिक, धार्मिक एवं आर्थिक गतिविधियों पर महामारी से बचाव के लिए प्रतिबंध/विराम लगा दिया गया था।

इस लॉकडाउन में भारत के सभी राज्यों की तरह उत्तराखंड भी प्रभावित हुआ भौगोलिक दृष्टि से उत्तराखंड में अधिकाशं पर्वतीय क्षेत्र न तो परंपरागत कृषि और न ही आधुनिक उद्योगों के लिए उपयुक्त है। परंपरागत रूप से उत्तराखंड के निवासी शिक्षा ग्रहण करने के लिए बाहर के अन्य राज्यों/प्रदेशों के लिए पलायन करते आए हैं। पूर्व में आबादी कम होने के कारण रोजगार आसानी से प्राप्त हो जाते थे। जिससे उत्तराखंड का प्रवासी अपनी तथा अपने परिवार की जरूरतों को पूरा कर लेता था,

लेकिन आबादी के बढ़ने और उसी अनुपात में रोजगार के अवसरों के न बढ़ने से आबादी का एक बहुत बड़ा हिस्सा बेरोजगार या सीमांत कर्मकारों के रूप में पंजीकृत है। वर्ष 2011 की जनगणना के अनुसार अनेक कारणों से (शादी को छोड़कर) लगभग 25 प्रतिशत आबादी ने पलायन किया। यह अंतर्राष्ट्रीय, अंतर्राज्यीय, अंतरजनपदीय के अतिरिक्त जनपद के अंदर आंतरिक प्रवास के रूप में हुआ।

कोविड-19 से रोकथाम के लिए अचानक लॉकडाउन लगाया गया, जिसके भय या बीमारी से सुरक्षा की चिंता बढ़ गई। संपूर्ण देश के विभिन्न उद्योगों, कृषि, भवन निर्माण, होटलों, पर्यटन, यातायात, संचार, कंपनियों में कार्यरत् प्रवासियों ने शासन के नियमानुसार अपने-अपने मूल राज्य की ओर वापसी (रिवर्स माईग्रेशन) करनी प्रारंभ कर दी, जिससे कानून आदि व्यवस्था की समस्या भी खड़ी हो गई और जिन प्रवासियों के पास अपने गंतव्य क्षेत्रों में व्यक्तिगत घर/स्थायी व्यवसाय आदि नहीं थे। उन्होंने अपने मूल गांवों जनन क्षेत्रों की ओर लौटना प्रारंभ किया, इनमें कुछ लोगों के पास सब कुछ होते हुए भी वे बीमारी के भय के कारण लौटे ।

की-वर्ड : कोविड-19, लॉकडाउन, अंतर्राष्ट्रीय, पलायन, प्रवासी।

भू-राजनीतिक परिदृश्य

भू-राजनीतिक दृष्टि से उत्तराखंड राज्य का स्थान महत्वपूर्ण है। आज के परिप्रेक्ष्य में इसका महत्व और अधिक बढ़ जाता है। उत्तराखंड की पूर्वी एवं उत्तरी अंतर्राष्ट्रीय सीमा नेपाल तथा तिब्बत (चीन) से लगी हुई है, वर्तमान में चीन के साथ किस प्रकार के आक्रामक संबंध चल रहे है सभी जानते है, वहीं नेपाल भी उत्तराखंड की उत्तरी-पूर्वी सीमा पर लीपूलेख से लांपिया धुरा वाले भू भाग को अपना होने का दावा प्रस्तुत कर रहा है। चीन ने लद्दाख से अरुणाचल प्रदेश तक पूरे तिब्बत में निगरानी हेतु अपने सामरिक अड्डे बना दिए हैं। उत्तराखंड का लीपूलेख से पश्चिमी हिमाचल की सीमा तक का क्षेत्र कई दर्रों/रास्तों से तिब्बत से जुड़ा है। उत्तराखंड का तिब्बत के साथ प्राचीनकाल से अटूट व्यापारिक संबंध रहे हैं। उत्तराखंड के पंडित नैनसिंह, राहुल सांकृत्यायन, स्वामी प्रवणानंद जैसे कई अंवेषणकर्त्ताओं एवं यात्रियों ने तिब्बत के क्षेत्र में शोध कर दुनिया में उसकी भौगोलिक स्थिति से अवगत कराया है। नेपाल के साथ मधुर संबंध होते हुए राजनीतिक अस्थिरता के चलते संबंधों में कटुता आई है।

उत्तराखंड की अंतर्राष्ट्रीय सीमाएं तिब्बत-चीन एवं नेपाल से लगी होने के कारण

सामरिक दृष्टि से इस क्षेत्र को आवागमन एवं आर्थिकी दृष्टि से सुदृढ़ करना पड़ेगा तथा इन क्षेत्रों से हुए पलायन पर भी ध्यान केंद्रित करना पड़ेगा, यदि क्षेत्र खाली हो जाते हैं तो सामरिक दृष्टि से विदेशियों के लिए अनुकूल स्थितियां बन जाएंगी जिसके लिए उत्तराखंड एवं भारत सरकार को विशेष योजना के तहत नई योजनाएं बनानी पड़ेंगी जिससे वे क्षेत्र पलायन से भी खाली न हों।

भारत के सत्ताइसवें राज्य के रूप में 9 नवंबर सन् 2000 को उत्तराखंड राज्य उत्तर प्रदेश से अलग होकर अस्तित्व में आया। वर्तमान उत्तराखंड का विस्तार 28^{0} 44' उत्तर से 31^{0} 25' उत्तरी अक्षांश एवं 77^{0} 45' पूर्वी से 81^{0} 1' पूर्वी देशांतर तक है। इसका कुल क्षेत्रफल 53,483 वर्ग किलोमीटर है, उत्तराखंड की पूर्वी सीमा नेपाल से काली नदी द्वारा, उत्तरी सीमा तिब्बत (चीन), पश्चिमी सीमा हिमाचल से तथा दक्षिणी सीमा उत्तर प्रदेश से निर्धारित होती है। वर्ष 2011 की जनगणना के अनुसार उत्तराखंड राज्य में 13 जनपद, 78 तहसीलें, 95 विकासखंड, 115 शहर तथा 15,745 गांव है।

कत्यूरी, चंद, परमारों तथा गोरखों से पहले अनेक शासकों ने उत्तराखंड या उत्तराखंड के भीतर छोटे-छोटे क्षेत्रों/राज्यों (जिन्हें गढ़ों के रूप में जाना जाता था) में शासन किया। कत्यूरियों और गोरखों का ही उत्तराखंड में एक छत्रराज रहा। कत्यूरी

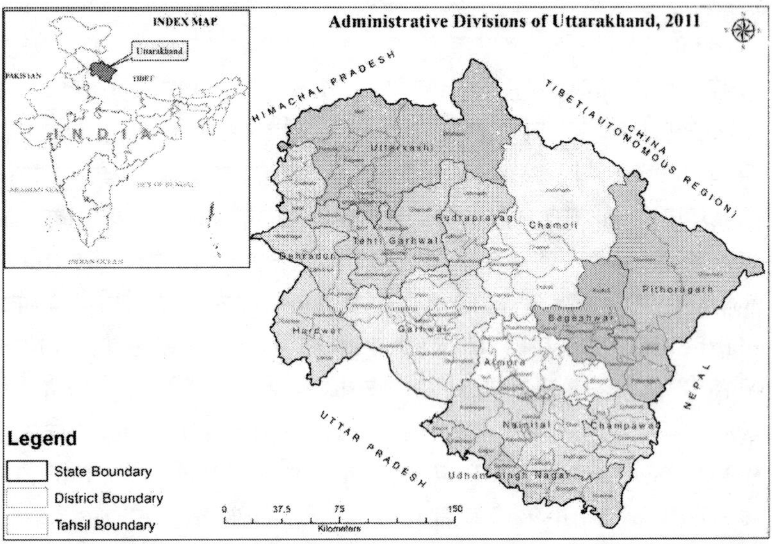

मानचित्र 1 : उत्तराखंड में प्रशासनिक ईकाइयां, 2001 (पंत एवं अन्य, 2020)

शासन के बाद उत्तराखंड चंद और परमार शासकों में बंट गया। गोरखों के बाद ब्रिटिश कंपनी द्वारा वर्ष 1815-16 में गढ़वाल का एक भाग अलकनंदा के पार का हिस्सा सुदर्शन शाह को देकर टिहरी रियासत बनाई गई, शेष उत्तराखंड ईस्ट इंडिया कंपनी और अंततः ब्रिटिश शासन के अंतर्गत आया। 1815-16 ई. में टिहरी छोड़ शेष उत्तराखंड का शासन बंगाल प्रेसीडेंसी से संबद्ध था। सन् 1834 ई. को आगरा प्रेसीडेंसी बनी जो दो साल वाद नार्थ-वेस्ट प्रॉविंस के रूप में अलग प्रांत बन गया। सन् 1856 में अवध को भी कंपनी सरकार के क्षेत्र में मिला लिया गया।

सन् 1877 ई. में अवध के जिलों को नार्थ-वेस्टर्न प्रॉविंसेज में मिलाकर नार्थ वेस्टर्न प्रॉविंस एंड अवध का नाम दिया गया और 1902 ई. में यूनाइटेड प्रॉविंस और 1950 ई. में उत्तर प्रदेश कहा जाने लगा। सन् 1815 से 1839 ई. तक कुमाऊं कमीश्नरी एक ही जिले के रूप में थी। 1839 ई. में ब्रिटिश गढ़वाल और 1891 में नैनीताल जिला बनाया गया और सन् 1842 ई. में तराई जिला बनाया गया था। जो नैनीताल जिला बनने तक चलता रहा। सन् 1949 में टिहरी रियासत को समाप्त कर यूनाइटेड प्रॉविंसेज, जो बाद में उत्तर प्रदेश कहलाया, में मिला लिया गया, को ही टिहरी गढ़वाल जिले के रूप में बनाया गया।

वर्ष 1951 की जनगणना के समय उत्तराखंड के अंतर्गत पूर्व में बने पांच जिले देहरादून, टिहरी गढ़वाल, पौड़ी गढ़वाल, अल्मोड़ा, नैनीताल तथा आंशिक रूप से सहारनपुर, मुजफ्फरनगर और बिजनौर जिले सम्मिलित थे। उत्तराखंड तीन मंडल (कमिश्नरियों) कुमाऊं (टिहरी गढ़वाल, गढ़वाल, अल्मोड़ा, नैनीताल), मेरठ (संपूर्ण देहरादून, आंशिक सहारनपुर और मुज्जफ्फर नगर) तथा रुहेलखंड (आंशिक बिजनौर का हिस्सा) था।

वर्ष 1961 की जनगणना के समय से पहले तक तीन नए जिले बन गए थे। अब आठ संपूर्ण जिले देहरादून, उत्तरकाशी, टिहरी गढ़वाल, गढ़वाल, चमोली, पिथौरागढ़, अल्मोड़ा, नैनीताल तथा आंशिक रूप से सहारनपुर, मुजफ्फर नगर जनपद सहित सन् 1961 तक उत्तराखंड चार कमिश्नरी में बंट गया था। उत्तराखंड मंडल में उत्तरकाशी, चमोली, पिथौरागढ़, कुमाऊं मंडल में टिहरी गढ़वाल, गढ़वाल, अल्मोड़ा तथा नैनीताल जनपद, मेरठ मंडल में देहरादून, सहारनपुर, आंशिक मुजफ्फर नगर जिले तथा रुहेलखंड मंडल का आंशिक रूप से बिजनौर जिला शामिल था। सन् 1971 की जनगणना से पहले उत्तराखंड के जिले प्रशासनिक तौर पर परिवर्तित हो गए थे। जिले तो सन् 1961 के ही रहे लेकिन जिलों को अलग-अलग कमीश्नरी

(मंडलों) का हिस्सा बनाया गया। गढ़वाल मंडल में उत्तरकाशी, टिहरी गढ़वाल, देहरादून, गढ़वाल तथा चमोली जिले मिलाए गए। कुमाऊं मंडल में अल्मोड़ा, पिथौरागढ़ तथा नैनीताल जनपद सम्मिलित किए गए। मेरठ मंडल के सहारनपुर तथा मुजफ्फर नगर आंशिक रूप से तथा रुहेलखंड का बिजनौर भी आंशिक रूप से सम्मिलित थे। सन् 1981 की जनगणना के समय जनपद तो पूर्ववत रहे मंडलों में केवल एक परिवर्तन किया गया बिजनौर जो पहले रुहेलखंड का हिस्सा था वह अब मुरादाबाद मंडल का हिस्सा बन गया था। वर्ष 1991 की जनगणना के समय उत्तराखंड में पूर्व में बने आठ जनपद–उत्तरकाशी, चमोली, टिहरी गढ़वाल, पौड़ी गढ़वाल, अल्मोड़ा, पिथौरागढ़, नैनीताल तथा सहारनपुर, मुजफ्फर नगर तथा बिजनौर जिलों को काटकर नव सृजित जनपद हरिद्वार को सम्मिलित कर दिया गया और वह मेरठ मंडल का हिस्सा ही रहा। जनगणना वर्ष 2001 आने तक उत्तराखंड के पूर्व के आठ जनपदों को पुनर्गठित कर पांच नए जनपद सृजित कर कुल 13 जनपदों में बांटा गया। गढ़वाल मंडल के अंतर्गत 7 जनपद उत्तरकाशी, चमोली, टिहरी (गढ़वाल), पौड़ी (गढ़वाल), रुद्रप्रयाग, देहरादून तथा हरिद्वार सम्मिलित किए गए जबकि कुमाऊं मंडल के अंतर्गत 6 जनपद पिथौरागढ़, अल्मोड़ा, बागेश्वर, चंपावत, नैनीताल तथा उधम सिंह नगर सम्मिलित किए गए। जनगणना वर्ष 2001 से 2011 के बीच प्रशासनिक ईकाइयों में फेरबदल नहीं किया गया। यद्यपि विभिन्न जनगणना वर्षों में क्षेत्रीय स्तर पर तहसील एवं पंचायतों को एक प्रशासनिक इकाई से दूसरे प्रशासनिक ईकाइयों में स्थानांतरित किया जाता रहा।

राज्य बनने से पूर्व उत्तराखंड क्षेत्र से मात्र 19 विधायकों द्वारा ही प्रतिनिधित्व किया जाता था व तीन-चार विधान परिषद् के सदस्य होते थे। राज्य निर्माण के साथ पहला चुनाव 70 विधानसभा क्षेत्रों के लिए हुआ। जिसमें लगभग 60 प्रतिशत विधायक पर्वतीय क्षेत्र के होते थे, लेकिन 2011 की जनगणना को आधार बनाकर विधानसभा क्षेत्रों का पुनर्गठन किया गया और पहाड़ का प्रतिनिधित्व 50 प्रतिशत से कम हो गया पर्वतीय क्षेत्रों से पलायन के कारण आबादी का कम होना इसके लिए उत्तरदायी माना गया। जन प्रतिनिधित्व राजनीतिक व्यवस्था में परिवर्तन देखने को मिला है। पर्वतीय अस्मिता लगभग समाप्त होने की स्थिति में है, क्योंकि मैदानी जनपदों में पर्वतीय आबादी निर्वाचन प्रकिया में कोई प्रभाव नहीं डाल पाती है। सन् 2021 या उसके बाद यह समस्या अधिक बढ़ जाएगी क्योंकि पुनः आबादी का अनुपात घट जाएगा और विधायकों की संख्या और कम हो जाएगी।

अध्ययन का उद्देश्य

प्रस्तुत शोध पत्र में उत्तराखंड की भू-राजनीतिक स्थिति का वर्णन करते हुए कोविड-19 के बाद सरकार द्वारा लॉकडाउन करने से बाद उत्तराखंड के प्रवासियों का जो मार्च से जून 2020 तक प्रदेश में वापसी हुई। उनका विवरण जनपद, विकासखंड स्तर पर वापसी, प्रवासी किन-किन व्यवसायों में संलग्न थे, उत्तराखंड राज्य के अंदर तथा बाहर से आने वाले प्रवासियों का विवरण का वर्णन तथा उत्तराखंड की बढ़ती आबादी के साथ पलायन परिदृश्य (2011) का अध्ययन करना है। मैदानी एवं पर्वतीय जनसंख्यात्मक विश्लेषण करना भी प्रस्तुत शोध पत्र का एक लक्ष्य है। उत्तराखंड के ऐतिहासिक दस्तावेजों में उल्लिखित महामारियों का विवरण प्रस्तुत करना भी है। उत्तराखंड में लौटे प्रवासियों के लिए राज्य सरकार ने क्या-क्या योजनाएँ बनाई हैं, का अध्ययन भी करना है। प्रस्तुत शोध पत्र में लॉकडाउन के बाद पर्यावरणीय प्रभाव एवं चुनौतियों के अध्ययन को भी सम्मिलित किया गया है।

अध्ययन विधि

प्रस्तुत अध्ययन में द्वितीयक आंकड़ों का विश्लेषण किया गया है। पूर्व में फैली महामारियों की जानकारी लिए ऐतिहासिक दस्तावेजों की सहायता ली गई है। जनगणना 2011 तथा उत्तराखंड सरकार द्वारा गठित ग्राम्य विकास एवं पलायन आयोग की रिपोर्ट 2020 को आधार बनाया गया है।

महामारियों का ऐतिहासिक प्रसंग

उत्तराखंड में ही नहीं, विश्व भर के अनेक राष्ट्रों में समय-समय पर अनेक महामारियों /बीमारियों का प्रकोप रहा। सन् 1941 से 1951 के दशक में स्वास्थ्य सुविधाओं की कमी के कारण औसत आयु आज से लगभग आधी थी। उत्तराखंड में भी अनेक बार अलग-अलग क्षेत्रों में हैजा, डायरिया, प्लेग, मलेरिया, तीव्र ज्वर, चेचक आदि का प्रकोप रहा। उन्नीसवीं शताब्दी में उत्तराखंड में प्लेग को महामारी के रूप में जाना जाता था। अधिक गर्म तापमान एवं तीव्र वर्षा के कारण संक्रमण वायरस या बीमारी के कीटाणुओं के प्रसार तीव्र गति से होता था, सर्वप्रथम मिस्टर गौविन जो उस समय कुमाऊं के कमिशनर थे, ने सन् 1838 में बीमारी से ग्रसित क्षेत्र की आख्या प्रस्तुत की थी। उन्होंने अपनी रिपोर्ट में वर्ष 1823 केदारनाथ मंदिर के मुख्य पुजारी रावल

के प्लेग की बीमारी से ग्रसित पाने का उल्लेख किया है। उसके बाद इस बीमारी के विषाणु पूरे गढ़वाल क्षेत्र में फैलने का भी उल्लेख किया है।

ऐतिहासिक दस्तावेजों के आधार पर वर्ष 1835-36 में एक बार पुनः उत्तराखंड के नागपुर एवं बधाण क्षेत्र में विषाणु पुनः फैल गए थे, वर्ष 1837-38 में यह वायरस परगने के कई गांवों में फैलते हुए पिंडर घाटी के उच्च क्षेत्रों तक फैल गया। वर्ष 1849 तक पश्चिमी रामगंगा घाटी को अपने जद में लेते हुए सरकोट गांव की पूरी आबादी को समाप्त कर दिया था। यह बीमारी कोसी नदी के उद्गम क्षेत्र वौरारों घाटी तक फैल गई थी। इस बीमारी से चांदपुर परगना से मरौड़ा तथा दूधातौली क्षेत्र में बड़ी संख्या में मौतें हो गईं। यह बीमारी पहाड़ों पर ही नहीं बल्कि तराई - भाबर तक फैल चुकी थी। वर्ष 1859 में प्लेग काशीपुर तथा चिलकिया क्षेत्र में फैला। निम्न तालिका 1 में कुमाऊं और गढ़वाल में प्लेग से मरने वालों का विवरण दिया है।

तालिका-1: प्लेग से मरने वालों की संख्या विवरण

जनपद	*पुरुष*	*महिला*	*बच्चे*	*कुल*
कुमाऊं	105	69	64	238
गढ़वाल	199	73	25	297

स्रोत : एटकिंसन 1884 (पुनः प्रकाशित 1973) हिमालयन गजेटीयर।

तालिका-2 : विभिन्न बीमारियों से मृत्यु वर्ष 1891 से 1902 के दौरान

वर्ष	*हैजा (प्रतिशत)*	*चेचक (प्रतिशत)*	*बुखार (प्रतिशत)*	*अतिसार/दस्त (प्रतिशत)*	*अंय (प्रतिशत)*	*कुल (प्रतिशत)*
1891	155	35	8,174	298	120	8,782
	(1.8)	(0.4)	(93.1)	(3.4)	(1.3)	(100.00)
1892	2,563	74	14,932	988	406	18,963
	(13.5)	(0.4)	(78.8)	(5.2)	(2.1)	(100.00)
1893	21	160	11,718	884	416	13,199
	(0.2)	(1.2)	(88.7)	(6.7)	(3.2)	(100.00)
1894	91	93	16,388	1034	526	18,132
	(0.5)	(0.5)	(90.4)	(5.7)	(2.9)	(100.00)

1895	-	28	14,512	761	483	15784
	(00)	(0.2)	(91.9)	(4.8)	(3.1)	(100.00)
1896	1,485	15	16,474	709	475	19,158
	(7.7)	(0.1)	(86.0)	(3.7)	(2.5)	(100.00)
1897	205	1,058	12,038	451	557	13,356
	(1.4)	(7.4)	(84.1)	(3.1)	(3.9)	(100.00)
1898	10	8	13,985	419	420	14,842
	(0.1)	(0.1)	(94.2)	(2.8)	(2.8)	(100.00)
1899	30	2	13,320	301	477	14,130
	(0.2)	(00)	(94.2)	(2.1)	(3.4)	(100.00)
1900	2	-	11,277	299	343	11,921
	(00)	(00)	(94.6)	(2.5)	(2.9)	(100.00)
1901	70	2	10,840	236	230	11,378
	(0.6)	(00)	(95.3)	(2.1)	(2.0)	(100.00)
1902	555	3	12,420	267	380	13,625
	(4.1)	(00)	(91.1)	(2.0)	(2.8)	(100.00)
कुल	5,187	1,478	15,6078	6,647	4,833	17,4223
	(3.0)	(0.8)	(89.6)	(3.8)	(2.8)	(100.00)

स्रोत : *नैनीताल गजेटियर* (नैविल पुनः प्रकाशित 2016)

तत्कालीन बीमारियों से केवल स्वास्थ्य ही प्रभावित नहीं हुआ बल्कि क्षेत्र की आर्थिक स्थिति भी प्रभावित हुई। उत्तराखंड में वर्ष 1874 में चेचक के प्रकोप से 16 व्यक्तियों की कुमाऊं से तथा 31 व्यक्तियों की गढ़वाल से मृत्यु हुई।

इन गांवों में 31 गांव ऐसे थे जिनमें 5 व्यक्तियों की मृत्यु हुई। 10 गांव ऐसे थे जिनमें 10 व्यक्तियों की मृत्यु हुई तथा एक गांव ऐसा था जहां 20 लोगों की मृत्यु का कारण चेचक जैसी महामारी थी। तराई के 594 गांवों में से 105 गांव चेचक से प्रभावित थे, छह गांव ऐसे थे जिनमें 20 व्यक्तियों से अधिक की मृत्यु हो गई थी। वर्ष 1979 में महामारी पुनः फैलने के कारण गढ़वाल की 17,2000 की आबादी पूरी तरह प्रभावित हुई इससे खेती पर भी बहुत बड़ा प्रभाव पड़ा। (एटकिंसन 1884)।

अपने नैनीताल गजेटियर में नैविल (1932) ने नैनीताल के तत्कालीन तराई

प्रदेश में किस प्रकार से महामारियों द्वारा बड़ी संख्या में मानव क्षति हुई, का उल्लेख किया है। उन्होंने वर्ष 1891 से 1902 तक प्रतिवर्ष विभिन्न बीमारियों से हुई मौतों का विवरण में दिया है (तालिका-2)। सन् 1891 से 1902 तक विभिन्न बीमारियों से 1,74,223 व्यक्तियों की मृत्यु हुई जिनमें से 89.6 प्रतिशत (15,6,078 व्यक्ति) केवल बुखार के कारण मृत्यु के शिकार हुए। इन बारह सालों में 3 प्रतिशत (5,187 व्यक्ति) हैजा, 0.8 प्रतिशत चेचक, 3.8 प्रतिशत अतिसार (दस्त), तथा 2.89 प्रतिशत की अंय बीमारियों के कारण मृत्यु हुई। तराई में बुखार का प्रकोप बहुत था क्योंकि तराई की जलवायु मच्छरों के विकसित होने के लिए उपयुक्त थी, इसी के कारण मलेरिया का बुखार भी होता है। जिसका उस समय किसी प्रकार का इलाज भी नहीं था। सन् 1892 में हैजे के कारण 13.5 प्रतिशत व्यक्तियों की मृत्यु हुई।

चार साल बाद सन् 1896 में भी नैनीताल में 7.71 प्रतिशत व्यक्तियों की मृत्यु हैजे के कारण हुई। अतिसार (दस्त) के कारण सन् 1892, 1893 एवं 1894 में अंय वर्षों से अधिक क्रमशः 5.2, 6.7, 5.7 प्रतिशत लोगों को काल का ग्रास बनना पड़ा। चेचक का सर्वाधिक प्रभाव 1897 में हुआ जब कुल मृतकों में से 7.4 प्रतिशत मृतक चेचक रोग से ग्रसित थे। इन बीमारियों का सर्वाधिक प्रभाव तराई एवं भाबर क्षेत्र में ही था जबकि पर्वतीय क्षेत्र की जलवायु उत्तम होने के कारण प्रभाव कम पड़ा। वनों के कटने एवं कृषि के विस्तार के कारण बीमारियों का प्रकोप धीरे-धीरे कम पड़ने लगा था।

उत्तराखंड का जनसंख्या परिदृश्य

भारत में सर्वप्रथम जनगणना का कार्य सन् 1872 में प्रारंभ हुआ। जो नौ वर्ष पर दूसरी बार 1881 में की गई, तब से प्रत्येक दस वर्ष में यह कार्य संपन्न किया जाता है, क्योंकि अनुमान लगाया जाता है कि जनसंख्या आधारित योजनाएं दस साल में अप्रासंगिक हो जाती हैं। जिससे पुनः जनगणना कर योजनाओं में आवश्यकतानुसार संशोधन एवं परिवर्तन किया जाता है। सन् 1901 से 1911 के बीच 8.20 प्रतिशत (16,2,392 व्यक्तियों) की आबादी में वृद्धि हुई, लेकिन 1911 से 1921 के बीच उत्तराखंड ही नहीं बल्कि संपूर्ण भारत की आबादी विभिन्न बीमारियों के प्रकोप के कारण घट गई थी। उत्तराखंड में औसत 1.23 प्रतिशत तथा संपूर्ण भारत की आबादी में भी 0.3 प्रतिशत की ऋणात्मक वृद्धि दर्ज की गई। उत्तराखंड की आबादी सन् 1921 से 1981 तक लगातार बढ़ती रही। 1981 से वृद्धि दर कम होने लग गई थी

तालिका : 3 उत्तराखंड में जनपदवार जनसंख्या वितरण, 2011

जनपद/प्रदेश	क्षेत्रफल	घनत्व	जनसंख्या			परिवार आकार	जनसंख्या 0.6 वर्ष	आबाद ग्राम	विकासखंड	तहसील	भाहर
	वर्ग किमी.	व्यक्ति/प्रति किमी.	व्यक्ति	पुरुष	महिला	व्यक्ति/ परिवार	(%कुल जनसंख्या)	संख्या	संख्या	संख्या	संख्या
उत्तरकाशी	8,016	41	33,0,086	16,8,597	16,1,489	5	14.0	694	6	6	3
चमोली	8,030	49	39,1,605	19,3,991	19,7614	4	13.3	1,170	9	6	6
रुद्रप्रयाग	1,984	122	24,2,285	11,4,589	12,7,696	5	13.2	653	3	3	2
टिहरी	3,642	170	61,8,931	29,7,986	32,0,945	5	13.7	1,774	9	7	7
देहरादून	3,088	549	16,96,694	89,2,199	80,4,495	5	11.9	731	6	6	22
पौड़ी	5,329	129	68,7,271	32,6,829	36,0,442	4	12.2	3142	15	9	8
पिथौरागढ़	7,090	68	48,3,439	23,9,306	24,4,133	4	13.1	1,572	8	6	3
बागेश्वर	2,241	116	25,989	1,24,326	13,5,572	4	13.7	874	3	4	1
अल्मोड़ा	3,144	198	62,2,506	29,1,081	33,1,425	4	12.9	2,184	11	10	5
चंपावत	1,766	147	25,9,648	13,1,125	12,8,523	5	14.3	662	4	4	4

नैनीताल	4,251	225	95,4605	49,3,666	460939	5	13.0	1097	8	8	11
ऊ.सिं. नगर	2,543	649	16,48,902	85,8,783	790119	5	13.9	674	7	7	19
हरिद्वार	2,360	801	18,90,422	10,05,295	885127	6	15.1	518	6	3	24
उत्तराखंड	**53,483**	**189**	**1,00,86,292**	**5137773**	**4948519**	**5**	**13.4**	**15745**	**95**	**78**	**115**
भारत	**3,28,7,469**	**368**	**1,21,05,69,573**	**62,31,21,843**	**58,74,47,730**	**5**	**13.6**	**59,7,608**	**6,612**	**5,464**	**7,933**

स्रोत : भारतीय जनगणना सार, 2011

तालिका-4 : उत्तराखंड में जनपदवार दशकीय जनसंख्या वृद्धि दर (प्रतिशत में)

	जनगणना वर्ष										
जनपद/प्रदेश	**1901-11**	**1911-21**	**1921-31**	**1931-41**	**1941-51**	**1951-61**	**1961-71**	**1971-81**	**1981-91**	**1991-2001**	**2001-11**
उत्तरकाशी	11.9	5.8	9.8	13.7	3.7	15.8	20.3	29.2	25.5	23.1	11.9
चमोली	11.7	1.2	10.0	12.8	6.2	19.5	17.0	24.1	22.6	13.9	5.7
रुद्रप्रयाग	11.7	2.4	10.0	13.0	5.5	13.3	13.1	25.1	18.1	13.4	6.5
टिहरी	11.9	5.8	9.8	13.7	3.7	13.0	14.3	24.7	16.5	16.2	2.3
देहरादून	15.3	3.6	8.5	15.6	36.1	18.6	34.6	31.9	34.7	25.0	32.3
पौड़ी	11.7	1.2	10.0	12.8	6.2	14.0	14.5	15.5	8.6	3.9	-1.4
पिथौरागढ़	15.9	0.9	10.0	17.8	12.5	19.1	14.4	16.4	14.1	11.0	4.6
बागेश्वर	15.9	0.9	10.0	17.8	12.5	14.3	24.0	19.6	14.8	9.3	5.2
अल्मोड़ा	15.9	0.9	10.0	17.8	12.5	13.6	15.2	15.8	8.9	3.7.	1.6
चंपावत	13.3	-1.3	8.8	16.4	12.7	30.5	45.1	25.3	26.4	17.6	15.6
नैनीताल	-0.1	-14.4	0.2	5.3	14.9	37.6	23.1	38.1	30.2	32.7	25.1

ऊ.सिं. नगर	-0.2	-14.4	0.2	5.3	14.9	121.1	49.7	48.1	38.3	33.6	33.45
हरिद्वार	-5.6	-4.9	11.4	13.1	14.6	18.0	32.9	32.7	26.3	28.7	30.6
उत्तराखंड	**8.2**	**-1.2**	**8.7**	**13.6**	**12.7**	**22.6**	**24.4**	**27.4**	**23.1**	**20.4**	**18.8**
भारत	**5.7**	**-0.3**	**11.0**	**14.2**	**13.3**	**21.5**	**24.8**	**24.7**	**23.9**	**21.5**	**17.7**

स्रोत : *पंत एवं अन्य,* 2020।

जो सन् 2011 में मात्र 18.81 प्रतिशत रही। उत्तराखंड की औसत वृद्धि दर में कमी आने के साथ-साथ पर्वतीय जनपदों में अत्यधिक कम ही नहीं बल्कि सन् 2001 से 2011 के बीच अल्मोड़ा तथा पौड़ी जनपदों में क्रमशः 1.6 प्रतिशत एवं 1.4 प्रतिशत ऋणात्मक वृद्धि पंजीकृत की गई। वहीं दूसरी ओर मैदानी क्षेत्रों में स्थित हरिद्वार (30.6 प्रतिशत), देहरादून (32.3 प्रतिशत) एवं ऊधमसिंहनगर (33.45 प्रतिशत) की आबादी में लगातार वृद्धि हुई। मैदानी भाग वाले जनपदों में वृद्धि बनी रही। मैदानी जनपदों में वृद्धि एवं पर्वतीय जनपदों में ह्रास का मुख्य कारक पलायन रहा। जो पर्वतीय क्षेत्रों से लोगों को अंतर्जनपदीय, अंतर्राज्यीय एवं अंतर्राष्ट्रीय पलायन के लिए प्रेरित करता रहा। पर्वतीय क्षेत्र में कृषि, जो केवल जीवन निर्वाह की प्रमुख जरूरत होती है और साल भर के लिए भी पूर्ति नहीं करती है के साथ उद्योगों एवं अन्य उद्यमों की कमी के कारण व्यक्तियों का क्षेत्र से पलायन निर्बाध रूप से चलता रहा।

तालिका-5 : उत्तराखंड के पर्वतीय एवं मैदानी क्षेत्रों में जनसंख्या वितरण एवं जनसंख्या वृद्धि, 1901-2011 (प्रतिशत)

वर्ष	*वितरण अनुपात (प्रतिशत)*			*वृद्धि (प्रतिशत)*		
	मैदानी	*पर्वतीय*	*उत्तराखंड*	*मैदानी*	*पर्वतीय*	*उत्तराखंड*
1901	32.28	67.72	100	0.00	0.00	0.00
1911	30.23	69.77	100	1.32	11.48	8.20
1921	29.33	70.67	100	-4.16	0.05	-1.23
1931	29.2	370.77	100	8.37	8.90	8.74
1941	28.97	71.03	100	12.64	14.03	13.63
1951	31.42	68.58	100	22.20	8.79	12.67
1961	34.21	65.79	100	33.44	17.59	22.57
1971	37.83	62.7	100	37.60	17.56	24.42
1981	40.53	59.47	100	36.53	21.93	27.45
1991	43.61	56.39	100	32.51	16.75	23.13
2001	46.70	53.30	100	28.94	13.80	20.41
2011	51.91	48.09	100	32.06	7.20	18.81

स्रोत : *पंत एवं अन्य,* 2020।

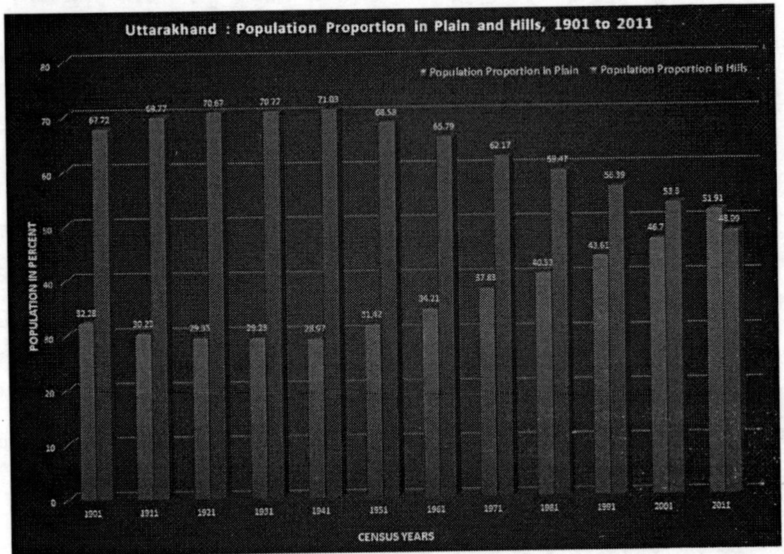

मानचित्र 2 : उत्तराखंड में पर्वतीय एवं मैदानी क्षेत्रों में जनसंख्या वितरण, 1901-2011

तालिका 5 से स्पष्ट हो रहा है कि सन् 1901 से 2001 तक आबादी का बड़ा हिस्सा पर्वतीय क्षेत्रों में रहा। जहां सन् 1901 से 1961 तक कुल आबादी 65 प्रतिशत से अधिक पर्वतीय भागों में रहती थी जिसका अनुपात धीरे-धीरे घट रहा था, लेकिन वर्ष 2011 में पर्वतीय क्षेत्र में मात्र 48.1 प्रतिशत तथा मैदानी जनपदों में 51.9 प्रतिशत रहा जो पूर्व से विपरित दृश्य दिखाई देने लगा है।

सन् 2011 की जनगणना में उत्तराखंड के छह पर्वतीय जनपदों में जनसंख्या वृद्धि लगभग 7 प्रतिशत से कम दर्ज हुई है। अनुमान लगाया जा सकता है सन् 2021 की जनगणना में ये जनपद भी ऋणात्मक वृद्धि दर्ज कर सकते हैं। तालिका 4 से पर्वतीय एवं मैदानी क्षेत्रों में किस प्रकार प्रतिदशक वृद्धि हुई, को भी दर्शाया गया है। सन् 1901 से 1941 तक पर्वतीय क्षेत्रों में ही अधिक वृद्धि हुई है। वर्ष 1911 से 1921 के बीच जब भारत के लगभग प्रत्येक राज्य के जनपद में आबादी में ऋणात्मक वृद्धि हुई तब उत्तराखंड के पर्वतीय क्षेत्र में ऋणात्मक नहीं हुई और मैदानी क्षेत्रों में 4.16 प्रतिशत ऋणात्मक वृद्धि दर्ज की गई। स्वतंत्रता प्राप्ति के बाद प्रत्येक दशकीय जनगणना में पर्वतीय क्षेत्र में कम वृद्धि तथा मैदानी क्षेत्र में औसत से बहुत अधिक वृद्धि रही। पर्वतीय क्षेत्र, जिसे प्रवास जनन क्षेत्र भी कहा जाता है की आबादी में पलायन के कारण कम वृद्धि दर्ज हुई जबकि प्रवास गंतव्य मैदानी

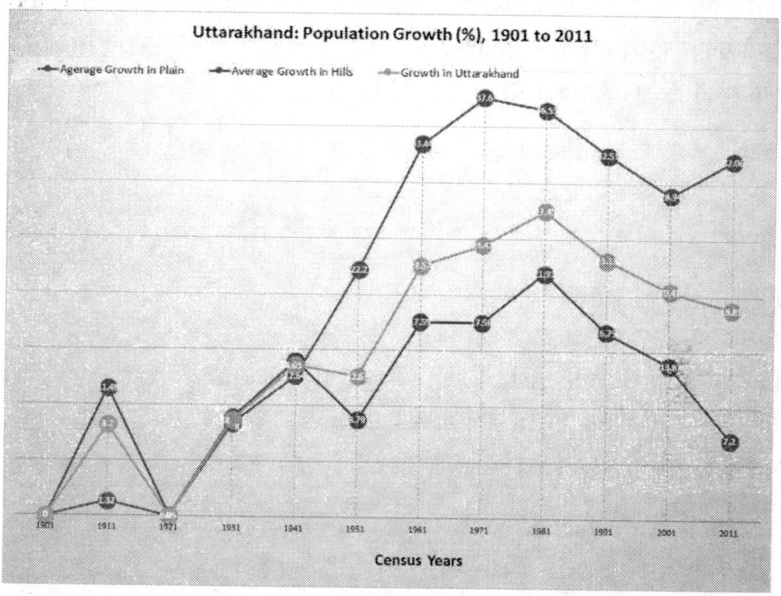

मानचित्र 3 : उत्तराखंड में पर्वतीय एवं मैदानी क्षेत्रों में जनसंख्या वृद्धि, 1901-2011

क्षेत्र में औसत से अधिक वृद्धि दर्ज हुई है। यहां पर यह भी उल्लेख करना समीचीन होगा कि प्रवास जनन क्षेत्र से अधिकांश पुरुषों का ही विभिन्न कारणों शिक्षा, रोजगार व्यापार आदि के लिए ही पलायन होता है इसलिए उन क्षेत्रों में लिंगानुपात अर्थात प्रति हजार परुषों में महिलाओं की संख्या अधिक होती है जबकि प्रवास गंतव्य क्षेत्रों में पुरुषों की संख्या अधिक होने से महिलाओं की संख्या कम हो जाती है जिससे सामाजिक असंतुलन भी उत्पन्न हो जाता है। प्रदेश के मैदानी क्षेत्रों में आप्रवास देश के अन्य क्षेत्रों से भी हुआ।

भारतीय जनगणना विभाग द्वारा 2011 के लिए जारी किए गए आंकड़ों के आधार पर उत्तराखंड की लगभग 44.2 प्रतिशत आबादी प्रवासी के रूप में है, यद्यपि इसमें शादी को भी पलायन के कारणों में सम्मिलित किया गया है। इस आबादी को यदि कम कर दिया जाए तो फिर भी लगभग 25 प्रतिशत आबादी प्रवासी श्रेणी के अंतर्गत होगी। प्रवासियों में 30.04 प्रतिशत पुरुष तथा 59.89 प्रतिशत महिलाएं हैं। जैसा कि पूर्व में उल्लेख किया गया है महिलाओं की शादी के कारण को सम्मिलित किया गया है इसलिए यह अनुपात इतना अधिक है। उत्तराखंड की कुल प्रवासी जनसंख्या में से 61.63 प्रतिशत ग्रामीण तथा 38.37 प्रतिशत नगरीय है।

गांव से गांव को 73.36 प्रतिशत तथा गांव से नगर को 27.03 प्रतिशत प्रवास हुआ है इसी प्रकार नगरीय प्रवासी आबादी में से 72.97 प्रतिशत नगर से नगर तथा नगर से गांव को 26.44 प्रतिशत प्रवास हुआ (तालिका-6)।

तालिका-6 : उत्तराखंड में प्रवास परिदृश्य, 2011

	प्रवास	*व्यक्ति*	*पुरुष*	*महिला*
कुल	44,57,986	44.20	30.04	58.89
ग्रामीण	27,47,243	61.63	47.47	69.12
नगरीय	17,10,743	38.37	52.53	30.88
गांव से गांव	23,14,424	73.56	57.42	80.50
गांव से नगर	26,9,261	27.03	26.69	27.36
नगर से नगर	72,6,867	72.97	73.36	72.64
नगर से गांव	83,1,813	26.44	42.58	19.58

स्रोत : भारत की जनगणना 2011 D-5 माइग्रेशन

तालिका-7 : उत्तराखंड में प्रवास के कारण (प्रतिशत में)

कारण	*व्यक्ति*	*पुरुष*	*महिला*
रोजगार	14.90	38.36	2.49
व्यापार	0.52	1.14	0.18
शिक्षा	3.11	5.49	1.85
शादी	42.64	1.36	64.49
अन्य	61.17	46.35	69.01

स्रोत : *भारत की जनगणना 2011* D-5 माइग्रेशन

सामाजिक दायित्वों की पूर्ति के लिए आवश्यक शादी को यदि प्रवास के कारणों से अलग किया जाए तो सर्वाधिक पलायन रोजगार के लिए ही होता है। शादी का कारण सम्मिलित करने पर भी लगभग 14.9 प्रतिशत प्रवास रोजगार के लिए होता है। इसी क्रम में 3.11 प्रतिशत शिक्षा के लिए होता है। उत्तराखंड में अब शिक्षण संस्थाओं के प्रचुर मात्रा में उपलब्ध होने के कारण शिक्षा के लिए प्रवास बहुत कम हो गया है। व्यापार के लिए भी पलायन बहुत कम होता है (तालिका-7)।

कोविड-19 का प्रभाव

वैश्विक बीमारी कोरोना वायरस के कारण 25 मार्च, 2020 से देश में संपूर्ण लॉकडाउन की व्यवस्था लागू की गई। इसका सबसे अधिक प्रभाव अस्थायी रूप से निजी प्रतिष्ठानों में कार्यरत कर्मकरों/श्रमिकों पर पड़ा। उत्तराखंड में प्रवासी श्रमिक के रूप में संख्या अधिक नहीं है। उत्तराखंड का अधिकांश प्रवासी या तो सरकारी या गैर-सरकारी संस्थानों में कार्यरत् होता है। श्रमिक शब्द का प्रयोग उत्तराखंड के संदर्भ में नहीं किया जा सकता है, क्योंकि श्रमिक, जो भवन निर्माण, कृषि कार्य या कच्चे सामान के निर्माण में हो या किसी भी प्रकार के निर्माण कार्य में अस्थायी रूप से संलग्न होता है, के लिए संबोधित करना उचित है। उत्तराखंड का निवासी प्रवासी इसलिए होता है कि यहां की भौगोलिक स्थिति कृषि एवं अन्य उद्यमों के लिए उपयुक्त नहीं है। इसलिए वह अपने मूल स्थान को छोड़कर सरकारी/गैर- सरकारी/निजी प्रतिष्ठानों/होटल रेस्तरां/कल-कारखानों/व्यावसायिक प्रतिष्ठानों/पर्यटन से संबंधित उद्यमों आदि हेतु पलायन करता है तथा धनोत्पार्जन कर अपने तथा अपने परिवार का भरण पोषण करता है। परंपरागत ढंग से पलायन की धारा निर्वाध रूप से बहती रही। पूर्व में अच्छी-अच्छी संस्थाओं में स्थायी रूप से कार्य मिलता रहा लेकिन आज प्रतिस्पर्धा के इस दौर में वैसा होना कठिन हो गया है फिर भी लोगों का पलायन जारी है।

कोविड-19 के प्रकोप के कारण हुए लॉकडाउन के बाद होटल, रेस्टोरेंट तथा प्रतिष्ठान बंद होने के कारण प्रवासी लोग अपने मूल गांव की ओर लौटे हैं। इनमें कई छात्र, छोटे व्यापारी एवं पेशेवर लोग भी हैं। इन प्रवासियों में कुछ के मूल परिवार गांव में थे, उन्हें अधिक परेशानी नहीं हुई तथा कुछ के गांव के घर रहने योग्य भी नहीं थे, वे अपने गांव में या अपने संबंधियों के घरों में लौटे हैं। उत्तराखंड के ग्राम्य विकास एवं पलायन आयोग द्वारा जारी अपनी आख्या में उल्लेख किया गया है कि मार्च 2020 तक उत्तराखंड में कुल 59,360 प्रवासी वापस (Reverse Migrants) लौटे हैं।

तालिका 8 से स्पष्ट हो रहा हैं कि मार्च 2020 तक उत्तराखंड के दस जनपदों में ही प्रवासी लौटे हैं। जिसमे सर्वाधिक 20.28 प्रतिशत प्रवासी पौड़ी जनपद में लौटे जबकि दूसरा स्थान 15.67 प्रतिशत के साथ अल्मोड़ा जनपद का रहा, तीसरे क्रम में 14.79 प्रतिशत के साथ टिहरी जनपद है। वर्ष 2011 की जनगणना में जनसंख्या

वृद्धि को देखें तो स्पष्ट हो रहा है कि इन्हीं दो–पौड़ी एवं अल्मोड़ा–जनपदों में सर्वाधिक ऋणात्मक वृद्धि दर्ज की गई है। अर्थात इन्हीं लोगों ने 2001 से 2011 के बीच में सबसे अधिक पलायन किया होगा। अन्य पर्वतीय जनपदों में भी वृद्धि दर कम है तो प्रवासियों की वापसी की संख्या भी अपेक्षाकृत कम ही है। मार्च 2020 तक मैदानी क्षेत्र (देहरादून, ऊधमसिंहनगर, हरिद्वार) जनपदों में प्रवासी अधिक होने के कारण संपूर्ण क्षेत्र की कुल आबादी भी कम हो गई है। मार्च तक लौटे प्रवासियों में से 25 से 30 प्रतिशत प्रवासी अपने ही प्रदेश के मैदानी नगरों से लौटे हैं जबकि 60 से 65 प्रतिशत प्रवासी अन्य राज्यों दिल्ली, हरियाणा, पंजाब, हिमाचल प्रदेश, राजस्थान, गुजरात, मध्य प्रदेश, छत्तीसगढ़, कर्नाटक, तमिलनाडु, गोवा, महाराष्ट्र व झारखंड से लौटे हैं। लगभग 3 प्रतिशत से 5 प्रतिशत विदेशों से जिनमें ओमान, आयरलैंड, चीन, न्यूजीलैंड, आस्ट्रेलिया इत्यादि देशों से भी लौटे हैं। प्रवासी लगभग सभी 35 से 45 वर्ष आयु वर्ग के हैं । प्रवासी क्षेत्र या उनसे संबंधित क्षेत्र, छोटे व्यवसाय, छात्र, पेशेवर आदि क्षेत्रों से लौटे हैं।

अप्रैल से जून 2020 तक तीन महीनों में उत्तराखंड में 21,5,575 प्रवासी प्रदेश में लौटे हैं इनमें से भी सर्वाधिक 28 प्रतिशत प्रवासी अकेले पौड़ी जनपद में लौटे जबकि अल्मोड़ा जनपद में लौटने वाले प्रवासियों की संख्या 20.29 प्रतिशत थी, तीसरे क्रम में 10.17 प्रतिशत के साथ ऊधमसिंह नगर जनपद है जहां मार्च तक कोई भी प्रवासी नहीं लौटा था। उत्तरकाशी, टिहरी एवं चंपावत जनपद में लौटे हुए प्रवासियों की संख्या के क्रम में चौथे, पांचवें और छठे क्रम पर थे। मैदानी जनपदों में उधमसिंह नगर पहले स्थान पर है क्योंकि ऊधमसिंह नगर जनपद में सामान्यतः पश्चिम बंगाल के विस्थापितों की आबादी अधिक है जिनके पास भूमि कम थी वे अपना भरण पोषण हेतु प्रवासित होते हैं। कुल लौटे प्रवासियों में (2,75,235) में से भी 26.33 प्रतिशत प्रवासी पौड़ी 19.29 प्रतिशत अल्मोड़ा जनपदों में से ही लौटे। टिहरी (10.18 प्रतिशत) तथा उत्तरकाशी (8.77 प्रतिशत) तीसरे एवं चौथे क्रम में हैं। ऊधमसिंहनगर एवं चम्पावत जनपदों में क्रमशः 7.98 एवं 7.56 प्रतिशत प्रवासी लौटे। यहां पर एक तथ्य स्पष्ट रूप से दृष्टिगोचर हो रहा है कि अत्यधिक दुर्गम क्षेत्र तथा भाबर से दूर स्थित पिथौरागढ़, बागेश्वर, चमोली, एवं रुद्रप्रयाग जनपदों में कम प्रवासी लौटे हैं अर्थात इन क्षेत्रों से बाहरी प्रवास भी कम हुआ होगा। भाबर से लगे हुए टिहरी, पौड़ी, अल्मोड़ा, चंपावत जनपदों में सर्वाधिक प्रवास हुआ तथा प्रवासी भी अधिक लौटे हैं। इन क्षेत्रों में बाहरी तथाकथित विकास एवं सुविधाओं का प्रभाव पड़ा है।

तालिका-8 : उत्तराखंड में वापस आए प्रवासियों की जनपदवार संख्या

वापस आए प्रवासियों की संख्या तक					*जून 2020 तक*	
जनपद	*मार्च 2020 तक*		*जून 2020 तक*		*कुल प्रवासी*	
	संख्या	*प्रतिशत*	*संख्या*	*प्रतिशत*	*संख्या*	*प्रतिशत*
अल्मोड़ा	9303	15.67	43784	20.29	53087	19.29
नैनीताल	4771	8.04	9650	4.47	14421	5.24
पिथौरागढ़	5035	8.50	5451	2.53	10486	3.81
चंपावत	5707	9.61	15097	7.00	20804	7.56
बागेश्वर	1541	2.60	1925	0.88	3466	1.26
ऊधम सिंह नगर	–	–	2195	810.17	21958	7.98
पौड़ी	12039	20.28	60440	28.00	72479	26.33
चमोली	3214	5.41	5877	2.72	9091	3.30
देहरादून	–	–	2254	1.04	2254	0.82
हरिद्वार	–	–	3136	1.45	3136	1.14
उत्तराकाशी	4721	7.95	19405	8.99	24126	8.77
टिहरी	8782	14.79	19242	8.91	28024	10.18
रुद्रप्रयाग	4247	7.15	7656	3.55	1190	34.32
कुल	59360	100.00	215875	100.01	275235	100.00

स्रोत : *ग्राम्य विकास एवं पलायन आयोग उत्तराखंड पौड़ी,* रिपोर्ट जुलाई 2020

विकास खंडवार प्रवासी

विकास खंडवार लौटे प्रवासियों के विवरण को अध्ययन करने से ज्ञात हो रहा है कि उत्तराखंड में सबसे कम कपकोट विकासखंड में मात्र 30 प्रवासी लौटे हैं जबकि सबसे अधिक 7759 प्रवासी पौड़ी जनपद के बीरोंखाल विकासखंड में वापस लौटे।

तालिका-9 : विकासखंडवार प्रवासी विवरण, जून 2020

वर्ग (प्रवासी सं)	*संख्या*	*प्रतिशत*	*विकासखंड*
500 से कम	19	20.0	बागेश्वर, बेरीनाग, खानपुर, मोरी, नरेंद्रनगर, रायपुर, विकासनगर, कनालीछीना, गंगोलीहाट, रुड़की, लक्सर चकराता, मुंस्यारी, जोशीमठ, थराली, सहसपुर, देवाल, कालसी एवं कपकोट
500-1500	28	29.5	भीमताल, नौगांव, गरुड़, मूनाकोट, डोइवाला, लमगड़ा, जाखड़ीधार, बहादराबाद, धारचूला, सितारगंज, ओखलकांडा, हल्द्वानी, पोखरी, पुरोला, जौनपुर, कर्णप्रयाग, डीडीहाट, भिलंगना, कोटाबाग, भगवानपुर, नारसन, धाट, दशौली, रामगढ़, धारी एवं उखीमठ।
1500-2500	121	2.6	बेतालघाट, बाराकोट, रामनगर, थौलधार, दुगड्डा, देवप्रयाग, बाजपुर, जसपुर, द्वाराहाट, गदरपुर, खिर्सू एवं चंबा।
2500-3500	121	2.6	लोहाघाट, जखोली, हवालबाग, कीर्तिनगर, जयहरीखाल, ताड़ीखेत, कोट, पौड़ी, भैंसियाछाना, पोखड़ा, ताकुला एवं गैरसैंण।
3500-4500	11	11.6	रिखणीखाल, एकेश्वर, खटीमा, काशीपुर, पाटी, अगस्त्यमुनि, धौलादेवी, द्वारीखाल, यमकेश्वर, पावो एवं कल्जीखाल।
4500-5500	3	3.2	चंपावत, डुंडा एवं स्याल्दे।
5500-6500	7	7.4	रुद्रपुर, भिकियासैंण, चौखुटिया, प्रतापनगर, चिन्यालिसौड़, भटवाड़ी एवं नैनीडांडा।
6500 से अधिक	3	3.2	बीरोंखाल (7,759), थलीसैंण (7,616) एवं सल्ट (7,523)।

स्रोत : *ग्राम्य विकास एवं पलायन आयोग उत्तराखंड पौड़ी,* रिपोर्ट जुलाई, 2020

तालिका 9 से स्पष्ट हो रहा है 19 (20 प्रतिशत) विकासखंडों में 500 से कम प्रवासी लौटे हैं। इनमें 5 विकासखंड मैदानी तथा शेष 14 विकासखंड पर्वतीय हैं। इसी प्रकार

500 से 1,500 तक जिन विकासखंडों में प्रवासी लौटे हैं उनकी संख्या 28 (29.5 प्रतिशत) है।

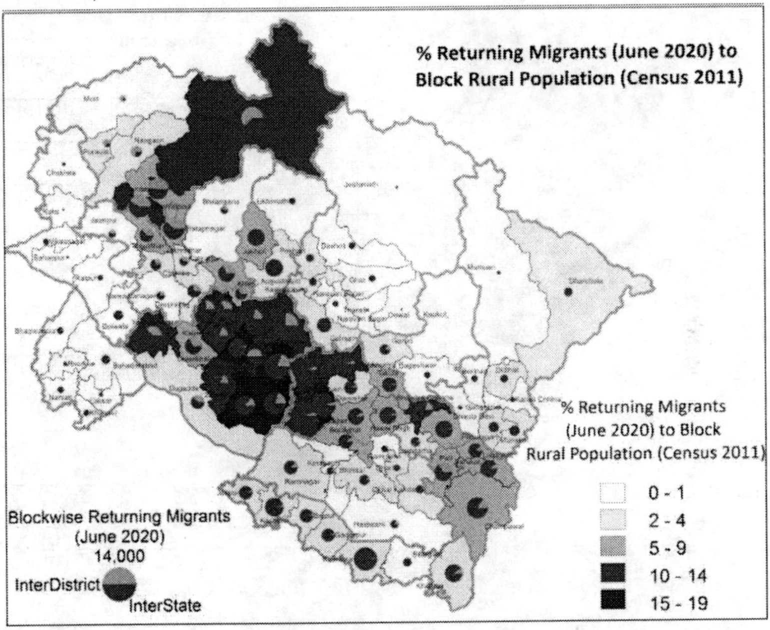

मानचित्र 3 : उत्तराखंड में विकासखंडवार प्रवासी विवरण, जून 2020 (Taragi, R. C. S. 2020. Facebook wall 2020)

बारह-बारह विकासखंडों में 1500-2500 तथा 2500-3500 के बीच प्रवासी लौटे हैं। 11 विकासखंडों में 3500-4500 तक प्रवासी लौटे जबकि उत्तराखंड के 13 विकासखंड जिनमें 4500 से अधिक प्रवासी लौटे हैं। इनमें रूद्रपुर एकमात्र विकासखंड है जो मैदान में स्थित है शेष सभी पर्वतीय क्षेत्र में स्थित हैं।

गंतव्य स्थान के आधार पर प्रवासी : तालिका 10 में केवल जून 2020 में उत्तराखंड लौटे प्रवासियों का विवरण उपलब्ध है। इस तालिका से स्पष्ट हो रहा है कि सर्वाधिक 80.68 प्रतिशत भारत के अन्य राज्यों से लौटे हैं जबकि प्रदेश के भीतर अन्य जनपदों से लौटने वाले प्रवासियों की संख्या 18.11 प्रतिशत है। प्रदेश के भीतर के जनपदों में लौटने वाले अधिकांश प्रवासी देहरादून, हरिद्वार, ऊधमसिंह नगर जनपद तथा पौड़ी, टिहरी एवं नैनीताल के मैदानी क्षेत्रों से सरकारी नौकरी वाले प्रवासी लौटे हैं। जनपद के अंदर से मात्र 0.92 प्रतिशत प्रवासी लौटे

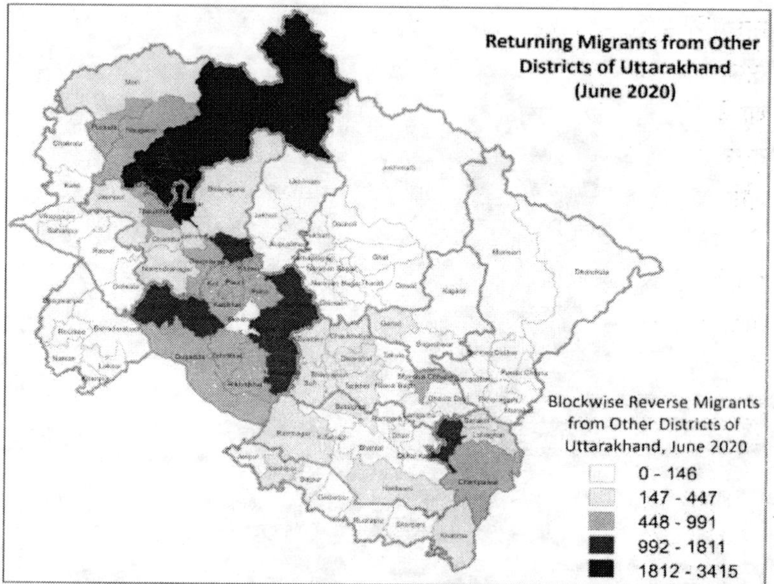

मानचित्र 3 : उत्तराखंड में विकासखण्डवार प्रदेश के अन्य जनपदों से प्रवासी विवरण, जून 2020 (Taragi, R. C. S. 2020. Facebook wall 2020)

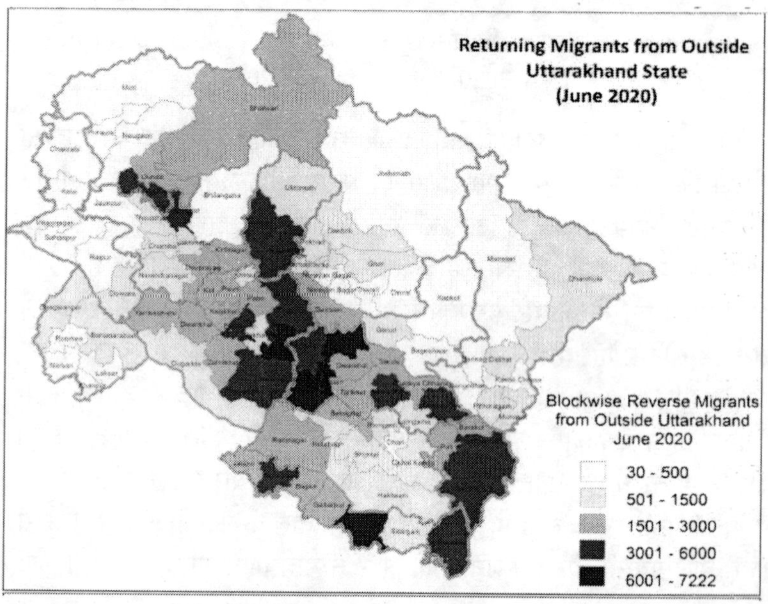

मानचित्र 3 : उत्तराखंड में विकासखण्डवार प्रदेश के अन्य भारत के अन्य राज्यों से प्रवासी विवरण, जून 2020 (Taragi, R. C. S. 2020. Facebook wall 2020)

हैं। उत्तराखंड में 616 व्यक्ति विदेशों से भी लौटे हैं। इनमें सर्वाधिक 274 व्यक्ति ऊधमसिंहनगर जनपद में हैं। यहां बसे हुए पंजाबी मूल के लोगों का कनाडा या अन्य देशों में व्यापार आदि का कार्य होता है जो इस लॉकडाउन में बंद हो गया था वे लौटे हैं। पौड़ी जनपद में भी 86 व्यक्ति लौटे हैं। लौटने वाली आबादी में दूसरे स्थान पर रहने वाले अल्मोड़ा जनपद में केवल 9 लोग ही विदेशों से वापस लौटे हैं।

व्यवसाय के आधार पर प्रवासियों का वर्गीकरण : तालिका 11 में लौटे हुए प्रवासियों साथ के व्यवसायों की जानकारी दी गई है। जनपदवार किसी में कम और किसी में अधिक प्रवासी हैं सरकारी नौकरियों में संपूर्ण उत्तराखंड में 3643 प्रवासी लौटे हैं इनमें सर्वाधिक 983 प्रवासी पौड़ी जनपद में लौटे हैं। दूसरे क्रम में 724 प्रवासियों के साथ अल्मोड़ा जनपद है। टिहरी, नैनीताल एवं रुद्रप्रयाग में भी क्रमशः 694, 657, 203 एवं 120 सरकारी नौकरी वाले प्रवासी लौटे हैं। ऊधमसिंह नगर में व्यावसायिक सूचना उपलब्ध नहीं है। शेष जनपदों में भी इस वर्ग के 100 से कम प्रवासी लौटे हैं। औसत रूप से 1.9 प्रतिशत प्रवासी सरकारी सेवाओं में सेवारत थे जो लॉकडाउन के चलते बीमारी के फैलने के भय के कारण अपने जनन क्षेत्र को लौटे। सर्वाधिक 58.17 प्रतिशत प्रवासी प्राइवेट (निजी) सेवा के साथ आतिथ्य क्षेत्र में कार्यरत थे, इस श्रेणी के सर्वाधिक 33,002 प्रवासी अल्मोड़ा जनपद में लौटे हैं। द्वितीय, तृतीय एवं चतुर्थ क्रम में पौड़ी, उत्तरकाशी, टिहरी एवं चंपावत जनपद हैं। जहां क्रमशः 27,772, 13,886, 10,412, तथा 8,749 गैर-सरकारी सेवाओं में कार्यरत प्रवासी लौटे हैं। तालिका 11 में कुल प्रवासी में से 8.8 प्रतिशत विद्यार्थी हैं जो भिन्न-भिन्न क्षेत्रों से अध्ययन करने गए थे, इसमें सर्वाधिक छात्र पौड़ी और टिहरी जनपद के हैं। अपने परिवारों में वापस आने वाली 7.2 प्रतिशत गृहिणियां भी वापस लौटीं। इस वर्ग में भी सर्वाधिक 6,822 पौड़ी, 2,052 अल्मोड़ा, 1738 टिहरी तथा 925 नैनीताल जनपद में लौटे हैं। जो प्रवासी पंडिताई (0.2 प्रतिशत) हेतु बाहर गए थे वे भी इस दौरान लौटे हैं, इसमें टिहरी प्रथम स्थान पर है। पंडिताई हेतु हरिद्वार, गंगोत्री बदरीनाथ, ऋषिकेश आदि स्थानों से भी लोग वापस अपने-अपने गांव की ओर लौटे हैं। तकनीकी ज्ञान रखने वाले मात्र 0.60 प्रतिशत प्रवासी लौटे हैं। इस वर्ग में उत्तरकाशी एवं टिहरी जनपद में सबसे अधिक हैं। मजदूर के रूप में 3.19 प्रतिशत प्रवासी ही लौटे हैं। मजदूरों में पिथौरागढ़ एवं हरिद्वार जनपद में सबसे

अधिक प्रवासी लौटे हैं। बेरोजगार प्रवासी मात्र 1.5 प्रतिशत थे। चंपावत जनपद में सर्वाधिक 2,288 बेरोजगार प्रवासी लौटे हैं, लगभग 1.5 प्रतिशत प्रवासियों के पास अपना रोजगार था जो छोड़कर लौटे हैं। सर्वाधिक 654 प्रवासी चंपावत जनपद में लौटे हैं।

तालिका-10 : वापस आए प्रवासियों के गंतव्य प्रवास के स्थान का विवरण

जनपद	*जनपद के भीतर*	*प्रदेश के अन्य जनपदों से*	*भारत के अन्य राज्यों से*	*विदेशों से*	*कुल*
अल्मोड़ा	23	2,478	41,274	9	43,784
नैनीताल	320	893	8,430	7	9,650
पिथौरागढ़	0	121	5,330	0	5,451
चंपावत	45	2,702	12,328	22	15,097
बागेश्वर	0	230	1,695	0	1,925
पौड़ी	1,271	14,000	45,073	86	60,440
चमोली	0	61	5,812	4	5,877
देहरादून	14	194	2,045	02	2,254
हरिद्वार	26	279	2,753	78	3,136
उत्तरकाशी	41	10,370	8,933	61	19,405
टिहरी	190	6757	12,221	74	19,242
रुद्रप्रयाग	0	1	7,655	0	7,656
उधम सिंह नगर	64	1,000	20,620	274	21,958
कुल	1,994	39,086	1,74,168	616	21,5,875
प्रतिशत कुल	0.92	18.11	80.68	0.29	100.00

स्रोत : *ग्राम्य विकास एवं पलायन आयोग उत्तराखंड पौड़ी*, रिपोर्ट जुलाई 2020

तालिका-11 : वापस आए प्रवासियों का व्यवसाय के आधार पर वर्गीकरण

जनपद	सरकारी क्षेत्र	प्राइवेट नौकरी एवं अस्थायी क्षेत्र	पंडिताई	तकनीकी	गृहणी	विद्यार्थी	मजदूर	बेरोजगार	स्वरोजगार	अन्य	कुल
अल्मोड़ा	724	33,002	2	47	2,052	1,920	176	26	278	5557	43,784
नैनीताल	657	4,102	15	106	925	945	720	104	144	1932	9,650
पिथौरागढ़	85	2,957	0	10	214	249	1,464	3	55	414	5,451
चंपावत	203	8,749	31	100	825	969	599	2,288	654	681	15,097
बागेश्वर	68	953	0	81	215	230	8	1	361	8	1925
पौड़ी	983	2,772	70	102	6,822	7,301	515	107	375	16,393	60,440
चमोली	47	40,771		84	310	352	48	0	53	905	5,877
देहरादून	52	1,258	14	10	186	219	209	0	87	219	2,254
हरिद्वार	7	833	0	84	33	16	1,767	78	103	215	3,136
उत्तरकाशी	3	13,866	2	242	0	1,341	0	167	287	3497	19,405

टिहरी	694	10,412	213	237	1,738	2,799	388	5	395	2,361	19,242
रुद्रप्रयाग	120	4813	0	0	707	665	71	143	52	1,085	7,656
उ.सि.नगर	अनुपलब्ध	अनुपलब्ध	अनुपलब्ध	अनुपलब्ध	अनुपलब्ध	अनुपलब्ध	अनुपलब्ध	अनुपलब्ध	अनुपलब्ध	अनुपलब्ध	21958
उत्तराखंड	3643	11,2,794	348	1103	14,027	17,006	5,966	2,920	2,844	33,267	21,5,875
प्रतिशत	1.90	58.17	0.20	0.60	7.20	8.80	3.10	1.50	1.50	17.00	100.00

स्रोत : ग्राम्य विकास एवं पलायन आयोग उत्तराखंड पौड़ी, जुलाई,

2020 अन्य प्रवासियों का एक अलग वर्ग बनाया गया है। जिसमें 17.0 प्रतिशत प्रवासियों को सम्मिलित किया गया है, इस वर्ग में सर्वाधिक पौड़ी (16,393) तथा अल्मोड़ा (5,557) में प्रवासी लौटे हैं। लगभग 81 प्रतिशत प्रवासियों के साथ रोजगार का संकट खड़ा हो गया है। इसमें अधिकांश प्रवासी स्थितियां ठीक होने पर लौटने की सोच रहे हैं। जबकि कुछ प्रवासी चाहते हैं कि यदि रोजगार/आय का साधन पहाड़ों पर ही मिल जाए तो अब यहीं रूकना चाहते हैं।

पुनर्वास हेतु योजनाएं एवं कार्यक्रम

प्रदेश के बाहर से लौटे प्रवासियों को आर्थिक संपन्नता प्रदान करने के लिए सरकार द्वारा कई कार्यक्रमों तथा योजनाओं का संचालन किया गया जिसमें प्रवासियों को वरीयता दी गई। इनमें कुछ योजनाएं निम्नलिखित हैं–

1. मुख्यमंत्री स्वरोजगार योजना।
2. महात्मा गांधी राष्ट्रय ग्रामीण रोजगार गारंटी कार्यक्रम
3. दीनदयाल अंत्योदय योजना
4. दीनदयाल ग्रामीण कौशल योजना
5. राष्ट्रीय आजीविका मिशन
6. सरकारी ऋण और अधिपोषण योजना
7. पशुपालन क्षेत्र।
8. कृषि क्षेत्र।
9. उद्यान क्षेत्र आदि अनेक कार्यक्रम हैं जिन्हें प्रवासियों के लिए चलाया गया है।

लॉकडाउन के प्रभाव

देश में महामारी को फैलने से रोकने के लिए अनायास लॉकडाउन लगाया गया। इससे जहां एक ओर अचानक प्रवासियों में अपने-अपने प्रदेशों में वापस लौटने संबंधित समस्याएँ उत्पन्न हो गईं वहीं दूसरी ओर पर्यावरण में कुछ अच्छे प्रभाव भी पड़े जिनमें कुछ प्रमुख इस प्रकार हैं–

1. शहरों में वायु प्रदूषण की मात्रा बहुत घट गई थी।
2. पर्वतीय क्षेत्रों में धुंध की मात्रा भी कम हो गई थी जिससे दृश्यता बहुत

बढ़ गई थी।

3. जल में प्रदूषण की मात्रा बहुत कम हो गई थी, प्रदेश से निकलने वाली नदियों का जल बहुत साफ हो गया था। दिल्ली में यमुना, प्रयागराज में गंगा बहुत निर्मल हो गई थी।
4. यातायात संबंधी एवं अन्य दुर्घटनाएं भी नहीं हुई।
5. अपराधों पर भी अंकुश लगा।
6. ईधन (पेट्रोल एवं डीजल) की बचत से भी प्रदूषण कम हुआ।
7. वन्य जीव जंतुओं को स्वच्छंद वातावरण मिला जिससे जंगली जानवर यत्र तत्र विचरण करते मिले।
8. फिजूल खर्च एवं दिखावे खर्च पर भी अंकुश लगा।

चुनौतियां

कोविड-19 के कारण संपूर्ण विश्व के साथ उत्तराखंड को भी अनेक चुनौतियों का सामना करना पड़ रहा है जो मुख्य निम्नलिखित हैं–

1. प्रवासियों को रोजगार उपलब्ध कराना।
2. कोविड-19 के मरीजों को उचित इलाज की व्यवस्था करना।
3. संक्रमण से निवासियों को बचाना।
4. राजकोषीय घाटे को कम करना।
5. आर्थिकी मजबूत करना।
6. पूर्व से चल रही योजनाओं को निरंतरता प्रदान करना।

सारांश

कोविड-19 से उत्तराखंड राज्य भी पूरी तरह से प्रभावित हुआ है। इससे बचाव के लिए संसाधनों का समुचित प्रयोग करने हेतु प्रवासी एवं युवाओं को प्रेरित करना अति आवश्यक है। लगभग 81 प्रतिशत प्रवासियों के साथ रोजगार का संकट खड़ा हो गया है। इसमें अधिकांश प्रवासी स्थितियां ठीक होने पर लौटने की सोच रहे हैं। जबकि कुछ प्रवासी चाहते हैं कि यदि रोजगार/आय का साधन पहाड़ों पर ही मिल जाए तो अब यहीं रुकना चाहते हैं। प्रदेश से बाहर से लौटे प्रवासियों को आर्थिक संपन्नता प्रदान करने के लिए सरकार द्वारा कई कार्यक्रमों तथा योजनाओं का

संचालन किया गया जिसमें प्रवासियों को वरीयता दी गई। देश में महामारी को फैलने से रोकने के लिए अनायास लॉकडाउन लगाया गया। इससे जहां एक ओर अचानक प्रवासियों में अपने-अपने प्रदेशों में लौटने संबंधित समस्याएँ उत्पन्न हो गई वहीं दूसरी ओर पर्यावरण में कुछ अच्छे प्रभाव भी पड़े।

उत्तराखंड की सीमाएं तिब्बत एवं नेपाल से लगी होने के कारण सामरिक दृष्टि से इस क्षेत्र को आवागमन एवं आर्थिकी को सुदृढ़ करना होगा तथा इन क्षेत्रों से हुए पलायन पर भी ध्यान केंद्रित कर विकास करना होगा, यदि ये क्षेत्र खाली हो जाते है तो सामरिक दृष्टि से विदेशियों के लिए अनुकूल स्थितियों बन जाएँगी, जिसके लिए उत्तराखंड एवं भारत सरकार को मिलकर विशेष योजना के तहत नई योजनायें बनानी पड़ेगी जिससे वे क्षेत्र पलायन से खाली न हों।

References

Anonymous, 2011. **Census of India**, 2011 (http://www. censusindia. gov.in).

Anonymous, 2011. **Census of India**, Provisional, D-5 Migrants by Place of Last Residence.

Anonymous, 2020. **Report of the Rural Development and Migration Commission**, Uttarakhand, Pauri, July 2020.

Atkinson, E. T., 1884. **The Himalayan Gazetteer**, (Reprint 1973) Cosmo Publications Delhi.

Nevill, H. R. 1904. **Nainital: A Gazetteer**, Govt. Printing Press Allahabad (Reprint 2016) Natraraj Publishers, Dehradun: 188-189.

Pant, B. R. (2020) Geo-Environmental Impacts and Challenges Before and After COVID -19: Uttarakhand A Case Study. **Journal of Maharashtra Bhugoleshastra Sansodhan Patrika, Pune**, Vol. 37 (1) 2020.

Pant, B. R., Chand, R. and Mehta B. S. (in press) **Uttarakhand: Jansankhya Paridrashya Evam Parivaritan**, PAHAR.

Pant, B. R., Chand, R. and Mehta B. S. 2020. Physical and Demographic Study of Uttarakhand. In Jules Lessard and Orson Riviere (Eds) **India: Environmental, Political and Social Issues.** Nova Science Publishers, Inc. 415 Oser Avenue, Suite N, Hauppauge, NY 11788 USA.: 1-52.

Taragi, R. C. S. 2020. Facebook wall 2020.

11

भारत चीन संबंध : 1947 से वर्तमान तक

कामना जैन

सार संक्षेप

समकालीन अंतर्राष्ट्रीय राजनीति में भारत व चीन का लगभग एक साथ ही पदार्पण हुआ। अपनी स्वतंत्रता के पश्चात् नेहरू ने माओ को उसके संघर्ष में पूर्ण सहयोग दिया। नेहरू से लेकर नरेंद्र मोदी तक भारत व चीन के संबंधों का विश्लेषण किया जाए तो भारत ने सदैव ईमानदारी व सदाशयता का परिचय दिया जबकि चीन ने दोस्ती की आड़ में धोखा एवं विस्तारवाद को बढ़ावा दिया। 1962 हो या 2020 उसने दोनों बार ही अपने कुटिल इरादे गलवान घाटी में प्रकट किए। विभिन्न प्रयासों के बाद भी कुछ ऐसे नाजुक मुद्दे हैं जो स्थिति को गंभीर बना देते है। मित्रता की बात करते-करते कब चीन दुश्मनी पर उतर आता है, उसको समझने के लिए भारत-चीन संबंधों की पृष्ठभूमि व उनके वर्तमान लक्ष्यों को समझना होगा। प्रस्तुत अध्याय में इसका विस्तृत विश्लेषण करने का प्रयास किया गया है।

कीवर्ड : चीन, भारत, तनाव बिंदु, भावी रणनीति, विस्तारवाद।

एशिया की सबसे बड़ी उभरती ताकत वाले दो पड़ोसी देश भारत व चीन हजारों वर्ष पुरानी सभ्यता के उत्तराधिकारी हैं। आजादी की लड़ाई के वर्षों में भी दोनों देशों के राष्ट्रवादी नेताओं के बीच संवाद बना रहा था। च्यांग काई शेक के साथ नेहरू जी की व्यक्तिगत मित्रता और माओ के नेतृत्व में लड़ रहे साम्यवादी छापामारों को राहत के लिए भेजी गई कांग्रेस पार्टी की चिकित्सा टीम इसी के उदाहरण हैं। भारत पहला जनतांत्रिक देश था जिसने जनवादी चीन को मान्यता दी। के.एम. पनिक्कर भारतीय राजदूत के रूप में चीन गए और भारत सरकार ने चीन को यू.एन. की सुरक्षा परिषद् में उसकी स्थायी सदस्यता दिलाने में सक्रिय भूमिका निभाई। चीन को बांडुंग शिखर सम्मेलन में आमंत्रित कर पंचशील

समझौते पर हस्ताक्षर किए।[1] किंतु जब हजारों वर्ष पुराने ऐतिहासिक, धार्मिक, सांस्कृतिक, व्यापारिक संबंधों को ताक पर रखकर 1962 में चीन ने भारत पर युद्ध थोपा तो करोड़ों भारतवासी स्तब्ध रह गए। हिंदी-चीनी भाई-भाई के सद्‌भाव पूर्ण संबंधों के भविष्य पर भी प्रश्नचिन्ह लग गया। तब से लेकर वर्तमान तक दोनों के मध्य रिश्ता रस्साकशी की तनातनी के समान कभी सामान्य व कभी गंभीर स्थिति पर पहुंच जाता है।

नेपोलियन ने कहा था, **'चीनी दैत्य अभी सो रहा है जब करवट लेकर जागेगा तो अन्तर्राष्ट्रीय राजनीति में भूचाल आ जायेगा।'**[2] अत्यंत महत्वाकांक्षी राष्ट्र चीन विस्तारवादी एवं साम्राज्यवादी नीति में विश्वास करता है। शांति की आड़ में चीन उग्रता के खतरनाक इरादे रखता है। एशिया व दक्षिण पूर्वी अफ्रीका आदि में वह अपने प्रभाव का विस्तार करने की नीति का ही पालन करता रहा है। चीन की विदेश नीति सिद्धांत व व्यवहार में अलग-अलग रही है। जिसमें क्रांतिकारी व अक्रांतिकारी के सिद्धांतों का सहारा लेते हुए दूसरे राष्ट्रों को भुलावे में रखने की नीति अपनाई गई।[3]

भारत व चीन सीमा विभाजन

1962 के युद्ध के बाद से भारत चीन के साथ 3,488 किलोमीटर लंबी सीमा साझा करता है, जिसे वास्तविक नियंत्रण रेखा (LAC) कहते हैं। ये सीमा जम्मू-कश्मीर, हिमाचल प्रदेश, उत्तराखंड, सिक्किम और अरुणाचल प्रदेश से होकर गुजरती है, जो तीन हिस्सों में बंटी है। अरुणाचल और सिक्किम वाला पूर्वी हिस्सा, उत्तराखंड और हिमाचल वाला मध्य भाग और लद्दाख वाला पश्चिमी भाग। हालांकि ऐतिहासिक दृष्टिकोण से 1914 में शिमला में हुए ब्रिटिश भारत, चीन और तिब्बत के प्रतिनिधियों के एक सम्मेलन में ब्रिटिश मंत्रिमंडल के सदस्य, आर्थर हेनरी मैकमोहन के द्वारा मानचित्र पर लाल पेंसिल से एक रेखा खींचकर भारत व चीन के मध्य सीमा विभाजन किया गया। इसे ही मैकमोहन रेखा कहा जाता है, किंतु चीन ने सदा साम्राज्यवादी रेखा कहकर इसकी निंदा की है।[4]

अक्टूबर 1949 की चीन क्रांति के पश्चात् विश्व पटल पर उभरे माओवादी चीन की विदेश नीति के निर्धारक तत्वों में यह अत्यंत महत्वपूर्ण तथ्य है कि चीन के जार शासकों द्वारा जो संधियाँ या समझौते आदि किए गए थे। उन्हें माओ ने मानने से इनकार कर दिया और अपने इरादे स्पष्ट करते हुए कहा कि वह छीनी हुई भूमि, खोए

हुए प्रदेश पुनः प्राप्त करना चाहता है।[5] प्रो. शरण कहते हैं, चीनी शासन की प्रत्यक्ष विशेषता इसकी भू-क्षेत्रीय महत्वाकांक्षा है।[6] और इसी कड़ी में वह भारत के साथ सीमा विवाद में उलझा हुआ है।

चीन की तिब्बत नीति से भारत प्रसन्न नहीं था, किंतु इस मुद्दे को लेकर भारत चीन के साथ अपनी मैत्री को प्रभावित नहीं करना चाहता था। भारत और चीन के तिब्बत क्षेत्र के मध्य वाणिज्य तथा अन्य संबंधों के विषय में भारत-चीन संधि पर 29 अप्रैल, 1954 को हस्ताक्षर किए गए। यह समझौता 8 वर्ष के लिए किया गया। भारत ने तिब्बत में अपने विशेष बहिर्देशीय अधिकार त्याग दिए और तिब्बत पर चीन की संप्रभुता स्वीकार कर ली।[7]

साम्यवादी क्रांति के कई वर्ष पश्चात् तक तो चीन ने सीमा के प्रश्न को कभी नहीं उठाया पर 1956 से ही चीन ने भारत की हजारों मील भूमि पर अपने दावे गलत नक्शों के प्रकाशन, भारतीय सीमा में अवैध घुसपैठ, सरकारी बयानों आदि के जरिये उछाले।[8] 1958 में चीन द्वारा *चाइना पिक्टोरियल* में प्रकाशित चीन के मानचित्रों में भारत के कुछ प्रदेशों को चीन के भाग के रूप में दिखाया गया। इन मानचित्रों में भारत के उत्तर-पूर्व के लगभग 36,000 वर्गमील प्रदेश को और उत्तर-पश्चिम के लगभग 1200 वर्ग मील प्रदेश को चीन के नक्शे में दिखाए जाने पर भारत ने जब आपत्ति जताई, तो चीन ने इसे पुरानी राष्ट्रवादी सरकार के मानचित्र कहकर टाल दिया। साथ ही कहा कि चीन को नए पर्यवेक्षण करने का अवसर नहीं मिला। जब तक चीन सरकार सर्वेक्षण नहीं करवा लेती, तब तक चीन की सीमाओं में फेर बदल का कोई प्रयत्न नहीं करेगी।[9] 23 जनवरी, 1959 को चाउ एन लाई ने पहली बार भारत के हजारों वर्ग मील के प्रदेशों पर अपना दावा प्रस्तुत किया, साथ ही, यह भी कहा कि तथाकथित मैकमोहन रेखा चीन के तिब्बत क्षेत्र के विरुद्ध आक्रमण की ब्रिटिश नीति की उपज थी। अतः चीन इसे अवैध मानता है। चाउ ने यह भी लिखा कि सीमा के प्रश्न को पहले इसलिए नहीं उठाया गया कि उसके लिए उपयुक्त समय नहीं था।[10] अतः स्पष्ट है कि चीन ने सोची-समझी रणनीति के तहत तिब्बत का भली-भांति अपने में एकीकरण करने के पश्चात् अपने सैनिकों को भारत-चीन सीमा पर नियुक्त कर, अपनी सुरक्षा चाक चौबंद कर विवाद प्रारंभ किया। तब से वर्तमान तक भारत-चीन सीमा विवाद विभिन्न क्षेत्रीय दावों को लेकर निरंतर चला आ रहा है।

भारत व चीन के मध्य तनाव के मुद्दे निम्नवत हैं–

1. **लद्दाख समस्या :** लद्दाख सदा से ही जम्मू-कश्मीर का अंग रहा है। शताब्दियों से भारत और चीन दोनों इस क्षेत्र की सीमा रेखा को मानते रहे थे और भारत के सभी मानचित्रों में इस सीमा रेखा को सदैव प्रदर्शित किया गया था। दोनों के मध्य संबंध जम्मू और कश्मीर के महाराजा गुलाब सिंह और दलाईलामा के मध्य 1814 में हुई संधि के अनुसार निर्धारित किए गए थे।[11] भारत द्वारा 1899 में चीन को भेजे एक पत्र में स्पष्ट कर दिया गया था कि अक्साई चिन भारतीय प्रदेश का भाग था। जम्मू-कश्मीर राज्य के राजस्व अभिलेखों में भी अक्साई चिन को कश्मीर के लद्दाख प्रांत का भाग स्वीकार किया गया था।[12]

   इस क्षेत्र में विवाद तब प्रारंभ हुआ जब 1955 के बाद चीन ने इस सीमा पर अपनी सैनिक गतिविधियां बढ़ा ली तथा 1956-57 में अपनी दीर्घकालिक योजना के तहत लद्दाख क्षेत्र के अक्साई चिन से सिक्यांग प्रांत (तिब्बत) को जोड़ने वाली सड़क का निर्माण किया जिससे इस क्षेत्र पर चीन का नियंत्रण स्थापित हो गया।[13]

   अक्साई चिन सड़क का सामरिक महत्व चीन के लिए वृहत्तर संदर्भ में है। लौप नौर (सिक्यांग प्रांत) में चीन का प्रक्षेपास्त्र परीक्षण स्थल है और मुक्त तिब्बत को नियंत्रण में रखने के लिए भी इस संचार व यातायात सुविधा की आवश्यकता पड़ती है।[14]

2. **अरुणाचल प्रदेश संबंधी विवाद :** अरुणाचल प्रदेश को नेफा (NEFA-उत्तर पूर्व सीमा एजेंसी) भी कहा जाता है। चीन की कपटपूर्ण दृष्टि प्रारंभ से ही अरुणाचल प्रदेश पर भी रही है, क्योंकि इसके द्वारा नेफा वाला पूर्वोत्तरी सीमांत भी चीन के लिए न केवल भारत वरन बांग्लादेश, भूटान आदि के संदर्भ में भी सामरिक महत्व का है। सारी हिमालयी सरहद संकट ग्रस्त रहने पर नेपाल पर भी दबाव बना रहता है। अगस्त 1959 के आरंभ में चीनी सेना नेफा में घुस गई। 18 सितंबर, 1959 को चीन ने औपचारिक रूप से भारत के लगभग 50,000 वर्गमील क्षेत्र पर अपना दावा प्रस्तुत किया। 1 अक्टूबर, 1959 में चीनी सेनाओं ने भारत के 9 जवानों की कोंगका दर्रे पर आकर हत्या कर दी और 10 को बंदी बना लिया।[15]

चीन अरुणाचल प्रदेश को तिब्बत का दक्षिणी भाग बताकर उस पर अपना दावा करता है। उसने अरुणाचल प्रदेश के 90,000 वर्ग किमी. और भारत-चीन सीमा के मध्य क्षेत्र के लगभग 2000 वर्ग किमी. पर अपना दावा कर रखा है। बीजिंग अरुणाचल प्रदेश को मान्यता नहीं देता।[16] 1986 में भारत द्वारा अरुणाचल प्रदेश को पूर्ण राज्य का दर्जा दिए जाने के फलस्वरूप चीन ने इसका कड़ा विरोध करते हुए कहा कि भारत को अरुणाचल को पूर्ण राज्य का दर्जा देने का कोई संवैधानिक अधिकार नहीं है। तत्कालीन चीनी प्रधानमंत्री झाओ झियांग ने कड़ी चेतावनी दी कि इसके लिए भारत को बड़ी कीमत चुकानी होगी। इस संबंध में 1987 में सुमडुरांग चु घाटी में दोनों देशों के बीच प्रत्यक्ष सैनिक मुठभेड़ भी हुई।[17] अरुणाचल प्रदेश में भारतीय प्रधानमंत्री की यात्राओं पर चीन को सदैव आपत्ति होती है। अरुणाचल प्रदेश को चीन के नक्शे में चीन के अंग के रूप में दिखाया जाता है।

3. **जम्मू व कश्मीर की स्थिति :** भारत व पाकिस्तान के मध्य विभाजन के बाद से ही जम्मू-कश्मीर क्षेत्र को लेकर विवाद बना रहा है और विडंबना यह है कि इस विवाद में चीन ने सदैव पाकिस्तान का समर्थन किया है। उसे हथियार व अन्य सुविधाएं प्रदान की हैं। चीन के साथ दोस्ती निभाते हुए पाकिस्तान ने 1963 में एक समझौते द्वारा पाक अधिकृत कश्मीर (POK) क्षेत्र में से 5,180 वर्ग किमी. भू-भाग चीन को उपहार स्वरूप दे दिया। इस भू-भाग के माध्यम से चीन और पाकिस्तान की सीमाऐं सीधे-एक दूसरे से मिल गईं। चीन ने अपने सिक्यांग प्रांत को पाकिस्तान से जोड़ते हुए इस क्षेत्र में कराकोरम हाइवे का निर्माण किया है।[18]
4. **तिब्बती धर्म गुरु दलाईलामा को शरण देने संबंधी विवाद :** 25 लाख वर्ग किलामीटर क्षेत्रफल वाला तिब्बत चीन व भारत के मध्य के साथ-साथ एशिया महाद्वीप के बीचो-बीच स्थित है। 1717 में जब तिब्बत पर हमला हुआ तो उसने चीन से सहायता मांगी और उसके बाद 1720 की संधि के आधार पर चीन तिब्बत पर अपना अधिकार जताता रहा। जबकि 1911 में मंचू साम्राज्य के खात्मे के साथ वह अधिकार भी समाप्त हो गया और तिब्बत स्वंतत्र देश के रूप में मौजूद रहा। अंतर्राष्ट्रीय विधि की दृष्टि से इस तथ्य का निर्णायक महत्व है। 1912 से ब्रिटेन ने भी तिब्बत के

साथ स्वतंत्र देश जैसा ही बर्ताव किया। 1943 में तिब्बत ने अपना विदेश विभाग भी स्थापित किया और तिब्बती पासपोर्ट को अंतर्राष्ट्रीय मान्यता भी मिली हुई थी। 1950 में चीन ने तिब्बत का बलात् अधिग्रहण किया और इसके साथ ही चीन भारत के दरवाजे पर आ खड़ा हुआ।[19] तिब्बत को पूरी तरह अपने नियंत्रण में लेने और वहां के स्थानीय लोगों के विरोध को कुचलने के लिए चीन द्वारा तिब्बती लोगों पर बर्बर अत्याचार व हिंसक हमले किए जा रहे थे। तब 1959 में दलाईलामा भाग कर भारत आ गए और उनके साथ 60,000 तिब्बतियों ने भी शरण मांगी। भारतीय परंपराओं के प्रति सम्मान व्यक्त करते हुए तथा लोकतंत्र की परिपाटी को जीवित रखने के लिए पं. नेहरू ने उन्हें धर्मशाला (हिमाचल प्रदेश) में रहने दिया साथ ही, उनको तिब्बती शरणार्थियों के पुनर्वास का दायित्व भी सौंपा।[20] दलाई लामा तिब्बत की स्वतंत्रता की मांग करते हैं। जो चीन को किसी भी कीमत पर स्वीकार्य नहीं है। संबंधों को सुधारने की दशा में चीन ने भारत से अनुरोध किया कि वह धार्मिक नेता दलाई लामा को अपनी भूमि का उपयोग राजनीतिक गतिविधियों को जारी रखने के लिए अनुमति न दे।[21] भारत ने सदैव चीन के इस अनुरोध का मान रखा।

5. **1962 का भारत चीन-युद्ध :** अथक प्रयासों के बाद भी चीन अपनी धूर्तता नहीं छोड़ सका और उसने भारत पर युद्ध थोप ही दिया। चीन ने 12 जुलाई, 1962 को लद्दाख की गलवान घाटी में स्थित भारतीय पुलिस चौकी पर कब्जा कर पुलिसकर्मियों को बंदी बना लिया और 25,000 वर्गमील क्षेत्र को अवैध रूप से अधिकृत कर लिया। 8 सितंबर, 1962 को नेफा में मैकमोहन रेखा पर कुछ अन्य क्षेत्रों पर भी अधिकार कर लिया। 20 अक्टूबर, 1962 तक बोमडिला पार करके चीनी सैनिक असम के मैदानी क्षेत्रों तक पहुंच गए। लद्दाख के जिस क्षेत्र पर चीनी अपना दावा कर रहे थे, वह उसके अधिकार में आ गया। 21 नवंबर, 1962 को चीन ने एक पक्षीय युद्ध विराम की घोषणा कर दी तथा 26 अक्टूबर, 1962 को भेजे गए अपने 3 सूत्री प्रस्ताव को पुनः दोहराया, जिसमें कहा गया था–

   (1) दोनों देशों द्वारा युद्ध विराम रेखा को वास्तविक नियंत्रण रेखा (एल.ओ.सी.) के रूप में स्वीकार करना और अपनी-अपनी सेनाओं को इस रेखा से 20 किलोमीटर हटा लेना था।

(2) यदि भारत न भी माना तो चीन अपनी सेना को नियंत्रण रेखा से 20 किलोमीटर उत्तर की ओर हटा देगा। शर्त यह थी कि दोनों देश नियंत्रण रेखा का सम्मान करेंगे।

(3) दोनों देशों के प्रधानमंत्री समस्या के निदान हेतु वार्ता करेंगे।

भारत ने चीन के इस प्रस्ताव को अस्वीकार करते हुए कहा कि वह सितंबर 1962 वाली यथास्थिति (Status quo ante) स्वीकार करे किंतु चीन ने इसे अस्वीकार कर दिया।[22]

चीन ने सीमा पर सदैव अग्रगामी नीति (दो कदम आगे और एक कदम पीछे) का अनुसरण किया है और दूसरों के क्षेत्रों को हड़पा है।

6. **सिक्किम समस्या :** 1890 में कलकत्ता समझौते के अंतर्गत चीन ने सिक्किम को ब्रिटेन का संरक्षित राज्य होने की मान्यता दी थी, किंतु इसके बीच जो सीमा रेखा निर्धारित की गई है, चीन उसका पालन नहीं कर रहा है।[23]

   1975 में सिक्किम के प्रधानमंत्री के अनुरोध तथा 97.5 प्रतिशत सिक्किम की जनता की सहमति के बाद ही 16 मई, 1975 को 36वें संवैधानिक संशोधन के तहत सिक्किम को भारत के 22वें राज्य का दर्जा दिया गया। चीन ने इसकी कटु आलोचना की, भारत पर विस्तारवादी होने का आरोप लगाया और सिक्किम की घटनाओं के लिए भारत को जिम्मेदार ठहराया। वर्ष 2003 में जब भारत ने औपचारिक रूप से तिब्बत को चीन के एक भाग के रूप में मान्यता दे दी, तब वर्ष 2004 में चीन ने सिक्किम को भारत के औपचारिक भाग के रूप में मान्यता दी।[24]

7. **भारत व चीन संबंध 1962 के पश्चात् :** 1962 के युद्ध के पश्चात् लगभग 2 दशकों तक भारत व चीन के संबंध तनावपूर्ण ही बने रहे। प्रधानमंत्री इंदिरा गांधी चीन के साथ सौहार्दपूर्ण संबंधों की इच्छुक थी, किंतु आत्मसम्मान या राष्ट्रहित की बलि देकर नहीं। 1971 के बांग्ला मुक्ति प्रकरण में भी चीन ने भारत का विरोध व पाकिस्तान का समर्थन किया। अपनी वीटो पावर द्वारा बांग्लादेश को यू.एन.ओ. का सदस्य नहीं बनने दिया।[25]

   1971 में भारतीय सोवियत मैत्री, हरित क्रांति से खाद्यान्न में आत्मनिर्भरता, मई 1974 में पोखरण परमाणु परीक्षण की सफलता आदि घटनाओं ने चीन को स्पष्ट कर दिया कि एशिया महाद्वीप में भारत ही चीन के एकाधिकार

को चुनौती दे सकता है।

भारत-चीन संबंधों को सामान्यीकरण की दिशा में बढ़ाते हुए 1979 में विदेश मंत्री अटल बिहारी बाजपेयी चीन की यात्रा पर गए किंतु चीन द्वारा गुटनिरपेक्ष देश वियतनाम पर किए गए आक्रमण के विरोध में बाजपेयी जी यात्रा बीच में छोड़कर वापस आ गए। वर्ष 1988 में प्रधानमंत्री राजीव गांधी की चीन यात्रा के पश्चात् यह तय किया गया कि चीन के साथ द्विपक्षीय क्षेत्रीय सीमा विवाद सुलझाने के प्रयास तो किए ही जाएंगे, इसके साथ ही, द्विपक्षीय व्यापारिक, सांस्कृतिक संबंधों में भी सहयोग बढ़ाया जाएगा।

1993 में वास्तविक नियंत्रण रेखा पर शांति के लिए दोनों देशों ने विश्वास निर्माण उपायों (सी.बी.एम.) को बढ़ावा देने की बात कही और 1996 में दोनों देशों ने सी.बी.एम. समझौते पर हस्ताक्षर किए। मई 1998 में भारत के पोखरण परमाणु परीक्षण पर चीन ने तीव्र प्रतिक्रिया व्यक्त करते हुए भारत से अपने परमाणु अस्त्रों को नष्ट करने की मांग की।

6 जून, 1998 में सुरक्षा परिषद द्वारा पारित प्रस्ताव संख्या 1174 में भारत के परमाणु परीक्षण तथा भारत द्वारा स्वयं को परमाणु अस्त्र संपन्न राज्य घोषित करने की निंदा की गई, तो चीन ने उसे पूर्ण समर्थन दिया।[26]

8. **डोकलाम विवाद :** 16 जून, 2017 को भारत व चीन के मध्य डोकलाम क्षेत्र में उत्पन्न तनातनी 72 दिनों बाद 28 अगस्त, 2017 को समाप्त हुई, जब भारत ने डोकलाम से अपनी सेनाऐं वापस सिक्किम में बुला लीं, साथ ही चीन ने भी सेना तथा सड़क निर्माण का सामान विवादित क्षेत्र से हटा लिया। डोकलाम चीन व भूटान के मध्य एक विवादित क्षेत्र है, जिस पर यह समझौता हुआ था कि, जब तक डोकलाम विवाद हल नहीं हो जाता, दोनों पक्ष वहां पर यथास्थिति बनाए रखेंगे, किंतु अपने स्वभावानुसार चीन भूटान के विरोध के बावजूद सड़क निर्माण कार्य करने लगा। इन परिस्थितियों में भूटान के आह्वान पर भारत ने डोकलाम पर अपनी सेनाएँ तैनात कर दीं, क्योंकि 1949 की भारत-भूटान मित्रता संधि के अंतर्गत यह उल्लिखित है कि दोनों एक-दूसरे की सुरक्षा में सहयोग करेंगे। डोकलाम भारत के लिए सामरिक दृष्टि से भी महत्वपूर्ण क्षेत्र है क्योंकि इस पहाड़ी क्षेत्र के नीचे ही भारत की मुख्य भूमि को उसके पूर्वी क्षेत्रों से

जोड़ने वाला संकरा दार्जीलिंग गलियारा (चिकन नेक) भी है और डोकलाम में सड़क निर्माण से चीन की सीधी पहुंच इस क्षेत्र तक हो जाती है।[27]

9. **भारत के विरुद्ध चीन-पाकिस्तान गठजोड़ :** कौटिल्य के मंडल सिद्धांत के अनुसार सीमा से लगा पड़ोसी कभी मित्र नहीं होता तथा शत्रु का शत्रु मित्र होता है। यह स्थिति भारत, चीन व पाकिस्तान के मध्य है। पाकिस्तान, चीन को कभी हर मौसम का दोस्त (all weather friend) तो कभी आयरन ब्रदर कहता है। चीन, भारत के परमाणु परीक्षण का पुरजोर विरोध और पाकिस्तान के परमाणु कार्यक्रम में पूर्ण सहयोग करता है। भारत-पाक के मध्य हुए युद्धों में भी चीन ने सदैव पाकिस्तान का ही समर्थन किया है। 2014 से चीन, पाकिस्तान के माध्यम से अरब सागर तक अपनी बढ़त बनाने हेतु आर्थिक गलियारे का निर्माण कर रहा है। 46 बिलियन डॉलर की लागत से बन रहे इस गलियारे में रोड, रेल नेटवर्क तथा विद्युत परियोजनाओं का निर्माण शामिल है। इसके जरिये चीन के झिंगझियांग प्रांत में स्थित कासगर शहर को पाक अधिकृत कश्मीर व पाक की मुख्य भूमि से होते हुए अरब सागर स्थित, पाकिस्तानी बंदरगाह ग्वादर से जोड़ना है। इससे चीन को हिंद महासागर तक पहुंचने का सुरक्षित मार्ग उपलब्ध हो जाएगा। वह गैस व तेल के व्यापार के लिए इस मार्ग का प्रयोग करेगा। भारत को आशंका है कि वे इसका प्रयोग भारत को सैनिक दृष्टि से घेरने के लिए भी कर सकते हैं। भारत की आपत्ति यह भी है कि यह गलियारा भारत व पाकिस्तान के मध्य उस विवादास्पद पाक अधिकृत कश्मीर से होकर गुजरेगा, जिसे भारत अपना मानता है। अंतर्राष्ट्रीय स्तर की बैठकों में भी चीन ने पाकिस्तान का साथ दिया है। चीन सदैव संयुक्त राष्ट्र की सुरक्षा परिषद् के उस प्रस्ताव को उछालता रहता है जो कश्मीर में जनमत संग्रह की बात करता है और जिसे भारत नहीं मानता। 5 अगस्त, 2019 को जब कश्मीर से धारा 370 को हटाया गया तो चीन के सहयोग से ही पाकिस्तान इस मुद्दे को संयुक्त राष्ट्र सुरक्षा परिषद् की बंद दरवाजा बैठक में चर्चा हेतु ले गया। सुरक्षा परिषद् की कमेटी द्वारा पुलवामा सहित भारत में कई आतंकवादी घटनाओं के साजिशकर्त्ता तथा पाक स्थित जैश-ए-मोहम्मद के मुखिया मसूद अजहर को पहले चीन के विरोध के कारण वैश्विक आतंकवादी घोषित नहीं किया जा सका और विभिन्न प्रयासों के बाद

अंततः जब उसे आतंकवादी घोषित किया गया तो चीन के दबाव के कारण उक्त प्रस्ताव में से अजहर द्वारा कश्मीर में किए गए आतंकवादी कार्यों का उल्लेख हटा दिया गया।[28]

10. **भारत, चीन व अन्य पड़ोसी देश :** 14 पड़ोसी देशों से घिरे चीन ने हाल ही के वर्षों में दक्षिण एशिया में अपनी पकड़ मजबूत करने के लिए स्थानीय, राष्ट्रीय और क्षेत्रीय स्तर पर त्रिशूल नीति अपनाई है।[29] पाकिस्तान तो चीन का परम विश्वसनीय राजनीतिक मोहरा है जिसका सहयोग करके चीन अप्रत्यक्ष रूप से भारत को उलझाए एवं दबाव बनाए रखता है। 1990 के दशक से चीन पड़ोसी देशों के माध्यम से भारत को घेरने की योजना पर काम कर रहा है। यह उसकी String of Pear नीति का परिणाम है। 2014 में चीन ने 21वीं शताब्दी Silk Route योजना के नाम से हिंद महासागर में प्रभाव बढ़ाने के लिए नई योजना शुरू की है। इसके अंतर्गत श्रीलंका, बांग्लादेश, मालदीव में चीन द्वारा बंदरगाह तथा अन्य सुविधाओं का विकास किया जाएगा। इस योजना से चीन हिंद महासागर होते हुए यूरोप तक समुद्री मार्ग का विकास करना चाहता है। भारत के अतिरिक्त अन्य एशियाई देशों ने इसे सहमति दे दी है।

    भारत व चीन के मध्य बफर स्टेट नेपाल की ऐतिहासिक, सांस्कृतिक परंपराएं भारत से जुड़ी होने के बाद भी आज नेपाल चीन के हाथ की कठपुतली बनकर भारत के खिलाफ बयानबाजी और गलत नक्शों का प्रकाशन कर रहा है। म्यांमार के साथ आर्थिक गलियारे के निर्माण पर सहमति बनाकर और श्रीलंका की निर्माण परियोजनाओं पर अपनी पकड़ मजबूत करके वह क्षेत्र में भारत विरोधी नीति को हवा दे रहा है।[30]

    दक्षिण एशिया में चीन का व्यापारिक कारोबार वर्ष 1990 में 1.18 तथा वर्ष 2000 में 5.57 अरब डॉलर से बढ़कर वर्ष 2018 में 127.36 अरब डॉलर हो गया। श्रीलंका के हब्बनटोटा, कोलंबो पोर्टसिटी से लेकर बांग्लादेश में पायरा बिजली परियोजना और ढाका चटगांव रेलवे में 3-3 अरब डॉलर निवेश करने तक और पाकिस्तान में चीन-पाकिस्तान आर्थिक गलियारा (CPEC) के तहत परियोजनाओं को पूरा करने के लिए 8.62 अरब डॉलर मुहैया कराने से लेकर भारत व नेपाल के सीमावर्ती इलाकों में रेलवे लाइन बिछाने की योजना बनाने तक बीजिंग ने नई दिल्ली के लिए

मुसीबतें खड़ी की है। भूटान अकेला पड़ोसी देश है जिसके साथ चीन के कूटनीतिक रिश्ते नहीं है। फिर भी भूटान में अपने आर्थिक, सांस्कृतिक प्रभाव को बढ़ाने हेतु सर्कस के कलाकार, नट-कलाबाज और फुटबॉलर, भूटानी छात्रों को चीनी विश्वविद्यालयों में पढ़ने के लिए छात्रवृत्तियां देने संबंधी प्रयास करता रहता है।[31]

11. **दक्षिण चीन सागर में चीन की जल कूटनीति :** जल-थल-नभ में अपनी ताकत अतुलनीय रूप से बढ़ाकर 2049 तक चीन वैश्विक महाशक्ति बनने की राह में है। अपनी विस्तारवादी-साम्राज्यवादी नीति को बढ़ाते हुए चीन पिछले एक दशक से जल कूटनीति द्वारा अपने सामाजिक, आर्थिक राजनीतिक, सामरिक हितों को साधना चाहता है। इसके लिए वह एक तरफ तो नदियों पर बांधों की शृंखला बनाकर पानी रोक रहा है और दूसरी तरफ दक्षिण चीन सागर व प्रशांत महासागर में जलीय सीमाओं का अतिक्रमण कर घेराबंदी कर रहा है। चीन व भारत की अर्थव्यवस्थाओं को तीव्र विकास हेतु ऊर्जा और कच्चे माल की आवश्यकता है।

    अतः दोनों अपने व्यापार और ऊर्जा आपूर्ति के अनधिकृत परिवहन हेतु समुद्री मार्गों पर ध्यान केंद्रित कर रहे हैं।[32] चीनी सेना (PLA) ने हिंद महासागर में प्रवेश किया है और अब अपनी ताकत बढ़ाने के लिए श्रीलंका, मालदीव, सिंगापुर, बांग्लादेश आदि देशों के साथ गठजोड़ मजबूत कर रहा है।[33]

12. **गलवान घाटी : तनाव का वर्तमान बिंदु :** गलवान घाटी में 15 जून, 2020 की घटना, वर्ष 2012 के बाद से भारत-चीन सीमा पर लगातार होने वाली गंभीर घटनाओं का परिणाम है। वर्ष 2013 में PLA ने वास्तविक नियंत्रण रेखा (LAC) पर घुसपैठ कर डेप्सांग में अपना तंबू गाढ़ दिया, जिसे ढाई हफ्ते की वार्ता के बाद पीछे हटाया गया। सितंबर 2014 में राष्ट्रपति शी जिनपिंग जिस दिन भारत की राजकीय यात्रा पर आए, 1000 से अधिक PLA सैनिक दक्षिण पूर्व लद्दाख के चुमार क्षेत्र में घुस गए और 3 हफ्ते बाद उसे खाली किया। इस वर्ष लद्दाख की घुसपैठ बड़ी थी क्योंकि वे LAC पर डेप्सांग, गलवान, हांट स्प्रिंग्स, पैंगोगत्सो और स्थानीय लद्दाखियों के अनुसार कुछ और क्षेत्रों में भी घुस आए थे।[34] 15 जून, 2020 को 16 बिहार रेजीमेंट के सैनिकों की एक टुकड़ी यह जांच

करने गई कि घाटी के ऊपर के पहाड़ी पाइंट-14 से PLA हट गई है या नहीं, जिस पर मई की शुरुआत से उन्होने कब्जा जमा रखा था। जब भारतीय सेना ने देखा कि चीनी सेना हटी नहीं तो भारतीय सैनिकों ने उनके तंबू उखाड़ने शुरू कर दिए, तो PLA सैनिकों ने लोहे की छड़ों और कील जड़ें मुग्दर से भारतीय सिपाहियों पर बर्बरतापूर्ण हमला कर दिया जिससे कमांडिग कर्नल व 20 भारतीय सैनिक शहीद हो गए।[35]

1949 में जब से चीन बना है तब से वह हमारे इलाकों को चूहे की तरह कुतरता रहा है। पैंगोगत्सो झील 135-136 किलोमीटर लंबी है, इसका करीब 37 कि.मी. इलाका भारत तथा शेष चीन में है।[36] हालांकि विशेषज्ञों के मुताबिक तो 1933 के मानचित्र में पैंगोगत्सो झील भारत में ही थी। वर्ष 1951 में चीन ने जो नक्शा छापा इससे दक्षिण में पैंगोगत्सो का हिस्सा चीन में आ गया और 1962 के युद्ध द्वारा चीन ने नक्शे के मुताबिक इस पर अपनी बढ़त बना ली। युद्ध खत्म होने के बाद चीन सिरिजाप तक तो लौटा पर दावेदारी आगे तक की करता रहा। सिरिजाप से आगे कई पहाड़ियां झील तक आती हैं, मानों फैली हुई उंगलियां हों। भारत ने इन्हें फिंगर-1 से फिंगर-8 तक नाम दिया है। भारत की तरफ से फिंगर-1 नजदीक व फिंगर 8 दूर है, भारत फिंगर-8 तक अपनी पैट्रोलिंग करता रहा है।[37] 58 साल पहले भी 1962 चीन ने इसी गलवान घाटी क्षेत्र में धोखा दिया था। गलवान क्षेत्र के सामरिक दृष्टि से महत्वपूर्ण होने के कारण चीन स्वयं अहम लोकेशन पर बने रहना चाहता था। चीन को ऐतराज भारत द्वारा निर्मित 260 किलोमीटर लंबी दारबुक श्योक दौलत बेग ओल्डी (DS-DBO) सड़क को लेकर है। जिससे केंद्र शासित प्रदेश लेह-लद्दाख से DBO सिर्फ 3 दिन में पहुंचा जा सकता है।[38]

13. **भारत-चीन आर्थिक संबंध :** वर्ष 1988 की प्रधानमंत्री राजीव गांधी की चीन यात्रा के पश्चात् से भारत-चीन आर्थिक संबंध लगातार प्रगति कर रहे हैं। 1978 में अपनी अर्थव्यवस्था को खोलने के बाद चीन ने मैन्युफैक्चरिंग में इतनी ताकत हासिल कर ली कि उसे दुनिया की फैक्टरी कहा जाने लगा।[39] चीन भारत का सबसे बड़ा व्यापारिक भागीदार है। हांगकांग को मिलाकर भारत के साथ उसका व्यापार 2019-20 में

> 109.8 अरब डॉलर है, जिसमें चीन को 54.6 अरब डॉलर की विशाल बढ़त है।[40]

डेटा एनालिसिक्स फर्म *ग्लोबल डेटा* के अनुसार हिंदुस्तान के स्टार्टअप में चीन का निवेश 2016 में 38.1 करोड़ डॉलर था जो 2019 में बढ़कर 4.6 अरब डॉलर हो गया।[41] भारत चीन से मोबाइल, दवाइयां, विद्युत उपकरण, उर्वरक, ऑटो पार्ट्स, संचार, रसायन, प्लास्टिक, इंजीनियरिंग, खिलौने, देवी-देवताओं की मूर्ति आदि बहुत कुछ आयात करता है, किंतु अब चीनी आक्रामकता के कारण भारत को चीन के साथ आर्थिक संबंधों का नवीनीकरण करना होगा। **चीन ने सुनत्जु की सीख, 'अदृश्य और इतने रहस्यमय बनो कि आवाज भी ना आए, तब तुम शत्रु के भाग्य को नियंत्रित कर सकते हो'।** को बड़ी निष्ठा से माना और मार्च 2019 में चीन की कम्युनिस्ट पार्टी द्वारा यह एलान किया गया कि चीनी कंपनियां कम्युनिस्ट पार्टी और राष्ट्रपति शी जिनपिंग के राजनीतिक दर्शन की ध्वजावाहक बनेंगी। वर्ष 2014 में साबरमती के तट पर जो भारत-चीन संबंधों को मजबूत बनाने की चर्चा की गई थी, उसकी अदृश्य डोर पकड़कर चीनी कंपनियां मेक इन इंडिया के शेर पर सवार हो गई। सरकारी घोषणाओं व दस्तावेजों पर आधारित ब्रुकिंग्स का अध्ययन बताता है कि 2017 तक भारत में 800 चीनी कंपनियां सक्रिय थीं। अतः अब सबसे पहले भारत को चीन से अपनी कारोबारी जमीन छुड़ानी होगी।[42] भारत ने चीन के 59 एप तथा इनके क्लोन माने जाने वाले 47 अन्य एप पर प्रतिबंध लगा दिया है। चीन की दूरसंचार कंपनियों पर रोक लगा दी है। देश की बिजली कंपनियों को भी चीनी सामान प्रयुक्त न करने के निर्देश दिए गए हैं।

चीन ने सदैव दोहरी चाल चली है, उसकी कथनी व करनी में फर्क होता है। जब तक सीमा विवाद हल नहीं हो जाता चीन के साथ आर्थिक, सांस्कृतिक संबंध बहाल नहीं किए जाने चाहिए। यदि हमें चीन की आवश्यकता है तो चीन को भी अपना निर्मित माल खपाने के लिए भारत जैसे विशाल बाजार की आवश्यकता है, अन्यथा भारत भी अपनी तकनीकी आवश्यकताओं को अन्य विकसित देशों, ताइवान, हांगकांग आदि से पूरा कर सकता है।

मोदी व शी जिनपिंग की वर्तमान रणनीति

राष्ट्रपति शी जिनपिंग खुद को आधुनिक चीनी इतिहास के तीसरे महान नेता के

तौर पर देख रहे हैं। माओत्से तुंग ने पुरानी व्यवस्था को ध्वस्त कर चीन को सामंतवाद और दमन से मुक्ति दिलाई। डेंग श्याओपिंग ने आधुनिक अर्थव्यवस्था की नींव रखी। शी जिनपिंग चीन को दबंग विश्व शक्ति में बदलना चाहते हैं।[43] और शायद इसी कारण चीन भारत, दक्षिण एशिया, अमेरिका आदि सभी के प्रति आक्रामक रुख बनाए हुए है। हालांकि एशिया में भारत के बढ़ते दबदबे से चीन चिंतित भी है। चीन के भय के निम्न कारण हैं–

1. मोदी ने चीन के महत्वाकांक्षी प्रोजेक्ट बेल्ट रोड एनिशिएटिव (BRI) जिसके द्वारा चीन विश्व व्यापार में अपना प्रभुत्व जमाना चाहता है, को समर्थन नहीं दिया।
2. मोदी ने क्षेत्रीय व्यापक आर्थिक साझेदारी (RCEP) पर भी हस्ताक्षर करने से मना कर दिया क्योंकि इसमें सभी सदस्य देशों को बराबरी का अवसर नहीं दिया गया।
3. जम्मू-कश्मीर से धारा 370 को हटाने के बाद चीन को भय है कि भारत POK का इलाका भी वापस ले लेगा। जिसका 5,180 वर्ग किमी. क्षेत्र चीन के पास है और उस पर चीन ने सड़क बनाई है।
4. WHO के कार्यकारी बोर्ड, जिसके मुखिया भारत के स्वास्थ्य मंत्री हैं, ने कोरोना वायरस के जन्म का सच जानने के लिए स्वतंत्र जांच कमेटी बनाई है। इस दबाव में भी चीन सीमा विवाद को हवा देने में लगा है।[44]
5. चीन भारत को सार्वजनिक रूप से नीचा दिखाना और इसकी हैसियत को कम करना चाहता है, क्योंकि शेष विश्व भारत को चीन का एक वैकल्पिक मॉडल मान रहा है।[45]

चीन को काबू में करने के लिए भारत को कूटनीतिक, आर्थिक, सैन्य सभी विकल्पों का इस्तेमाल अत्यंत सोच-समझकर सावधानी के साथ करना चाहिए। मोदी सरकार ने शी जिनपिंग के साथ रिश्ता बनाने में अच्छी खासी राजनीतिक पूंजी निवेश की है। 6 साल में 18 शिखर बैठकें, जिसें 2018 की **'वुहान स्प्रिट'** और 2019 की **'चेन्नई इफेक्ट'** भी सम्मिलित है। एक विशेषज्ञ के अनुसार चीनियों ने इस मेल मुलाकातों में मोदी के अहं को सहलाते हुए लड़े बिना जीतने का प्रयास किया। दूसरी तरफ यह भी कहा जा सकता है कि मोदी की पूरी कोशिश दो पाटों के बीच बंधी रस्सी पर चलने की रही है ताकि चीन को तब तक दुश्मन बनने से रोका जा सके

जब तक कि हम खुद को इतना ताकतवर न बना ले कि उसका सीधा मुकाबला कर पाएँ, जैसा कि **डेंग श्याओ पिंग ने अपनी 24 कैरेट राजनीति में चीन को नसीहत दी कि चुपचाप देखो, खुद को मजबूत करो, अपनी ताकत छिपाओ, अपने वक्त का इंतजार करो।**[46] मजबूत दिखाई देते चीन में कुछ आंतरिक चिंताएं भी हैं, जिन्होंने शी जिनपिंग को चिंतित किया हुआ है। बेरोजगारी में वृद्धि, नागरिक स्वतंत्रता पर पाबंदी, अल्पसंख्यकों का उत्पीड़न आदि के कारण चीनी कम्युनिस्ट पार्टी के खिलाफ असंतोष बढ़ रहा है। सार्वजनिक सूचनाओं के अनुसार पार्टी को सख्त नियंत्रित करते हुए 2013 से 2018 के बीच जिनपिंग ने 23 लाख से अधिक कर्मचारियों को बर्खास्त और कैद किया, जिनमें PLA के वरिष्ठ अधिकारी और नौकरशाह शामिल हैं।

इन परिस्थितियों में बहुत ही बुद्धिमत्तापूर्ण कूटनीति से चलते हुए चीन को नियंत्रित करना होगा–

- भारत को उन अंतर्राष्ट्रीय संगठनों से जुड़ना होगा। जो चीनी रवैये को लेकर चिंतित हैं।
- चीन से आयात में कटौती करनी होगी। स्वदेशी जागरण मंच के राष्ट्रीय सहसंयोजक अश्विनी महाजन का कहना है कि यदि भारत और अमेरिका व्यापार के मोर्चे पर हाथ मिला लें तो चीन ताश के पत्तों की तरह ढह जाएगा।
- जिस प्रकार से चीन सीमा क्षेत्र में तेजी से निर्माण कार्य कर रहा है, उसी प्रकार भारत को भी अपनी क्षमताएँ बढ़ाकर LAC के आस-पास बुनियादी ढांचे का निर्माण कराना होगा ताकि सैन्य नियंत्रण मजबूत किया जा सके।
- पड़ोसी देशों के साथ भारत को द्विपक्षीय रिश्ते मजबूत करने होंगे। प्राकृतिक आपदाओं, जलवायु परिवर्तन जैसी समस्याओं के लिए एक संयुक्त कार्य योजना बनाने की पहल करने के साथ ही नई प्रौद्योगिकी, शिक्षा, मेडिकल टूरिज्म आदि को बढ़ावा देना होगा। वीजा जारी करने की प्रक्रिया को सरल बनाना तथा सीमा शुल्क की पुनर्समीक्षा करनी होगी।
- विश्व जनमत भी भारत के पक्ष में है आसियान के देश, दक्षिण चीन सागर तथा भारत के साथ अनावश्यक विवाद खड़ा करने को लेकर चीन की आलोचना कर रहे हैं।
- हांगकांग के संबंध में 1997 समझौते का उल्लंघन कर वहां की जनता के लोकतांत्रिक अधिकारों को सीमित करने का जो कानून पारित किया है

उसका सभी लोकतांत्रिक देशों द्वारा भारी विरोध किया जा रहा है।

भारत चीन-संबंधों के विस्तृत विश्लेषण के पश्चात् कहा जा सकता है कि भारत प्रारंभ से ही पंचशील समझौते के माध्यम से चीन के साथ मैत्रीपूर्ण संबंध बनाए रखने का इच्छुक था। दोनों ही एशिया की उभरती हुई ताकतें हैं। यह सत्य है कि अंतर्राष्ट्रीय राजनीति में राष्ट्रीय हित सर्वोपरि होते हैं, किंतु अनावश्यक रूप से केवल अपने साम्राज्य विस्तार एवं वैश्विक महाशक्ति बनने की उत्कंठा को पूरा करने के लिए चीन साम, दाम, दंड, भेद की नीति को अपनाता रहा है। इसके विपरीत भारतीय संस्कृति सद्भाव पूर्ण संबंधों के साथ शांतिपूर्ण सहअस्तित्व में विश्वास रखती है। चीन ने सदैव ही चालाकी के साथ भारत की इंच-इंच जमीन से हजारों वर्ग किमी. भू भाग पर अपना कब्जा कर लिया। इन परिस्थितियों में भारत को भी अपने अस्तित्व, अखंडता एवं संप्रभुता को बचाए रखने हेतु 'शठे शाठ्यं समाचरेत्' (जैसे को तैसा) की भाषा में ही जवाब देना समुचित कदम होगा।

संदर्भ सूची

1. पुष्पेश पंत, *21 वीं शताब्दी मे अंतः संबंध,* टाटा मैक्ग्राहिल प्रकाशन, पृ. 38-42, 2008
2. पुष्पेश पंत, श्रीपाल जैन, *अंतर्राष्ट्रीय संबंध सिद्धांत और व्यवहार,* मीनाक्षी प्रकाशन मेरठ, 2011, पृ. 363-364
3. बी.सी. नरूला, *प्रमुख राष्ट्रों की विदेश नीति,* अर्जुन पब्लिकिशंग हाउस, नई दिल्ली, 2012, पृ. 128,
4. वी.एन. खन्ना, लिपाक्षी अरोड़ा, *भारत की विदेश नीति,* विकास पब्लिशिंग हाउस, नई दिल्ली, 2008 पृ. 154,
5. बी.सी. नरूला, पूर्वोक्त 118
6. यू.आर. घई, *अंतर्राष्ट्रीय राजनीति,* न्यू एकेडिमिक पब्लिशिंग हाउस जलंधर, 2008 पृ. 713
7. वी.एन., खन्ना, पूर्वोक्त, पृ. 149
8. पुष्पेश पंत, श्रीपाल जैन, पूर्वोक्त पृ. 512-517
9. वी.एन. खन्ना, पूर्वोक्त, पृ. 150-151
10. उपरोक्त, पृ. 156
11. वी.सी. नरूला, पूर्वोक्त, पृ. 161
12. वी.एन. खन्ना, पूर्वोक्त, पृ. 155
13. बी.सी. नरूला, पूर्वोक्त,
14. पुष्पेश पंत, पूर्वोक्त, पृ. 518

15. वी.एन. खन्ना, पूर्वोक्त, पृ. 156-157
16. अशोक कुमार, विपुल कुमार, *भारत की आंतरिक सुरक्षाः मुख्य चुनौतियाँ*, टाटा मैक्ग्राहिल, प्रकाशन, 2017, पृ. 157
17. बी.एम. जैन, *प्रमुख देशों की विदेश नीतियां*, राजस्थान हिन्दी ग्रंथ अकादमी, जयपुर, 1995, पृ. 224
18. *प्रतियोगिता दर्पण*, 2018, पृ. 74
19. पुष्पेश पंत, श्रीपाल जैन, पूर्वोक्त पृ. 531-533
20. वी.पी. दत्त, *स्वतंत्र भारत की विदेश नीति*, अनुवाद नरेंद्र तोमर, राष्ट्रीय पुस्तक न्यास, भारत, 2015, पृ. 23
21. बी.एम. जैन, पूर्वोक्त, पृ. 224
22. वी.एम. खन्ना, पूर्वोक्त, पृ. 161
23. बी.सी. नरूला, पूर्वोक्त, पृ. 162
24. तपन बिस्वास, अंतर्राष्ट्रीय संबंध, अध्याय-भारत की विदेश नीति, साल्विन पाल, मैक्मिलन पब्लिशर, नई दिल्ली, 2013 पृ. 110,
25. वी.एन. खन्ना, पूर्वोक्त, पृ. 166
26. उपरोक्त, पृ. 179
27. *प्रतियोगिता दर्पण*, अरुणोदय बाजपेयी, 'भारत व चीन-डोकलम विवाद व उसके बाद', जनवरी 2018, पृ. 74
28. *प्रतियोगिता दर्पण*, अरूणोदय बाजपेयी, 'भारत व चीन तथा चेन्नई संकट', फरवरी 2020, पृ. 69-70
29. हिंदुस्तान, महेंद्र पी. लामा, 'पड़ोसी की त्रिशूल नीति के जवाब में हमारी रणनीति', 14 जूलाई 2020, पृ. 8
30. हिंदुस्तान, अरविंद गुप्ता, कहीं हमसे दूर न हो जाएं पड़ोसी 1 अगस्त 2020, पृ. 8
31. *इंडिया टुडे*, बर्टिल लिंटनर, 'मुद्दा जमीन का बिल्कुल नहीं सीधे दादागिरी का है', 29 जुलाई 2020, पृ. 35
32. वी.एन. खन्ना, पूर्वोक्त, पृ. 158
33. *प्रतियोगिता दर्पण*, शंकर प्रसाद तिवारी, मई 2017, पृ. 88
34. *इंडिया टुडे*, शिवशंकर मेनन, 'भारत चीन' आपसी संबंधों को नए सिरे से गढ़ने की जरूरत', 29 जुलाई 2020, पृ. 26
35. *इंडिया टुडे*, संदीप उन्नीयन, 'पहाड़ों पर गुत्थम गुत्था', 1 जूलाई 2020, पृ. 26
36. *हिंदुस्तान*, मोहन भंडारी, 'हमारी जमीन कुरेदता ड्रैगन', 1 सितंबर 2020
37. *हिंदुस्तान*, 17 जून 2020, पृ. 11
38. *इंडिया टुडे*, संदीप, उन्नीथन, पूर्वोक्त, पृ. 29
39. हिंदुस्तान, विवेक काटजू, 'आत्म निर्भर भारत ही असली जवाब', 18 जून 2020, पृ. 10

40. *प्रतियोगिता दर्पण*, रविप्रताप सिंह, 'आर्थिक और सामरिक क्षेत्र में भारत-चीन विवाद में भारत की रणनीति', सितंबर 2020, पृ. 55
41. *इंडिया टुडे*, एम.जी. अरूण, 'ड्रैगन के कब्जे मे देसी यूनीकार्न', 15 जुलाई 2020, पृ. 40
42. *इडिया टुडे*, अंशुमान तिवारी, 'चीन की युद्ध कला', 1 जुलाई 2020, पृ. 13
43. *इडिया टुडे*, बर्टिल लिंटनर, पूर्वोक्त पृ. 34
44. हिंदुस्तान, शशांक, 'शांति की दरकार दोनों को है', 17 जून 2020, पृ. 10
45. *इंडिया टुडे*, राज चेंगप्पा, संदीप उन्नीयन और जे. मैथ्यु, 'चीन को कैसे डालें नकेल', 1 जुलाई 2020, पृ. 16
46. उपरोक्त

12

भारत-नेपाल संकट वर्तमान परिस्थितियों के परिप्रेक्ष्य में

प्रियंका विश्वकर्मा

सारांश

भारत और चीन के मध्य एक 'बफर स्टेट' के अतिरिक्त नेपाल के भारत के साथ सामाजिक, आर्थिक, राजनीतिक अनेक प्रकार के घनिष्ठ संबंध हैं। नेपाल का एक हिंदुवादी राष्ट्र होना तथा गौतम बुद्ध की जन्मभूमि होना भारत को नेपाल से सांस्कृतिक रूप से भी जोड़ता है। भारतवासियों को नेपाल जाने के लिए और नेपाल के नागरिकों को भारत आने के लिए वीजा-परमिट की आवश्कता नहीं है। भारत के लोग नेपाल को 'विदेश' कहने से भी कतराते हैं क्योंकि दोनों देशों की भौगोलिक विशेषताएं इतनी समान हैं कि उनमें अंतर कर पाना मुश्किल है। नेपाल एक ऐसा इकलौता विदेशी राष्ट्र है जिसके नागरिक भारतीय सेना के 'गोरखा रेजीमेंट' में भर्ती किए जा सकते हैं। इस सबके बावजूद भारत-नेपाल के मध्य वैचारिक एवं राजनीतिक तनातनी किसी से छिपी नहीं है। नेपाल का मानना है कि भारत मधुर संबंध स्थापित करने के बहाने उससे उसकी 'संप्रभुता' छीनना चाहता है और उस पर 'कब्जा' करना चाहता है।

भारत और नेपाल के बीच नवीनतम टकराव का मुद्‌दा 'नक्शे का विवाद' है। हालिया महीनों में भारत की ओर से नेपाल सीमा के पास सड़क निर्माण के काम की वजह से तनाव बढ़ा है। भारत और नेपाल के बीच करीब 1880 किमी. सीमा खुली हुई है। दोनों देशों ने 98 फीसदी सीमा को घेरने वाले नक्शे को अंतिम रूप दिया। लेकिन पश्चिमी नेपाल में लिपुलेख, कालापानी और लिंपियाधुरा वे क्षेत्र हैं, जिनको भारत ने अपने नक्शे में दर्शाया है। इसके बाद दोनों देशों के बीच तनाव

चरम पर है।

प्रस्तुत शोध पत्र भारत-नेपाल के बीच तनाव की पृष्ठभूमि, उसके पीछे के वास्तविक कारणों एवं भावी समाधानों का विश्लेषण करने का प्रयास करता है।

कीवर्ड : बफर स्टेट, भौगोलिक विशेषताएँ, वीजा परमिट, संप्रभुता, भारतीय सेना, गोरखा रेजीमेंट, नेपाल कांग्रेस, नक्शा विवाद, पश्चिमी नेपाल।

प्रस्तावना

नेपाल में वर्ष 2007 में लोकतंत्रीय संविधान (अंतरिम) की स्थापना हुई। इससे पूर्व यह एक राजतंत्रीय देश था। उस छोटे से देश के प्राचीन इतिहास को खंगाला जाए तो यह एक शक्तिशाली एवं प्रगतिशील देश रहा है जिसने अपनी क्षमताओं का भरपूर उपयोग किया है। भारत और नेपाल के संबंध आदिकाल से हैं। नेपाल हिमालय में स्थित भारत का पड़ोसी देश है जो सार्क, विम्सटेक और नैम का भी सदस्य है। वर्तमान विवादों को देखकर यह निष्कर्ष नहीं निकाला जाना चाहिए कि दोनों देशों के आपसी रिश्ते हमेशा तनावपूर्ण ही रहे हैं। समय-समय पर दोनों देश गहरी मित्रता का परिचय भी देते रहे हैं। इसका अंदाजा इसी बात से लगाया जा सकता है कि दोनों देशों के बीच आवागमन के लिए सीमा खुली है जबकि प्रायः दूसरे देशों में प्रवेश के लिए वीजा एवं अन्य कानूनी दस्तावेजों की आवश्यकता पड़ती है। दोनों देशों के मध्य 1850 किमी. से अधिक साझा सीमा है जिससे भारत के पांच राज्य-सिक्किम, पश्चिम बंगाल, बिहार, उत्तरप्रदेश व उत्तराखंड जुड़े हैं। सीमा के संबंध में लगभग 98% क्षेत्र पर आपसी सहमति बन चुकी है। कुछ क्षेत्रों को लेकर हालिया मतभेद उभरे हैं लेकिन आशा की जा रही है कि इन्हें शांतिपूर्ण बातचीत के माध्यम से सुलझाया जा सकेगा।

नेपाल दक्षिण एशिया की दो प्रमुख महाशक्तियों की प्रतिद्वंद्विता का गढ़ बना हुआ है। आधुनिक नेपाल के उदय की बात की जाए तो महाराजा पृथ्वी नारायण शाह, जिन्हें आधुनिक नेपाल का जनक कहा जाता है, ने सन् 1779 में तत्कालीन प्रमुख रियासतों पर विजय प्राप्त करके एक सुदृढ़ और एकीकृत राज्य की स्थापना की। उस समय नेपाल को 'गोरखा राज्य' के नाम से जाना जाता था। पृथ्वी नारायण शाह ने इसे गोरखा राज्य से 'नेपाल' में परिवर्तित कर दिया। वर्ष 2018 के आंकड़ों के अनुसार नेपाल की कुल जनसंख्या 2.81 करोड़ है तथा कुल क्षेत्रफल 1,47,516 वर्ग किमी. है। तिब्बत पर चीन के अधिकार के बाद नेपाल भारत और चीन के मध्य

'बफर स्टेट' के रूप में उभरा। भारत के उत्तर-पूर्व में स्थित नेपाल का भारत के लिए सामरिक महत्व है। चीन द्वारा तिब्बत को हड़प लेने के बाद भारत के लिए इसका महत्व और अधिक बढ़ गया है। यही कारण है कि भारत अपने इस महत्वपूर्ण पड़ोसी को खोना नहीं चाहता। इसके अतिरिक्त दोनों देशों के बीच आजीविका के साथ-साथ विवाह और पारिवारिक संबंधों की मजबूत नींव है। इस नींव को ही ''रोटी-बेटी का रिश्ता' नाम दिया गया है।

इस सबके बावजूद पिछले कुछ वर्षों से, विशेषतः 2015 में नए संविधान के निर्माण के बाद मधेशियों के अधिकारों को लेकर और उसके उपरांत 2019 में उपजे नक्शा-विवाद को लेकर दोनों देशों के मध्य तनाव चरम बिंदु पर है। प्रस्तुत शोध पत्र भारत की स्वतंत्रता के बाद से लेकर वर्तमान तक बने मतभेद के माहौल और उसकी परिणति को समझने का प्रयास करता है। तथा इस मतभेद के भावी समाधान क्या हो सकते हैं, का विश्लेषण करने का प्रयास करता है।

उद्देश्य

- भारत-नेपाल संबंधों की पृष्ठभूमि को समझना।
- दोनों देशों के बीच तनाव के कारणों का विश्लेषण करना।
- भावी समाधानों की खोज करना।

पद्धति

शोध पद्धति : विश्लेषणात्मक पद्धति : शोध पत्र के गठन हेतु विश्लेषणात्मक पद्धति का प्रयोग किया गया है।

शोध पत्र के माध्यम से भारत की स्वतंत्रता के पश्चात से लेकर वर्तमान तक भारत एवं नेपाल के संबंधों का विश्लेषण करने का प्रयास किया गया है।

तथ्यों के आधार : द्वितीयक दत्त : शोध अध्ययन हेतु द्वितीयक आधार सामग्री का प्रयोग किया गया है। साहित्यिक समीक्षा हेतु पुस्तकों, समाचार पत्रों आदि का अध्ययन किया गया है।

साहित्यिक समीक्षा भारत-नेपाल संबंध : पृष्ठभूमि

ब्रिटिश इंडिया के पश्चात संबंध : 15 अगस्त, 1947 को अंग्रेजों ने भारत की स्वतंत्रता की घोषणा कर दी। नेपाल को पूर्व में ही अंग्रेजों द्वारा स्वतंत्र राज्य का दर्जा

दिया जा चुका था। प्रथम विश्वयुद्ध के बाद भारत-नेपाल के बीच 1923 का 'शांति एवं मैत्री समझौता' अब तक प्रभावी था इसलिए भारत की स्वतंत्रता के बाद संबंधों की शुरुआत मित्रतापूर्ण हुई। यह समझौता भारत और नेपाल के बीच प्रथम लिखित समझौता था। इस समझौते के अनुसार अंग्रेजों ने औपचारिक रूप से नेपाल को स्वतंत्र एवं संप्रभु राज्य स्वीकार कर लिया तथा नेपाल को भारतीय मार्ग से गोला-बारूद आयात करने की छूट दे दी।

- **यथास्थिति समझौता, 1947 :** 1947 में भारत-नेपाल के बीच एक 'यथास्थिति समझौता' हुआ। इस समझौते द्वारा दोनों देशों ने 1923 के समझौते को बनाए रखने के लिए तब तक मान्यता दी जब तक कि कोई दूसरा समझौता नहीं हो जाता। इस समझौते के द्वारा भारत को अपनी सेनाओं में गोरखा सैनिकों की भर्ती का अधिकार प्राप्त हुआ।
- **शांति एवं मैत्री तथा व्यापार एवं वाणिज्य समझौता, 1950 :** जुलाई, 1950 में दोनों देशों के मध्य शांति एवं मैत्री तथा व्यापार एवं वाणिज्य समझौते के रूप में एक नया समझौता हुआ जिससे पिछली दो संधियों (1816 की सुगौली संधि एवं 1923 की शांति एवं मैत्री संधि) की समाप्ति हो गई।
- **नेहरू का प्रभाव :** स्वतंत्रता के प्रारंभिक वर्षों में भारत-नेपाल संबंधों पर भारत के प्रधानमंत्री जवाहरलाल नेहरू के व्यक्तित्व का अत्यधिक प्रभाव पड़ा। दोनों देशों के बीच परस्पर वार्ताओं के दौरान नेहरू ने इस बात पर जोर दिया कि वह नेपाल को एक गणतंत्र के रूप में देखना चाहते हैं। नेहरू के ही प्रयासों के परिणामस्वरूप भारतीय कांग्रेस की तर्ज पर अप्रैल, 1950 में नेपाली कांग्रेस नामक राष्ट्रीय राजनीतिक दल का गठन किया गया। नेपाली कांग्रेस प्रजातंत्र की समर्थक थी जबकि नेपाल की शासन सत्ता को संभाले हुए राणा शासक पुरानी राजतंत्रात्मक सामंतवादी व्यवस्थाओं को जारी रखना चाहते थे। अतः नेपाली कांग्रेस और राणा शासन के प्रतिनिधियों के बीच संघर्ष प्रारंभ हो गया जिससे वहां के आंतरिक प्रशासन में अस्थिरता उत्पन्न हो गई। परिणामस्वरूप नेपाल में एक भीषण जनक्रांति हुई। गंभीर स्थितियों को देखते हुए नेहरू ने नई दिल्ली में नेपाली कांग्रेस को वार्ता के लिए आमंत्रित किया। नेहरू ने स्पष्ट किया कि वह नेपाली कांग्रेस को पूर्ण समर्थन देंगे। यही नहीं भारत ने 1951 के 'अंतरिम सरकार अधिनियम' की

सरंचना में भी नेपाल की सहायता की। भारत की इन गतिविधियों पर विरोध जताते हुए राणा प्रशासन ने आरोप लगाया कि भारत नेपाल के आंतरिक मामलों में हस्तक्षेप कर रहा है।

- **राणाशाही की समाप्ति :** इन आरोप-प्रत्यारोपों के बावजूद दिल्ली समझौते के तहत अक्टूबर, 1951 में नेपाली मंत्रिपरिषद का समापन कर दिया गया। इस तरह नेपाल के प्रशासन से सदियों पुरानी राणाशाही समाप्त हो गई।
- **पंचायती लोकतंत्र की स्थापना :** नवंबर, 1951 में नेपाल से राणाशाही की समाप्ति के बाद पंचायती लोकतंत्र की स्थापना हुई जिसमें नेपाली कांग्रेस के प्रतिनिधि मंत्रिका प्रसाद कोईराला को प्रधानमंत्री नियुक्त किया गया। नेपाल से राणाशाही तो समाप्त हो गई थी लेकिन लोकतंत्र विरोधी तेवर अब भी जीवित थे। भारत नेपाल के इस पंचायती लोकतांत्रिक व्यवस्था से संतुष्ट नहीं था। यह व्यवस्था जहां एक ओर लोकतंत्र के समर्थकों का तुष्टिकरण करने का प्रयास कर रही थी वही दूसरी ओर नरेश को प्रशासनिक प्रधान घोषित करती थी। प्रधानमंत्री की नियुक्ति नरेश द्वारा की जाती थी। 1955 में महराजा त्रिभुवन की मृत्यु के बाद महेंद्र सत्ता में आए। वे देश में लोकतंत्र नहीं चाहते थे नरेश महेंद्र के सत्तासीन होने के साथ ही भारत नेपाल संबंधों में तनाव उत्पन्न हो गया। नरेश महेन्द्र ने भारत समर्थक एम.पी. कोईराला की सरकार का समापन करके चीन के साथ अपने संबंधों को प्रगाढ़ करने के उद्देश्य से चीनी समर्थक टंक प्रसाद आचार्य को प्रधानमंत्री नियुक्त कर दिया।
- **नेहरू महेंद्र वार्ता :** जनवरी 1962 में नेपाल नरेश महेंद्र भारत की यात्रा पर आए। भारत के प्रधानमंत्री से वार्ता के दौरान उन्होंने कहा कि मित्र राष्ट्रों को नेपाल की संप्रभुता एवं स्वतंत्रता का सम्मान करना चाहिये तथा नेपाल के आंतरिक मामलों में हस्तक्षेप नहीं करना चाहिए। नेपाल नरेश ने नेहरू से 'पंचायती लोकतंत्र' के लिए समर्थन प्राप्त करना चाहा लेकिन उनका यह प्रयास असफल रहा। साथ ही उन्होंने भारत से 1950 के व्यापार एवं वाणिज्य समझौते में भी संशोधन की अपील की। भारत के नेपाल की नीतियों के प्रति निराशाजनक रवैये देखते हुए जहां नेपाल नरेश ने भारत की कटु आलोचना शुरू कर दी वहीं चीन की तरफ नेपाल का झुकाव बढ़ने लगा।
- **भारत-चीन युद्ध, 1962-** इसी बीच अक्टूबर 1962 में भारतीय सीमाओं पर

चीन के आक्रमण से नेपाल स्तब्ध रहा गया। उसे अपनी सुरक्षा खतरे में दिखाई देने लगी। परिणामस्वरूप दोनों देशों की एक-दूसरे के प्रति नीतियों में परिवर्तन आया। भारत-चीन युद्ध के दौरान नेपाल की सहानुभूति और समर्थन भारत के प्रति था।

- **पंचायती शासन को मान्यता :** युद्धोपरांत दोनों देशों द्वारा आपसी रिश्तों को सहज बनाने का प्रयास किया गया। नेपाल ने व्यापार एवं वाणिज्य को पूर्व की भांति चलाए जाने के लिए मान्यता दी तथा भारत ने नरेश महेंद्र को प्रत्यक्ष पंचायती शासन व्यवस्था के लिए समर्थन दिया। भारत ने नेपाल की स्वतंत्रता और संप्रभुता को सम्मान देने का वादा किया।
- **भारत-पाकिस्तान युद्ध, 1965 :** भारत-पाक युद्ध के दौरान भी नेपाल का समर्थन भारत के प्रति था। इस युद्ध के पूर्व ही नेपाल नरेश ने कश्मीर के प्रश्न पर तटस्थ बने रहने की घोषणा कर दी थी। 1965 की अपनी भारत यात्रा के दौरान नेपाल नरेश ने कश्मीर के मुद्दे पर पाकिस्तान के आत्मनिर्णय के सिद्धांत का विरोध करते हुए कहा कि आत्मनिर्णय का सिद्धांत आश्रित क्षेत्रों पर ही लागू किया जा सकता है किसी संप्रभु राष्ट्र के अभिन्न भाग पर नहीं। साथ ही, उन्होंने 'जनमत निर्णय' को भी समर्थन देने से साफतौर पर मना कर दिया। इस युद्ध के बाद नेपाल को यह स्पष्ट हो गया था कि भारत का विरोध उसके हित में नहीं है।
- **व्यापार एवं पारगमन समझौता, 1971 :** अगस्त, 1971 में भारत की शर्तों पर दोनों देशों के बीच वाणिज्य एवं पारगमन समझौता हुआ। इस समझौते के तहत दोनों देश अपने क्षेत्र में निर्धारित मार्ग में पारगमन की स्वतंत्रता देने हेतु तैयार हो गए। इसी वर्ष चीन और अमेरिका के विरोध के बावजूद भारत के प्रभाव से 'बांग्लादेश' नामक एक नए देश के निर्माण से दक्षिण एशिया की राजनीति में एक बड़ा परिवर्तन आया। 1970 का दशक विश्व स्तर पर भारत का औहदा बढ़ाने में महत्वपूर्ण साबित हुआ। संयुक्त राष्ट्र संघ में नवनिर्मित बांग्लादेश को सदस्यता दिलाने के संदर्भ में हो अथवा 1974 में सिक्किम का भारतीय संघ में विलय करवाने के संदर्भ में, भारत की ृाक्ति लगातार बढ़ रही थी। मई, 1974 में ही भारत ने परमाणु परीक्षण किया जिसने उसे दुनिया की पांचवी परमाणु शक्ति के रूप में स्थापित कर दिया। अब सभी देश भारत से मित्रतापूर्ण संबंध बनाना चाहते थे, नेपाल

भी उनमें से एक था।

- **शांति क्षेत्र का प्रस्ताव :** नेपाल नरेश वीरेंद्र ने घोषणा की कि नेपाल पड़ोसी राष्ट्रों के साथ गुटनिरपेक्षता और शांतिपूर्ण सह-अस्तित्व की नीति अपनाएगा तथा विश्व राजनीति में उपनिवेशवाद का विरोध करते हुए निःशस्त्रीकरण को बढ़ावा देगा। साथ ही, नेपाल नरेश ने भारत के समक्ष शांति क्षेत्र का प्रस्ताव रखा जिसमें भारत ने रुचि नहीं दिखाई।
- **व्यापार एवं पारगमन समझौता, 1978 :** 1977 में भारत में जनता सरकार के गठन के बाद दोनों देशों के बीच उदार नीतियों को बढ़ावा दिया गया। मार्च, 1978 में भारत और नेपाल के बीच व्यापार और पारगमन समझौता हुआ जो जनता सरकार की 'पड़ोसियों से मित्रता' वाली विदेश नीति पर आधारित थी। दोनों देशों में इस बात पर सहमति बनी कि सुरक्षा के मुद्दों पर दोनों देश आपस में सूचना का आदान-प्रदान करेंगे। आर्थिक क्षेत्र में भी भारत नेपाल को प्राथमिकता देगा। लेकिन शांति क्षेत्र के प्रस्ताव को लेकर दोनों देशों में तनाव व्याप्त रहा। नेपाल की सरकार ने 1984 में इस मांग को पुनः दोहराया तथा 1990 तक इस प्रस्ताव पर चीन और पाकिस्तान सहित 112 देशों का समर्थन हासिल किया।
- **व्यापार एवं पारगमन समझौता, 1989 :** 1950 के व्यापार एवं वाणिज्य समझौते के दो बार कार्यकाल में वृद्धि होने के बाद अंततः मार्च, 1989 में इस संधि का कार्यकाल समाप्त हो गया। दिसंबर, 1991 में नेपाली प्रधानमंत्री गिरिजा प्रसाद कोईराला ने भारत की यात्रा की तथा दोनों देशों के बीच व्यापार और पारगमन पर एक नया समझौता हुआ।
- **नेपाल की पहल :** भारत-नेपाल संबंधों की महत्वपूर्ण शुरुआत तब हुई जब अप्रैल, 1995 में नेपाल के प्रधानमंत्री मनमोहन अधिकारी ने भारत आगमन पर 1950 की शांति एवं मैत्री संधि के पुनर्विलोकन की पहल की।

भारत नेपाल संबंध : वर्तमान परिदृश्य : अप्रैल, 2006 में राजा ज्ञानेंद्र द्वारा सभी शक्तियां निर्वासित प्रतिनिधियों को सौंपने के साथ नेपाल में राजशाही का अंत हो गया। इसके साथ ही 1996 से शुरु हुए गृहयुद्ध का भी अंत हो गया।

- **अंतरिम संविधान का निर्माण :** नेपाल में नई लोकतांत्रिक शासन व्यवस्था के निर्माण के लिए सभी दलों ने मिलकर एक अंतरिम सरकार का निर्माण

किया। अंतरिम सरकार को ही शासन का कार्यभार सौंपा गया और उसे ही संविधान का निर्माण करना था। 2007 में नेपाल का अंतरिम संविधान बनकर तैयार हुआ। मई, 2008 में पहली बार लोकतांत्रिक ढंग से चुनाव हुए। नेपाली कांग्रेस के प्रतिनिधि गिरिजा प्रसाद कोईराला को नेपाल का प्रथम प्रधानमंत्री नियुक्त किया गया तथा मधेशी नेता रामबरन यादव राष्ट्रपति बने। गिरिजा प्रसाद कोईराला की सरकार केवल तीन महीने चली और अगस्त, 2008 में उन्होंने अपने पद से त्यागपत्र दे दिया। उसके उपरांत नेपाली गृहयुद्ध में महत्वपूर्ण भूमिका निभाने वाले 'माओवादी दल' की सरकार बनी। पुष्प कमल दहल 'प्रचंड' को प्रधानमंत्री नियुक्त किया गया। नेपाल का अंतरिम संविधान जो हाल ही में बनकर तैयार हुआ था, पर कई मतभेद उठ खड़े हुए जिससे नए और अधिक उदार संविधान की आवश्यकता महसूस होने लगी। सितंबर, 2008 में प्रधानमंत्री 'प्रचंड' ने भारत की यात्रा की। उन्होंने नए संविधान के निर्माण में भारत से सहायता की अपील की तथा नेपाल के आधारभूत ढांचे में निवेश के लिए भी भारत को आमंत्रित किया। मई, 2009 में सेनाध्यक्ष की बर्खास्तगी के मुद्दे पर 'प्रचंड' को पद से इस्तीफा देना पड़ा। 'प्रचंड' ने नेपाल की आंतरिक अस्थिरता के लिए भारत को जिम्मेदार ठहराया जिससे दोनों देशों के बीच रिश्ते तनावपूर्ण हो गए। प्रचंड के इस्तीफे के बाद माधव कुमार नेपाल को इस पद पर नियुक्त किया गया जिसे माओवादियों ने 'भारत की कठपुतली सरकार' की संज्ञा दी। माओवादी समर्थकों ने माधव कुमार की सरकार के समक्ष 'नागरिक सर्वोच्चता' स्थापित करने की मांग रखी। फलतः फरवरी, 2011 में उन्होंने पद से इस्तीफा दे दिया। अगस्त, 2011 के चुनावों में माओवादी दल के बाबूराम भट्टारई ने नेपाली कांग्रेस के उम्मीदवार आर.सी. पौड़ियाल को पराजित कर प्रधानमंत्री पद ग्रहण किया।

- **नये संविधान के निर्माण की प्रक्रिया :** नेपाली जनता की अत्यंत प्रबल मांगों और सर्वोच्च न्यायालय के स्पष्ट आदेश के बावजूद देश के लिए नवीन संविधान तैयार करने और उसे लागू करने की समय सीमा समाप्त हो जाने के कारण अंततः अंतरिम सरकार के प्रधानमंत्री बाबूराम भट्टाराई ने इस संविधान को भंग करते हुए नई संविधान सभा के गठन हेतु तिथि 22 नवंबर, 2012 निर्धारित की। लेकिन राजनीतिक गतिरोध के चलते चुनाव संपन्न

नहीं हो सके। इसक उपरांत मार्च, 2013 में सर्वोच्च न्यायालय के पूर्व मुख्य न्यायाधीश खिलराज रेग्मी को कार्यवाहक प्रधानमंत्री नियुक्त किया गया। उन्होंने दूसरी संविधान सभा हेतु 12 नवंबर, 2013 को चुनाव संपन्न कराए जिसमें नेपाली कांग्रेस सबसे बड़े दल के रूप में उभरी। फरवरी, 2014 में संविधान सभा की बैठक में नेपाली कांग्रेस के नेता सुशील कोईराला को नेपाल के सातवें प्रधानमंत्री के रूप में चुना गया।

- **नया संविधान लागू :** अक्टूबर, 2015 में नया संविधान लागू होने के बाद हुए चुनावों में सुशील कोईराला को सी.पी.एन.यू.एम.एल. दल के नेता खड्ग प्रसाद ओली के हाथों हार का सामना करना पड़ा। के.पी. शर्मा ओली ने प्रधानमंत्री पद ग्रहण करने के बाद फरवरी, 2016 में सबसे पहली विदेश यात्रा भारत की की। जुलाई, 2016 में अल्पमत में आ जाने के बाद उन्होंने राष्ट्रपति को अपना त्यागपत्र सौंप दिया।
- **मधेशी आंदोलन :** 2015 में नए संविधान के लागू होने के साथ ही मधेशियों ने इसका विरोध करना शुरू कर दिया। मधेशी आंदोलन के तेज होने के कारण शुरुआत से ही भारत-नेपाल संबंधों में उतार-चढ़ाव शुरू हो चुका था। मधेशियों ने संविधान में उनके समुदाय को उचित दर्जा न दिए जाने को लेकर विरोध जताते हुए भारत-नेपाल सड़क जाम कर दी। जिसके चलते भारत से नेपाल को जाने वाली वस्तुओं की आवाजाही बंद हो गई। लेकिन फिर भी 2016 की अपनी भारत यात्रा को के.पी. ओली ने सुखद बताया उन्हें आशा थी कि मधेशियों के विवाद को नेपाल का आंतरिक मामला मानकर भारत नए संविधान पर सहमति प्रदान करेगा। लेकिन भारत मधेशियों के अधिकारों पर खड़ा रहा। इससे ओली का रुख भारत विरोधी होने लगा। अगस्त, 2016 में 'प्रचंड' दोबारा नेपाल के प्रधानमंत्री पद पर आसीन हुए। पूर्व प्रधानमंत्री ओली और 'प्रचंड' के बीच मतभेद की खबरें काफी गरम रहीं। ओली ने आरोप लगाया कि 'आमतौर पर नेपाली कांग्रेस पार्टी को ही भारत की नीतियों का समर्थक माना जाता रहा है लेकिन कुछ सालों से देखा जा रहा है कि 'प्रचंड' का रुझान भी भारत की ओर है।'
- **त्रिपक्षीय संबंध स्थापित करने की इच्छा :** अपने शासनकाल के दौरान 'प्रचंड' ने भारत और चीन के साथ त्रिपक्षीय संबंध स्थापित करने की इच्छा जाहिर की। वह भारत से मित्रता चाहते थे लेकिन चीन को भी किनारे नहीं

करना चाहते थे। 'प्रचंड' ने प्रधानमंत्री पद ग्रहण करने के बाद पहली आधिकारिक विदेश यात्रा के लिए भारत को चुना। सिंतबर, 2016 में भारत यात्रा पर आए। भारत ने उनका भव्य स्वागत किया। दोनों देशों के बीच कई महत्वपूर्ण मुद्दों पर चर्चा हुई और कुछ महत्वपूर्ण समझौतों पर हस्ताक्षर हुए। 'प्रचंड' की भारत यात्रा से दोनों देशों के बीच बिगड़ते रिश्तों में कुछ सुधार हुआ।

- **द्विपक्षीय संबंधों की प्रगाढ़ता पर जोर :** मई, 2017 में 'प्रचंड' ने अपने पद से इस्तीफा दिया। उसके उपरांत नेपाली कांग्रेस के नेता शेर बहादुर देउबा जून, 2017 में नेपाल के नए प्रधानमंत्री नियुक्त हुए। देउबा प्रधानमंत्री का पद संभालने के बाद अपने पहले विदेश दौरे के तहत अगस्त, 2017 में भारत पहुंचे। देउबा ने अपनी यात्रा के दौरान भारत के साथ द्विपक्षीय संबंधों को प्रगाढ़ करने की इच्छा जाहिर की। देउबा ने दोनों देशों की आपसी वार्ता के दौरान मधेशियों के मुद्दे का जल्द समाधान किए जाने का आश्वासन दिया। फरवरी, 2018 में देउबा के पद से हटने के बाद के.पी. शर्मा ओली को पुनः प्रधानमंत्री बनाया गया। ओली की नीतियां 2015 से ही भारत विरोधी रही हैं लेकिन अप्रैल, 2018 की उनकी भारत यात्रा ने इस पूर्वाग्रह को गलत साबित कर दिया। उन्होंने भारत के साथ नेपाल के संबंधों में सुधार लाने के प्रति तीव्र इच्छा जाहिर की। इसके साथ ही इस यात्रा का जो सबसे सुखद पहलू था वह था—काठमाण्डू एवं रक्सौल के बीच रेल संपर्क को लेकर हुआ समझौता। इस समझौते को भारत-नेपाल संबंधों में एक अन्य महत्वपूर्ण घटनाक्रम माना गया। इसके बाद प्रधानमंत्री नरेंद्र मोदी ने भी दोनों देशों के संबंधों में उत्साह बढ़ाने के लिए मई, 2018 में नेपाल का दौरा किया। भारतीय प्रधानमंत्री ने अपने एक ही कार्यकाल (2014-2019) के दौरान नेपाल के तीन दौरे किए। नेपाल के प्रधानमंत्री ओली मई, 2019 में पुनः भारत यात्रा पर आए और दोनों देशों के बीच दक्षिण एशिया की पहली क्रॉस-बार्डर पाइपलाइन की शुरुआत पर सहमति बनी।

इसके बावजूद नवंबर, 2019 से भारत-नेपाल के संबंध अत्यंत खराब दौर से गुजर रहे हैं। वर्तमान समय में भारत-नेपाल के बीच निम्नलिखित मुद्दों पर विवाद है—

सीमा विवाद : भारत-नेपाल के बीच सीमा विवाद समय-समय पर उभरते

रहे हैं लेकिन वर्तमान समय में स्थिति चरम पर है। दरअसल नवंबर, 2019 में जम्मू-कश्मीर के विभाजन के बाद भारत सरकार ने देश का नया मानचित्र जारी किया। यह मानचित्र जम्मू-कश्मीर और लद्दाख को भारत के केंद्र शासित प्रदेश के रूप में दर्शाता है। इसी मानचित्र में लिंपियाधुरा, कालापानी और लिपुलेख को भी भारतीय क्षेत्र के रूप में दर्शाया गया है। इस मानचित्र के जारी होते ही नेपाल ने इसका विरोध जताना शुरु कर दिया। नेपाल ने इस संबंध में वर्ष 1816 में हुई 'सुगौली संधि' का जिक्र किया है। एंग्लो-नेपाल युद्ध (1814-16) के बाद वर्ष 1816 में नेपाल और ब्रिटिश भारत द्वारा सुगौली की संधि पर हस्ताक्षर किए गए थे। उल्लेखनीय है कि इस संधि में विवादित क्षेत्र को नेपाल की पश्चिमी सीमा के रूप में परिभाषित किया गया है। हाल ही में भारत सरकार द्वारा उत्तराखंड के धारचूला को लिपुलेख दर्रे से जोड़ने वाली सड़क का निर्माण किया गया है। नेपाल का दावा है कि कालापानी के पास पड़ने वाला यह क्षेत्र नेपाल का हिस्सा है और भारत ने नेपाल से वार्ता किए बिना इस क्षेत्र में सड़क का कार्य किया है।

मधेशी विवाद : भारत नेपाल के बीच दूसरा सबसे प्रमुख विवाद मधेशियों को लेकर है। यह विवाद सितंबर, 2015 में नेपाल में नए संविधान के निर्माण के बाद शुरू हुआ। मधेशियों का कहना है कि नए संविधान में उनके समुदाय की अनदेखी की गई है और उन्हें पर्याप्त प्रतिनिधित्व नहीं दिया गया है। मधेशी नेपाल के वे नागरिक हैं जिनका मूल भारत में है। वर्तमान समय में भारत से विस्थापित बड़ी संख्या में लोग नेपाल के नागरिक हैं जिनकी जनसंख्या 50 से 60 लाख तक होने का अनुमान है। मधेशियों द्वारा किए जा रहे विरोध प्रदर्शनों में अब तक सैंकड़ों लोग अपनी जान गंवा चुके हैं और उससे भी अधिक लोग घायल हो गए हैं। भारत मधेशियों के अधिकारों की लड़ाई में उनका साथ दे रहा है। नेपाल का आरोप है कि मधेशियों का उग्र आन्दोलन भारत द्वारा समर्थित षड्यंत्र है।

चीन का समर्थन : यह सर्वविदित है कि दक्षिण एशिया में भारत और चीन एक-दूसरे के कट्टर विरोधी हैं। नेपाल भारत और चीन के मध्य एक 'बफर स्टेट' का कार्य करता है। तिब्बत को हड़पने के बाद चीन की नजर अब नेपाल पर है लेकिन भारत ऐसा नहीं होने देना चाहता। इसलिए प्रायः भारत और चीन के बीच नेपाल को लेकर खींचतान चलती रहती है। सांस्कृतिक

एवं भौगोलिक परिस्थितियों पर गौर किया जाए तो नेपाल को भारत की ज्यादा आवश्यकता है लेकिन पिछले कुछ दशकों से नेपाल का झुकाव चीन की तरफ बढ़ता जा रहा है। नेपाल के सभी शीर्ष नेता पुष्प कमल दहल 'प्रचंड' से लेकर के.पी. शर्मा ओली तक प्रायः चीन की तरफ नातेदारी बढ़ाने के लिए उत्सुक नजर आते हैं। ओली लंबे समय से त्रिपक्षीय संबंधों को बढ़ावा देने पर जोर दे रहे हैं जबकि प्रचंड के माओवादी दल को चीन का प्रबल समर्थक माना जाता है। 2016 की अपनी पहली विदेश यात्रा के रूप में ओली चीन जाने के इच्छुक थे लेकिन आंतरिक दबावों के चलते उन्होंने चीन से पहले भारत का दौरा किया। भारत का मानना है कि नेपाल के समक्ष भारत की नकारात्मक छवि बनाने के पीछे चीन का हाथ है।

भारत की छवि : भारत और नेपाल के संबंधों को मित्रतापूर्ण कहना अतिशयोक्ति होगी क्योंकि स्वेच्छापूर्ण मित्रता और थोपी गई मित्रता में अंतर होता है। दोनों देशों में समान स्तर पर मित्रता का होना संभव भी नहीं है क्योंकि यदि सांस्कृतिक-भौगोलिक परिस्थितियों के इतर भारत-नेपाल की तुलना की जाए तो उनके क्षेत्रफल, आर्थिक, राजनीतिक परिस्थितियों में अत्यधिक अंतर है। नेपाल का संपूर्ण क्षेत्रफल भारत के किसी एक राज्य से अधिक नहीं है। आर्थिक परिस्थितियों की बात की जाए तो दक्षिण एशिया में चीन के बाद भारत सबसे बड़ी शक्ति है। वहीं नेपाल की राजनीतिक परिस्थितियों में भारत से भिन्नता का अंदाजा इसी बात से लगाया जा सकता है कि भारत को 1947 में स्वतंत्रता के दौरान ही संपूर्ण प्रभुत्वसंपन्न, लोकतंत्रात्मक गणराज्य घोषित कर दिया गया था जबकि नेपाल में अंततः 2015 में पूर्ण लोकतंत्र की स्थापना हुई। यह उल्लेखनीय है कि यदि भारत का दबाव न होता तो शायद नेपाल आज भी एक राजतंत्रात्मक व्यवस्था वाला देश होता।

नेपाल की हर सामाजिक, आर्थिक राजनीतिक व्यवस्था पर भारत की छाप दिखती है। कहने को नेपाल एशिया का एकमात्र ऐसा देश है जो ब्रिटिश शासन का उपनिवेश नहीं रहा लेकिन भारत में ब्रिटिश हुकूमत का नेपाल पर प्रत्यक्ष प्रभाव पड़ा और अंततः सुगौली की संधि करके अपने भूक्षेत्र के एक बड़े हिस्से से हाथ धोना पड़ा। ब्रिटिश इंडिया के पूर्व भी ऐसे अनेक उदाहरण मिलते हैं जब भारतीय आक्रमणों ने नेपाल की आंतरिक व्यवस्था

को तहस-नहस कर दिया। नेपाल में लोकतंत्र की स्थापना हो अथवा 1950 में नेपाली कांग्रेस पार्टी की स्थापना, भारत की विशेष भूमिका रही है। नेपाल भारत के 'बड़े भाई' वाले दबाव से कई बार बाहर निकलने का प्रयास कर चुका है लेकिन परिस्थितियां उसे भारत से मदद मांगने पर मजबूर कर देती है भारत ने नेपाल के 'शांति क्षेत्र के प्रस्ताव' को ठुकरा दिया। नेपाल का आरोप है कि नेपाल में भारत द्वारा समर्थित जिन भी परियोजनाओं पर कार्य करवाया जाता है भारत उसमें अनावश्यक विलम्ब करवाता है। रक्षा से संबंधित मुद्दों पर भी भारत को जानकारी देनी होती है। जहां तक नेपाल का प्रश्न है संघीय लोकतंत्र की स्थापना होने के बाद नेपाल में जितने भी प्रधानमंत्री हुए उन्होंने कार्यभार संभालने के बाद पहली विदेश यात्रा भारत की की। बिगड़े रिश्तों को संभालने के लिए 1995 में नेपाली प्रधानमंत्री द्वारा 1950 की शांति एवं मैत्री संधि का पुनर्विलोकन करने की पहल की गई। इस सबके बावजूद नए संविधान के निर्माण के बाद मधेशियों के आंदोलन को समर्थन देने, सुगौली संधि के अनुसार पश्चिमी नेपाल के क्षेत्र को भारत के नक्शे में दर्शाकर भारत की तरफ से भारत-नेपाल के रिश्तों में एक गहरा तनाव उत्पन्न हो गया है। यही कारण है कि नेपाल का लगाव भारत से घटकर चीन की तरफ बढ़ता जा रहा है और चीन इस मौके का फायदा उठा रहा है।

निष्कर्ष एवं सुझाव

नेपाल हिमालय की गोद में बसा एक छोटा सा देश है जो एक संप्रभु देश जैसी परिस्थितियों के लिए सदियों से तरस रहा है। भारत और चीन आपसी शत्रुता के बीच ये भूल गए हैं कि नेपाल की उन दोनों के मध्य एक 'बफर स्टेट' के अतिरिक्त एक स्वतंत्र पहचान भी है। नेपाल की आंतरिक व्यवस्था के अंदर भी गहरे मतभेद व्याप्त हैं। यही कारण है 2015 में पूर्ण लोकतांत्रिक गणराज्य बनने के 5 साल के भीतर वहां पांच प्रधानमंत्री बदल चुके हैं। कोई भी प्रधानमंत्री अब तक दो साल का कार्यकाल भी पूरा नहीं कर पाया है। पिछले दिनों प्रधानमंत्री के.पी. ओली एवं पूर्व प्रधानमंत्री 'प्रचंड' के मतभेद खुलकर सामने आए। भारत को लेकर भी नेपाल की नीतियों में लगातार परिवर्तन होता रहा है। वर्तमान परिस्थितियों को देखकर लगता है कि नेपाल को अभी एक प्रजातांत्रिक राष्ट्र के रूप में सुदृढ़ होने में दशकों लग

जाएंगे और तब तक वहां की आर्थिक परिस्थितियों में भी सुधार होना मुश्किल है। नेपाल अभी उन परिस्थितियों से गुजर रहा है जो स्वतंत्रता के बाद भारत में थीं। पड़ोसी देशों के रूप में नेपाल भारत और चीन में से किसी पर भी भरोसा करने की स्थिति में नहीं है क्योंकि दोनों देश समय-समय पर उसे अपनी शक्ति का एहसास कराते आए हैं। अतः ऐतिहासिक परिप्रेक्ष्य और वर्तमान स्थितियों का विश्लेषण करते हुए भारत-नेपाल के रिश्तों के संबंध में निम्नलिखित सुझाव दिए जा सकते हैं–

- जैसा कि हाल में नेपाल के पूर्व प्रधानमंत्री बाबूराम भट्टाराई ने बयान दिया है कि 'भारत को यह मानना होगा कि नेपाल स्वतंत्र देश है' भारत को उसे उसके हाल पर छोड़ देना चाहिए।
- भारत ने जो गुटनिरपेक्षता की नीति शीत युद्ध के समय अमेरिका और सोवियत संघ के संबंध में अपनाई थी वर्तमान समय में नेपाल वही नीति भारत और चीन के संबंध में अपना रहा है। किसी भी शक्तिशाली राष्ट्र से बैर मोल न लेना एक कमजोर राष्ट्र की मजबूरी भी होती है और जरूरत भी।
- वर्तमान नक्शा विवाद को दोनों देशों द्वारा आपसी सहमति से सुलझाया जाना चाहिए। भारत को इस ओर ध्यान देना चाहिए कि सुगौली संधि और उसके उपरांत सिक्किम का भारत संघ में विलय होने के बाद नेपाल का काफी क्षेत्र भारत में सम्मिलित हो चुका है। भारत द्वारा नेपाल के पश्चिमी क्षेत्र को भारत के नक्शे में दर्शाया जाना भारत की विस्तारवादी नीति को दर्शाता है जो विश्व पटल पर उसकी छवि को खराब कर रहा है।
- भारत को अपनी तरफ से नेपाल की आर्थिक, राजनीतिक सहायता की पहल नहीं करनी चाहिए। नेपाल स्वयं अपना भला-बुरा सोचने में सक्षम है अतः उसके अनुरोध पर ही भारत को सहायता का हाथ बढ़ाना चाहिए।
- नेपाल को 'बफर स्टेट' के रूप में उपयोग करने के बजाए भारत को उसे अपने एक शक्तिशाली भावी पड़ोसी के रूप में देखना चाहिए जो आने वाले समय में भारत से सहायता लेने में नहीं अपितु देने में भी सक्षम होगा।
- जहां तक मधेशियों का प्रश्न है भारतीय मूल के होने से भी बड़ा सच यह है कि अंततः वह नेपाल के नागरिक हैं। उनकी सुरक्षा एवं अधिकारों की जिम्मेदारी नेपाल की है। अतः जहां तक संभव हो भारत को इस विवाद से

दूर रहना चाहिए।

- भारत की अर्थव्यवस्था लगातार गिरती जा रही है। कोरोना महामारी के बाद देश की जी.डी.पी. -60 पर पहुंच गई है, जो यह दर्शाता है कि भारत दिवालिया होने की कगार पर है। अतः फिलहाल उसे अपने देश की अर्थव्यवस्था को सुदृढ़ करने में ध्यान लगाना चाहिए, न कि नेपाल की व्यवस्था पर।
- नेपाल के शीर्ष नेता पदलोलुपता और आपसी वैमनस्य के शिकार हैं जिसके परिणामस्वरूप वहां का आर्थिक-राजनीतिक विकास प्रभावित हो रहा है। सबको अपना आपसी अहंकार भुलाकर देश के विकास के लिए कार्य करना चाहिए। हमेशा नेपाल में व्याप्त अस्थिरता का ठीकरा भारत पर फोड़ने के बजाए अपनी गलतियों से सबक लेकर उन्हें सुधारना चाहिए।
- नेपाल की आबादी का एक बड़ा भाग मधेशियों का है जो वहां की आर्थिक, राजनीतिक परिस्थितियों को परिवर्तित करने में सक्षम हैं। नेपाल एक बहुलवादी देश है इसलिए उसे नए संविधान में संपूर्ण जनता एवं प्रत्येक समुदाय के हित को स्थान देना चाहिए था। लेकिन यदि तब ऐसा नही किया गया तो अब संविधान में संशोधन करके उनके अधिकारों को शामिल करना चाहिए।

संदर्भ सूची

1. Jha, Prashant. (20 Jan, 2015). 'How India was both right and wrong to Nepal'. *Hindustan Times.*
2. एजेंसी, नई दिल्ली. (7 अप्रैल, 2018). तीन दिवसीय भारत यात्रा पर पहुंचे नेपाल के प्रधानमंत्री ने मोदी से की मुलाकात. *अमर उजाला.*
3. एजेंसी, (09 अगस्त, 2016). नेपाल और चीन के साथ त्रिपक्षीय संबंध स्थापित करना चाहता है नेपाल : प्रचंड. *नवभारत टाइम्स.*
4. एजेंसी, (04 अक्टूबर, 2015). भारत-नेपाल संबंध. Vivace Panorama, Hindi.
5. एथिराजन, अनबरासन. (11 जून, 2020). भारत-नेपाल नक्शा विवाद : चीन इस झगड़े को भड़का रहा है?. *बीबीसी न्यूज.*
6. एनडीटीवी खबर. (24 अगस्त, 2017). नेपाल के प्रधानमंत्री देउबा चार दिवसीय यात्रा पर भारत पहुंचे, आज पीएम मोदी से मुलाकात. *एनडीटीवी इंडिया.*
7. कनौजिया, सोनू. (02 जुलाई, 2020). नेपाल : प्रधानमंत्री केपी शर्मा ओली की कुर्सी खतरे में. *एच डब्ल्यू हिंदी न्यूज.*

8. किशोर, तारेंद्र. (30 जून, 2020). नेपाल-भारत विवाद में ओली और प्रचंड के बीच मतभेद से बढ़ा तनाव. *बीबीसी न्यूज.*
9. कुमार, रजनीश. (02 सितंबर, 2020). भारत-नेपाल में हिंदुओं का होना विदेशी संबंध में मायने नहीं रखता : नेपाल. *बीबीसी न्यूज.*
10. खनाल, उमाकांत. (12 अक्टूबर, 2020). नेपाल-भारत-चीन सीमा : 2 साल में सीमा चौकियों की संख्या दोगुनी होगी. *बीबीसी न्यूज.*
11. झा, हरिबंश. (14 अप्रैल, 2018). ओली की दिल्ली यात्रा : नेपाल-भारत संबंधों में मील का पत्थर. *हिंदी पोस्ट.*
12. द वायर, स्टाफ. (19 फरवरी, 2019). भारत को यह मानना होगा कि नेपाल स्वतंत्र देश है : पूर्व नेपाली प्रधानमंत्री. *द वायर,* हिंदी.
13. पांडे, पवन. (15 जून, 2020). भारत-नेपाल के बीच रोटी-बेटी का रिश्ता, दुनिया की कोई भी ताकत इस संबंध को तोड़ नहीं सकती : राजनाथ सिंह. *एनडीटीवी इंडिया.*
14. *भाषा.* (15 जून, 2020). नेपाल के वरिष्ठ अर्थशास्त्री ने कहा : भारत का विकल्प चीन नहीं हो सकता. *एनडीटीवी इंडिया.*
15. *भाषा.* (03 जुलाई, 2020). नेपाल के साथ संबंध मजबूत करने के लिए भारत प्रतिबद्ध : विदेश मंत्रालय. *एनडीटीवी इंडिया.*
16. *भाषा.* (04 अगस्त, 2020). बहनों की जिद के आगे झुके भारत और नेपाल, कुछ समय के लिए खोली सरहद. *एनडीटीवी इंडिया.*
17. मीना, राकेश कुमार. (20 सिंतबर, 2016). नेपाल प्रधानमंत्री प्रचंड की भारत यात्रा. Indian Council of world affairs, Sapru House, New Delhi.
18. राजन, आलोक. (09 अगस्त, 2016). क्या प्रचंड के दौरे से भारत-नेपाल संबंधों में आई खटास दूर होगी? आई चैक न्यूज.
19. राजहंस, गौरीशंकर. (20 सितंबर, 2016). भारत-नेपाल संबंध : दोनों देशों के संबंध सैकड़ों वर्ष पुराने, भारत को भरोसे में लेकर आगे बढ़े नेपाल. *जागरण.*
20. रामन, सुनील. (16 सितंबर, 2008). प्रचंड की भारत यात्रा की अहमियत और नजरियां. *वन इंडिया,* हिंदी.
21. शर्मा, कादंबिनी. (18 अगस्त 2020). भारत को पड़ोसियों की शंकाएं और नाराजगी दूर करना जरूरी. *एनडीटीवी इंडिया.*
22. सिंह, राहुल. (26 जनवरी, 2020). गणतंत्र दिवस, 2020 : गणतंत्र दिवस पर भारत ने नेपाल को तोहफे में दी 30 एंबुलेंस और 6 बसें. *एनडीटीवी इंडिया.*
23. सोनल, स्वप्नल. (17 नवंबर, 2015). भारत-नेपाल रिश्तों में मधेशी आंदोलन ने घोली कड़वाहट. आज तक.
24. संपादक. (16 मई, 2016). नेपाल और भारत में बढ़ती दूरियां. *नवभारत टाइम्स.*

13

भारत और सार्क

मनोज कुमार

सारांश

वर्तमान भारत की ऐतिहासिक व आर्थिक पृष्ठभूमि पर विचार करने से हमें यह जानकारी मिलती है कि उसका सामाजिक, आर्थिक व राजनीतिक विकास किन परिस्थितियों में हुआ। वर्तमान आर्थिक व राजनीतिक व्यवस्था के मुख्य पहलुओं पर विचार करने से पहले यह समझना होगा कि इसका भारत के वर्तमान और भविष्य की कल्पना के लिए क्या महत्व है। शीतयुद्ध के समाप्त होते ही भारत की तटस्थता की नीति का महत्व कम हो गया है। जिस कारण क्षेत्रीय सहयोग पर जोर दिया जा रहा है। यद्यपि यहां पर भी रुख सहयोग से ज्यादा स्पर्धा का है। भारत के द्वारा विदेशी व्यापारियों को उद्योगों में पूंजी लगाने के लिए प्रेरित किया जा रहा हैं, और देश के साधनो के उपयोग पर ज्यादा जोर दिया जा रहा है। इस बीच देश की सैनिक व आर्थिक शक्ति बढ़ी है, और आर्थिक व सामाजिक ढांचे का अनेक दिशाओं में विस्तार हुआ है। अगले कुछ वर्षों में विदेशी सहायता की दरकार होगी, किंतु यह व्यापारिक सौदा होगा, राजनीतिक रियायत या मदद नहीं। अंतर्राष्ट्रीय स्थिति में बदलाव से नए देशों का उदय हो रहा है। जिससे विभिन्न क्षेत्रों में संघर्ष पैदा हुए है। बड़े राष्ट्र भारत-चीन के क्षेत्र में यथास्थिति बनाए रखना चाहते हैं। भारत को विश्व के बजाए अपने क्षेत्र की ओर देखना होगा। पड़ोसी राष्ट्र के प्रति नए रुख अपनाने होंगे और क्षेत्रीय संदर्भ में परमाणु बम बनाने के प्रश्न पर विचार करना होगा।

सार्क (दक्षेस) का विकास शनैः शनैः हुआ है। दक्षिण एशियाई देशों का क्षेत्रीय संगठन बनाने का विचार बांग्लादेश के पूर्व राष्ट्रपति जिया-उर-रहमान ने दिया था। सार्क का मूल आधार क्षेत्रीय सहयोग पर बल देना है। सार्क के माध्यम से दक्षिण

एशियाई देश नियमित रूप से मिल बैठकर अपनी समस्याओं पर चर्चा करते है। इसका गठन किसी महाशक्ति के इशारे पर नहीं हुआ बल्कि क्षेत्रीय आवश्यकताओं के कारण हुआ है। द्वितीय विश्व-युद्ध के बाद क्षेत्रीय सहयोग के संगठनों की बढ़ोत्तरी हुई। क्षेत्रीय संगठनों की स्थापना का उद्‌देश्य आर्थिक और सामाजिक समस्याओं का समाधान करना एवं क्षेत्रीय सुरक्षा व्यवस्था को पुख्ता करना है। क्षेत्रीय संगठनों के माध्यमों से स्वतंत्र एवं संप्रभु राष्ट्र क्षेत्रीय हितों की पूर्ति के लिए प्रयत्नशील रहते है।

कीवर्डः सार्क, संप्रभु, शीतयुद्ध, शिखर सम्मेलन, मंत्रिपरिषद्, स्थायी समिति, तकनीकी समितियां, कार्यकारी समिति, सचिवालय, रियायत, राष्ट्राध्यक्ष, शासनाध्यक्ष।

प्रस्तुत शोध पत्र का उद्‌देश्य : प्रस्तुत शोध पत्र का उद्‌देश्य भारत और सार्क से संबंधित पहलुओं का ऐतिहासिक व विश्लेषणात्मक अध्ययन करना। विभिन्न बिंदुओं पर प्रकाश डालना और भविष्य के लिए सुझाव प्रस्तुत करना हैं।

शोध प्रविधि : प्रस्तुत शोध पत्र में शोधार्थी द्वारा द्वितीयक स्रोतों में लेखकों की पुस्तकों, शोध पत्रों, पत्रिकाओं एवं इंटरनेट द्वारा अध्ययन किया गया है।

प्रस्तावना

भारत में नए युग के प्रभाव से जो प्रतिक्रिया हुई, उससे पुरानी परंपरा और संस्कृति के प्रति नया बोध उत्पन्न हुआ। जिससे भारत आधुनिक विश्व में अपना स्थान प्राप्त कर सके, साथ ही, भारतीयता की भावना ने भी नया रूप, नया बल और नया अर्थ प्राप्त किया। इस प्रकार भारतीय पुनर्जागरण के नेताओं ने वर्तमान में परिवर्तन किया और भविष्य की नई कल्पना की। राष्ट्र और समाज की नई कल्पना का आधार केवल यही नहीं था कि अतीत में हम क्या थे, बल्कि यह भी था कि भविष्य में हमें क्या होना हैं। द्वितीय विश्वयुद्ध ने प्रथम विश्वयुद्ध की अपेक्षा अधिक संपूर्णता तथा प्रगतिशीलता के साथ मानव-जीवन को प्रभावित किया। सबसे ज्यादा बर्बाद यूरोप और एशिया हुआ। द्वितीय विश्वयुद्ध के दौरान जापान ने एशिया एशियावासियों के लिए के नारे के विरुद्ध ब्रिटिश सरकार ने भारतीयों को युद्ध सहायता के बदले डोमिनियन स्टेट का दर्जा देने का आश्वासन दिया। 1947 में भारत को स्वतंत्र घोषित किया और भारतीय साम्राज्य को भंग करके भारत और पाकिस्तान के रूप में दो हिस्सों में बांट दिया। जो आज भी भारत के लिए सिर दर्द बना हुआ है।

सार्क के अभी तक 18 शिखर सम्मेलन आयोजित हो चुके हैं। अपने जीवनकाल में सार्क ने शोध और प्रशिक्षण के अनेक क्षेत्रीय केंद्र स्थापित किए है।

आतंकवाद, बच्चों, स्त्रियों और नशीले पदार्थों के अवैध व्यापार को रोकने के लिए अनेक क्षेत्रीय समझौते पर हस्ताक्षर किए हैं। पूरे क्षेत्र में समारोहों व महासम्मेलनों का आयोजन किया गया है।

सार्क (साउथ एशियन एसोसिएशन फॉर रीजनल को-ऑपरेशन)

इसकी स्थापना बांग्लादेश की राजधानी ढाका में 7-8 दिसंबर 1985 को दक्षिण एशिया के सात देशों के राष्ट्राध्यक्षों के सम्मेलन में हुए निर्णयानुसार हुई। इसका मुख्यालय काठमांडू (नेपाल) में है। सार्क के संस्थापक सदस्य देश हैं–भारत, पाकिस्तान, नेपाल, बांग्लादेश, भूटान, श्रीलंका और मालदीव। सार्क के आठवें और नवीनतम सदस्य के रूप में अफगानिस्तान का अनुमोदन 13वें शिखर सम्मेलन (ढाका, 2005) में किया गया था और 14वें शिखर सम्मेलन (नई दिल्ली, 3 अप्रैल, 2007) से यह सदस्य के रूप में सम्मिलित हो गया। इसकी बैठक प्रतिवर्ष आयोजित होती है जिसमें सदस्य देशों के राष्ट्राध्यक्ष भाग लेते हैं। ज्ञातव्य है कि सार्क बनाने का सर्वप्रथम विचार बांग्लादेश के पूर्व राष्ट्रपति जिया-उर-रहमान ने 1977 में दिया था। 1980 में दक्षिण एशियाई देशों के बीच इस मुद्दे पर आपस में व्यापारिक साझेदारी बढ़ाने के उद्देश्य से इसके गठन पर सहमति बनी। इस दिशा में पहला ठोस कदम उठाते हुए, अप्रैल 1981 में सात देशों के विदेश सचिवों की पहली बार कोलंबो में बैठक हुई। जिसमें 5 विषयों पर क्षेत्रीय सहयोग पर सहमति बनी जो इस संगठन की बुनियाद बना। बाद के वर्षों में सहयोग के बिंदु बढ़कर 16 तक पहुंच गए।

अगस्त 1983 में दिल्ली में संपन्न विदेश मंत्रियों की बैठक में सार्क के घोषणा पत्र को स्वीकार किया गया और सहयोग के 9 विभिन्न क्षेत्रों से संबंधित **'इंटीग्रेटेड प्रोग्राम ऑफ एक्शन'** को प्रारंभ किया गया। 8 दिसंबर 1985 को सातों दक्षिण एशियाई राष्ट्रों के राष्ट्राध्यक्षों/शासनाध्यक्षों की ढाका में संपन्न बैठक में सार्क के चार्टर को स्वीकृति प्रदान की गई।

सार्क का चार्टर : सार्क के चार्टर में 10 धाराएं हैं। इनमें सार्क के उद्देश्यों, सिद्धांतों, संस्थाओं तथा वित्तीय व्यवस्थाओं को परिभाषित किया गया है। जो निम्न प्रकार से हैं–

उद्देश्य

चार्टर के अनुच्छेद 1 के अनुसार सार्क के मुख्य उद्देश्य हैं—

1. दक्षिण एशिया क्षेत्र की जनता के कल्याण एवं उनके जीवन स्तर में सुधार करना।
2. दक्षिण एशिया के देशों की सामूहिक आत्मनिर्भरता में वृद्धि करना।
3. क्षेत्र के आर्थिक, सामाजिक तथा सांस्कृतिक विकास में तेजी लाना।
4. आर्थिक, सामाजिक, सांस्कृतिक, तकनीकी और वैज्ञानिक क्षेत्र में सक्रिय सहयोग एवं पारस्परिक सहायता में वृद्धि करना।
5. सामान्य हित के मामलों पर अंतर्राष्ट्रीय मंचों पर आपसी सहयोग मजबूत करना।
6. आपसी विश्वास, सूझ-बूझ तथा एक-दूसरे की समस्याओं का मूल्यांकन करना।
7. अन्य विकासशील देशों के साथ सहयोग में वृद्धि करना।

सिद्धांत : चार्टर के अनुच्छेद 2 के अनुसार सार्क के मुख्य सिद्धांत निम्नलिखित है—

1. आपसी सहयोग द्विपक्षीय और बहुपक्षीय उत्तरदायित्वों का विरोध नहीं होगा।
2. संगठन के ढांचे के अंतर्गत सहयोग, समानता, क्षेत्रीय अखंडता, राजनीतिक स्वतंत्रता, दूसरे देशों के आंतरिक मामलों में हस्तक्षेप न करना तथा आपसी लाभ के सिद्धांतों का सम्मान करना।
3. इस प्रकार का सहयोग द्विपक्षीय और बहुपक्षीय सहयोग का स्थान नही लेगा बल्कि उनका पूरक होगा।

संरचना : चार्टर के अंतर्गत सार्क की निम्न संस्थाओं का उल्लेख किया गया है-

(क) शिखर सम्मेलन,
(ख) मंत्रिपरिषद्,
(ग) स्थायी समिति,
(घ) तकनीकी समितियाँ,
(ङ) कार्यकारी समिति,
(च) सचिवालय।

(क) **शिखर सम्मेलन :** सार्क चार्टर के तीसरे अनुच्छेद में वार्षिक शिखर बैठकों का प्रावधान है हालांकि सार्क चार्टर के अनुसार राज्य या सरकार के प्रमुखों को वर्ष में एक बार मिलने की आवश्यकता होती है। शिखर सम्मेलन आम तौर पर लगभग हर अठारह महीने में होते है, किंतु सार्क की अब तक केवल 18 बैठकें ही संपन्न हो सकी हैं। यह दक्षिण एशियाई क्षेत्रीय सहयोग संगठन (सार्क) के सम्मेलन की एक सूची है–

शिखर सम्मेलन	*शहर*	*देश*	*तिथि सहित वर्ष*
पहला	ढाका	बांग्लादेश	7-8 दिसंबर, 1985
दूसरा	बंगलौर	भारत	17 नवंबर, 1986
तीसरा	काठमांडू	नेपाल	4 नवंबर, 1987
चौथा	इस्लामाबाद	पाकिस्तान	31 दिसंबर, 1988
पांचवां	माले	मालदीव	23 नवंबर, 1990
छठवां	कोलंबो	श्रीलंका	21 दिसंबर, 1991
सातवां	ढाका	बांग्लादेश	11 अप्रैल, 1993
आठवां	नई दिल्ली	भारत	4 मई, 1995
नवां	माले	मालदीव	14 मई, 1997
दसवां	कोलंबो	श्रीलंका	31 जुलाई, 1998
ग्यारहवां	काठमांडू	नेपाल	6 जनवरी, 2002
बारहवां	इस्लामाबाद	पाकिस्तान	6 जनवरी, 2004
तेरहवां	ढाका	बांग्लादेश	12 नवंबर, 2005
चौदहवां	नई दिल्ली	भारत	3-4 अप्रैल, 2007
पंद्रहवां	कोलंबो	श्रीलंका	2-3 अगस्त, 2008
सोलहवां	थिंपू	भूटान	28-29 अप्रैल, 2010
सत्रहवां	अड्डू सिटी	मालदीव	10-11 नवंबर, 2011
अठारहवां	काठमांडू	नेपाल	27-28 नवंबर, 2014
उन्नीसवां	**इस्लामाबाद***	**पाकिस्तान***	**4 नवंबर, 2016**

नोट : यह चार्ट प्रो. श्रीप्रकाश मणि त्रिपाठी की पुस्तक *अंतर्राष्ट्रीय संगठन* से लिया गया है।

***18 सितम्बर, 2016 को जम्मू-कश्मीर के उरी में हुए आतंकी हमले के बाद भारत ने साल 2016 में इस सम्मेलन में शामिल न होने का निर्णय लिया था।**

(ख) **मंत्रिपरिषद्** : यह सदस्य देशों के विदेश मंत्रियों की परिषद् है। इसकी बैठक 6 माह में एक बार होती है किंतु आवश्यकता पड़ने पर यह बैठक कभी भी बुलाई जा सकती है। संघ की नीति-निर्धारित करना, सामान्य हित के मुद्दों के बारे में निर्णय करना, सहयोग के नए क्षेत्र खोजना आदि मंत्रिपरिषद् के कार्यों में शामिल हैं।

(ग) **स्थायी समिति** : यह सदस्य देशों के सचिवों की समिति होती है। इसकी बैठकें आवश्यकतानुसार कभी भी हो सकती है परंतु वर्ष में एक बैठक होना अनिवार्य है। सहयोग के कार्यक्रमों का प्रबंधन करना, अंतर-क्षेत्रीय प्राथमिकताएं निर्धारित करना, अध्ययन के आधार पर सहयोग के नए क्षेत्रों की पहचान करना इस समिति के कार्यों में शामिल है। स्थायी समिति कार्यकारी समिति की भी व्यवस्था करती है। यह सदस्य देशों द्वारा प्रोजेक्ट के लागू करने से संबंधित कार्यवाही समिति स्थापित कर सकती है। इसमें दो से अधिक सदस्य देश शामिल हो सकते है। लेकिन सभी सदस्य देश शामिल नही हो सकते है।

(घ) **तकनीकी समितियाँ** : इसमें सभी सदस्य देशों के प्रतिनिधि शामिल होते हैं। यह अपने-अपने क्षेत्र में कार्यक्रम लागू करने, उनमें समन्वय पैदा करने और उनकी देखभाल करने के लिए उत्तरदायी होती है तथा अपनी रिपोर्ट स्थायी समिति को सौंपती है। ये समितियां स्वीकृत क्षेत्रों में क्षेत्रीय सहयोग के क्षेत्र और संभावनाओं का पता लगाती हैं। प्रत्येक तकनीकी समिति की अध्यक्षता प्रायः प्रत्येक दो वर्षो के अंतराल पर वर्णानुक्रम के अनुसार सदस्य देशों के बीच घूमती रहती है। इस समय 12 तकनीकी समितियां, कृषि संचार, वातावरण, स्वास्थ्य और जनसंख्या क्रियाएं, ग्रामीण विकास, विज्ञान और प्रौद्योगिकी, पर्यटन, परिवहन हैं। ये समितियां सार्क सहयोग के स्वीकृत क्षेत्रों को व्यक्त करती हैं और 'स्पा' के अंतर्गत आती है जो सार्क प्रक्रिया का एक मुख्य अंग है।

(ङ) **कार्यकारी समिति** : इसमें वरिष्ठ कर्मचारी शामिल होते है। यह सचिवालय के बजट को सही करने, कार्य-कलापों की वार्षिक सूची को अंतिम रूप देने तथा स्थायी समिति द्वारा सौंपे गए किन्हीं मामलों को निपटाने का काम करती है। यह स्थायी समिति के सत्रों से पहले अपनी बैठकें करती है।

(च) **सचिवालय** : सार्क के सचिवालय की स्थापना द्वितीय सार्क सम्मेलन (बेंगलुरू) के बाद 16 जनवरी, 1987 को की गई थी। सचिवालय का अध्यक्ष महासचिव कहलाता है जिसका कार्यकाल 2 वर्ष का होता है। महासचिव का पद

सदस्यों को बारी-बारी से प्रदान किया जाता है। सचिवालय सात भागों में विभक्त है और प्रत्येक भाग के अध्यक्ष को निदेशक कहते हैं।

वित्तीय प्रावधान : सदस्यों का अंशदान ऐच्छिक होता है। कार्यक्रमों के व्यय को सदस्य देशों में बांटने के लिए तकनीकी समिति की सिफारिशों का सहारा लिया जाता है। सार्क सचिवालय के व्यय को पूरा करले के लिए सदस्य देशों के अंशदान को निम्न प्रकार निर्धारित किया गया है—भारत 32 प्रतिशत, पाकिस्तान 25 प्रतिशत, नेपाल, बांग्लादेश एवं श्रीलंका प्रत्येक 11 प्रतिशत और भूटान एवं मालदीव प्रत्येक का 5 प्रतिशत।

सदस्य व प्रेक्षक देश

सार्क के वर्तमान सदस्य :

- भारत
- पाकिस्तान
- बांग्लादेश
- नेपाल
- भूटान
- श्रीलंका
- मालदीव
- अफगानिस्तान

प्रक्षेक देश :

- चीन जनवादी गणराज्य
- यूरोपीय संघ
- ईरान
- जापान
- मॉरिशस
- म्यांमार
- दक्षिण कोरिया
- संयुक्त राज्य अमेरिका

अन्य संस्थाओं के साथ सहयोग

सार्क ने अंतर्राष्ट्रीय एवं क्षेत्रीय संगठनों के साथ सहयोग स्थापित किया है। यह सहयोग की व्यवस्था विभिन्न संस्थाओं के साथ राजीनामे पर हस्ताक्षर द्वारा होती है। फरवरी 1993 में व्यापार-विश्लेषण तथा सूचना पद्धति पर सार्क-अंकटाड समझौता प्रपत्र पर हस्ताक्षर किए गए। यह सार्क का एक अंतर्राष्ट्रीय संगठन के साथ सहयोग का पहला राजीनामा था। इसी तरह फरवरी 1994 में सार्क और इस्कैप के बीच सहयोग हुआ। सार्क ने संयुक्त राष्ट्र विकास कार्यक्रम के साथ 18 अगस्त 1996 को तथा दिसंबर, 1995 में यूरोपीय समुदाय के साथ महत्वपूर्ण आर्थिक समझौते किए।

सार्क कोष

वित्तीय कठिनाइयों को दूर करने के उद्देश्य से सार्क के तहत निम्न कोष स्थापित किए गए हैं–

1. **सार्क-जापान विशेष कोष :** सार्क-जापान विशेष कोष की स्थापना 27 दिसम्बर, 1993 में काठमांडू में हुई सार्क महासचिव एवं जापान के राजदूत के बीच इस कोष की रूपरेखा से संबंधित पत्रों का आदान-प्रदान हुआ। इस कोष की धनराशि 5 लाख अमेरिकी डॉलर है।
2. **दक्षिण एशियाई विकास कोष :** सन् 1991 में क्षेत्रीय परियोजनाओं के लिए सार्क कोष 2.50 लाख डॉलर की प्रारंभिक पूंजी के साथ स्थापित किया गया साथ ही, सार्क क्षेत्रीय कोष की स्थापना भी की गई जिसका उद्देश्य **'कार्य के एकीकृत कार्यक्रम'** के अंतर्गत वित्त उपलब्ध कराना था जो वित्तीय कठिनाइयों के कारण पूरी नहीं हो पाई थी। आठवें सार्क सम्मेलन के दौरान दक्षिण एशियाई विकास कोष की स्थापना का निर्णय लिया गया था। जिसमें पहले के दोनों कोषों का मिला दिया गया। इसकी निम्न तीन शाखाएं हैं–1. प्रोजेक्ट की पहचान एवं विकास करने के लिए, 2. संस्थागत तथा मानव संसाधन विकास प्रोजेक्टों के लिए, व 3. सामाजिक विकास तथा आधारभूत ढांचे के विकास से संबंधित प्रोजेक्टो के लिए।
3. **सार्क विकास फंड :** इसके लिए 14वें शिखर सम्मेलन के चार्टर पर

समझौता किया गया। सार्क डेवलपमेन्ट फंड सार्क के सदस्य राष्ट्रों के आर्थिक, सामाजिक एवं ढांचागत विकास को वित्तीय सहायता उपलब्ध करा रहा है। वर्तमान में इस फंड में दक्षिण एशियाई विकास फंड (SADF) का स्थान ले लिया है।

व्यापार और विपणन सहयोग

सार्क ने सदस्य देशों के बीच महत्वपूर्ण क्षेत्रों में सहयोग के लिए कदम उठाए हैं, जिनमें व्यापार और विपणन 'सार्क व्यापार समझौता' या वरीयता है।

दक्षिण एशियाई वरीयता व्यापार समझौता- साप्टा (SAPTA)

सार्क देशों के बीच व्यापार एवं विपणन सहयोग करने हेतु 7 दिसंबर, 1995 से साप्टा समझौता लागू किया गया। इसकी उत्पत्ति 1991 में व्यापार विपणन-विनिमय विनिर्माण और सेवाओं के क्षेत्र में एक क्षेत्रीय अध्ययन से हुआ। परिणामस्वरूप ढाका में सातवें सार्क सम्मेलन के दौरान 11 अप्रैल, 1993 को सदस्य देशों के मंत्रियों ने साप्टा समझौते पर हस्ताक्षर किए जिसमें एक प्रस्तावना और 25 धाराएं थीं। साप्टा के अंतर्गत सार्क देशों के बीच व्यापार और आर्थिक सहयोग के संबर्द्धन के प्रयोजन से टैरिफ रियायतों प्रशुल्कों पर व्यापार करने का यह सार्क वरीयता व्यापार समझौता 7 दिसंबर 1995 से प्रभावी हो गया। नई रियायती व्यापार प्रणाली को 1995 में शुरू करने का निर्णय मई 1995 में नई दिल्ली में संपन्न आठवें शिखर सम्मेलन में लिया गया था। साप्टा प्रणाली के तहत सार्क देशों के बीच प्रारंभ में 226 वस्तुओं के व्यापार पर 10 प्रतिशत से 100 प्रतिशत तक की रियायती प्रशुल्क दरों की व्यवस्था की गई। सर्वाधिक 106 वस्तुओं पर भारत सरकार द्वारा रियायत प्रस्तुत की, जिसमें 62 सार्क के लिए हैं। पाकिस्तान द्वारा 35, श्रीलंका द्वारा 31, मालदीव द्वारा 17, नेपाल द्वारा 14, बांग्लादेश द्वारा 12 तथा भूटान द्वारा 11 वस्तुओं पर रियायत प्रस्तुत की।

दक्षिण एशियाई मुक्त व्यापार समझौता- साफ्टा (SAFTA)

11 अप्रैल, 1993 को सार्क देशों ने ढाका में सार्क क्षेत्र के अंतर्गत टैरिफ को कम करने के लिए एक समझौते पर हस्ताक्षर किए। साउथ एशियन प्रिफरेंशियल ट्रेडिंग अरेंजमेंट (SAFTA) 7 दिसंबर, 1995 को अस्तित्व में आई। साप्टा के बाद साफ्टा (साउथ एशियन फ्री ट्रेड एरिया) की पृष्ठभूमि तैयार हो गई। 25 अनुच्छेदों

वाली साफ्टा संधि पर 6 जनवरी, 2004 को इस्लामाबाद शिखर सम्मेलन में सहमति हुई और 1 जनवरी, 2006 में प्रभावी हुआ। अफगानिस्तान फरवरी, 2008 में साफ्टा का सदस्य बना।

सार्क को सार्थक बनाने हेतु सुझाव : सार्क की सफलता के लिए निम्नलिखित सुझाव दिए जा सकते हैं–

- जहां तक हो सके सार्क को महाशक्तियों के क्षेत्र से दूर रखा जाए।
- द्विपक्षीय और बहुपक्षीय सहयोग को बढ़ावा देने पर जोर दिया जाए।
- अंतर्राष्ट्रीय मंचों पर सार्क देशों द्वारा सर्वसम्मत दृष्टिकोण अपनाया जाए।
- व्यापार, उद्योग, वित्त, ऊर्जा, मुद्रा और अन्य क्षेत्रों में सहयोग को बढ़ावा दिया जाए।
- जहां तक हो सके विवादित मुद्दों को आपसी बातचीत द्वारा हल किया जाए।
- सांस्कृतिक संपर्क एवं आदान-प्रदान को प्रोत्साहन दिया जाए।

निष्कर्ष

सार्क जनसंख्या की दृष्टि से दुनिया का सबसे बड़ा क्षेत्रीय संगठन है। संपूर्ण दक्षिण एशिया भौगोलिक संरचना के संदर्भ में एक राष्ट्र की तरह है, जिससे आपस में किसी भी तरह के आदान-प्रदान के लिए परिस्थितियां अतिशय अनुकूल हैं। सांस्कृतिक दृष्टि से सार्क के देशों में अत्यधिक समानता है। सार्क चार्टर सदस्य देशों की द्विपक्षीय तनाव पर बहस की अनुमति नहीं देता। इस मंच पर राजनीतिक विवाद एवं सीमा जनित समस्यायों पर चर्चा नहीं हो सकती। इस समय दुनिया में यूरोपीय संघ, आसियान, एपेक जैसे कई संगठन हैं जिन्होंने व्यापार को नई बुलंदियों तक पहुंचाया है, इसकी तुलना में सार्क में आपसी व्यापार का स्तर बहुत कम है। गरीबी और पिछड़ेपन से ग्रस्त इस क्षेत्र के लिए सार्क ने कई महत्वाकांक्षी योजनाएं तैयार की हैं लेकिन वे मात्र कागजों तक ही सीमित रहीं। पहले यूरोपीय यूनियन की तरह ही दक्षिण एशियाई क्षेत्र के आर्थिक एकीकरण करने और एकल मुद्रा अपनाने की चर्चा जोरों पर थी, लेकिन अब इस विचार का लगभग परित्याग कर दिया गया है।

सार्क की गणना एक क्षेत्रीय आर्थिक समूह के रूप में होती है, जिसका मुख्य उद्देश्य है 'आर्थिक एकीकरण'। आर्थिक एकीकरण की दिशा में सार्क की प्रगति नाममात्र के बराबर है। अभी तक सदस्य देशों में आर्थिक एकीकरण के उद्देश्य पर भी सहमति नहीं बन पाई है। सार्क के किसी भी सरकारी दस्तावेज में इस शब्द का

उल्लेख नही मिलता। 1997 के शिखर सम्मेलन ने प्रतिष्ठित व्यक्तियों की एक समिति का गठन किया था। 1998 में अपनी रिपोर्ट में इस समिति ने सिफारिश की कि 2010 तक एक सामान्य सीमा शुल्क प्रणाली लागू हो जाए और 2020 तक इस क्षेत्र को एक आर्थिक संघ में परिणत कर दिया जाए, पर इन उद्देश्यों के ऊपर अब तक राजनीतिक स्तर पर सहमति नहीं हो पाई।

सार्क के मार्ग में विविध पर की बाधाएं हैं—

1. भारत और पाकिस्तान के बीच इस क्षेत्र में दीर्घ अवधि से तनाव बना हुआ है। जिस कारण सार्क का एजेंडा आगे नहीं बढ़ पा रहा है।
2. सार्क के देश आर्थिक सहयोग के किसी निर्णायक लक्ष्य तक नहीं पहुंच पा रहे हैं जिसके कारण इस संगठन की स्थापना का मुख्य उद्देश्य ही पूर्ण नहीं हो पा रहा है।
3. चीन-पाकिस्तान गठबंधन और इसके माध्यम से सार्क में चीन के प्रवेश की आकांक्षा और तत्संबंधी प्रयास से भी सार्क की प्रगति पर प्रतिकूल प्रभाव पड़ता है।

सार्क के गठन के पहले से भारत-पाक संबंधों में कटुता रही है। संगठन की स्थापना के दौरान यह कटुता स्पष्ट रूप से दिखी थी। इसी कारण क्षेत्रीय शांति एवं सहयोग पर कोई सफल व प्रभावी फॉर्मूला नही बन पाया। राष्ट्रीय सुरक्षा के मोर्चे पर भारत और पाकिस्तान के बीच प्रगति और सहमति होने पर सार्क की कठिनाइयों पर नियंत्रण किया जा सकेगा। सार्क के माध्यम से दक्षिण एशियाई देश नियमित रूप से मिलकर सरकारी स्तर पर अपनी समस्याओं के बारे में चर्चा करते है जो क्षेत्र के लिए एक महत्वपूर्ण उपलब्धि है। इसका गठन किसी महाशक्ति के इशारे पर न होकर क्षेत्रीय आवश्यकताओं के कारण हुआ है। अतः यह आशा की जा सकती है कि सार्क शांति सद्भाव एवं शोषण मुक्त अंतर्राष्ट्रीय राजनीति के लिए मार्ग प्रशस्त करेगा। इससे संभावनाओं के द्वार खुलेंगे और यूरोपीय संघ तथा आसियान की तरह सार्क भी मजबूत, सशक्त और सफल संगठन बन पाएगा।

संदर्भ ग्रंथ सूची

1. कोठारी रजनी, *भारत में राजनीति*, ओरियंट ब्लैक स्वान, दिल्ली, दूसरा संस्करण-2013
2. पंत, डॉ. पुष्पेश/जैन पाल, *प्रमुख देशों की विदेश नीतियां*, मीनाक्षी प्रकाशन, मेरठ-2010

3. पंत डॉ. पुष्पेश/जैन पाल/पंचौला डॉ. राखी, *अंतर्राष्ट्रीय संबंध, सिद्धांत और व्यवहार,* मीनाक्षी प्रकाशन, मेरठ, 12वां संस्करण- 2013-14
4. पंत, पुष्पेश, *21वीं शताब्दी में अंतर्राष्ट्रीय संबंध,* मैग्राहिल एजुकेशन, प्रा. लि. नई दिल्ली, द्वितीय संस्करण-2013
5. त्रिपाठी, प्रो. श्रीप्रकाश मणि, *अंतर्राष्ट्रीय संगठन,* प्रत्यूष पब्लिकेशन, दिल्ली, द्वितीय संस्करण-2013
6. दत्त वी.पी, *बदलती दुनिया के भारत की विदेश नीति भाग-1(1950-1987),* हिंदी माध्यम कार्यान्वय निर्देशालय दिल्ली, प्रथम संस्करण- जून, 2011
7. दत्त, वी.पी, *बदलती दुनिया के भारत की विदेश नीति भाग-2* (1987 के उपरांत), हिन्दी माध्यम कार्यान्वय निर्देशालय दिल्ली, प्रथम संस्करण-2003, द्वितीय संशोधन- 2009
8. राय, विजय कुमार, *अंतर्राष्ट्रीय एवं राष्ट्रीय संस्थाएं और प्रमुख व्यक्तित्व,* विवाक पनोरमा प्रकाशन, दिल्ली
9. गाबा ओम प्रकाश, *तुलनात्मक राजनीति की रूपरेखा,* मयूर बुक्स, नई दिल्ली, 13वां पुनर्मुद्रण संस्करण- 2018
10. देव, अर्जुन/देव, इंदिरा अर्जुन, *समकालीन विश्व का इतिहास : 1890-2008,* ओरियंट ब्लैक स्वान, दिल्ली
11. वर्मा, दीनानाथ/ सिंह शिव कुमार, *विश्व इतिहास का सर्वेक्षण,* भारती भवन पब्लिशर्स एण्ड डिस्ट्रीब्यूटर्स, पटना, तृतीय संस्करण-1991

14

कोरोना राष्ट्रवाद : भारत और वैश्विक व्यवस्था का परिदृश्य

संजय कुमार

सारांश

भारत व विश्व ने विभिन्न महामारियों के प्रकोप का सामना किया है पुनः इस बार कोविड-19 महामारी ने विश्व के अधिकांश देशों में लाखों की संख्या में जनहानि व आर्थिक विकास को प्रभावित किया। विश्व को एक संदेश भी मिला है कि यदि बढ़ती आबादी, पर्यावरण प्रदूषण, शहरों का बढ़ता जनसंख्या घनत्व आदि पर समय रहते काबू नहीं किया गया तो वह दिन दूर नहीं जब संपूर्ण मानवजाति के जीवन पर प्रश्नचिह्न भी लग सकता है। इसीलिए अंतर्राष्ट्रीय संस्थाओं में अधिक से अधिक निवेश कर उनकी विश्वसनीयता को मजबूत बनाये रखना अति आवश्यक है, मात्र आक्रामक राष्ट्रवाद से न तो एक देश सुरक्षित रखा जा सकता है और न ही विश्व सुरक्षित रह पाएगा। अधिकांश देश अपनी सैन्य शक्ति बढ़ाने में अधिक निवेश कर रहे हैं, जबकि आवश्यकता है प्रत्येक देश को आपसी मतभेदों से ऊपर उठकर चिकित्सा विज्ञान को और अधिक विकसित कर नई-नई वैक्सीन की खोज पर अधिक सहयोग करना चाहिए।

कीवर्ड : महामारी, वायरस, सार्वदेशिक (Pandemic) कोविड-19, वैक्सीन, स्पेनिश फ्लू, वैक्सीन राष्ट्रवाद, GAVI, हाइड्रोक्सीक्लोरोक्वीन ।

भारत एवं विश्व में महामारी का प्रकोप प्राचीनकाल से ही देखा गया है स्पेनिश फ्लू, हैजा (भारत), ब्लैकडेथ (इटली), एंतोनाइन प्लेग, जस्टिनियन प्लेग (यूरोप), एच-1 एन-1 फ्लू आदि कई महामारियों से लाखों-करोड़ों जनहानि हुई है। कोई भी ऐसी बीमारी जो एक देश से दूसरे देश या एक महाद्वीप से दूसरे महाद्वीप तक फैल

जाए तो उसे सार्वदेशिक (Pandemic) रोग के नाम से जाना जाता है। विभिन्न शब्दकोषों में वैश्विक महामारी को परिभाषित करते हुए 'Pandemic over the large region'[1] एवं 'A disease that spread over a whole country or the whole world'[2] कहा गया है। यह महामारी जीवाणु या विषाणु से उत्पन्न होती है। भारत के उत्तर प्रदेश माध्यमिक शिक्षा परिषद् के इंटरमीडिएट पाठ्यक्रम के जन्तु विज्ञान की पुस्तक में कोरोना वायरस संक्रमण के बारे में पूर्व में ही लिखा गया है, लेकिन वह एक सामान्य फ्लू का संक्रमण है, जबकि कोविड-19 एक विशिष्ट बीमारी है जोकि महामारी से भी आगे बढ़कर वैश्विक महामारी बन चुकी है।[3] WHO के अनुसार किसी बीमारी का प्रकोप पहले की अपेक्षा बहुत व्यापक स्तर पर फैलने लगे तो इसे ही महामारी के नाम से जाना जाता है।

कोरोना वायरस क्या है

वर्तमान समय में देश व विश्व की विभिन्न फ्लू से संक्रमित बीमारियों में एक बहुत ही भयावह एवं प्रभावशील कोरोना वायरस का नाम जुड़ गया है। जिसे कोविड-19 के नाम से पहचाना गया है, यह कोरोना परिवार का एक नया वायरस है, जिसका प्रादुर्भाव माह दिसंबर-2019 से चीन के वुहान शहर से बताया जाता है। जिसमें खांसी, बुखार आना, थकान लगना एवं सांस लेने में तकलीफ जैसी समस्याओं का सामना व्यक्ति को करना पड़ता है। यह वायरस एक व्यक्ति से दूसरे व्यक्ति के संपर्क में आने से फैलता है। विश्व स्वास्थ्य संगठन के मुताबिक 10 वर्ष से कम आयु के बच्चों तथा 60 वर्ष से अधिक आयु के व्यक्ति इसकी चपेट में जल्दी आ रहे हैं, जिसका सीधा संबंध मानवीय आंतरिक रोग प्रतिरोधक क्षमता (Immunity system) से जोड़ा जा रहा है। इम्यूनिटी कमजोर व्यक्ति को संक्रमण का खतरा अधिक रहता है जबकि अभी तक इसकी रोकथाम से संबंधित कोई वैक्सीन या दवाई नहीं बन पाई है।

वायरस, वैक्सीन और नई दुनिया

कोविड-19 जैसी घातक बीमारी को देखते हुए विश्व के अधिकांश देश इसकी वैक्सीन बनाने में जुटे हुए हैं। ब्रिटेन के वैक्सीन मैन्युफैक्चरिंग एंड इनोवेशन सेंटर के चीफ मैथ्यूज डजर्स का मानना है कि *'हमने टाइमलाइन को हटाकर तकरीबन आधा कर दिया है, हम 2022 के अंत तक वैक्सीन तैयार करने की उम्मीद कर रहे*

थे, लेकिन हम इसके 2021 से शुरू होने की उम्मीद कर रहे है।'[4] लेकिन अंतर्राष्ट्रीय वैक्सीन गठजोड़ (Global Alliance for Vaccines and Immunisation) का मानना है कि विकसित देशों तक वैक्सीन को पहुंचाना आसान नहीं है, क्योंकि विकसित देशों का वैक्सीन कंपनियों से पहले ही करार हो जाएगा और उनको इसकी आपूर्ति भी हो जाएगी परंतु विकासशील व अल्पविकसित देशों के लिए यह चुनौती से कम नहीं होगा। GAVI के सी.ई.ओ. वर्कले कहते हैं कि, *'उनके सामने सबसे बडी चुनौती वैक्सीन राष्ट्रवाद की होगी।'*[5]

वर्कले का यह भी मानना है कि विकासशील देशों को वैक्सीन सुरक्षा के लिए कांच की शीशियों एवं रेफ्रिजरेशन की आवश्यकता होगी, जो इनके लिए कठिनाई पैदा करेगी क्योंकि वैक्सीन के लिए न्यूनतम तापमान की आवश्यकता होगी साथ ही, हवाई परिवहन से लेकर सड़क परिवहन तक उचित स्थान पर वैक्सीन को पहुंचाना विकासशील देशों के लिए एक कठिन काम होगा। प्रश्न उठता है कि वैक्सीन को किन व्यक्तियों को देने की प्राथमिकता दी जानी चाहिए, ये प्रश्न प्रत्येक देश की अपनी प्राथमिकता हो सकती है जैसा कि रूस ने वैक्सीन की प्रथम डोज डॉक्टर व द्वितीय शिक्षक समुदाय को देने का प्रावधान किया।

वैक्सीन राष्ट्रवाद

'जब कोई देश अपने नागरिकों के लिए वैक्सीन की खातिर मैन्युफैक्चर के साथ प्री-परचेज एग्रीमेंट करता है तो यही वैक्सीन राष्ट्रवाद है।'[6] विश्व स्वास्थ्य संगठन के प्रमुख ने वैक्सीन राष्ट्रवाद व इसके जमाखोरी पर अपनी चिंता जाहिर करते हुए कहा है कि यदि कोई देश वैक्सीन बनाने में सफलता प्राप्त करता है तो उसे विश्व के सभी देशों को सहयोग करना आवश्यक है। जिससे covid-19 से विश्व को बचाया जा सके, इसी को ध्यान में रखते हुए विश्व स्वास्थ्य संगठन ने विश्व के सभी देशों को कोवैक्स वैक्सीन फैसिलिटी में शामिल होकर सहयोग प्रदान करने की अपील की है, क्योंकि अमीर व विकसित देश दवा निर्माता बड़ी कंपनियों से अपने नागरिकों की सुरक्षा के लिए प्री-परचेज एग्रीमेंट कर लेंगे जिससे इसकी जमाखोरी भी बढ़ेगी तथा इसकी कीमत में बहुत अधिक वृद्धि होने से विश्व की लगभग 08 करोड़ आबादी या गरीब देशों तक इसकी पहुंच कठिन हो जाएगी, क्योंकि 2009 में एच-1 एन-1 फ्लू के प्रकोप के समय आस्ट्रेलिया प्रथम देश था जिसने वैक्सीन बनाने में सफलता प्राप्त की तथा अन्य देशों के लिए अपना निर्यात रोक दिया था,

उसी प्रकार कई विकसित देशों में कोरोना के वैक्सीन को बनाने की प्रक्रिया पहले से चल रही है तथा कई देश ह्यूमन ट्रायल भी प्रारंभ कर चुके हैं जिसमें ब्रिटेन, रूस व चीन प्रमुख हैं। इसलिए वैक्सीन राष्ट्रवाद से ऊपर उठकर हमें विश्व राष्ट्रवाद को प्रमुखता देनी होगी तभी इस कोरोना जैसी महामारी से विश्व को बचाया जा सकता है, इस संकटकाल में भारत ने अग्रणी भूमिका का निर्वहन किया विश्व के कई देशों को हाइड्रोक्सीक्लोरोक्वीन व पैरासिटामोल आदि दवाइयां देकर एक प्रभावशाली कार्य किया।[7] जबकि विश्व के सभी देशों को कोवैक्स वैक्सीन फैसिलिटी में शामिल होने की अंतिम तिथि विश्व स्वास्थ्य संगठन ने 31 अगस्त, 2020 रखी थी।

COVID-19 को लेकर विश्व के कई देशों में हुई इम्यूनिटी सामूहिक रोग प्रतिरोधक क्षमता (हर्ड इम्यूनिटी) की संकल्पना उत्पन्न हुई है। ब्रिटेन की सुप्रसिद्ध ऑक्सफोर्ड यूनिवर्सिटी ने ब्रिटेन में हर्ड इम्यूनिटी होने का दावा किया था, जबकि विशेषज्ञयों का मानना है कि देश में 70 प्रतिशत आबादी में वायरस को रोकने के लिए एंटीबाडीज का उत्पन्न होना जरूरी है तभी वायरस के प्रभाव को कम किया जा सकता है परंतु अभी यह एक संकल्पना ही है।

कोरोना के बाद की दुनिया

कोविड-19 के बाद की दुनिया का स्वरूप कैसा होगा ? विभिन्न विचारकों का मानना है कि विश्व में अलग-अलग स्वरूप दिख सकते हैं, कुछ का मानना है कि अमेरिका का वर्चस्व कम होगा जबकि चीन की स्थिति मजबूत होगी, क्योंकि चीन ने बहुत जल्दी कोरोना पर काबू पाया तथा संक्रमण एवं मत्यु दर भी कम हुई, जबकि अमेरिका में स्थिति बिल्कुल विपरीत रही है। ऐसे भी कयास लगाए जा रहे हैं कि विश्व राष्ट्रवाद में मजबूती आएगी क्योंकि वायरस ने विश्व की स्वास्थ्य व्यवस्था को कठघरे में खड़ा कर दिया है। कुछ विचारकों का यह भी मानना है कि विश्व में उग्र राष्ट्रवाद बढ़ सकता है तथा वैश्वीकरण का पक्ष कमजोर होगा, जबकि दूसरी ओर महामारी की आड़ में कुछ देश व राजनीतिक नेतृत्वकर्त्ता अपनी मनमानी व निरंकुशता को बढ़ाकर आम जनता के अधिकारों पर पाबंदियां थोप सकते हैं।

टोलेडो इंटरनेशनल सेंटर फॉर पीस के उपाध्यक्ष श्लोमो बेन एमी का मानना है कि महामारियों के समय परिवर्तन आना स्वाभाविक बात है, क्योंकि ऐसे समय में किसी भी देश के स्वास्थ्य आंतरिक व्यवस्था की पोल खुलती है और वह देश आम नागरिकों के स्वास्थ्य की कितनी चिंता करता है, सब कुछ सामने आ जाता है, कई

पुरानी मान्यताएं टूटती हैं और नई व्यवस्था व मान्यता नया रूप लेती है क्योंकि जब स्वास्थ्य व्यवस्था चरमरा जाती है तो किसी भी देश के लिए सोशल डिसटेंसिंग ही अंतिम विकल्प रह जाता है।

साहित्य के नोबेल विजेता फ्रेंच अल्जीरिन लेखक अल्बेयर कामू ने वर्तमान कोरोना महामारी को विश्व पटल पर देखने के नजरिये को अपने उपन्यास *द प्लेग* में लिखते हुए कहते हैं कि चीनी सरकार ने कोरोना से संक्रमित संख्या को दबाने की कोशिश की जिससे कि वह विश्व पटल पर आलोचना का पात्र न बन सके, जबकि अमेरिकी राष्ट्रपति ने तो इसे सीजनल फ्लू बताकर महामारी को गंभीर रूप दिया जो अब तक लाखों जीवन को अपने आगोश में ले चुका है। फरीद जकारिया कहते हैं कि 'The US president largely dismissed international warnings about the disease,and when he finally acted, did so unilaterally, not even bothering to inform his closest European allies before announcing travel bans on those countries. Predictably, Brazil''s Jair Bolsonaro and india''s Narendra Modi –populist nationalists like Trump-approached the pandemic with a similar distrust of any kind of global efforts or multilateral solutions.Modi reminded Indians of dangers of global supply chains and urged that they be 'vocal for local' buying and promting allthings made by country.'[8] इसी प्रकार ग्रेबियल गर्सिया मरकश ने अपने विश्व प्रसिद्ध पुस्तक Love in the Time of Cholera में महामारी के समय मनुष्य के जीवन संघर्ष और परिवर्तित मनोविज्ञान का चित्रण किया है जोकि वर्तमान कोरोना काल में किसी भी देश या समाज के व्यक्तिगत व सामुदायिक मनोविज्ञान को समझने के लिए सहायक हो सकता है। दूसरे अर्थों में साहित्य की इन दो प्रमुख रचनाओं के माध्यम से वैश्विक स्तर पर मनुष्य जीवन में होने वाले बदलाव को समझा जा सकता है। कोरोना महामारी ने विश्व के अधिकांश देशों को जिस प्रकार प्रभावित किया है वास्तव में इसे अकल्पनीय आपदा ही कहा जा सकता है।

श्लोमो का मानना है कि पूर्व की महामारियों ने भी आर्थिक संकट व सामाजिक विषमता को बढ़ाया है, चाहे दूसरी सदी में आए एंतोनाइन प्लेग हो या 541-542 ई. पूर्व में आया जस्टिनियन प्लेग, दोनों ने कई शतक तक अपना प्रभाव बनाए रखा

जिससे लाखों की संख्या में जनहानि हुई, लेकिन इसके लिए तत्कालीन रोम के शासकों ने ईसाई धर्मावलंबियों को जिम्मेदार माना, जबकि 14वी सदी में जब ब्लैकडैथ महामारी आई तो उस समय ईसाई धर्मावलम्बियों का संपूर्ण साम्राज्य में दबदबा था लेकिन उसका दोष यहूदियों पर मढ़ दिया गया, ऐसी ही स्थिति वर्तमान में कोविड-19 महामारी में भी देखने को मिली, कुछ देश की सरकारों ने एक विशेष वर्ग जाति व धर्म के लोगों को महामारी फैलाने का दोषी माना जबकि माहामारी ने अमीर-गरीब हर धर्म समुदाय के लोगों को अपनी चपेट में लिया।

श्लोमो बेन एकी आगाह करते हैं कि 'दो विश्व युद्धों से ये बात साबित हो गई थी कि संकीर्ण राष्ट्रवाद के साथ दुनिया में शांति और स्थिरता नहीं रह सकती, इस महामारी ने संकेत दे दिए हैं कि नेशन-स्टेट और अंतर्राष्ट्रीय संस्थाओं के बीच तत्काल एक नए संतुलन की जरूरत है इसके बिना कोरोना वायरस की महामारी और भी भयावह रूप लेगी।'[9]

युवाल नोआह हरारी जो कि एक इतिहासकार व दार्शनिक हैं और *सेपियंस एक ब्रीफ हिस्ट्री ऑफ ह्यूमन* जैसी प्रसिद्ध पुस्तक के लेखक हैं। उनका मानना है कि कोरोना के कारण अब सर्विलेंस प्रणाली को प्रमुखता दी जा सकती है। इसमें जनमानस में सरकारें बायोमैट्रिक ब्रेसलेट पहनाकर उनकी शारीरिक प्रत्येक गतिविधियों का डेटा जुटा सकती है। व्यक्ति को अपनी बीमारी का पता लगने से पहले सरकार तक उसकी रिर्पोट पहुंच जाएगी ऐसे में मानव समाज की जानकारी 'ओवर द स्किन' की जगह 'अंडर द स्किन' में बदल जाएगी क्योंकि बायोमैट्रिक ब्रेसलेट पहनने से डेटा सरकारी एल्गोरिध में एकत्रित होता रहेगा। जिसके माध्यम से बीमार व्यक्ति व उसकी बीमारी का विश्लेषण होता रहेगा उसकी प्रत्येक गतिविधियों को रिकॉर्ड कर संक्रमण फैलने से पूर्व ही रोका जा सकता है। वास्तव में यह एक बहुत क्रातिकारी परिवर्तन ला सकता है और सुनने में भी बहुत अच्छा लग रहा है, लेकिन इसके दूरगामी परिणाम क्या होंगे? क्योंकि खुशी, गम, प्रेम, करुणा, सहानुभूति, क्रोध यह सब मानवीय संवेदनाएं एवं भावनाएं हैं क्या उपरोक्त पद्धति से यह सब क्रियाकलाप सरकार की निगरानी में नहीं आ जाएंगे ? और हमारी प्रत्येक भावनाओं को सरकार हमारे विरूद्ध ही उपयोग कर हमें अपने बस में नहीं कर लेगी। हरारी कहते हैं, 'कोरोना वायरस का फैलाव नागरिकों के अधिकारों व कर्त्तव्यों का बड़ा इम्तहान है, अगर हमने सही फैसले नहीं लिए तो हम अपनी सबसे कीमती आजादियां खो देंगे। हम यह मान लेंगे कि सरकारी निगरानी सेहत की रक्षा करने

के सही फैसला है।'[10]

नोबेल पुरस्कार विजेता अर्थशास्त्री अमर्त्यसेन का मानना है कि कोरोना महामारी से दुनिया में विषमता की समस्या बढ़ी है और वर्तमान में भी यही विषमता समानता का रूप धारण नहीं कर पा रही है क्योंकि ब्राजील से बोलिविया और पोलैंड से हंगरी तक लोकतांन्त्रिक विरोध उत्पन्न हुआ है, जिसका परिणाम महामारी के समय विश्व को झेलना पड़ रहा है। अमर्त्यसेन का मानना है कि UNO, IMF, WORLD BANK, WHO जैसी संस्थाओं का जन्म द्वितीय विश्व युद्ध के परिणाम रहे हैं, विश्व युद्ध के बाद ब्रिटेन जैसा समृद्धशाली देश खाद्य संकट व कुपोषण से प्रभावित हुआ, लेकिन विश्व स्तरीय संस्थाओं के सहयोग से इस संकट को कम करने में सफल रहा। अमर्त्यसेन विषमता का उदाहरण देते हुए कहते हैं कि अमेरिका के शिकागो शहर में अफ्रीकी अमेरिकन की संख्या मात्र एक-तिहाई है, जबकि कोरोना से मरने वालों में 70 प्रतिशत अफ्रीकी अमेरिकन है। विषमता वाले देशों में कोरोना महामारी का फैलाव ज्यादा हुआ है चाहे वह भारत, ब्राजील या हंगरी ही क्यों न हो, सेन कहते हैं 'भारत एक और समस्या से जूझ रहा है लोकतंत्र के मायनों पर हमला किया जा रहा है और मीडिया की स्वतंत्रता पर शिकंजा कसता जा रहा है।'[11]

स्टीफन एम बॉल्ट हार्वर्ड यूनिवर्सिटी में इंटरनेशनल रिलेशन के प्रोफेसर हैं, जिनका मानना है कि कोरोना वायरस से देश अधिक मजबूती से राष्ट्रवाद की ओर बढ़े हैं, कोविड-19 के बाद दुनिया में एक बहुत बड़ा परिवर्तन देखने को मिलेगा कि पश्चिमी विश्व की ताकत पूर्व की ओर शिफ्ट हो सकती है, क्योंकि पूर्वी विश्व के देश सिंगापुर, दक्षिण कोरिया एवं चीन ने कोरोना महामारी को बहुत जल्दी काबू करने में आंशिक सफलता प्राप्त की।

इसी प्रकार काउन्सिल ऑफ फॉरेन रिलेशन के प्रमुख रिर्चड एन ह्रास भी मानते हैं कि अमेरिका प्रत्येक महामारी गें असफल रहा है, चाहे वह 2008 की मंदी हो या अब कोरोना महामारी हो, अमेरिका व चीन ने वैश्वीकरण को भी कठघरे में खड़ा किया है, क्योंकि जब दोनों सक्षम देशों को कोविड-19 की महामारी में मिल जुलकर काम करना था तो ऐसे दौर में दोनों देश एक-दूसरे पर आरोप-प्रत्यारोप लगाते रहे हैं जिससे लोगों व विश्व मे वैश्वीकरण की विचारधारा पर संदेह बढ़ा है।

फ्रैडरिका मोगेरिनी जो कि यूरोपीय यूनियन में विदेशी मामलों और सुरक्षा नीति की प्रतिनिधि रही है, उन्होने अपने प्रोजेक्ट 'सिंडिकेट' में मुख्यतः तीन बातों पर

प्रकाश डाला है प्रथमतः जब कोई महामारी फैलती है तो वहां किसी मुल्क, सरहद, जाति, धर्म, नस्ल, लिंग या राष्ट्रीयता आदि का कोई महत्व नहीं रह जाता, सबके साथ एक जैसा ही संक्रमण होता हैं। द्वितीय, महामारी में अपने पड़ोसी की देखभाल व सहयोग बहुत जरूरी है, क्योंकि यदि पड़ोसी देश महामारी से जूझ रहा है तो हमारे स्वास्थ्य का कोई मायने नहीं रह जाता, हम भी कहीं न कहीं प्रभावित अवश्य होते हैं। तृतीय बिंदु बहुत ही महत्वपूर्ण है, क्योंकि आज फैलते आक्रामक राष्ट्रवाद को कम करके वैश्विक समन्वय बढ़ाने की बहुत जरूरत है, तथा हमें अपने अंतर्राष्ट्रीय संस्थानों को संदेह के घेरे में न लाकर उन पर अपना विश्वास बढ़ाना चाहिए तथा उनमें अधिक से अधिक निवेश बढ़ाकर विश्व की रक्षा करनी चाहिए।

इंटरनेशनल इंस्टीट्यूट फॉर स्ट्रैटेजिक स्टडीज की उपमहानिदेशक कोरी शेक्स का मानना है कि विश्व में अमेरिका का वर्चस्व कम हुआ है, क्योंकि वह इस महामारी को समय रहते काबू में नही कर सका जबकि चीन ने समय रहते इस पर नियंत्रण कर अपने नागरिकों को सुरक्षा प्रदान की। अतः अब वैश्वीकरण चीन केंद्रित होती जाएगी, क्योंकि अमेरिकी आबादी का भरोसा वैश्वीकरण व अंतर्राष्ट्रीय संगठनों में कम हुआ है। राष्ट्रपति ट्रम्प द्वारा कई बार अंतर्राष्ट्रीय संगठन डब्ल्यू.एच.ओ. पर मनमानी करने का आरोप लगाया गया।

कोविड-19 से प्रभावित दुनिया एवं पाँच अग्रणी देशों की स्थिति

(18 नवंबर 2020 तक)

क्रम संख्या	*देश का नाम*	*संक्रमित मामले*	*मृत्यु*	*रिकवरी*
	विश्व	5,59,61,380	13,43,716	3,89,67,285
1.	संयुक्त राज्य अमेरिका	1,16,95,711	12,54,255	70,87,796
2.	भारत	89,12,907	1,31,031	83,35,109
3.	ब्राजील	59,11,758	1,66,743	53,61,592
4.	फ्रांस	20,36,755	46,273	1,43,152
5.	रूस	19,71,013	33,931	14,75,904

स्रोत : विभिन्न समाचार पत्रों से संकलित

कोरोना पश्चात् की आशंकाएं एवं संभावनाएं

कोरोना वायरस से जूझ रहे पूरे विश्व में अब भी अनिश्चितता की स्थिति है। प्रश्न यह उठता है कि कोरोना महामारी से व्यवस्था कब पटरी पर आएगी और आने के बाद विश्व में बदलाव की कई संभावनाएं बनने की उम्मीद है। मानवीय संवेदनाओं के साथ नई सोच व प्रतिमान बनाने की जरूरत होगी, क्योंकि इस महामारी ने व्यक्तिगत एवं सामाजिक दूरी को बढ़ावा दिया है, आपसी संबंधों व भाईचारे में संदेह का दायरा बढ़ा है जिसका सीधा प्रभाव हमारे संबंधों में दिखाई दे रहा है। इसीलिए समाज को पूर्व की भांति अपने आपसी संबंधों में अधिक विश्वास बढ़ाने की जरूरत है।

कोरोना काल व उसके पश्चात् यदि कोई व्यक्ति आक्रामक व्यवहार करता है तो उसे सामान्य व्यवहार की तरह लेना होगा, क्योंकि चिकित्सक, पुलिसकर्मी, विदेशों से आए लोग, विमान सेवा में कार्यरत लोगों से एक सामाजिक विषमता दिखाई देती है, जबकि ये वे लोग हैं जिन्होंने अपने कर्तव्य से मानवीय धर्म का पालन किया। अतः इन लोगों के साथ सदैव सहानुभूति से पेश आना चाहिए।

कोरोना वायरस ने सबसे अधिक शहरी क्षेत्र के लोगों को प्रभावित किया, क्योंकि भारत ही नहीं, विश्व में शहरीकरण की संस्कृति बढ़ती जा रही है, जिसके कारण बहुमंजिली इमारतें, घनी आबादी, अधिक कारखानों का निर्माण, जिसके कारण पर्यावरण प्रदूषण का बढ़ना आदि से शहरी क्षेत्रों की आबो-हवा खराब होती जा रही है कई शहर तो गैस चेंबर बनते जा रहे है। इस महामारी ने लोगों को बहुत गंभीर कष्ट दिया है क्योंकि मई-जून की भीषण गर्मी एवं 40 डिग्री से अधिक तापमान में चलते लू के थपेड़ों में सैकड़ों से हजारों किलोमीटर भूखे-प्यासे रात-दिन चलते जाना, साथ में अबोध बच्चों का दर्द, इतनी आसानी से भूल नही पाएंगे। इसीलिए हमारे वैज्ञानिकों, सरकारों व एन.जी.ओ. सभी को मिलकर बड़े शहरों को ग्रामीण क्षेत्रों में विकेंद्रीकरण करने का भी कोई प्लान तैयार करना होगा जिससे बड़े शहरों का बोझ कम हो सके।

महामारी के बाद व्यैक्तिक स्वास्थ्य (Personal Hygiene) के मानक बदलेंगे क्योंकि यही माना जाएगा कि किसी देश व राष्ट्र की स्वास्थ्य सेवाएँ कितनी समृद्ध व सुदृढ़ है। अंतर्राष्ट्रीय स्तर पर विकास और शक्ति की परिभाषा में परिवर्तन होगा, वास्तव में विकसित और शक्तिशाली देश वही माना जाएगा जो कि अपने नागरिकों की स्वास्थ्य संबंधी सुरक्षा को बेहतर तरीके से अंजाम देगा साथ ही वैश्विक स्तर पर अल्पविकसित और विकासशील देशों के स्वास्थ्य संबंधी आपदा का

संकटमोचक बनेगा।

सन्दर्भ

1. *Webster new world,* dictionary and thesaurus second edition,page no. 460.
2. Oxford advanced learner''s dictionary ,seventh edition -2005,page no.1096
3. गुप्ता रमेश, *आधुनिक जंतु विज्ञान,* प्रकाश पब्लिकेशन, मुजफ्फरनगर पृ. 1072।
4. http:\\www.bbc.com\hindi\international-52243699
5. http:\\www.bbc.com\hindi\international-52243699
6. *अमर उजाला,* संस्करण नई दिल्ली 06 मई, 2020।
7. navbharattimes.indiatime.com
8. Zakaria,Fareed, *Ten Lessons for a Post-Pandemic World,* Penguin Random House UK-2020
9. http:\\www.bbc.comèhidièinternational-52243699
10. http:\\www.bbc.comèhindièinternational-52243699
11. http:\\www.bbc.comèhindièinternational-52243699

15

वर्तमान वैश्विक राजनीति में शक्ति संतुलन और भारत

अमित कुमार शर्मा, आशा राणा

सारांश

विगत कुछ वर्षों में वैश्विक स्तर पर शक्ति संतुलन तथा अंतर्राष्ट्रीय राजनीति में परिवर्तन तीन दशकों की तुलना में तीव्र गति से हुआ है। इस परिवर्तन के परिणामस्वरूप विश्व राजनीति के केंद्र के रूप में क्रमशः भारत का उदय हुआ है दशकों से वैश्विक राजनीति के केंद्र के रूप में स्थापित अमेरिका-रूस, अमेरिका-खाड़ी देश अथवा अमेरिका-उत्तर कोरिया संबंध धीरे-धीरे वैश्विक राजनीति की परिधि पर पहुंचते जा रहे हैं। वर्तमान समय में चीन-वियतनाम, चीन-जापान, और चीन-अमेरिका संबंधों का ध्रुवीकरण क्रमशः भारत-चीन, भारत-पाक तथा भारत-अमेरिका संबंधों के रूप में परिवर्तित होता जा रहा है। इस वैश्विक परिस्थिति में रूस एक मौन सदस्य के रूप में लगभग तटस्थ राजनीतिक शक्ति के रूप में उभर रहा है जो संभवतः द्वितीय विश्वयुद्ध में अमेरिका के पूर्व राष्ट्रपति रूजवेल्ट की भूमिका निभाना चाहता है। वर्तमान समय में भारत आर्थिक, राजनीतिक एवं सामरिक दृष्टि से प्रमुख वैश्विक शक्तियों के लिए प्रमुख स्थान रखता है। प्रस्तुत शोध पत्र वर्तमान परिस्थितियों में वैश्विक, आर्थिक, राजनीतिक एवं सामरिक शक्ति के रूप में भारत की केंद्रीय भूमिका के साथ-साथ भारत पर वर्तमान परिस्थितियों के प्रभाव की विवेचना करने का प्रयास करता है।

कीवर्ड : वैश्विक व्यवस्था, अवमूल्यन, विघटन, परराष्ट्र, संवर्द्धक, तटस्थ, प्रौद्योगिकी, सामरिक, परिस्थिति।

प्रस्तावना

विश्व के सभी राष्ट्र अपनी विकासात्मक आवश्यकताओं के संदर्भ में परराष्ट्र संबंधों का निर्धारण करते हैं। राष्ट्र अपने राष्ट्रहितों की पूर्ति हेतु अन्य राष्ट्रों से प्राथमिकता के आधार पर अपने संबंधों का निर्धारण एवं संचालन करते हैं। भारत शांतिप्रिय देश है एवं अहिंसा और सहअस्तित्व के सिद्धांत का समर्थक रहा है। वर्तमान समय में अंतर्राष्ट्रीय राजनीतिक परिदृश्य अत्यंत जटिल और चुनौतिपूर्ण होता जा रहा है। अतंर्राष्ट्रीय राजनीति के क्षेत्र में नए-नए राजनीतिक, आर्थिक एवं सामरिक गठबंधन अस्तित्व में आ रहे हैं एवं दूसरी ओर पुराने गठबंधन भंग हो रहे है। वैश्विक राजनीति में शक्ति के नए समीकरण आकार ले रहे हैं शक्ति के अनेक केंद्र अस्तित्व में आ गए हैं जो वैश्विक आर्थिक और सामरिक शक्ति अमेरिका को एवं उसके दृष्टिकोण को विभिन्न माध्यमों एवं स्वरूपों में चुनौती दे रहे हैं। वैश्विक परिस्थितियों में परिवर्तन के फलस्वरूप वैश्विक महाशक्तियां शक्ति संतुलन को अपने पक्ष में बनाये रखने के लिए नए गठबंधनों के लिए प्रयासरत् हैं। ऐसी परिस्थितियों में भारत की भूमिका महत्वपूर्ण हो गई है।

वैश्विक राजनीति में शक्ति संतुलन

26 दिसंबर, 1991 को सोवियत संघ रूस टूट कर बिखर गया। इससे पूर्व तक वैश्विक राजनीति में दो ध्रुव थे, लेकिन इस ऐतिहासिक घटनाक्रम के पश्चात् संयुक्त राज्य अमेरिका विश्व में एक मात्र शक्ति रह गया, सोवियत संघ ने 1991 के पूर्व तक अमेरिका को वैश्विक राजनीति के हर क्षेत्र में संतुलित और संयमित रखा। विघटन के पश्चात् सोवियत संघ के उत्तराधिकारी रूस में नए संकटों का दौर शुरू हुआ, रूस अब इतना शक्तिशाली नहीं था कि वह अमेरिका का सामना कर सके और उसे आर्थिक चुनौतियों का भी सामना करना पड़ रहा था।

सन् 1994 में रूस और चेचन्या के बीच संघर्ष का दौर शुरू हुआ आर्थिक चुनौतियों के संदर्भ में रूस ने अगस्त 1998 में सार्वजनिक रूप से घोषणा कि वह अपने ऋण एवं प्रतिभूतियों को चुकाने में सक्षम नहीं है इस समय रूसी मुद्रा का अवमूल्यन भी तीव्र गति से होने लगा और रूबल की कीमत 70 प्रतिशत तक गिर गई। रूस को चेचन्या के विद्रोहियों के साथ-साथ जार्जिया की क्रांति, यूक्रेन संकट, सीरिया संकट आदि से भी जूझना पड़ रहा था।

चेचन्या युद्ध के दौरान ही दिसंबर 1999 में राष्ट्रपति वोरिस येल्तसिन ने त्यागपत्र दे दिया। येल्तसिन ने व्लादिमीर पुतिन को रूस का कार्यवाहक राष्ट्रपति बना दिया, पुतिन के नेतृत्व में रूस अपनी खोई हुई शक्ति को प्राप्त करने में निरंतर अग्रसर है। सन् 1999 में व्लादिमीर पुतिन प्रधानमंत्री के पद पर नियुक्त हुए इसके पश्चात् 2000 से 2008 तक वह राष्ट्रपति पद पर चुने गए। इसके पश्चात् 2008 से 2012 तक पुतिन फिर प्रधानमंत्री पद पर रहे और 2012 से वर्तमान तक रूस के राष्ट्रपति के रूप में पद पर बने हुए हैं।

पुतिन के नेतृत्व में फरवरी 2014 में रूस ने पश्चिमी देशों के व्यापक विरोध के बाद भी यूक्रेन में हस्तक्षेप करके उसके स्वायत्तशासी क्षेत्र क्रीमिया पर कब्जा कर लिया और वैश्विक राजनीति में अपनी शक्ति का प्रदर्शन किया। पुतिन के नेतृत्व में रूस इतना शक्तिशाली हो गया कि पश्चिमी देशों के साथ अपने संबंधों, संधि-समझौतों को अपने अनुसार परिभाषित करने लगा है।

रूस ने सीरिया के राष्ट्रपति बशर-अल-असद का साथ दिया और सीरिया की सेना के साथ गठबंधन भी किया। मध्य पूर्व में सीरिया, अमेरिका और अन्य पश्चिमी देशों की आंखों की किरकिरी बना हुआ था, लेकिन रूस का साथ मिलने पर पश्चिमी देश सीरिया में चाहकर भी कुछ नहीं कर पाए। रूस, सीरिया का साथ देने पर विश्व के अन्य देशों को वह यह संदेश देने में सफल रहा कि वह अपने मित्र देशों का साथ कभी नहीं छोड़ता ।

सन् 2012 में ब्लादिमीर पुतिन के राष्ट्रपति बनने के पश्चात् शायद ही कोई ऐसा अंतर्राष्ट्रीय विषय हो जिसमें प्रत्यक्ष या अप्रत्यक्ष रूप से रूस की भूमिका ना रही हो, रूस हर क्षेत्र में अमेरिका के सामने दिखाई देता है। इन मामलों से पता चलता है कि रूस एक बार फिर वैश्विक परिदृश्य में अपना स्थान अर्जित कर चुका है।

सीरिया के साथ-साथ मध्य पूर्व के देशों में भी रूस का कूटनीतिक हस्तक्षेप निरंतर बढ़ रहा है। कुछ ही वर्षों में रूस ने यहां अपनी स्थिति को सुदृढ़ किया है और अमेरिका की स्थिति इस क्षेत्र में कमजोर हुई है। मध्य पूर्व में रूस की कूटनीतिक सफलता सीरिया और ईरान से उसके अच्छे संबंध के साथ-साथ इन देशों के धुर विरोधी इजराइल के साथ भी श्रेष्ठ सामंजस्य के रूप में दृष्टिगोचर होती है। रूस और तुर्की के दोस्ताना संबंध भी वैश्विक जगत में अचरज का विषय है। रूस ने दशकों बाद अफगानिस्तान में अपनी सक्रियता से विश्व राजनाति में हलचल पैदा

कर दी है। सबसे उल्लेखनीय विषय रूस द्वारा अमेरिकी चुनाव में हस्तक्षेप की घटना रही हैं। अमेरिकी विद्वानों के अनुसार रूस अपने वर्चस्व को स्थापित करने के लिए कुछ भी करने को तैयार है। विघटन के पश्चात् वैश्विक राजनीति में आई रिक्तता को बहुत हद तक रूस ने भर दिया है। अमेरिका के सहयोगी देश विश्व राजनीति में अमेरिका के कम होते वर्चस्व के कारण रूस और उसके सहयोगी देशों के साथ सहयोगात्मक संबंधों को बढ़ाने पर जोर दे रहे हैं। पुतिन के नेतृत्व में वैश्विक राजनीति में रूस सुदृढ़ राजनीतिक शक्ति के रूप में उभरकर सामने आया है।

शक्ति संतुलन में परिवर्तन

अंतर्राष्ट्रीय राजनीति में समय के साथ-साथ परिवर्तन होता रहता है संचार साधनों एवं प्रौद्योगिकी में क्रांतिकारी परिवर्तन से एक ऐसी वैश्विक व्यवस्था का सृजन हो रहा है, जिसमें शक्ति को धारण करने वाले एक-दो प्रमुख राष्ट्र न होकर अनेक राष्ट्र हैं जो शक्ति को धारित करते हैं। वर्तमान समय में अंतर्राष्ट्रीय राजनीति का परिदृश्य ऐसा है जिसमें अंतर्राष्ट्रीय मामलों के निर्धारण की क्षमता अनेक प्रमुख राष्ट्रों के पास है अंतराष्ट्रीय क्षेत्र में यह स्थिति दो ध्रुवीय या एक ध्रुवीय व्यवस्था से बिल्कुल भिन्न है।

तकनीक एवं संचार साधनों के विकास से विश्व भर के राष्ट्रों में परस्पर सहयोग एवं निर्भरता का सृजन हुआ है। विश्व राजनीति एवं अर्थव्यवस्था का केंद्र पश्चिमी राष्ट्रों से परिवर्तित होकर एशिया प्रायद्वीप बन गया है। विश्व राजनीति में एशिया वैश्विक प्रतिस्पर्धा का मंच बन गया है। एशिया के दो बडे राष्ट्र क्रमशः चीन और भारत वैश्विक अर्थव्यवस्था और राजनीति में महत्वपूर्ण भूमिका रखते हैं। एशिया क्षेत्र में चीन के उत्थान से विश्व के अनेक राष्ट्र सशंकित हैं कि वह वैश्विक भू-राजनीति में किस प्रकार की भूमिका निभाएगा। विश्व राजनीतिक पटल पर शक्ति संतुलन में परिवर्तन से नई चुनौतियां सृजित हुई हैं भारत दक्षिण एशिया, मध्य एशिया, दक्षिण-पूर्व एशिया में अनेक स्तरों पर परस्पर शक्ति संतुलन में उलझा हुआ है।

वर्तमान विश्व राजनीति के दृष्टिगत भारत के लिए अंतर्राष्ट्रीय राजनीति में अनेक संभावनाएं दिखाई पड़ती है। अनेक राष्ट्र वैश्विक जगत में भारत की सकारात्मक भूमिका एवं उसके बढ़ते प्रभाव को मान्यता प्रदान करते हैं।

भारत और विश्व समुदाय

पंडित नेहरू ने वैदेशिक संबंधों के संचालन में एक नवीन सिद्धांत की रचना की, परिणामस्वरूप एक ऐसी विदेश नीति सामने आई जिसका लक्ष्य साम्राज्यवाद, उपनिवेशवाद का विरोध, शक्ति ध्रुवों का विरोध करते हुए संयुक्त राष्ट्र के निर्णयों के क्रम में की जाने वाली प्रभुत्व की होड़ को मर्यादित करना था।[1] भारत ने स्वतंत्रता के पश्चात् अपने वैदेशिक संबंधों और परराष्ट्र नीति को तत्कालीन मांग के अनुरूप निर्मित किया। रूस और अमेरिका अंतर्राष्ट्रीय संबंधों के संचालन और विश्व के राष्ट्रों की विदेश नीति के व्यवहार के लिए महत्वपूर्ण कारकों में से एक रहे हैं। भारत ने शीत युद्ध में रत दोनों परस्पर विरोधी गठबंधनों से अलग रहने का निर्णय लिया और प्रत्येक अंतर्राष्ट्रीय वाद-विवाद में श्रेष्ठता, योग्यता के आधार पर निर्णय लेने की स्वतंत्रता का अवलंबन किया। इस नीति का अभिप्राय विश्व समुदाय से अलगाव या तटस्थ रहना बिल्कुल भी नहीं था बल्कि इसका अभिप्राय यह था कि अंतर्राष्ट्रीय मामलों का अधिक गंभीरता और जिम्मेदारी के साथ निर्णय लिया जाए और अनावश्यक मामलों से अपने आप को पृथक किया जाए। भारत ने परस्पर विरोधी वैश्विक विचारधाराओं का त्याग करते हुए, राष्ट्र निर्माण एवं सामरिक हितों के दृष्टिगत विश्व की दोनों ही प्रमुख शक्तियों के साथ अपने संबंधों का संचालन सुनिश्चित किया। भारत ने अपने विकास के लिए समाजवादी मिश्रित अर्थव्यवस्था का अनुसरण किया और अंतर्राष्ट्रीय क्षेत्र में शांति, मैत्री और सहअस्तित्व, अनाक्रमण आदि सिद्धांतों को अपनाया।

भारत और अमेरिका दोनों ही देशों के इतिहास में साम्यता दिखाई देती है। दोनों ही देशों ने एक लंबे समय तक पराधीनता से मुक्ति के लिए संघर्ष किया और इसके फलस्वरूप प्राप्त सफलता के पश्चात् दोनों ही देशों ने लोकतांत्रिक शासन प्रणाली को अपने-अपने देशों के लिए उपयुक्त समझा। अमेरिका विश्व का सबसे प्राचीन लोकतांत्रिक मूल्यों वाला राज्य है, तो दूसरी ओर भारत विश्व का सबसे बड़ा लोकतांत्रिक व्यवस्था वाला देश है। भारत और अमेरिका में लोकतांत्रिक साम्यता के बाद भी अपने-अपने राष्ट्रहितों, राष्ट्रविकास और वैश्विक संबंधों के निर्धारण में व्यापक गतिरोध रहा है और इस गतिरोध के कारण दोनों देशों के संबंधों में प्रारंभिक दौर में कोई प्रगति नहीं हुई। अमेरिका विश्व में पूंजीवादी विचारधारा का पोषक, संवर्द्धक एवं नेतृत्वकर्त्ता रहा है, वहीं दूसरी ओर भारत विचारधारा के रूप में तटस्थ

रहा और उसने गुटनिरपेक्ष आंदोलन का नेतृत्व किया। सन् 1955 अनेक प्रकार से भारत के लिए अंतर्राष्ट्रीय क्षेत्र में महत्वपूर्ण वर्ष था। विदेश नीति और सुरक्षा संबंधी उन दुविधाओं के संबंध में यह निर्णायक वर्ष था, जिनका भारत को छठे दशक के प्रारंभिक वर्षों तक सामना करना पड़ा।[2] सन् 1950-60 के दशक से अमेरिका द्वारा भारत के पड़ोसी और परंपरागत शत्रु पाकिस्तान को भारी मात्रा में आर्थिक और सैन्य सहायता उपलब्ध कराई जाने लगी। सन् 1954 में अमेरिका और पाकिस्तान के बीच एक सैनिक संधि हुई जिसके अंतर्गत भारत के विरोध के बावजूद पाकिस्तान को विशाल पैमाने पर शस्त्र देने का निर्णय लिया गया।[3] पाकिस्तान वर्ष 1954-55 में बगदाद संधि और सीटो (साउथ ईस्ट अटलांटिक ट्रीटी) जैसे अमेरिकी सैनिक गठबंधनों का सदस्य बन चुका था जो भारत के लिए चिंता का विषय था। भारत ने अपनी सीमाओं की सुरक्षा एवं राष्ट्रीय विकास, तकनीक, सैन्य विकास के संदर्भ में सोवियत संघ से अपने संबंधों का संचालन सुनिश्चित किया जिसके फलस्वरूप 1955 में सोवियत संघ के राष्ट्रपति ख्रुश्चेव भारत यात्रा पर आए और भारत में रूस के सहयोग से कईं परियोजनाएं प्रारंभ हुई भारत और रूस के सहयोगात्मक संबंधों के बाद गुटनिरपेक्ष आंदोलन का प्रथम सम्मेलन इंडोनेशिया के बांडुंग में हुआ। इस गुटनिरपेक्ष सम्मेलन में एशिया-अफ्रीका के नवोदित राष्ट्रों ने प्रतिभाग लिया। भारत गुटनिरपेक्ष राष्ट्रों के नेता के रूप में उभरा और उसे अधिकांश एशिया-अफ्रीका के राष्ट्रों का समर्थन प्राप्त हुआ। भारत के नेतृत्व में गुटनिरपेक्ष सदस्यों ने शांति एवं मैत्रीभाव के साथ वैश्विक विचारधाराओं से पृथक रहते हुए अपने-अपने राष्ट्रों के विकास का संकल्प लिया। भारत गुटनिरपेक्ष आंदोलन के संस्थापक सदस्यों में से एक रहा है। गुटनिरपेक्ष आंदोलन के नेतृत्वकर्त्ता के रूप में विश्व समुदाय में भारत की प्रभावशीलता में उल्लेखनीय वृद्धि हुई है ।

सन् 1955 में सोवियत राष्ट्रपति ख्रुश्चेव की यात्रा से भारत और रूस के संबंध मैत्रीपूर्ण रहे हैं। रूस ने भारी मशीनरी, खनन, ऊर्जा उत्पादन और इस्पात संयंत्रों, तकनीक हस्तांतरण आदि के क्षेत्रों में निवेश एवं तकनीकी सहयोग किया जिससे भारत को आर्थिक निर्भरता का लक्ष्य प्राप्त हुआ। भारत पर जब भी क्षेत्रीय या अंतर्राष्ट्रीय दबाव पड़ा, रूस भारत के अभिन्न सहयोगी के रूप में नजर आया, फलस्वरूप भारत का भी यही दृष्टिकोण रहा। भारत के युद्धों और वैश्विक प्रकृति के मामलों में रूस भारत का एक मजबूत मित्र रहा है। जब भी अमेरिकी और पश्चिमी देशों ने रूस को वैश्विक परिदृश्य से छिन्न-भिन्न करने का प्रयास किया,

भारत ने सदैव रूस का सहयोग और समर्थन किया। भारत और रूस की 1971 की शांति-मैत्री एवं सहयोग संधि दोनों देशों के साझा लक्ष्यों की अभिव्यक्ति थी, इसके साथ ही यह संधि क्षेत्रिय एवं वैश्विक शांति का प्रारूप भी थी। सोवियत संघ के विघटन के बाद रूस के कमजोर होने पर भी भारत और रूस के संबंधों में गतिहीनता नहीं आई दोनों देशों द्वारा 1993 में शांति-मैत्री एवं सहयोग की एक नई संधि को अपनाया गया तथा 1994 में द्विपक्षीय सैन्य सहयोग समझौते पर हस्ताक्षर किए। रूस दशकों से परमाणु ऊर्जा, तेल और गैस, अंतरिक्ष आदि महत्वपूर्ण क्षेत्रों में भारत का अग्रणी साझेदार रहा है, अक्टूबर 2000 में अटल बिहारी वाजपेयी और पुतिन द्वारा भारत सामरिक साझेदारी की घोषणा पर हस्ताक्षर किए गए। इसके पश्चात् रूस भारत का प्रथम रणनीतिक साझेदार बन गया।

दोनों देशों के संबंधों में पारस्परिक सहयोग बना रहा। भारत को रूस की तकनीक और प्रौद्योगिकी का हस्तांतरण एवं आपूर्ति होती रही और भारत भी रूस की आर्थिक आवश्यकताओं को पूरा करने में सहयोग करता रहा। भारत और रूस के नेतृत्व की यात्राओं से दोनों देशों के संबंधों में गतिशीलता बनी रही, भारत को सामरिक एवं वैश्विक मुद्दों पर रूस का सहयोग और समर्थन प्राप्त होता रहा, रक्षा क्षेत्र से जुड़ी आवश्यकताओं को भी रूस ने समय समय पर पूर्ण किया।

मार्च 1997 में भारत-रूस शिखर सम्मेलन संपन्न हुआ। इस सम्मेलन में दोनों देशों के बीच प्रमुख समझौतों पर सहमति बनी और रूस ने संयुक्त राष्ट्र संघ में भारत की स्थायी सदस्यता का समर्थन किया। सन् 2004 में भारत के रक्षा अनुसंधान एवं विकास संगठन एवं रूस के फेडरल स्टेट यूनिटरी एंटरप्राइज के संयुक्त उद्यम ब्रह्मोस एयरोस्पेस ने कई परीक्षण किए। सन् 2007 में पूर्वी सागर में संयुक्त नौ सेना का अभ्यास हुआ, इसी वर्ष भारतीय वायु सेना और रूस की वायु सेना का संयुक्त युद्धाभ्यास भी रूस में पूर्ण हुआ। सन् 2012 में पुतिन की भारत यात्रा के दौरान 42 नई सुखोई विमानों के उत्पादन का समझौता किया गया। सन् 2016 में दोनों देशों ने ब्रह्मोस की नई पीढ़ी को विकसित करने के लिए समझौता किया। सन् 2018 में भारत रूस शिखर सम्मेलन के दौरान भारत रूस रक्षा समझौता, अमेरिका के द्वारा रूस, ईरान, उत्तर कोरिया पर लगाए गए व्यापार प्रतिबंधों के बाद भी पूर्ण किया गया। इस रक्षा समझौते से भारत और रूस के सहयोगात्मक संबंधों की निरंतरता और मैत्रीपूर्ण संबंधों की आत्मीयता को समझा जा सकता है।

शीत युद्ध के दौरान भारत-अमेरिका के संबंधों में निरंतरता व सहयोग का

अभाव दृष्टिगोचर होता है। भारत-अमेरिका संबंधों के निर्धारण में भारत-पाक, भारत-चीन और भारत-सोवियत संबंधों की पृष्ठभूमि रही है। अमेरिका-भारत की गुटनिरपेक्ष नीति एवं समाजवादी विचारधारा वाले एक नए देश चीन को मान्यता देने से अप्रसन्न था। समय-समय पर सोवियत संघ और चीन द्वारा वैश्विक सामरिक स्थितियों को परिवर्तित करने का प्रयास किया गया तो अमेरिका द्वारा रूस और चीन के कदमों का विरोध किया गया। इन विरोध प्रस्तावों में भारत ने अमेरिका का सहयोग व समर्थन नहीं किया। अमेरिका द्वारा पाकिस्तान को दी जा रही सैन्य आर्थिक सहायता ने भी भारत-अमेरिका संबंधों को सही मार्ग पर नहीं आने दिया। दोनों देशों की परस्पर विरोधी नीतियों से भी संबंधों को आघात पहुंचा, भारत ने अंतर्राष्ट्रीय क्षेत्र में शांतिपूर्ण सहअस्तित्व की नीति का अनुसरण किया और अमेरिका के सैनिक गठबंधनों से अपने को अलग रखा।

शीत युद्ध के पश्चात् वैश्विक परिदृश्य में परिवर्तन के साथ ही अमेरिका विश्व की एकमात्र शक्ति रह गया और भारत द्वारा अपनी अर्थव्यवस्था में उदारीकरण के प्रयासों के कारण दोनों देशों के संबंधों पर जमी बर्फ पिघलने लगी। भारतीय अर्थव्यवस्था में उदारीकरण की प्रक्रिया के फलस्वरूप दोनों देशों के संबंधों का नवीन दृष्टिकोण विकसित हुआ। दोनों देशों के बीच व्यापार बढ़ने लगा। भारत की ढ़ांचागत विकास परियोजनाओं में अमेरिकी निवेश तेजी के साथ बढ़ा।

अमेरिका के राष्ट्रपति की भारत यात्रा (सन् 2000) से दोनों देशों के संबंधों को नया आयाम मिला और भारत के प्रति अमेरिकी नीति में परिवर्तन हुआ सन् 1998 में भारत ने परमाणु परीक्षण किया जिसके फलस्वरूप अमेरिका ने भारत पर आर्थिक प्रतिबंध लगाए सन् 2001 में अमेरिका ने आर्थिक प्रतिबंधों को हटा लिया।

इस दौर में भारत-अमेरिका संबंधों में प्रगति दोनों ही देशों की आवश्यकता रही है। भारत को वैश्विक मंचों पर अमेरिका के समर्थन की आवश्यकता थी, वहीं अमेरिका को चीन के बढ़ते प्रभाव को संतुलित करने हेतु दक्षिण एशिया में एक स्थायी और मजबूत सहयोगी की आवश्यकता थी। दोनों देशों के प्रगाढ़ होते संबंधों का प्रमाण सिविल परमाणु सहयोग समझौता है, जिसे दोनों ही देशों ने (2008) अंतिम रूप देने में सफलता प्राप्त की।

सन् 2010 में अमेरिका के राष्ट्रपति बराक ओबामा ने भारत की यात्रा की और भारत में निवेश, व्यापार, तकनीकी हस्तांतरण जैसे अनेक मुख्य विषयों पर समझौते किए दोनों ही देशों ने आर्थिक सहयोग और व्यापार वृद्धि लक्ष्य रखा। सन् 2015

में बराक ओबामा दूसरी बार भारत यात्रा पर आए और भारत-अमेरिका संबंधों ने एक नए स्तर को प्राप्त किया। दोनों देशों ने जलवायु परिवर्तन, अंतर्राष्ट्रीय आतंकवाद, मानवाधिकार जैसे अंतर्राष्ट्रीय मुद्दों पर सहयोग और सहमति बनी।

विश्व में केंद्रीय भूमिका में भारत

भारत की वैश्विक भूमिका के संबंध में 2014 से 2020 का कालखंड महत्वपूर्ण रहा है इस कालखंड में भारत की वैश्विक भूमिका एवं प्रभाव में वृद्धि हुई है।

मोदी भारत में (2014) सत्ता में आई मोदी सरकार ने अपने शपथ ग्रहण कार्यक्रम में सार्क देशों के राष्ट्राध्यक्षों को आमंत्रित किया मोदी सरकार के इस कदम को पड़ोसी देशों के साथ संबंधों को सुधारने की पहल के रूप में देख गया।

मोदी सरकार ने भारत के वैश्विक प्रभाव एवं साख में वृद्धि हेतु विश्वभर के प्रमुख देशों की यात्राएं कीं। मोदी के विदेश दौरों और दूरदर्शी नीति के कारण भारत के अंतर्राष्ट्रीय संबंधों में प्रगति हुई।

नवंबर 2015 में भारत और फ्रांस दोनों ही देशो ने मिलकर सोलर अलायंस का गठन किया।

जून 2016 में भारत मिसाइल टेक्नोलॉजी कंट्रोल रिजिम (MTCR) का सदस्य बना।

नवंबर 2016 में भारत विश्व की सबसे बड़ी न्यूक्लियर लैब (CERN) का सदस्य बना।

जून 2017 में शंघाई सहयोग संगठन (SCO) की बैठक में पूर्ण सदस्य के रूप में सम्मिलित हुआ, (SCO) का सदस्य बनने में भारत को रूस का सहयोग प्राप्त हुआ।

रक्षा सहयोग

भारत-अमेरिका

भारत ने अमेरिकी कंपनी बोइंग से 2015 में 22 अपाचे और 15 चिनूक हेलीकॉप्टर खरीदने का समझौता किया

भारत-जापान

जापान ने भारत की अंतरिक्ष और रक्षा क्षेत्र से संबंधित छह संस्थाओं को फॉरेन

एवं यूजर्स लिस्ट से हटा दिया है जिससे रक्षा तकनीक में परस्पर सहयोग हो सके, दोनों देश यू-एस 2 को भारत में ही निर्मित करने का कार्य करने पर सहमत हुए।

भारत-जर्मनी

मोदी ने जर्मनी यात्रा से पूर्व जर्मनी की रक्षा मंत्री ने भारत की यात्रा की जिसमें उन्होंने **'क्षेत्रीय और अंतर्राष्ट्रीय सुरक्षा के साथ रक्षा के साथ द्विपक्षीय सम्बन्धों को सुदृढ़'** बनाने की बात कही। प्रधानमंत्री मोदी की जर्मनी यात्रा ने द्विपक्षीय संबंधों को नया आयाम दिया।

भारत-फ्रांस

भारत और फ्रांस दोनों देशों ने बहुप्रतिष्ठित रॉफेल विमानों के सौदे को पूर्ण किया है। जिसमें भारत को कुछ रॉफेल विमानों की खेप प्राप्त भी हो चुकी है।

भारत-रूस

पुतिन-मोदी विचार-विमर्श में मोदी ने कहा भारत-रूस के साथ परमाणु ऊर्जा, अंतरिक्ष, व्यापार और निवेश संबंधों को नवीन स्तर तक ले जाएगा। स्टॉकहोम इंटरनेशनल पीस रिसर्च इंस्टीट्यूट के अध्ययन के अनुसार प्रमुख हथियारों के आयात करने का आंकड़ा पूर्व की तुलना में 140 प्रतिशत बढ़ा है।

भारत-इजरायल

भारत और इजरायल के बीच दो अरब डॉलर का रक्षा सौदा हुआ, जिसके तहत इजरायल भारत को जमीन से हवा में मार करने वाला मिसाइल सिस्टम देगा। इजरायल की (सरकारी) रक्षा कंपनी (आई.ए.आई.) मेक इन इंडिया के अंतर्गत (DRDO) के साथ विकसित करेगी।

मोदी की विदेश नीति में **नेबरहुड फर्स्ट पॉलिसी** एवं **एक्ट ईस्ट पॉलिसी** को प्राथमिकता दी गई। भारत ने अपने पड़ोसी देशों से संचालित होने वाले उग्रवादी, आतंकवादी घटनाओं के संबंध में भी कठोर निर्णय लेते हुए **हाट परस्यूड (10 जून, 2015)**, **सर्जिकल स्ट्राइक (29 सितंबर 2016)**, **एयर स्ट्राइक (26 फरवरी, 2019)** जैसे ऑपरेशन के माध्यम से म्यमांर और पाकिस्तान की सीमा में घुसकर आतंकी कैंपों पर कार्रवाई की। भारत की कार्रवाई को विश्व के प्रमुख राष्ट्रों का समर्थन प्राप्त

हुआ और भारत आतंकवाद के विषय पर पाकिस्तान को अलग-थलग करने में सफल रहा, कश्मीर के मुद्दे पर पाकिस्तान को चीन के अतिरिक्त किसी देश का सहयोग नहीं मिला, मोदी की कूटनीति से अरब राष्ट्रों का सहयोग और समर्थन भी भारत को प्राप्त हुआ। अमेरिका के **ह्यूस्टन में हाउडी मोदी** जैसे कार्यक्रम करके मोदी ने प्रवासी भारतीयों को भारत में निवेश करने के लिए को प्रोत्साहित किया।

डोकलाम विवाद में भारत के मुखर होने के कारण चीन को भी यहां से पीछे हटना पड़ा। मोदी 1 में भारत की विदेश नीति में महत्वपूर्ण परिवर्तन यह रहा कि भारत की नीति पाकिस्तान से हटकर चीन केंद्रित हो गई है।

यह निष्कर्ष **'बुलेटिन ऑफ एटॉमिक साइंटिस्टस'** में प्रकाशित एक अध्ययन का है, इस अध्ययन के अनुसार यह परिवर्तन **2017 के डोकलाम गतिरोध** के बाद से हुआ है।

मोदी-2 कार्यकाल में **5 अगस्त को** भारत ने जम्मू-कश्मीर के राज्य के स्तर को समाप्त करके दो केंद्र शासित प्रदेशों के रूप में परिवर्तित कर दिया। **धारा 370** को भी समाप्त कर दिया गया। दिसंबर में संसद द्वारा पारित नागरिकता संशोधन अधिनियम (सी.ए.ए.) पर पाकिस्तान और चीन ने भारत का विरोध किया।

चीन का विश्व के अधिकांश देशों के साथ विवाद रहा है। दक्षिण चीन सागर में चीन का ताइवान, फिलीपींस, मलेशिया, ब्रुनेई, इण्डोनेशिया, सिंगापुर, जापान और वियतनाम आदि देशों से विवाद है। पूर्वी चीन सागर में चीन का जापान से विवाद, पूर्वी चीन सागर के सेनकाकुश द्वीपों की शृंखला को लेकर है।

चीन के अमेरिका और ब्रिटेन के साथ हांगकांग और उइगर मुस्लिमों के मानवाधिकारों के विषयों को लेकर गतिरोध है।

चीन का रूस और भारत के साथ भी सीमा संबंधी विवाद है भारत की वैश्विक, आर्थिक, राजनीतिक एवं सामरिक शक्ति के केंद्र के रूप में उदय के कारण चीन भारत को अपने घरेलू विषयों में ही उलझा के रखना चाहता है।

दिसंबर 2019 में चीन के वुहान शहर से निकली कोरोना वायरस ने विश्व के अधिकांश देशों को अपनी चपेट में ले लिया। चीनी नेतृत्व पर दुनिया से कोरोना वायरस के तथ्यों को छुपाने के आरोप लगे, जिसके कारण कोरोना वायरस दूसरे देशों में पहुंचकर महामारी में परिवर्तित हो गया। कोविड 19 से विश्व के अधिकांश देशों में 10 लाख लोगों की मृत्यु हो गई। भारत ने 62 देशों के साथ यूरोपियन यूनियन व आस्ट्रेलिया की ओर से कोरोना वायरस फैलाने के जिम्मेदार कारणों की जांच की

मांग करने वाले प्रारूप, प्रस्ताव को मंजूरी देते हुए उस पर हस्ताक्षर कर दिए हैं।

विश्व के प्रमुख देशों का ध्यान कोरोना महामारी से हटाने के लिए चीन अपनी सीमाओं पर और दक्षिणी चीन सागर में आक्रामक रणनीति का सहारा ले रहा है और युद्धाभ्यास जैसी सैनिक गतिविधियों में संलग्न है। भारत के लद्दाख राज्य के गलवान वैली में भी चीनी सेनाओं ने अतिक्रमण करने की कोशिश की जिसका भारतीय सेनाओं ने समय रहते जवाब दिया जिसका समर्थन विश्व के प्रमुख देशों ने किया।

भारत की सीमाओं पर और दक्षिण चीन सागर में चीन ने युद्ध जैसे हालात बना रखे हैं। कोविड 19 के पश्चात् नई वैश्विक व्यवस्था में भारत आर्थिक और सामरिक रूप से केंद्रीय भूमिका में उभरकर सामने आया। अमेरिका, आस्ट्रेलिया, जापान, दक्षिणी चीन सागर में चीन को संतुलित करने के लिए भारत से सहयोग की अपेक्षा कर रहे हैं और क्वाड (दि क्वाड्रिलैटरल सिक्योरिटी डायलॉग) के माध्यम से अपनी सामरिक स्थिति को सुदृढ़ करना चाहते हैं। यूरोपियन यूनियन और विश्व के प्रमुख देश अपने अपने व्यापारिक गतिविधियों को चीन से समेट रहे हैं और भारत इस संबंध में बड़ी भूमिका निभाने की तैयारी में है

निष्कर्ष

विश्व व्यवस्था, क्षेत्रीय संतुलन और सामरिक दृष्टि से महत्वपूर्ण सीमावर्ती इलाकों, सागरीय संप्रभुता से खिलवाड़ करने वाले चीन के व्यवहार को नियंत्रित और संयमित करने के लिए भारत ने यथार्थवादी दृष्टिकोण अपनाया है। भारत चीन के संबंध में रूस और अमेरिका दोनों के साथ महत्वपूर्ण संबंधों को बनाए हुए है, यूरोपियन यूनियन के देशों फ्रांस, जर्मनी से भी भारत के संबंधों में नए आयाम देखने को मिले हैं। दक्षिणी चीन सागर में आस्ट्रेलिया, जापान, ताइवान देशों के साथ भारत नई भूमिका में है। विश्व में भारत की यह स्थिति विदेश नीति में हुए परिवर्तनों का परिणाम है।

संदर्भ

1. कोठारी, रजनी, *भारत में राजनीति* (2005) वाणी प्रकाशन, नई दिल्ली, पृ. 413।
2. दीक्षित, जे.एन., *भारतीय विदेश नीति* (2008) प्रभात प्रकाशन, नई दिल्ली, पृ. 55।
3. शर्मा, डॉ. मथुरालाल, *अंतर्राष्ट्रीय संबंध*, कॉलेज बुक डिपो प्रकाशक, जयपुर, पृ. 342।

4. राव, निरूपमा (विदेश सचिव का संबोधन), *भारत की वैश्विक भूमिका* (20/09/2010) mea.gov.in विदेश मंत्रालय, भारत सरकार।

5. मेनन, शिव शंकर (राष्ट्रीय सुरक्षा सलाहकार) *वैश्विक राजनीति में परिवर्तन एवं संक्रमण* (22/10/2011) mea.gov.in विदेश मंत्रालय, भारत सरकार।

6. झा, महेश, सोवियत संघ : जन्म से मृत्यु तक (19/08/2011) DW हिंदी, ऑनलाइन पोर्टल।

7. भाटिया, के. राजीव, महानिदेश ICWA, *उभरती हुई वैश्विक व्यवस्था में भारत : राजनीतिक, रणनीतिक और आर्थिक गतिशीलता* (10/11/2014) विश्व मामलों की भारतीय परिषद, सप्रू हाउस, नई दिल्ली

8. वरदराजन, सिद्धार्थ, वरिष्ठ पत्रकार, *भारत रूस : पुरानी दोस्ती के नए इम्तिहान।* (12/12/2014) BBC News हिंदी ऑनलाइन पोर्टल।

9. जोशी मनोज, नए शक्ति संतुलन में भारत (21/11/2014) *अमर उजाला* हिंदी ऑनलाइन पोर्टल।

10. डोगरा, भारत, *राजनीति : विश्व अर्थव्यवथा और चुनौतियां* (10/12/2018) *जनसत्ता* ऑनलाइन पोर्टल।

11. गुप्त, संजय, सी.ई.ओ *दैनिक जागरण, दुनिया में भारत की बढ़ती धमक* (29/01/2018) नई दुनिया ऑनलाइन पोर्टल।

12. थरूर, शशि, सरन समीर, *कोविड 19, अव्यवस्था और नई विश्वव्यवस्था में भारत की भूमिका* (08/04/2020) Orfonline.org. ऑनलाइन पोर्टल।

16

क्षेत्रीय संगठन के रूप में सार्क की भूमिका : एक विवेचना

गीता तिवारी, हेम चंद्र, गिरिश चंद्र थुवाल

संक्षिप्त सार

प्रस्तुत शोध पत्र में क्षेत्रीय संगठन के रूप में सार्क के उदय की पृष्ठभूमि को देखते हुए वर्तमान समय तक की स्थिति का विश्लेषणात्मक अध्ययन किया गया है। सार्क की स्थापना दिसंबर 1985 में ढाका में हुए 7 राष्ट्रीय राज्यों के शिखर सम्मेलन में की गई। सार्क की स्थापना का प्रस्ताव 1977 में तत्कालीन बांग्लादेश के राष्ट्रपति जिया-उर-रहमान ने किया था। सार्क की कुल आबादी विश्व की लगभग 21 प्रतिशत है। यह क्षेत्र अत्यंत असंगठित है, इस संगठन के देशों के बीच आपसी व्यापार मात्र 5 प्रतिशत ही है। जिस कारण यह आज तक एक शक्तिशाली संगठन का रूप नही ले सका है। भारत पाकिस्तान के कटु संबंध भी इसकी असफलता का प्रमुख कारण हो सकते है। दक्षिण एशियाई देशों को सार्क की महत्ता को देखते हुए, एक व्यापक सुझाव तथा वर्तमान में चल रही कोविड-19 संबंधी महामारी से निपटाने हेतु भी महत्वपूर्ण परस्पर सांझेदार बनना होगा। क्योंकि आज विश्व भी क्षेत्रीय सहयोग की उपयोगिता को स्वीकार करने लगा है। अतएव आज सार्क देशों को आपसी मनमुटावों को भूलाकर सहयोगात्मक रूख अपनाना चाहिए। जिससे सामाजिक, सांस्कृतिक, आर्थिक, तकनीकी विकास को बढ़ाने की दिशा में यह संगठन अग्रसर हो सके।

की-वर्ड : क्षेत्रीय सहयोग, संगठन, सार्क, दक्षिण एशियाई विकास कोष, भारत, पाकिस्तान, एकीकृत कार्यक्रम।

प्रस्तावना

दक्षिण एशिया के आठ राष्ट्रों भारत, अफगानिस्तान, पाकिस्तान, नेपाल, भूटान, बांग्लादेश, श्रीलंका, मालदीव द्वारा राष्ट्रीय साधनों के पूर्ण विदोहन, क्षेत्रीय स्तर पर पारस्परिक सहयोग, आर्थिक विकास की प्रक्रिया को गति प्रदान करने हेतु दक्षेस संघगठित किया गया। आज वैश्विक परिदृश्य में सभी महाशक्तियां क्षेत्रीय नीतियों की ओर अग्रसर हो रही है।[1] सार्क की स्थापना दिसंबर 1985 में ढाका में हुए 7 राष्ट्रों के शिखर सम्मेलन में की गई। सार्क की स्थापना का प्रस्ताव 1977 में बांग्लादेश के तात्कालीन राष्ट्रपति जिया-उर-रहमान ने किया था। नवोदित बांग्लादेश में कुछ मात्रा में स्थायित्व और शांति की स्थापना की इच्छा से तथा वहां की जनता को सनातन निर्धनता और दुख से उबारने के विचार से राष्ट्रपति जिया-उर-रहमान ने क्षेत्रीय सहयोग के विचार का प्रसार किया।

दक्षिण एशियाई क्षेत्रीय सहयोग का विचार 1977 में भारत, पाकिस्तान, नेपाल और श्रीलंका की यात्रा करते हुए राष्ट्रपति जिया-उर-रहमान ने प्रसारित किया था। इस आधार पर बांग्लादेश की सरकार ने एक कार्य पत्र (working paper) तैयार करके क्षेत्र के सभी देशों को भेजा। इसका शीर्षक था—दक्षिण एशिया में क्षेत्रीय सहयोग' और इसमें यह सुझाव दिया गया कि विदेश सचिव स्तर पर इस प्रस्ताव पर विचार किया जाए और क्षेत्रीय सहयोग की संभावना का पता लगाया जाए। विचार-विमर्श और तैयारी का कार्य 1981 तक चला। औपचारिक रूप से यह प्रस्ताव राष्ट्रपति रहमान द्वारा मई 1980 में संबंधित सरकारों के पास विचार के लिए प्रेषित किया गया। विदेश सचिवों की पहली मीटिंग अप्रैल 1981 में कोलंबो में हुई इसके पश्चात् अन्य राजधानियों में और भी बैठकें हुई। सातों देशों के विदेश मंत्री भी ढ़ाका शिखर सम्मेलन से पूर्व कई बार विचार-विमर्श करने के लिए मिले।

नई दिल्ली में 1983 में विदेश मंत्रियों के सम्मेलन में एक 'एकीकृत कार्यक्रम' तैयार किया गया। इस कार्यक्रम की घोषणा **नई दिल्ली घोषणा पत्र** के द्वारा की गई। ढ़ाका शिखर सम्मेलन 1985 से पूर्व जो विचार-विमर्श हुए उसमें यह तय किया गया कि प्रस्तावित सार्क राज्यों की संप्रभु समानता, प्रादेशिक अखंडता की रक्षा तथा एक-दूसरे के आंतरिक मामलों में हस्तक्षेप न करने की नीति के आधार पर, आर्थिक क्षेत्रीय सहयोग के लिए कार्य करेगा।

दक्षिण एशियाई क्षेत्रीय सहयोग संगठन (साकं) स्थापित करने का प्रारंभिक कार्य

जुलाई 1984 में हुई विदेश मंत्रियों की माले बैठक और थिंपू की मई 1985 की बैठक में पूरा कर लिया गया। इन सम्मेलनों में नई दिल्ली 1983 सम्मेलन के कार्य को पूरा किया गया और निश्चय किया गया कि सात दक्षिण एशियाई देशों का शिखर सम्मेलन ढाका में 7-8 दिसंबर को बुलाया जाएगा। ढाका शिखर सम्मेलन की अध्यक्षता बांग्लादेश के राष्ट्रपति एच.एम. इरशाद ने की। भारत का प्रतिनिधित्व प्रधानमंत्री राजीव गांधी ने किया। पाकिस्तान के राष्ट्रपति जिया उल हक, श्रीलंका के राष्ट्रपति जयवर्धने, नेपाल और भूटान के नरेश तथा मालदीव के राष्ट्रपति मौमून अब्दुल गयूम थे। ढाका सम्मेलन अत्यंत सौहार्दपूर्ण वातावरण में संपन्न हुआ।

सार्क के 8 सदस्य राष्ट्रों की कुल आबादी 1.6 अरब से अधिक है, जो विश्व की कुल आबादी का लगभग 21 प्रतिशत है। इन क्षेत्रों की आबादी का 40 प्रतिशत गरीबी रेखा से नीचे जी रहा है और अशिक्षा की दर 50 प्रतिशत है। ढाका सम्मेलन में औपचारिक रूप से सार्क की स्थापना की तथा उसका एक 10 सूत्री चार्टर भी स्वीकार किया। सम्मेलन में यह भी निश्चय किया गया और चार्टर में प्रावधान भी किया गया कि सार्क के मंच पर द्विपक्षीय मामले या विवाद विचार के लिए नहीं उठाए जाएंगे। यह भी निर्णय किया गया कि सार्क का एक स्थायी सचिवालय स्थापित किया जाएगा। इसकी विस्तृत रूपरेखा तैयार करने का कार्य विदेश मंत्रियों को सौंपा गया। सचिवालय स्थायी रूप से ढाका में स्थापित किया गया और श्री अब्दुल हसन को सार्क का महासचिव नियुक्त किया गया। आगे चलकर विदेश मंत्रियों ने स्थायी सचिवालय काठमांडू (नेपाल) में स्थापित करने का निर्णय किया। वही सार्क सचिवालय स्थापित और कार्यरत है ।

सार्क के उद्देश्य और सिद्धांत

1. दक्षिण एशियाई देशों के लोगों के कल्याण को प्रोत्साहन देना और उनके जीवन स्तर में सुधार करना।
2. आर्थिक विकास सामाजिक प्रगति और सांस्कृतिक विकास को गति प्रदान करना।
3. सामूहिक आत्मनिर्भरता को प्रोत्साहित और सुदृढ़ करना।
4. आर्थिक, सामाजिक, सांस्कृतिक, तकनीकी और वैज्ञानिक क्षेत्रों में पारस्परिक सहायता को प्रोत्साहन देना।

5. पारस्परिक विश्वास और एक-दूसरे की समस्याओं को समझने में सहयोग देना।
6. अन्य विकासशील देशों के सहयोग को मजबूत करना।
7. राष्ट्रीय मंच पर आपसी सहयोग को सुदृढ़ करना।
7. क्षेत्रीय एवं अंतरर्राष्ट्रीय संगठनों के साथ सहयोग करना।

चार्टर में जिन सिद्धांतों का उल्लेख है वो निम्नलिखित है -:

1. सार्क के माध्यम से क्षेत्रीय सहयोग, संप्रभुता, समानता के सिद्धांत के प्रति पारस्परिक सम्मान, प्रादेशिक अखंडता, राजनीतिक स्वतंत्रता, एक दूसरे के आंतरिक मामलों में हस्तक्षेप न करना और पारस्परिक लाभ के सिद्धांतों पर आधारित होगा।
2. क्षेत्रीय सहयोग, द्विपक्षीय सहयोग और बहुपक्षीय सहयोग का स्थान नहीं लेगा, परंतु उसका पूरक होगा।
3. क्षेत्रीय सहयोग द्विपक्षीय एवं बहुपक्षीय उत्तरदायित्व के विरुद्ध नहीं होगा, इस प्रकार सार्क चार्टर में क्षेत्रीय सहयोग पर बल अवश्य है। परंतु द्विपक्षीय बहुपक्षीय उत्तरदायित्वों में हस्तक्षेप किए बिना, और संप्रभु समानता का आदर करते हुए अपनी प्रादेशिक अखंडता एवं सदस्य राष्ट्रों कि स्वतंत्रता बनाए रखते हुए ही दक्षिण एशियाई सहयोग को प्रोत्साहन दिया जाएगा।

शोध विधि एवं उद्देश्य

प्रस्तुत शोध पत्र का उद्देश्य क्षेत्रीय संगठन के रूप में सार्क के उदय की पृष्ठभूमि को समझते हुए वर्तमान समय तक की स्थिति का विश्लेषणात्मक अध्ययन करना है। यह शोध पत्र विश्लेषणात्मक व द्वितीयक स्त्रोतों पर जो विभिन्न पुस्तकों, ऑनलाइन पत्र-पत्रिकाओं, अंतर्राष्ट्रीय जर्नल्स में प्रकाशित हुए शोध आलेख पर आधारित है।

सार्क के सदस्य राष्ट्र

भारत, पाकिस्तान, बांग्लादेश, नेपाल, श्रीलंका, मालदीव, और भूटान संस्थापक राष्ट्र हैं, एवं अप्रैल 2007 के सम्मेलन में अफगानिस्तान इसका सदस्य बन गया एवं 9 प्रेक्षक राष्ट्र जिनमें ऑस्ट्रेलिया, चीन, यूरोपीय संघ, ईरान, जापान, मॉरिशस, म्यांमार, दक्षिण कोरिया व संयुक्त राज्य अमेरिका हैं।

सार्क की उपलब्धियां

दक्षिण एशियाई विकास कोष-1996

भूटान के नरेश ने 1991 के कोलंबो सार्क शिखर सम्मेलन में एक दक्षिण एशियाई विकास कोष स्थापित करने का विचार व्यक्त किया था। इस कोष को स्थापित करने का उद्देश्य यह था कि सार्क देशों की विकास परियोजनाओं में क्षेत्रीय स्तर पर पूंजी निवेश को प्रोत्साहन दिया जा सके। इस बात की भी आवश्यकता थी कि पूंजी निवेश सर्वेक्षण किया जाएगा, ताकि उत्पादन क्षमता और निर्यात योग्य वस्तु की पहचान की जा सके। भूटान नरेश के प्रस्ताव को 1995 के नई दिल्ली शिखर सम्मेलन ने विधिवत स्वीकार कर लिया। दक्षिण एशियाई विकास कोष की औपचारिक स्थापना जून 1996 में की गई । इसकी स्थापना की घोषणा बांग्लादेश के पूंजी निवेश निगम के प्रबंध निदेशक खैरुल हुडा ने की थी। खैरुल हुडा को दक्षिण एशियाई विकास बोर्ड का अध्यक्ष नियुक्त किया गया था। विकास कोष का मुख्यालय और सचिवालय ढ़ाका में स्थापित किया गया। विकास कोष का मुख्य उद्देश्य ऐसी परियोजनाओं को स्थापित और प्रोत्साहित करना है, जिनसे दक्षिण एशियाई क्षेत्र के दो या दो से अधिक देशों को लाभ होता हो। इस कोष की आरंभिक पूंजी के रूप में 1996 तक सदस्य देशों ने 50 लाख अमेरिकी डॉलर की राशि जमा कर ली थी। इसमें सबसे अधिक राशि 16,05,000 भारत ने दिए, जबकि पाकिस्तान ने 11,92,500 डॉलर का योगदान दिया। बांग्लादेश ने 5,67,500 डॉलर तथा इतनी ही राशि का योगदान श्रीलंका ने दिया। दो कोष जो पहले से स्थापित थे, क्षेत्रीय परियोजनाओं के लिए सार्क कोष तथा सार्क क्षेत्रीय कोष। उन दोनों का इसी नए विकास कोष में विलय कर दिया गया।[2]

सार्क विकास निधि (South Development Fund) 2010

इसका गठन सार्क देशों के सदस्यों ने 2010 में किया था। जिसका मुख्यालय थिंपू (भूटान) में है। इसके प्रबंध निकाय में सभी सार्क देशों के वित्त मंत्री शामिल हैं। एसडीएफ ने अब तक 12 विकास परियोजनाओं पर कार्य किया है। जिसमें अधिकतर सामाजिक परियोजनाएं हैं, लेकिन अब यह बुनियादी ढांचा परियोजना पर भी काम करने की योजना बना रहा है।

दक्षिण एशियाई उपग्रह (South Asian Satelite)

भारत में सार्क देशों के उपयोग हेतु 'दक्षिण एशियाई उपग्रह' का निर्माण किया है। इस उपग्रह का प्रक्षेपण 5 मई को किया जाएगा। यह उपग्रह प्राकृतिक संसाधनों का मानचित्रण, टेलीमेडिसिन, शिक्षा, आईटी कनेक्टिविटी अथवा लोगों से लोगों के संपर्क को बढ़ावा देने के कारण यह उपग्रह संपूर्ण दक्षिण एशियाई क्षेत्र की प्रगति के लिए वरदान सिद्ध होगा। इस प्रोजेक्ट की शुरुआत 2014 में नेपाल में हुई सार्क की बैठक में की गई थी। पाकिस्तान के अलावा अन्य सभी देश में इसमें शामिल हुए थे। इस उपग्रह प्रक्षेपण की लागत 235 करोड़ रूपये है, जो धनराशि भारत सरकार द्वारा वहन की जाएगी।

एक संगठन के रूप में ऐतिहासिक प्रदर्शन तथा समकालीन रूप से यह क्षेत्र दक्षिण एशियाई पहचान को प्रतिबिंबित करता है। इसके अतिरिक्त इसकी अपनी भौगोलिक पहचान भी है। इस क्षेत्र में सांस्कृतिक, भाषाई, धार्मिक एवं खानपान संबंधी समानता भी विद्यमान है। यह तत्व दक्षिण एशिया को एक एकीकृत क्षेत्र के रूप में परिभाषित करते हैं।

दक्षिण एशियाई देश अपनी सामाजिक, राजनीतिक राज्य की पहचान के अंतर्गत बंधे हुए हैं। उनके द्वारा समान रूप से आतंकवाद, समान आर्थिक चुनौतियां, आपदा इत्यादि खतरों एवं चुनौतियों का सामना मिलकर किया जाता है।[3]

सार्क कोविड-19 आकस्मिक कोष - 15 मार्च, 2020

भारत के प्रधानमंत्री ने इस फंड के लिए भारत की तरफ से शुरुआती सहयोग के रूप में 10 मिलियन अमेरिकी डॉलर देने की घोषणा की। बांग्लादेश की प्रधानमंत्री ने भविष्य में दक्षिण एशिया क्षेत्र में ऐसी स्वास्थ्य संबंधी चुनौतियों से निपटने और उनकी रोकथाम के लिए आपसी सहयोग से एक चिकित्सा संस्थान की स्थापना किए जाने का सुझाव दिया है।[4]

तालिका-1 : सार्क के शिखर सम्मेलन

क्रमांक	*दिनांक/वर्ष*	*सम्मेलन आयोजक देश*	*सम्मेलन आयोजित शहर*	*राष्ट्राध्यक्ष*
प्रथम	7 दिसंबर 1985	बाग्लादेश	ढाका	एच.एम. इरशाद
द्वितीय	16-17 नवंबर 1986	भारत	बेंगलरू	राजीव गांधी
तृतीय	2-4 नवंबर 1987	नेपाल	काठमांडू	रिचमान सिंह श्रेष्ठ
चतुर्थ	29-31 दिसंबर 1988	पाकिस्तान	इस्लामाबाद	बेनजीर भुट्टो
पांचवा	21- 23 नवंबर 1990	मालदीव	मलेमॉमून	अब्दुल गय्यूम
छठा	І21 दिसंबर 1991	श्रीलंका	कोलम्बो	रणसिहें प्रेमदासा
सांतवा	10-11 अप्रैल 1993	बांग्लादेश	ढ़ाका	खालिदा जिया
आठवां	2-4 मई 1995	भारत	दिल्ली	पी.वी. नरसिम्हा राव
नौवां	12-14 मई 1997	मालदीव	मलेमॉमून	अब्दुल गययूम
दसवां	29-31 जुलाई 1998	श्रीलंका	कोलम्बो	चंद्रिका कुमारतुंगा
ग्यारहवां	4-6जनवरी 2002	नेपाल	काठमांडू	शेर बहादुर देउवा
बारहवां	2-6 जनवरी 2004	पाकिस्तान	इस्लामाबाद	मीर जफरूल्लाह खान जमाली
तेरहवां	12-13 नवंबर 2005	बाग्लादेश	ढाका	खालिदा जिया

चौदहवां	3-4 अप्रैल 2007	भारत	नई दिल्ली	मनमोहन सिंह
पंद्रहवां	1-3 अगस्त 2008	श्रीलंका	कोलंबो	महेंद्रा राजपक्षे
सोलहवां	28-29 अप्रैल 2010	भूटान	थिंफू	जिग्मे थिनले
सत्रहवां	10-11 नवंबर 2011	मालदीव	अडडू	मोहम्मद नशीद
अठारहवा	26-27 नवंबर 2014	नेपाल	काठमांडू	सुशील कोईराला
उन्नीसवां	9-10 नवंबर 2016	पाकिस्तान	इस्लामाबाद	रद्द
बीसवां	निर्धारित होना शेष			

स्रोत : https:èhi.m. Wikipedia.org

सार्क की चुनौतियां

1. **गरीबी उन्मूलन :** दुनिया के सबसे गरीब देशों के संगठन के रूप में गरीबी उन्मूलन के इस महत्वपूर्ण उद्देश्य पर ध्यान देना सार्क की पहली प्राथमिकता में से एक है। सार्क के 8 सदस्य राष्ट्रों की कुल आबादी 1.6 अरब से अधिक है, जो विश्व की कुल आबादी का लगभग 21 प्रतिशत है। इन क्षेत्रों की आबादी का 40 प्रतिशत गरीबी रेखा से नीचे जी रहा है, और अशिक्षा की दर 50 प्रतिशत है। यह कार्य बहुत आसान नहीं है, लेकिन स्थिर क्षेत्रीय सहयोग के दृढ़ विश्वास और दृष्टि के साथ यह उपलब्धि हासिल की जा सकती है।[5]
2. वर्ष 2006 में सार्क देशों के बीच व्यापार को बढ़ावा देने के लिए किया गया दक्षिण एशियाई मुक्त व्यापार क्षेत्र (साफ्टा) समझौता वास्तविकता में बहुत सफल नहीं रहा।
3. दक्षिण एशियाई क्षेत्र के देशों के मध्य बेहतर तालमेल और सहयोग का अभाव जैसे बीबीआई मोटर वाहन समझौता जैसी उप क्षेत्रीय पहलें रुकी पड़ी हैं, सार्क की वीजा प्राप्ति में राहत योजना का लाभ केवल कुछ गण्यमान्य व्यक्तियों को ही प्राप्त है।
4. सार्क देशों के समाजों में बुनियादी सुविधाओं का अभाव जिसमें उन्नत शिक्षा, पोषण, कौशल, प्रौद्योगिकी एवं चिकित्सा सुविधाएं आदि प्रमुख हैं।
5. हालिया परिदृश्य में देखा जाए तो पाकिस्तान एवं नेपाल द्वारा भारत से मानचित्र, सीमा संबंधी विवाद, आतंकवाद को बढ़ावा देना आदि प्रमुख हैं। जो सार्क की प्रासंगिकता को कम कर रहे हैं, इसका उदाहरण 2016 में पाकिस्तान द्वारा सीमापारीय आतंकवाद को बढ़ावा देते हुए उरी हमला किया गया जिसके कारण सार्क का 19वां सम्मेलन रद्द कर दिया गया जो कि इस्लामाबाद में होना था ।
6. वर्तमान में कोविड-19 से उपजी महामारी से निपटना और दक्षिण एशियाई क्षेत्र के राष्ट्रों में उत्तम स्वास्थ्य सुविधाएं उपलब्ध कराना एवं मानव मात्र की सुरक्षा करना सार्क के सम्मुख वर्तमान समय में महत्वपूर्ण एवं अग्रिम चुनौती है।
7. यहां ये बात भी ध्यान देने वाली है कि सार्क के चार सदस्य देशों की

सीमाएं चीन से लगी हुई हैं, जो कोरोना वायरस के शुरू होने का केंद्र है हांलाकि तिब्बत स्वायत्त शसित क्षेत्र में कोरोना वायरस से संक्रमित लोगों की संख्या कम थी और चीन का यही क्षेत्र है जिसकी सीमाएं सार्क देशों से लगी हुई हैं।[6]

निष्कर्ष एवं सुझाव

सार्क की कुल आबादी विश्व की लगभग 21 प्रतिशत है। यह क्षेत्र अत्यंत असंगठित है, इस संगठन के देशों के बीच आपसी व्यापार मात्र 5 प्रतिशत ही है। जिस कारण यह आज तक एक शक्तिशाली संगठन का रूप नहीं ले सका है। भारत-पाकिस्तान कटु संबंध भी इसकी असफलता का प्रमुख कारण हो सकते हैं। दक्षिण एशियाई देशों को सार्क की महत्ता को देखते हुए, एक व्यापक सुझाव तथा वर्तमान में चल रही कोविड-19 संबंधी महामारी से निपटाने हेतु भी महत्वपूर्ण परस्पर साझेदार बनना होगा, क्योंकि आज विश्व भी क्षेत्रीय सहयोग की उपयोगिता को स्वीकार करने लगा है। अतएव आज सार्क देशों को आपसी मनमुटावों को भुला कर सहयोगात्मक रुख अपनाना चाहिए। जिससे सामाजिक, सांस्कृतिक, आर्थिक, तकनीकी विकास को बढ़ाने की दिशा में यह संगठन अग्रसर हो सकें। यह कदम सार्क के 8 सदस्य देश तथा 9 प्रेक्षक देश साथ मिलकर उठा सकते हैं। सार्क के सुझाव, जो इसे प्रासंगिक बनाते हैं, निम्न प्रकार से हैं--

1. सार्क संगठन को अपने हितों तथा अंतर्राष्ट्रीय स्तर के हितों को एक सम्मेलन में व्यापक तौर पर उठाना चाहिए, परंतु पाकिस्तान संबंधी विवादों को निपटाना कहीं न कहीं एक अग्रिम कदम होना चाहिए, क्योंकि हम जानते हैं कि पाकिस्तान के क्रूर कार्यवाही के कारण 2016 का सम्मेलन हमें रदद् करना पड़ा था और सार्क अपनी प्रासंगिकता को खोता जा रहा था, इसीलिए आवश्यक है कि इसका जल्द से जल्द निपटान किया जाए। व्यापार को बढ़ावे को ध्यान में रखकर सार्क के सभी देशों को आपस में टैरिफ और गैर-टैरिफ बाधाओं को दूर करने के लिए काम करना चाहिए।
3. विश्व बैंक का एक अध्ययन यह कहता है कि दक्षिण एशिया क्षेत्र को मुख्य रूप से ऊर्जा, बिजली, परिवहन, दूरसंचार और पर्यावरण में बुनियादी ढांचे के बीच अंतर को कम करने की आवश्यकता है।

4. कोविड-19 के कारण अर्थव्यवस्था, जो विभिन्न राष्ट्रों की नकारात्मक हो गई है उसे उभारने के लिए सभी सदस्य देशों को साथ मिलकर एक वैश्विक सहयोग संगठन के रूप में सामने आना होगा।
5. पाकिस्तान विरोधी बयानबाजी तथा भारत-पाकिस्तान व भारत-नेपाल के बीच सीमा तथा मानचित्र विवाद का निपटान जल्द से जल्द होना चाहिए। साथ ही चीन का LAC line of actual control वास्तविक नियंत्रण रेखा) विवाद भी सार्क देशों को परस्पर मिलकर निपटाना होगा, क्योंकि चीन सार्क देशों के साथ एक प्रेक्षक की भूमिका को निभाता है।
6. भारत पर कई बार आरोप लगे हैं कि भारत सार्क देशों पर अपना वर्चस्व बढ़ा रहा है, इस बात को नकारते हुए भारत को एक शीर्ष नेतृत्वकर्त्ता के रूप में उभरने की आवश्यकता है, जो भारत लगातार करते आ रहा है।

संदर्भ सूची

1. शर्मा, भावना, *नई अंतराष्ट्रीय अर्थव्यवस्था व दक्षिण एशियाई देश,* 2017, ISBN : 9788131608692.
2. जैन, पुखराज व खन्ना, वी.एन. *राजनीति विज्ञान* आगरा : एस.बी.पी.डी. पब्लिकेशन, 2016, पृ. स.-152-157.
3. *दृष्टि* आई.ए.एस., *अंतराष्ट्रीय संबध,* 2 मई 2020, www.drishtiias.com
4. दृष्टि आई.ए.एस., 'सार्क कोविड-19 इमरजेंसी फंड', 16 मार्च 2020, पृ.सं. 02. www.drishtiias.com
5. Shaheen, Irum, 'South Asian Associtìon for Regional Cooperation (SAARC): its Role, Hurdles and Prospects' : IOSR *Journal of Humanities and social science,* vol.15, issue 6(sep-oct 2013), ISSN 2279-0837, p.no. 03.
6. वाइहोम, के 'कोविड 19 : वैश्विक संकट के दौर में भारत की सार्क डिप्लोमेसी' 4 अप्रैल 2020, orfonline.org
7. Muni, S.D., *The Emerging Dimensions of SAARC, Foundation Books,* 2010, Online ISBN : 9788175968615.

17

भारत-रूस संबंधों के समक्ष चुनौतियां
(सन् 1991 से समकालीन समय तक)

नुसरत

सारांश

भारत की आजादी के बाद से ही भारत और रूस के संबंध बहुत अच्छे रहे हैं, शीत युद्ध के समय भारत और सोवियत संघ मे मजबूत रणनीतिक, सैनिक, आर्थिक एवं राजनयिक संबंध रहे है। सोवियत संघ के विघटन को बाद भी दोनों के संबंध पूर्वक्त बने रहे। प्रस्तुत शोध पत्र भारत तथा रूस के संबंधों का बनाए रखने के लिए क्या-क्या चुनौतियां एक-दूसरे देशों के समक्ष आई है, से संबंधित है। 1991 में सोवियत संघ के विघटन के पश्चात् ही दोनों देश अपने द्विपक्षीय संबंधों को बनाए रखने के लिए प्रयत्नशील है भारत तथा रूस दोनों ही देशों को अपने संबंधों को बनाए रखने के लिए अनेकों चुनौतियों का सामना करना पड़ा है, समकालीन समय में भी भारत तथा रूस दोनों देश अपने-अपने हितों की पूर्ति करने के लिए अनेक चुनौतियों का सामना कर रहे है।

कीवर्ड : संबंध, समक्ष, चुनौतियां, समकालीन।

उद्देश्य

1. दोनों देशों के समक्ष अपने हितों की प्राप्ति करने के लिए क्या चुनौतियां है? का अध्ययन करना।
2. भारत तथा रूस के सक्रिय राजनयिकों की भूमिका का अध्ययन करना।
3. वर्तमान समय में दोनों देशों के संबंधों का अध्ययन करना।

शोध क्रियाविधि

प्रस्तुत शोधपत्र में विषयों से संबंधित तथ्यों के संकलन हेतु द्वितीयक स्त्रोतो जैसे-पुस्तक, पत्रिकाओं व शोध ग्रंथों का अध्ययन किया गया है एवं साथ ही विश्लेषणात्मक एवं वर्णनात्मक पद्धति का प्रयोग किया गया है।

भारत-रूस संबंध

किसी भी देश की विदेश नीति, जिसे विदेशी संबंधों की नीति भी कहा जाता है, वह अपने राष्ट्रीय हितों की रक्षा करने के लिए और अंतर्राष्ट्रीय संबंधो के वातावरण में अपने लक्ष्यों को प्राप्त करने के लिए राज्य द्वारा चुनी गई स्वहितकारी रणनीतियों का समूह होती है। किसी देश की विदेश नीति दूसरों के साथ आर्थिक, राजनीतिक, सामाजिक तथा सैन्य विषयों पर पालन की जाने वाली नीतियों का एक समुच्च्य है। इसी प्रकार भारत तथा रूस की विदेश नीति भी अपने-अपने हितो की पूर्ति के लिए प्रयासरत रही है तथा भारत के समक्ष अनेक चुनौतियां रही हैं, जिसका सामना भारत की विदेश नीति को करना पड़ा है।

इसी तरह यदि हम भारत तथा रूस की विदेश नीति को देखें तो अनेक चुनौतियां दोनों देशों के बीच रही है। दिसंबर 1991 में सोवियत संघ के पूर्ण विघटन के बाद रूस विश्व की महाशक्ति सोवियत संघ के उत्तराधिकारी के रूप में उभरा। तभी से भारत तथा रूस अपने द्विपक्षीय संबंधों को नई इच्छित दिशा देने में जुटे हुए हैं। दोनों ही समकालीन राजनीति में अपने-अपने राजनीतिक-आर्थिक-राजनीतिक हितों को पूरा करने के लिए एक-दूसरे के महत्व के बारे में सचेत हैं। दिसंबर, 1991 में सोवियत संघ के पूर्ण विघटन होने के बाद 9 सोवियत गणतंत्रों द्वारा स्वतंत्र संघ राष्ट्रों का एक राष्ट्रमंडल स्थापित किया गया। रूस कानूनी रूप में रूस भू. पू. सोवियत संघ का उत्तराधिकारी बना तथा संयुक्त राष्ट्र संघ की सुरक्षा परिषद् में निषेधाधिकार तथा स्थायी सदस्यता रूस को दे दी गई। सोवियत संघ परमाणु शस्त्र भंडार की चाबी भी भू.पू. सोवियत संघ के राष्ट्रपति गोर्वाच्योव द्वारा रूस के राष्ट्रपति बोरिस येल्तसिन को सौंप दी गई।[1]

सोवियत संघ के विघटन से भारत को बहुत हानि हुई, क्योंकि इसकी समाप्ति का इसके लिए अर्थ था, उच्च कोटि के व्यापारिक-औद्योगिक तथा तकनीकी संबंधों और सुरक्षा शस्त्रों की आपूर्ति के युग का अंत, भारत के लिए अपनी सुरक्षा मशीनरी

तथा विमानों के पुर्जों की प्राप्ति का विषय सिरदर्द बन गया। सोवियत संघ जैसी महाशक्ति की प्रगाढ़ मित्रता तथा सहयोग के अंत से, वह भी एक ऐसे समय में जब पाकिस्तान जम्मू-कश्मीर तथा पंजाब में युद्ध जैसी स्थिति बनाए हुए था। जो किसी भी समय वास्तविक युद्ध में परिवर्तित हो सकती थी, सुरक्षा साधनों की आपूर्ति की समस्या ने भारत के विदेश-संबंधों को सीमित कर दिया। 1989-91 में भारत सोवियत संघ की दुर्बलता तथा अस्थिरता से उत्पन्न समस्या को भली-भांति भांप गया था। तभी इसने रूस के राष्ट्रपति बोरिस येल्तसिन के साथ घनिष्ठता स्थापित करने के प्रयत्न कर दिए थे। तथापि सोवियत संघ के अस्तित्व के बने रहने तक भारत के लिए राष्ट्रपति गोर्बाच्योव तथा राष्ट्रपति येल्तसिन के साथ संबंधों में संतुलन बनाए रखना कठिन था, क्योंकि दोनों के बीच काफी मतभेद थे।

नवंबर, 1991 में भारत के विदेशी मामलों के मंत्री श्री माधव सिंह सोलंकी ने सोवियत संघ तथा अपने संबंधों को फिर से ढर्रे पर लाने के प्रयत्न किए जो सोवियत संघ के भू-क्षेत्रों की पुनः संरचना के कारण पटरी से उतर गए थे। उसने सोवियत संघ के अधिकारियों के साथ संबंध स्थापित करने तथा सोवियत संघ की तुलना में रूस के साथ संबंधों की स्थिति का पहले से ही अंदाज़ा लगाने के लिए इस अवसर का लाभ उठाया। वे सोवियत तथा रूसी प्रशासनों, दोनों के ही अधिकारियों से मिले। इस यात्रा से उन्हें सोवियत संघ की बुनियादी स्थिति का पता चल गया। उस समय यहां के सभी सोवियत गणराज्यों ने भारत के साथ व्यापार करने की रुचि तथा रूपया-रूबल समानता जैसी समस्याओं के लिए, जब कभी आवश्यकता हो, उपाय सुझाने का विश्वास दिलाया।

वहां रूस की सरकार ने यह घोषणा की, कि रूस अपने देश की धरती पर तीसरे देशों तथा सोवियत संघ के द्वारा व्यापार करने के लिए किए गए विशेष समझौतों को मान्यता नहीं देगा (ऐसे समझौतों में भारत तथा सोवियत संघ का रूपया-रूबल समझौता भी शामिल था)। यहां तक कि जब मि. सोलंकी मास्को में ही थे, रूसी विदेश मंत्री केसीरोव (Kasirov) ने टी.वी. साक्षात्कार में कहा कि रूस भारत के साथ स्वेच्छा से कूटनीतिक संबंध बनाना चाहेगा। इस कथन का अर्थ यह था कि शेष सोवियत गणतंत्रों के लिए भी ऐसा करने के दरवाजे खुले हैं। इसलिए इस यात्रा से 1991 की रूस की राजनीतिक व्यवस्था का परिवर्तित तथा ढीला-ढाला स्वरूप प्रकाश में आया। इसके साथ-साथ ही रूस के साथ भारत के संबंधों के विकास के रास्ते में आने वाली संभावित कठिनाइयों का भी पता चला।[2]

भारत-रूस संबंधों की आरंभिक चुनौतियाँ (Initial Challenges in Indo-Russian Relations)

जब दिसंबर, 1991 में सोवियत संघ पूर्णतया विघटित हो गया तो रूस के साथ संबंधों की स्थापना भारत के लिए विशेष-रूप से महत्वपूर्ण हो गई क्योंकि रूस भूतपूर्व सोवियत संघ का सबसे बड़ा तथा शक्तिशाली गणतंत्र राज्य था, जो सोवियत संघ का उत्तराधिकारी बना जिसके साथ भारत का 70 प्रतिशत व्यापार चलता था। रूस के राष्ट्रपति येल्तसिन ने यह कहने में तनिक भी देर नहीं की कि उनका विश्वास है कि भारत को दिए वचन पूरे किए जाएंगे। फिर भी उस समय भारत, रूस की अर्थव्यवस्था की बिगड़ी हुई स्थिति, स्पष्ट रूसी नीति का अभाव, यथार्थवादी विनिमय दर के निर्धारण के साथ संबंधित समस्या तथा रुपया-रूबल व्यापार समस्या के कारण, अनिश्चय की स्थिति में था। भारत के लिऐ रूसी सैनिक, मशीनों के कल-पुर्ज़ों की आपूर्ति की समस्या रूसी रूबल तथा रूपये की विनिमय दर के निर्धारण की, व्यापार संबंध पुनः स्थापित करने की समस्या तथा भूतपूर्व सोवियत संघ के गणतंत्रों के साथ संबंधों से संबंधित गंभीर मुद्दों पर असहमतियों को दूर करने की समस्या थी। ऐसी कठिनाइयों पर नियंत्रण पाने के लिए भारत ने तात्कालिक कदम उठाए।

1992 के आरंभ में भारत तथा रूस ने आर्थिक संबंधों को पुनः स्थापित करने के लिए दृढ़ कदम उठाये जोकि भू. पू. सोवियत संघ में अप्रत्याशित राजनीतिक उथल-पुथल तथा विघटन के कारण टूट गए थे। विशेषतया आर्थिक क्षेत्र में भारत-रूस संबंधों को तर्क-संगत बनाने के लिए दृढ़ प्रयत्न किए गए रूपया-व्यापार (भारतीय मुद्रा का विनिमय इकाई के रूप में प्रयोग) को समाप्त करने तथा कठोर मुद्रा (Hard currencies) का प्रयोग करने का निर्णय लिया गया। ऐसा इसलिए किया गया ताकि पुरानी रुपया-रूबल समानता के निर्धारण तथा पुनः निर्धारण की समस्या से छुटकारा पाया जा सके, यह निर्णय इसलिए भी आवश्यक था क्योंकि दोनों ही देश मंडीकृत आर्थिक व्यवस्था के रास्ते पर चल पड़े थे। जिसमें दोनों पर विदेशी मुद्रा की आवश्यकता अधिक आ पड़ी थी। भारत-रूस व्यापार सरकारी एकाधिकार से भी मुक्त किया गया था। दोनों ही देशों ने निजी कंपनियों को वस्तुओं को खरीदने तथा बेचने के लिए एक-दूसरे के देश के बाजार में प्रवेश करने की अनुमति दी थी। इस निर्णय से भारत तथा रूस के बीच आयात-निर्यात संबंधों को बल मिला। इसके

अतिरिक्त अपनी दिल्ली की यात्रा के दौरान रूस के विदेश मंत्री गेनेडी बरबुलिस (Gannedy Burbulis) ने यह वायदा किया कि रूस भारत को सुरक्षा कार्यों के लिए प्रयुक्त होने वाली मशीनों के कल-पुर्ज़ों की निर्विघन आपूर्ति करता रहेगा।

इसके साथ-साथ भारत के लिए रूस द्वारा भेजे जाने वाले सुरक्षा कल-पुर्ज़ों की आपूर्ति जारी रही। भारत के भू0 पू0 रक्षा मंत्री श्री शरद पवार (Sh. Sharad Pawar) ने यहां तक घोषणा की थी कि भारत की सुरक्षा कार्यो के लिए प्रयुक्त होने वाली मशीनो के कल-पुर्जो की आपूर्ति को और अधिक तेज करके तथा रूस से तकनीकी सहायता प्राप्त करके बनाए रखी जाएगी। यह आपूर्ति तथा सहायता रूस के राष्ट्रपति येल्तसीन (Yeltsin) द्वारा भारत को 40 करोड़ डॉलर के कर्जे के अंतर्गत देनी थी। परिशोधित मिग-29 विमानों को भी भारत ने रूस से प्राप्त करना था।

रूस के राष्ट्रपति बोरिस येल्तसिन द्वारा स्वीकार्य भारतीय सशस्त्र सेनाओं के लिए आधुनिक उपकरण खरीदने के लिए दिए जाने वाले 83 करोड़ डॉलर के ऋण की सहायता पर टिप्पणी करने के इनकार करते हुए भी श्री गोंसालविस (Gonsalvis) ने कहा कि रूस, भारत के साथ सामरिक सहयोग के पक्ष में है जो मात्र केंद्रीय एशिया तथा पश्चिम एशिया में इस्लामी कट्टरवाद की बढ़ती शक्ति की स्थिति को ध्यान में रखकर मात्र सुरक्षा तक ही सीमित नहीं होगा। उन्होंने आगे कहा कि मि. कॉजीरेव (Kozyrev) ने भी उन्हें यह विश्वास दिलाया था कि रूस भारत को पहले की तरह ही अधिमान देता रहेगा। रूस के विदेश मंत्री ने दोनों देशों के बीच नियमित परामर्शों तथा सहयोग पर एक समझौते का मसौदा तैयार किया था तथा यह समझौता जनवरी, 1993 में मि. येल्तसिन की भारत यात्रा के दौरान हस्ताक्षरबद्ध किया जाना था। मि. गोन्सालविस (Gonsalvis) ने भी कहा कि रूसी नेताओं ने उन्हें विश्वास दिलाया था कि रूस के दीर्घकालीन सामरिक हित भारत के साथ अच्छे संबंध स्थापित करने में ही समाहित थे। एशिया, विशेषतया भारत, चीन, दक्षिण कोरिया तथा टर्की के पक्ष में रूस की विदेश नीति में थोड़े से झुकाव की ओर इंगित करते हुए सेवा मुक्त हो रहे राजदूत ने कहा कि दोनों देशों के बीच प्रतिरक्षा संबंध सामान्य संबंधों में महत्वपूर्ण भूमिका प्रदान करते रहेंगे, क्योंकि दोनों को यह विश्वास था कि दोनों देश मिलकर विश्व के नाज़ुक क्षेत्रों तथा केंद्रीय एशिया तथा पश्चिमी एशिया में प्रमुख भूमिका निभा सकते थे।

यह स्पष्ट करते हुए कि भारत तथा रूस के संबंध में अपनी उड़ान सीमा तक

पहुंच चुके थे तथा अनिश्चितता का दौर समाप्त हो चुका था, मि. गोन्सालविस (Gonsalvis) ने कहा था कि दोनों देशों के बीच आने वाले समय में प्रतिरक्षा तथा ऊर्जा के क्षेत्र में और इसके साथ-साथ दीर्घकालीन योजनाओं के क्षेत्र में सहयोग बना रहेगा। रूस व्यापार तथा सुरक्षा योजनाओं को वित्तीय सहायता देता रहेगा। उन्होंने कहा, 'प्रतिरक्षा के लिए वित्तीय सहायता एक बड़ा कदम है। ऐसी सहायता किसी अन्य को नहीं दी जा रही।'' (Financing in defence is a major step, such a assistance is not given to anyone else.) रूस ने इसके कुछ समय बाद ही भारत के तत्कालीन रक्षा मंत्री श्री शरद पवार की मास्को की यात्रा के दौरान यह बात स्वीकार कर ली।[3]

मित्रता तथा सहयोग की नई संधि (A new Treaty of Friendship and Co-operation)

मित्रता तथा सहयोग की नई संधि, आने वाले 20 वर्षों में भारत-रूस संबंधों का निर्धारण करने के लिए की गई। इसके अनुसार यह निर्धारित किया गया कि भारत तथा रूस, कोई भी ऐसा कार्य नहीं करेंगे जो एक-दूसरे के सुरक्षा हितों को बुरी तरह प्रभावित करे। संधि के अनुसार दोनों देश व्यापक तबाही करने वाले शस्त्रों को समाप्त करने तथा परमाणु निःशस्त्रीकरण की प्रक्रिया का समर्थन करने की आवश्यकता पर भी सहमत हुए। इसके साथ ही दोनों देशों ने कम से कम ऐसी आवश्यकता प्रतिरक्षा सामर्थ्य रखने की आवश्यकता पर भी बल दिया, जो इस क्षेत्र तथा विश्व में सुरक्षा तथा स्थायित्व को सुदृढ़ करेगी। यह संधि जो रूस के 1991 में स्वतंत्र गणतंत्र बनाने के बाद भारत-रूस संबंधों को निर्देशित करने वाला एक पहला प्रमुख दस्तावेज था, दोनों देशों की संसदों द्वारा पुष्टि के बाद 20 वर्षों तक वैद्य रहनी थी। इस संधि, जिसमें सुरक्षा धारा नहीं थी, ने 1971 की भारत-सोवियत संधि का स्थान ले लिया। यह संधि एक प्रस्तावना से शुरू हुई, जिसमें 1971 की संधि का जिक्र था और जिसके अंतर्गत यह लिखा गया था कि भारत तथा भूतपूर्व सोवियत संघ किसी भी आक्रमण के समय एक दूसरे के साथ परामर्श करेंगे तथा एक दूसरे की सहायता करेंगे।

दोनों देशों के लिए, समय की यह पुकार बनी कि वे इस नींव पर लाभप्रद तथा विस्तृत ढंग से ऐसे संबंधों की स्थापना करें जो शांति सुरक्षा तथा विकास के साझे उद्देश्यों की प्राप्ति में सहायक सिद्ध हो। परंतु जुलाई, 1993 में रूस ने अमेरिकी

दबाव के अधीन आकर यह निर्णय लिया कि वह भारत को क्रायोजेनिक राकेट इंजन तकनीक का हस्तांतरण नहीं करेगा तथा इसके बदले में वह भारत को क्रायोजेनिक राकेट इंजन दे देगा। रूस का यह निर्णय उसकी पूर्व की नई घोषणाओं के विरूद्ध था। रूस ने निश्चय ही यह निर्णय अमेरिकी दबाव के अधीन तथा अमेरिका पर अपनी आर्थिक निर्भरता के कारण किया, परंतु इसके द्वारा भारत तथा अन्य देशों को यह आभास हुआ कि रूस अंतर्राष्ट्रीय राजनीति में अपनी स्वतंत्र भूमिका निभाने में पूर्णतया सक्षम नहीं।

भारत ने रूस संबंधों की पूर्ण समीक्षा उस समय की गई जब भारत के विदेश मंत्री ने अगस्त 1995 में रूस की यात्रा की तथा रूसी विदेश मंत्री तथा अन्य अधिकारियों से बातचीत की। इस यात्रा में दोनों देशों के संबंध दृढ़ हुए। विदेश मंत्री श्री प्रणव मुखर्जी ने यह कहा कि यद्यपि NPT, CTBT तथा कुछ अन्य विषयो पर भारत तथा रूस में कुछ मतभेद थे तथापि दोनों देश आपसी संबंधों और सहयोग को बढ़ाने के लिए दृढ़ निश्चय किए हुए हैं और भारत-रूस मित्रता एवं सहयोग आने वाले समय में तीव्रता से विकसित होगा।

मार्च 1996 में भारत रूस ने नई दिल्ली तथा मास्को के बीच लगातार सीधे संचार संपर्क (Hot Line) तथा शैक्षणिक, वैज्ञानिक तथा सांस्कृतिक विनियमों के लिए दो समझौते किए। भारत यात्रा पर आए रूसी विदेश मंत्री ने यह भी कहा कि रूस, कश्मीर पर भारत के इस पक्ष को मानता है कि कश्मीर एक द्विपक्षीय मुद्‌दा था जिसका हल शिमला समझौते के अंतर्गत होना था। 1991-98 के मध्य भारत ने रूस से सैनिक साज-समान तथा हथियारो की खरीद के लिए तथा भारतीय सेना के पास विद्यमान रूसी विमानो के आधुनिकीकरण के लिए कई समझौते किए। भारत रूस मित्रता तथा सहयोग की प्रक्रिया एक स्वस्थ रूप में आरंभ हो गई तथा दोनों देशों ने यह पहचान लिया कि भविष्य में अधिक सहयोगात्मक संबंधो की स्थापना दोनों देशों के हितो की सुरक्षा के लिए आवश्यक थी।[4]

भारत-रूस संबंध 2007-2010 (India-Russia Relations, 2007-2010)

भारत-रूस सातवीं शिखर बैठक 25-26 जनवरी, 2007 को भारत रूस सातवां शिखर सम्मेलन नई दिल्ली में संपन्न हुआ। जब प्रधानमंत्री डॉ. मनमोहन सिंह तथा राष्ट्रपति पुतिन ने सभी विपक्षीय और अंतर्राष्ट्रीय मुद्‌दों पर व्यापक वार्तालाप किया।

इस वार्तालाप के बाद यह घोषित किया गया कि भारत और रूस ने तमिलनाडु की कुंडालतम परियोजना में चार तथा अन्य नए स्थानों पर परमाणु रिएक्टरों का निर्माण करने की सहमति बनाई थी, बाद में दोनों देशों के बीच 9 समझौते किए गए। सबसे प्रमुख बात यह रही की भारत अमेरिका नागरिक परमाणु समझौता होने के बाद रूस भारत में परमाणु ऊर्जा क्षेत्र में आपसी सहयोग को और व्यापक बनाने के लिए समझौते किए। भारत में रूसी हवाई जहाजों के ईंधन के उत्पादन तथा एक नए यातायात वायुयान के साझे रूप में विकास के लिए भी समझौते किए गए। जिन द्विपक्षीय दस्तावेजो पर हस्ताक्षर किए गए, उनमें से एक अत्यंत महत्वपूर्ण समझौता यह था कि अब भारत Russian Global Navigation Satelite System-GLONASS में भागीदार बन गया और इस व्यवस्था से सूचनाएं प्राप्त करने का अधिकारी हो गया।

इस शिखर सम्मेलन ने एक बार फिर स्पष्ट रूप में यह प्रकट किया कि भारत और रूस दोनों ही आपसी संबंधों को व्यापक बनाने के प्रति वचनबद्ध थे। इस शिखरवार्त्ता में दोनों देशों ने चीन के साथ मिलकर त्रिपक्षीय सहयोग स्थापित करने की आवश्यकता को स्वीकार किया परंतु साथ ही, चीन द्वारा उपग्रह को अंतरिक्ष में नष्ट करने के संबंध में जो प्रयोग किया गया था उसका विरोध भी किया गया। दोनों देशों ने यह माना कि अंतरिक्ष का परमाणुकरण और सैनिकीकरण नहीं किया जाना चाहिए।

2007-10 के समय में भारत और रूस संबंध अपने परंपरागत सकारात्मक स्वरूप में लगातार बढ़ते रहे और दोनों देशो ने सुरक्षा क्षेत्र में आपसी सहयोग को बढ़ाने के साथ-साथ परस्पर आर्थिक और व्यापारिक संबंधों को लगातार भी विस्तृत किया। दोनों देशो में साझे शोध और प्रशिक्षण कार्यक्रम नियमित रूप में संचालित होते रहे और आज भी हो रहे हैं। अप्रैल 2007 में दोनों देशों की समुद्री सेनाओं ने जापान सागर में अभ्यास किए और इसके बाद सितंबर 2007 में दोनों देशों की हवाई सेनाओं ने अपने साझे सैनिक अभ्यास किए। ऐसे ही अभ्यास नवंबर दिसंबर 2008 में भी किए गए।

आज भी दोनों देश सुरक्षा क्षेत्र में साझे प्रोजेक्ट अधीन पांचवीं पीढ़ी के लड़ाकू हवाई जहाज और बहुभूमिका वाले मालवाहक जहाज के उत्पादन के लिए कार्य कर रहे हैं। ब्रह्मोस क्रूज मिसाइल कार्यक्रम की सफलता ने दोनों देशो को अपने सुरक्षा सहयोग को आगे बढ़ाने के लिए उत्साहित किया है और दोनों देश कई एक साझे

सैनिक उत्पादन कार्यक्रम चला रहे हैं। भारत और रूस ने अपने वार्षिक शिखर सम्मेलनों द्वारा आपसी संबंधों को विशेष रूप से आर्थिक संबंधों और प्रतिरक्षा सहयोग को अधिक विकसित करने की प्रयास जारी रखें। भारत रूसी सैनिक साजो-समान खरीदने वाला एक बड़ा देश बना रहा। हवाई जहाज सक्षमता वाला रूसी सुमद्री जहाज एडमिरल गोर्शकोव की भारत द्वारा प्राप्ति की प्रक्रिया विद्यमान रही और यह समझा गया कि इसकी लागत के संबंध जो मतभेद पैदा हुए थे, वे दोनों देश मिलकर दूर कर लेंगे। लगभग 8,000 करोड़ रु. के मूल्य के रुपया ऋण फंड (Rupee Debt. Fund) के संबंध में विद्यमान मतभेदों को कुछ सीमा तक सफलतापूर्वक समाधान करने की प्रक्रिया में भारत रूस सफल रहे।

मई-जून 2009 में भारत में 15वीं लोकसभा के चुनावों के पश्चात् लगातार दूसरी बार प्रधानमंत्री डॉ. मनमोहन सिंह के नेतृत्व में कांग्रेस-यू.पी.ए. गठबंधन सरकार सत्ता में आई। इस बार यह सरकार अधिक स्थायी सरकार थी तथा दूसरे राजनीतिक दलों के बाहरी समर्थन पर अधिक निर्भर नहीं थी। इससे यह संभावना बनी कि यह सरकार रूस के साथ भी संबंधों के विस्तार को अब पहले से भी अधिक प्राथमिकता देगी। मई 2009 से जून 2010 के दौरान भारत-रूस उन रेखाओं के आधार पर लगातार विकसित होते रहे जोकि 1995 से अस्तित्व में आई थी। दोनों देशों के नेताओं में नियमित रूप से यात्राओं का आदान-प्रदान किया। अपने द्वि-पक्षीय संबंधों तथा व्यापार रिश्तों को सकारात्मक रूप में विकसित किया।

राष्ट्रपति प्रतिभा पाटिल ने स्पष्ट रूप में यह घोषित किया कि भारत की रूस के साथ संबंध अपने-आप में स्थिर आधारों पर खड़े थे और यह किसी अन्य देश अथवा देशों की कीमत पर संचालित नहीं किए जा रहे थे। इसी कारण ये पिछले समय में लगातार विकसित हुए हैं और आज भी हो रहे हैं। प्रधानमंत्री पुतिन ने भी कहा कि रूस, भारत के साथ संबंधों को पूर्ण महत्व देता है और यह महत्व उस समय स्पष्ट रूप में सामने आया जब रूस ने परमाणु आपूर्ति समूह की बैठक में भारतीय परमाणु ऊर्जा आवश्यकता को देखते हुए भारत को परमाणु संयंत्र तथा पुनः प्रक्रिया टैक्नोलोजी (Reprocessing) हस्तांतरित करेगा और जैसे कि पहले समझौता हो चुका था, रूस तीसरी पीढ़ी के चार VVER-1200 रिएक्टर जिनकी ऊर्जा उत्पादन क्षमता 1177 मेगावाट होगी, भारत को आपूर्ति करेगा।

12 मार्च, 2010 के दिन रूस के प्रधानमंत्री पुतिन भारत पहुंचे। उनकी यात्रा का उद्देश्य दोनों देशो के बीच संबंधों को आगे विकसित करना था। इस यात्रा के

दौरान दोनों देशों ने पांच द्वि-पक्षीय समझौतों पर हस्ताक्षर किए तथा इनमे से दो समझौतों का संबंध द्वि-पक्षीय नागरिक परमाणु ऊर्जा सहयोग के साथ था। प्रधानमंत्री डॉ. मनमोहन सिंह तथा प्रधानमंत्री पुतिन इस बात पर सहमत हुए कि, दोनों देशों को नागरिक परमाणु ऊर्जा, अंतरिक्ष उन्नत प्रतिरक्षा टैक्नोलोजी, हाइड्रोकार्बन व्यापार तथा संचार के क्षेत्रों में आपसी द्वि-पक्षीय सहयोग को पहले से अधिक बढ़ाना चाहिए। दोनों देशों ने यह दोहराया कि वे परमाणु सहयोग का प्रयोग शांतिपूर्ण उद्देश्यों के लिए ही करेंगे।[5]

समकालीन समय में भारत-रूस संबंधों की चुनौतियां

1. रूस भारत के साथ अधिक व्यापक आर्थिक और व्यापारिक संबंध स्थापित करना चाहता है, क्योंकि भारतीय अर्थव्यवस्था एक तेजी से विकसित हो रही अर्थ-व्यवस्था है। फिर रूस विश्व व्यापार संगठन में प्रवेश के संबंध में भी भारत का सहयोग चाहता है।
2. अपने आर्थिक आवश्यकताओं को देखते हुए रूस भारत को प्रतिरक्षा संबंधी उपकरण बेचने का इच्छुक है और भारत अपनी सुरक्षा आवश्यकताओं को देखते हुए रूस से उच्च तकनीक के प्रतिरक्षा उपकरणों तथा सैनिक हवाई जहाजों को खरीद का इच्छुक है। दोनों देशों में प्रतिरक्षा के क्षेत्र में सहयोग को विकसित करने के लिए बहुत संभावना विकसित है। दोनों ही देश ब्रह्मोस मिसाइल के साझे उत्पादन के क्षेत्र में विकसित हुए सहयोग से संतुष्ट हैं तथा दोनों ही ऐसे सहयोग को और अधिक विस्तृत करना चाहते हैं।
3. भारत और रूस आपसी व्यापार दोनों देशों की आर्थिक व्यवस्थाओं को शक्तिशाली बना सकता है। दोनों देशों में काफी पुरानी मित्रता है तथा दोनों देश इस बात को स्वीकार करते हैं कि वे अपने संबंधों के सभी क्षेत्रों में अपने सहयोग को बहुत अधिक व्यापक बना सकते हैं। दोनों देशों में कोई भी मतभेद अथवा झगड़ा नहीं है। ऐसी स्थिति में दोनों देश आपसी संबंधों को अधिक-से-अधिक सहयोगी बनाने के इच्छुक हैं।
4. दोनों ही देश अंतर्राष्ट्रीय आतंकवाद की समाप्ति के उद्देश्य से प्रेरित हैं, क्योंकि दोनों ही इस्मालिक आतंकवाद से पीड़ित है। दोनों यह चाहते हैं कि अंतर्राष्ट्रीय आतंकवाद के सभी स्वरूपों की समाप्ति के लिए सभी देश

आपस में सहयोग करें तथा अंतर्राष्ट्रीय आतंकवाद की समाप्ति के लिए कोई भी देश अपनी विदेश नीति के हितों के आधार पर ही कार्य न करें।

5. रूस यह चाहता है कि दक्षिण एशिया में अमेरिका का प्रभाव सीमित रहे। भारत के साथ संबंधों के विकास को रूस की विदेश नीति में केंद्रीय महत्व का स्थान प्राप्त है।
6. दोनों देश प्रतिरक्षा उत्पादन, तेल की खोज तथा खनन में सहयोग बढ़ाने के महत्व को स्वीकार करते हैं। भारत यह चाहता है कि सकलेन तीन के तेल-क्षेत्र में भारत को अधिक व्यापक भूमिका प्राप्त होनी चाहिए।
7. भारत और रूस दोनों इस चुनौती को स्वीकार करते हैं कि चीन के साथ मिलकर त्रिपक्षीय समझ तथा सहयोग का विकास किया जाना विश्व-शक्ति एवं सुरक्षा के हित में आवश्यक है। कोई भी देश अमेरिका पर पूरी तरह निर्भर नहीं बनाना चाहता।[6]

भारत-रूस समकालीन संबंध

भारत एवं रूसी संघ मध्य संबंध विश्वास आपसी समझ बूझ और निरंतरता की कसौटी पर खरे उतरे हैं। भारत एवं रूस के मध्य मैत्री एवं सहयोग का रिश्ता प्राचीन काल से है दोनों जरूरत के समय एक-दूसरे के साथ खड़े हुए हैं। दोनों देशों के नेताओं ने एक-दूसरे के वहां यात्राएं की तथा रक्षा एवं व्यापार संबंधित कई समझौते सपन्न किए। रूस के साथ भारत के संबंध प्राथमिकता के रहे हैं। वर्तमान समय में यदि हम देखें तो दोनों देशों के मध्य सहयोगात्मक संबंध है रूस का कहना है कि 'भारत हमारा करीबी और महत्वपूर्ण सहयोगी देश है' दोनों देशों ने विभिन्न आपसी महत्व के महत्वपूर्ण समझौतों पर हस्ताक्षर करते हुए एक संयुक्त वक्तव्य **'21 वी सदी का एक दृष्टिपत्र'** नाम से जारी किया है। दोनों देशों के मध्य अटूट संबंधों का आधार प्रेम, सम्मान और दृढ़ विश्वास रहा है। कुछ ऐसे महत्वपूर्ण बिंदु हैं जिनके आधार पर हम दोनों देशों के संबंधों को सहयोगात्मक दृष्टि से देख सकते है जैसे–

1. दोनों देश एक बहुध्रुवीय अतर्राष्ट्रीय राजनीति और सुरक्षा अवसंरचना को बढ़ावा देना चाहते हैं।
2. दोनों रक्षा हाडवयेर और प्रौद्योगिकी, परमाणु ऊर्जा एवं तेल और गैस जैसे

क्षेत्रों में सहयोग कर रहे हैं।

3. दोनों देशों के संबंध, वैश्विक भू-राजनीतिक परिस्थितियों में हर परिवर्तनों के बावजूद स्थिर बने हुए है।[7]

निष्कर्ष

समकालीन समय में भारत-रूस व्यापक रूप में विकसित हो रहे हैं। भारत और रूस की मित्रता और सहयोग परस्पर आवश्यकताओं पर आधारित हैं। दोनों देश ही आपसी संबंधों और सहयोग को अधिक-से-अधिक विकसित करने के लिए उत्सुक हैं, क्योंकि दोनों की विदेश नीतियो के उद्‌देश्यों में काफी समानताएं हैं। उल्लेखनीय है कि पिछले दशक में भारत-रूस के संबंधो मे एक निराशाजनक पैटर्न रहा है, लेकिन दोनों देशों ने बहुत व्यापक, कुशल और उत्पादक ढंग से अपने संबंधों को संचलित किया है तथा सभी क्षेत्रों में आपसी सहयोग को लगातार विकसित किया है। आज भारत तथा रूस के मध्य संबंधों के तीव्र एवं व्यापक विकास की बहुत अधिक संभावना है और साथ ही विदेश नीति के समक्ष अनेक चुनौतियां भी हैं। अतः नई सहस्राब्दी में दोनों देशों को विश्व में मौजूद चुनौतियों और अवसरों को देखते हुए अपने संबंधों को एक नई दिशा देने की जरूरत है।

संदर्भ

1. दत्त, वी.पी., *इंडियन फॉरेन पोलिसी,* विकास पब्लिकेशन, 1990
2. कोहली, सी.एम., *अंतर्राष्ट्रीय संबंध,* साहित्यगार पब्लिकेशन, 2000
3. विस्वाल, तपन, *अंतर्राष्ट्रीय संबंध,* मैकमिलियन पब्लिशर्स, दिल्ली, 2003
4. मिश्रा, अखिलेश, *अंतर्राष्ट्रीय राजनीति के मूल तत्व,* उ. प्र. हिंदी ग्रथं, अकादमी, लखनऊ, 1974
5. घई, यू.आर., *भारतीय विदेश नीति,* न्यू एकेडमिक पब्लिशिंग कंपनी, जालंधर, 2013
6. वेदाषकार, हरिदत्त, अंतर्राष्ट्रीय संबध : सरस्वती सदन, दिल्ली, 1971

18

भारत-चीन संबंध वर्तमान परिप्रेक्ष्य में (व्यवहारवादी राजनीतिक विश्लेषण पर आधारित)

बीना जोशी

भारत व चीन के बीच लंबे समय से चले आ रहे सांस्कृतिक संबंधों के बावजूद 1949 में साम्यवादी सरकार की स्थापना के बाद से संबंध कठिनाइयों से घिरा है। भारत की सामाजिक, राजनीतिक, आर्थिक व्यवस्थाओं तथा संस्थाओं की भिन्नता, चीन की साम्राज्यवादी, विस्तारवादी विचारधारा, साम्यवादी व्यवस्थाएं व संस्थाएं माओवादी नीति की प्रेरणाओं से है। चीन एशिया पर एकाधिकार चाहता है। भारत पर उसका आक्रमण न करने का कारण उसकी शांतिप्रिय नीति नहीं वरन हिमालय की दुर्गम पर्वतमालाएं हैं। तिब्बत को चीन को सौपने की गलती भारत ने की जिस कारण चीन द्वारा भारत पर आक्रमण आसान हो गया। आर्थिक क्षेत्र में चीन का वर्तमान में 10वां भागीदार है। BASIC (Brazil, Argentina,s, Africa, India, China) के जलवायु परिर्वतन सम्मेलन (कानकुन), AFRICAN FOURM SUMMIT (26 अक्टूबर, 2015), BCIM (Brazil, China, India, Myanmar) गलियारा 1999 जिसे सिल्क रोड भी कहा जाता है। 12 अक्टूबर से 22, अक्टूबर 2015 तक दोनों देशों के बीच 5वां संयुक्त सैन्याभ्यास BDCA (सीमा सुरक्षा सहयोग समझौता) अक्टूबर 2013 आदि दोनों संबंधों की निकटता को उद्घृत करते है जबकि व्यवहार में यह अपवाद है।

दक्षिणी चीन सागर पर PCA (Permanent Court of Arbitration) के फैसले के बाद चीन की भारत को चेतावनी भारत की विदेशों मे तैल अन्वेषण शाखा (ONGC विदेश लि.) की वियतनाम की कंपनी (Petro Vietnam) के बीच दक्षिण चीन सागर में तेल अन्वेषण संबंधी समझौते करने पर दी गई चेतावनी जो सीमा विवाद सुलझाने की प्रगति की शर्त बन गई। UNSC में स्थायी सदस्यता

की मांग पर चीन का नकारात्मक दृष्टिकोण तथा जापान की पैरवी छोड़ने की भारत को सलाह, BRICS के 8वें शिखर सम्मेलन में (15-16 अक्टूबर, 2016 गोवा में) चीन का आतंकवाद पर पाक को समर्थन, One China Policy के संदर्भ में ताइवान के साथ भारत का परोक्ष संबंध, चीन की समुद्री सिल्क रूट परियोजना (MSR), जो भारत के विवादाग्रस्त क्षेत्र पी.ओ.के. से गुजरती है, में भारत को भरोसे पर न लेना, आदि टकराव संबंधी तथ्यों का राजनीतिक विश्लेषण विस्तृत लेख में किया जाएगा।

मोदी सरकार के आने के बाद संबंधों पर क्या प्रभाव पड़ा? का राजनीतिक विश्लेषण अनुभवात्मक, यथार्थवादी, अंतर अनुशासनात्मक, व्यवहारवादी दृष्टिकोण के आधार पर किया जाएगा। जैसा कि प्रधानमंत्री मोदी ने चीनी नेताओं से कहा कि—'दोनों देशों के बीच रिश्तों को रणनीतिक व दीर्घकालिक नजरिये से देखना होग' चीन LAC (Line of Actual Control) को स्वीकार नहीं करता जबकि मोदी LAC को स्पष्ट करने की बात करते है। चीन की दोहरी नीति कैसे संबंधों को नजदीक लायेगी चिंता का विषय है।

प्राक्कथन

वर्तमान शोध लेख इस मान्यता पर आधारित है कि भारत-चीन संबंधों का इतिहास सदैव चुनौतिपूर्ण रहा है। दोनों देशों के संबंधों का विभिन्न दृष्टिकोणों से विभिन्न संदर्भों में अध्ययन किया जा चुका है। भारत एक विकासशील देश होने के कारण व्यवहारवादी यथार्थवादी उपागम दोनों देशों के राजनीतिक, सामाजिक, आर्थिक, वैचारिक, सांस्कृतिक प्रकियाओं को संपूर्णता के संदर्भ में समझने में सहायक है। अध्ययन में संबंधों की समस्याओं को अलग-अलग समझने का प्रयास किया गया है। अध्ययन द्वारा जो भी तथ्य प्रकाश में आए उनको एक अवधारणाक ढांचे के रूप में प्रस्तुत करने का प्रयास है।

निकटता

BASIC समूह तथा भारत-चीन संबंध : BASIC समूह में ब्राजील, द. अफ्रिका, भारत व चीन आते हैं। मैक्सिको के कानकुन जलवायु सम्मेलन में इस समूह से दो देशों द. अफ्रीका व ब्राजील ने कानूनी रूप से बाध्यकारी समझौते का समर्थन किया जबकि समर्थन न करने का लेकर दोनों देश एक साथ नजर आए। BASIC

आर्थिक गलियारा बांग्लादेश, चीन, भारत, म्यांमार से संबंधित बैठक जो क्रमशः 1 नवबंर 1998 दिल्ली में, अगस्त1999 में चीन में संपन्न हुई। इस गलियारे के जरिये चारों देशों के आपसी संपर्क बुदियादी ढांचे ऊर्जा संसाधन, कृषि, व्यापार निवेश को बेहतर बनाने के प्रावधान है जो लगभग16 लाख वर्ग किलो मी. क्षेत्र घेरेंगा जिसके तहत चीन के युनान प्रांत बंग्लादेशः म्यांमार, उत्तर भारत के लगभग 44 करोड़ लोग सड़क रेल व जलमार्ग द्वारा आपस में जुड़ जाएंगे। इसे Silk Route भी कहा जाता है। चीन-भारत निकट आते प्रतीत होते हैं।[1]

भारत-चीन संबंध व अफ्रीकी देश

1970-80 के दशक में अफ्रीकी देश भारतीय कारोबारियों—मारवाड़ी, गुजराती को पसंद नहीं करते थे अब इस तरह का दृष्टिकोण चीनियों के प्रति है जिन्हें शोषक की तरह देखा जाता है। यदि भारत चीनी अमेरिकी तथा यूरोपीय कंपनियों से प्रतिस्पर्धा कर विश्वसनीयता हासिल कर लेता है तो अफ्रीकी देशों में द्विपक्षीय व्यापार को अगले दशक में पांच गुना तक पहुचा सकता है। द. अफ्रीका, नाइजीरिया, सूडान, अंगोला, लीबिया, कीनिया, मोजांबिक में भारत के बड़े कारोबारी साझेदार हैं। रिलायंस (एस्सार) दोनों ही कंपनियां जांबिया, मलावी, वोत्ससवाना, नामीबिया में कारोबार कर रही हैं। ONGC, IOC ने दक्षिणी सूडान, नाइजीरिया, मिस्र व लीबिया में निवेश किया है।

प्रधानमंत्री मोदी अफ्रीका पर ध्यान केंद्रित करना चाहते है India-Africa-Forum Summit (26-29 Oct. 2015) नई दिल्ली में यह बात उभरकर सामने आई कि भारत उन्हें गंभीरता से नहीं लेता और बहुत कम राष्ट्राध्यक्षों को ही उसने अब तक अपने यहां आने का आमंत्रण दिया।[2] 54 अफ्रीकी देशों ने यू.एन. के विस्तार पर दावेदारी के समर्थन की बात कही। ज्यादातर देशों ने अपना विकल्प खुला रखा। अफ्रीका के भारत के संबंधों पर भारत के प्रति दृष्टिकोण व्यक्त करते हुए चीन के विदेश विभाग के प्रवक्ता लू कांग के शब्द 'ऐसे बयान फैलाए जा रहे हैं कि भारत व चीन के बीच प्रतिद्वंद्विता है, जबकि वास्तविकता यह है कि भारत व चीन के गहरे संबंध हैं, और हमारे हित एक समान हैं, तथा बेहतर समन्वय तंत्र है।[3] भारत व चीन के बीच 5वां संयुक्त सैन्य अभ्यास 12 अक्टूबर - 22 अक्टूबर 2015 तक, जिसका उद्देश्य आतंकवाद विरोधी अभियानों के आपसी अनुभवों को साझा करने, दोनों सेनाओं के बीच आपसी विश्वास को बढ़ाने के कदम के रूप में देखा जा सकता है।

टकराव

बी.आर.आई.सी.एस. (ब्रिक्स) तथा भारत-चीन संबंध (10 जुलाई, 2015) सम्मेलन में जिस तरह से 26/11 मुंबई हमले के वांछित आतंकी जकीउर रहमान लखवी के लिखाफ यू.एन.ओ. में लाए गए प्रस्ताव पर चीन ने पाकिस्तान की प्रशंसा की से पता चलता है कि रिश्तों में फांस जरूर है।[4] गोवा में 15-16 अक्टूबर 2016 को भारत की अध्यक्षता में बी.आर.आई.सी.एस. का 8वां शिखर सम्मेलन संबंधों में आई कटुता के बीच हुआ जो मसूद अजहर पर चीन के रवैया से हुआ। परिणामस्वरूप दिवाली पर चीनी सामान की बिक्री कम कराकर भारत को नीति संतुलित करने पर बाध्य होना पड़ा।

दक्षिण चीन सागर विवाद का भारत-चीन संबंध पर प्रभाव

दक्षिणी चीन सागर पर पी.सी.ए. (Permanent Court of Arbitration) के फैसले के बाद चीन ने भारत को संबंध खराब न करने की चेतावनी दी।[5] विशालता व अनेक देशों के हित जुड़े होने के कारण दक्षिण चीन सागर की स्फीति काफी तनावपूर्ण है। एक पक्ष चीन है तो दूसरा पक्ष ब्रुनेई, वियतनाम, ताइवान, मलेशिया, फिलीपींस जैसे देश है। यह विवाद केवल स्प्रेटली व पाराद्वीप समूह को लेकर नहीं है वरन इन दक्षिण पूर्व एशियाई देशों के द्वीप व समुद्री दावों से जुड़े कई विवाद हैं मुख्य विवाद 'नाइन डेस लाइन' क्षेत्र का है जिस पर चीन अपने अधिकार का दावा कर रहा है पी.सी.ए. ने जब चीन के दावे के खिलाफ निर्णय दिया तथा दावे के ऐतिहासिक तथ्यों को सिरे से खारिज कर दिया। दक्षिण चीन सागर के समुद्री मार्ग का उपयोग करने वाले भारत समेत सभी राष्ट्र चाहते हैं कि यह अंतर्राष्ट्रीय जल क्षेत्र बना रहे जैसा कि यू.एन. समुद्र कानून संधि में कहा गया है। चीन जान बूझकर आक्रामक तेवर दिखाकर भारतीय हितों को नुकसान पहुंचाना चाहता है। भारत की विदेशों में तेल अंवेषण शाखा ओ.एन.जी.सी. विदेश लिमिटेड ने वियतनाम की कंपनी 'Petro Vietnam' के साथ दक्षिण चीन सागर के कुछ क्षेत्रों में तेल खोज के लिए 3 वर्षीय अनुबंध किया। इस पर चीनी विदेश मंत्रालय ने प्रतिक्रिया दी 'दक्षिण चीन सागर व उसके द्वीपों पर चीन की निर्विवाद संप्रभुता है'[6] चीनी विदेश मंत्री ने नई दिल्ली यात्रा के दौरान चीनी सरकारी दैनिक अखबार में स्पष्ट चेतावनी दी, 'भारत को अनावश्यक रूप से उलझने से बचना चाहिए।'[7]

Disputed claims in the South China Sea

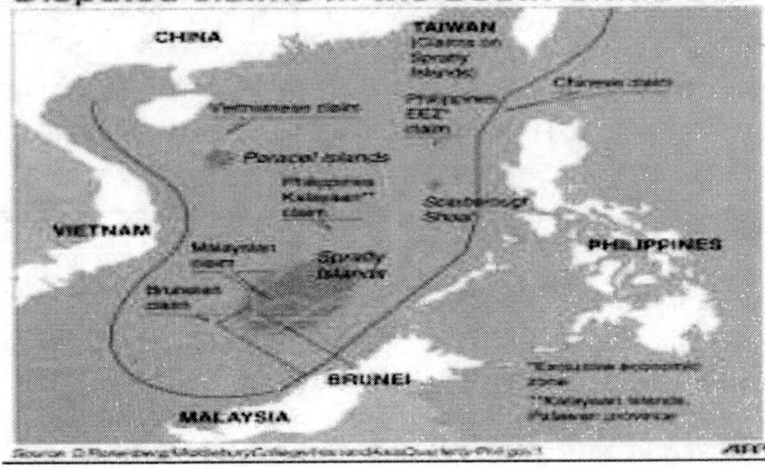

क्या चीन द. चीन सागर के लिए जंग करेगा ?

चीन विवादित सागर में लड़ाकू विमान व बांबर तैयार करने को एयरक्राफ्ट हैंगर का निर्माण कर चुका है। चीनी शोध संस्था के निदेशक ग्रेगरी पोलक के शब्दों में– 'अगर चीन लड़ाकू विमान तैयार कर लेता है तो इससे चीन व यू.एस.ए. समेत अन्य देश आमने-सामने हो जाएंगे। चीन की तरफ से तैनाती होने पर यू.एस.ए. के लिए विवादित सागर का Petroling करना मुश्किल हो जाएगा।'[8] चीन दक्षिण सागर पर एकाधिकार बनाए रखना चाहता है। जिससे दोनों देशों के बीच तल्खी बढ़नी तय है। हैंगर इतने बड़े हैं कि चीनी वायु सेना के सबसे बड़े लड़ाकू विमान भी तैनात किया जा सकता है। सैटेलाइट से प्राप्त चित्रों के मुताबिक चीन ने यहां 60-70 फुट से लेकर 200 फुट तक के एयर टेल हैंगरों का निर्माण किया है। यहां वह अपने H-6Bomber, H-6U-Refueling Trainers, y-6 transport Air craft को तैनात कर सकता है। Kj 200 Airborne warning system[9] दक्षिण चीन सागर पर लगातार चीन की दखलअंदाजी से परेशान वियतनाम इस अहम समुद्री क्षेत्र में भारत की मजबूत रणनीतिक उपस्थिति चाहता है। वियतनाम के प्रधानमंत्री मिन्ह के शब्दों में, 'भारत व वियतनाम का भविष्य व संबंध भी द. चीन सागर व हिन्द महासागर पर निर्भर है। वह भारत को तीन नए ब्लॉक देगा।'[10]

जी-4 तथा भारत-चीन संबंध : प्रधानमंत्री मोदी ने अमेरिकी यात्रा के दौरान

26 सितंबर 2015 को न्यूयॉर्क शहर में जी-4 के शिखर सम्मेलन में यू.एन.एस. सी. की स्थायी सदस्यता की मांग की। मोदी के शब्दों में–'हमारे संस्थान खासकर यू.एन.एस.सी. उस शताब्दी की जिसमें हम रह रहे हैं।'[11]

1987-2010 तक के बीच जी-4 देशों में से जापान 5 बार, जर्मनी 4 बार यू.एन.एस.सी. की गैर स्थायी सदस्यता प्राप्त करने में सफल रहे जबकि भारत केवल 2 बार। यू.एन.एस.सी. की स्थायी सदस्यता देने के पक्ष में पी-5 देश नहीं हैं। जी-4 के देश भी रोड़ा अटका रहे हैं। चीन भी विरोध कर रहा है। चीन की शर्त है कि वह जापान की पैरवी बंद कर दे तभी समर्थन करेगा। one china policy पर भारत people's Republic of china को मान्यता देता है जबकि ताइवान के साथ भी परोक्ष संबंध रखता है।

समुद्री Silk Route का भारत चीन-संबंध पर प्रभाव : वर्तमान चीनी राष्ट्रपति शी जिन पिंग की महत्वाकांक्षी परियोजना (MSR) को लेकर भारत की स्थिति स्पष्ट नहीं है क्योंकि चीन ने इस पर पारदर्शिता को नहीं अपनाया जिस पर विश्लेषकों का कहना है 'परियोजना के बारे में भारत को अगर चीन पूरी जानकारी देता है तो इससे भारत अपने नफा-नुकसान की गणना कर इसे समर्थन देने पर फैसला ले सकता है।'[12] इसके विपरीत भारत अपने Spice Route पर ध्यान दे रहा है।

चीन-पाक रिश्तों का संबंध पर प्रभाव : JNU के प्रोफेसर अंतर्राष्ट्रीय मामलों के जानकार चिंतामणी महापात्रा के शब्दों में 'चीन-पाक संबंधों के प्रतीक आर्थिक

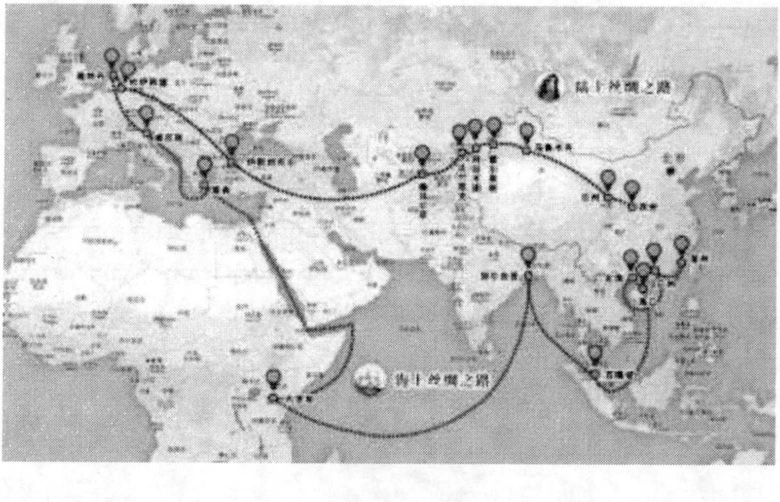

गलियारा, चीन-पाक कोरीडोर के नाम से जाना जाता है। दोनों देशों के गहरे रिश्ते को दर्शाता है।'[13] पहले चीन भारत संबंधों की चीड़िया के नाम से पुकारा जाता है। 1962 के बाद चीन-पाक रिश्तों में घनिष्ठता बढ़ती जा रही है जो भारत के खिलाफ रही हैं। चीन-पाक कोरीडोर बलूचिस्तान के ग्वादर पोर्ट से शुरू होगा गिलगित बाल्टिस्तान होते हुए चीन के शिजिंयांग प्रांत पर खत्म होगा। चीन को इसका रणनीतिक तौर फायदा हो सकता है। जबकि स्थानीय लोग चीन से खुश नहीं हैं। पाकिस्तानी सामंती सरकार से इसकी इजाजत मिलना मुश्किल तो चीन पाक कोरीडोर रास्ता बदल दिया गया है अब यह पाकिस्तान के पंजाब प्रांत से होकर जाएगा। इससे पख्तूनख्वा के लोग नाखुश हैं।

उद्देश्य तथा निष्कर्ष

दोनो देशों के बीच रिश्तों को रणनीतिक व दीर्घकालिक नजरिये से देखा जाना चाहिए जैसा कि प्रधानमंत्री मोदी ने चीनी नेताओं को कहा कि मुद्दों पर विचार करना चाहिए जो सहयोग के बीच आड़े आते हैं। 1950 के दशक में दोनों देश सीमा के बारे में कुछ भी कहने से हिचकते थे। हैरत है कि 1959 में चीन ने अचानक यह मुद्दा उठाया। एक तरफ चीनी नेता कहते हैं कि पाकिस्तान से उसके रिश्तों का प्रभाव नहीं पड़ेगा जबकि 1980 से चीन पाक को परमाणु हथियारों के विकास तथा मिसाइलों के विकास में पर्याप्त मदद करता आया है। भारत चाहता है कि चीन अक्साई चिन पर अपना दावा छोड़ दें जबकि चीन अरुणाचल की शर्त रखता है जिसे उसने दक्षिणी तिब्बत कहना शुरू कर दिया। हाल मे तुवांग क्षेत्र जो दलाईलामा का जन्म स्थल है पर भी उसने अपना दावा किया। जहां 17वीं शताब्दी का प्रसिद्ध मठ है।

भारत चीन के बीच रिश्ते सामान्य हो सकते हैं व सीमा विवाद हल हो। जबकि 2012 में भारत चीन सीमा पर परामर्श व समन्वय के लिए संचालन तंत्र संबंधी समझौता BDCA (Border Defence Corporation Agreement) आदि। 2014 के लद्दाख के चुनार क्षेत्र में चीनी घुसपैठ से पता चलता है कि चीन LAC (Line of Actual Control) को स्वीकार नहीं करता जबकि भारत LAC को स्वीकार नहीं करता जबकि भारत LAC को स्वयं करना चाहता है। आर्थिक सहयोग के बाद भी रणनीतिक अविश्वास कम नहीं हुआ है।

हमारी विदेश नीति देश की सीमाओं की रक्षा करने मे विफल सिद्ध हुई है। आज

भी चीन व पाकिस्तान हमारे सैकड़ों वर्ग मील के प्रदेश दबा रखे हैं तथा हमारी विदेश नीति उन्हें मुक्त नहीं कर सकी है। मित्र व शत्रु को हमें सफलता प्राप्त करते हुए Spice Route की नीति तथा Look East Policy की नीति का समर्थन अध्ययन इसका उद्देश्य है। हर राष्ट्र की अपनी सभ्यता और संस्कृति होती है तथा वह अन्य देशों में अपनी संस्कृति के प्रसार के कार्य करता है तथा सांस्कृतिक उद्देश्यों को प्राप्त करने के लिए व विदेशों में सांस्कृतिक प्रतिनिधि मंडल भेजे जाते है। साहित्य बांटता है तथा सांस्कृतिक प्रभाव के माध्यम से अपने राष्ट्रीय हितों की पूर्ति करता है। डॉ. वेदप्रकाश वैदिक के शब्दों 'उन देशों में भारतीय भाषा, वेशभूषा, भोजन, भजन और भेषज की कूटनीति चलाना होना चाहिए'।[15]

विदेश में भारतीय भोजन काफी लोकप्रिय है। विदेश मंत्रालय भारतीय रेस्तरा सारी दुनिया में स्थापित कर सकते है। भारत अरबों डॉलर विदेशी मुद्रा अर्जित कर सकता है। भारतीय संगीतज्ञों को सुनने में अमेरिका में इतनी भीड़ जुटती है जितनी वहां के राष्ट्रपति को सुनने के लिए भी नहीं। इसी प्रकार भारतीय साड़ी के प्रति वहां की महिलाओं में अदम्य आकर्षण, भजन व भेषज केवल डॉलर कमाने के साधन नही है वरन संदेश वाहक भी । प्राकृतिक चिकित्सा तथा योग के माध्यम से भी हम चीन जैसे देशों में अपना प्रभाव स्थापित कर सकते हैं। भारत को सदैव चीन की चाल से सतर्क रहने की जरूरत है।

संदर्भ

1. *अमर उजाला,* दैनिक समाचार पत्र 18 जुलाई, 2015।
2. सुरेंद्र कुमार, पूर्व राजदूत का *अमर उजाला को साक्षात्कार,* 2015
3. लूवांग की प्रतिक्रिया, चीनी सरकारी समाचार पत्र *People's Daily.*
4. *अमर उजाला* (11 जुलाई, 2015, दैनिक समाचार)।
5. लेख, प्रशांत दीक्षित, 'चीन की चाल से सतर्कता', *अमर उजाला*।
6. चीन सरकारी दैनिक समाचार पत्र *People's Daily*।
7. चीन सरकारी समाचार पत्र *People's Daily*।
8. वाशिंगटन स्थिर शोध संस्थान- Center for Strategic and international studies के निदेशक ग्रेगरी पोलिंग का Aljazeera को साक्षात्कार।
9. उपरोक्त ।
10. Asean think tank के उद्घाटन अवसर, मिन्ह का भाषण।
11. *अमर उजाला*-दैनिक जागरण पत्र, प्रधानमंत्री का जी-4 सम्मेलन में संबोधन 26 सितंबर 2015

12. China west normal university में भारतीय अध्ययन केंद्र के निदेशक लॉगशिन चुन का भाषण।
13. लेख-*अमर उजाला*, मनोज जोशी 'राजनीतिक विशलेषक नए मुकाम की ओर चीन पाक रिश्ते'।
14. मनोज जोशी, 'राजनीति विश्लेषक', *अमर उजाला* लेख उपरोक्त।
15. डॉ. वेद प्रकाश वैदिक, *भारतीय विदेश नीति नए दिशा संकेत*, पृ. 116।
16. Harish Kapoor 'China in world politicsA
    (A) Internet images

KEY WORDS

BASIC – Brazil, S.Africa, India, China, Argentina.

BRICS – Brazil, Russia, India, China, S.Africa.

PCA –Permanent Court of Arbitration.

BDCA – Border Defence Co-Operation Agreement.

19

भारत-पाकिस्तान संबंध

नीमा

सारांश

भारत और पाकिस्तान में संबंध हमेशा से ही ऐतिहासिक और राजनीतिक मुद्दों की वजह से तनाव में रहे हैं। स्वतंत्रता प्राप्ति के पश्चात् इन दोनों राष्ट्रों के संबंध बहुत वर्षों तक आपसी सामंजस्य और मधुरता से परे अत्यधिक तनावपूर्ण थे, जिसका सृजन उनकी आधार भूमि, दो भिन्न देशों के दर्शन, उनके बिल्कुल भिन्न दृष्टिकोण और असमान उद्देश्यों सहित व्यापक रूप से भिन्न प्रकार की नीतियों के कारण हुआ था। जब से भारत का विभाजन होकर ये दोनों राष्ट्र बने तब से लेकर आज तक दोनों के मध्य विवाद होते रहे हैं। विवादों के कई कारण थे जो इस प्रकार हैं - कश्मीर मुद्दा, सिंधु नदी जल-विवाद मुद्दा, सियाचिन विवाद, सरक्रीक विवाद, आतंकवाद का मुद्दा व चीन-पाक आर्थिक गलियारा। जिनमें से कश्मीर विवाद इन दोनों देशों को आज तक उलझाए हुए है और इसके कारण ही दोनों देश एक-दूसरे पर कई बार सैनिक कार्रवाई कर चुके हैं। आतंकवाद भी दोनों देशों के मध्य बड़ा विवादित मुद्दा रहा है, जो वर्तमान में भी इनके संबंधों को बिगाड़े हुए है। आज भी इन दोनों में तनाव मौजूद है। जबकि दोनों ही देश एक-दूसरे के इतिहास, सभ्यता, भूगोल और अर्थव्यवस्था से जुड़े हुए हैं। 1947 से लेकर दोनों देशों के मध्य कई विवाद, समझौते, संधि होते रहे और संबंधों में कभी मिठास तो कभी खठास आती रही है, परंतु दोनों के संबंध कभी सामान्य व शांतियुक्त नहीं हुए हैं। जैसे ही दोनों के संबंधों में थोड़ी मधुरता आती है। वैसे ही कश्मीर एवं आतंकवाद का मुद्दा उसे फिर से कटु बना देता है। ऐतिहासिक काल (1947 के बाद) से लेकर वर्तमान तक कई विवादों द्वारा इन देशों के संबंधों में कटुता आती रही है। भारत-पाक संबंधों को प्रभावित करने वाली समस्याएं जैसे विभाजन से उत्पन्न समस्याएं, भारत

विरोधी नीति से उत्पन्न समस्याएं, पाक की सीटों, सेंटो की सदस्यता व भारत की किलेबंदी से उत्पन्न होने वाली समस्या का विस्तारपूर्वक विश्लेषण शोध पत्र में करेंगें।

कीवर्ड : सीमा पार आतंकवाद, संयुक्त राष्ट्र संघ, दक्षिण एशिया, नदी जल-विवाद।

प्रस्तावना

भारतीय उपमहाद्वीप में विभाजन के साथ कट्टर प्रतिद्वंद्विता के कारण पाकिस्तान का निर्माण हुआ और यह ऐतिहासिक आधार भारत-पाकिस्तान के संबंधों को आज भी प्रभावित कर रहा है। जहां भारत का निर्माण लोकतांत्रिक पंथनिरपेक्ष एवं बहुलवादी राज्य के रूप मे हुआ, वहीं पाकिस्तान का निर्माण धार्मिक आधार पर हुआ तथा इसने भारत विरोधी नीति को मूल आधार बनाया। भारत-पाकिस्तान के संबंध पिछले कई दशकों के दौरान दुखपूर्ण, तनावों, उत्तेजक बयानों, बाहरी दखलदाजी, पारस्परिक सार्वजनिक भर्त्सना तथा अंतर्राष्ट्रीय मंचों पर अपनी इज्जत घटा देने वाले कार्यों से भरपूर रहे हैं। ब्रिटिश शासन से आजादी मिलने के बाद पाकिस्तान और भारत के रूप में दो देशों की उत्पत्ति हुई। भारत पाकिस्तान के साथ भौगौलिक, आर्थिक, सांस्कृतिक आदि संबंध साझा करता है, लेकिन इसके बाद भी दोनों देशों के संबंध आपसी मतभेद, शत्रुता और संदेह के कारण परस्पर सामंजस्यपूर्ण नहीं बन सके। आजादी के बाद से अब तक दोनो के बीच चार युद्ध हो चुके है। रिश्तों को सुधारने के लिए शिमला समझौते और लाहौर घोषणा-पत्र जैसे कदम उठाए गए लेकिन पाकिस्तान के दोहरे रवैये के कारण ये कदम फलीभूत ना हो सकें।

एशिया महाद्वीप में ब्रिटिश उपनिवेशवाद की समाप्ति के साथ एक नए संघर्ष की शुरुआत हुई। जिसके परिणामस्वरूप इस क्षेत्र से 'शांति' शब्द का लोप हो गया। यह संघर्ष है दो पड़ोसी देशों का संघर्ष, जिसे भारत-पाक संघर्ष के नाम से जाना जाता है। भारत-पाक संघर्ष की प्रकृति को सही रूप से समझने के लिए भारत-विभाजन में निहित तथ्यों का वस्तुनिष्ठ अध्ययन अपरिहार्य है। विभाजन की घटना ने दो समुदायों के मध्य घृणा, अविश्वास और वैमनस्य को क्रूरतम ढंग से उजागर किया है। विभाजन के बाद सभी समस्याओं के स्वतः ही सुलझ जाने का सपना देखने वालों ने जब वास्तविकता पर नजर दौड़ाई तो उन्हें घोर निराशा हुई। पाकिस्तान के जन्म से समस्याएं सुलझने की अपेक्षा अधिक उलझ गई और इससे दक्षिण एशिया में नए

संघर्ष का सूत्रपात हुआ जो अपनी प्रकृति से कहीं अधिक गहरा और पेचीदा था। जो वर्तमान में भी विकट समस्या रही है। आज इन समस्याओं का स्वरूप थोड़ा बदल गया है और इसका परिणाम जनमानस को जानमाल की हानि द्वारा चुकाना पड़ रहा है। कभी सीमा को लेकर विवाद तो कभी आतंकवाद द्वारा भारत को धमकाने की नापाक कोशिशें तो कभी संयुक्त राष्ट्र संघ व अन्य मंचों पर पाकिस्तान के भारत के खिलाफ जहर उगलना या अंतर्राष्ट्रीय न्यायालय में कुलभूषण जाधव के मामले को ले जाना, चीन के साथ अपने रिश्तों को मजबूत करना, भारत के साथ आर्थिक संबंधों को मजबूत करने के बजाय पाकिस्तान का चीन के साथ व्यापारिक समझौते करना आदि वर्तमान में नए विवाद व मुद्दे दोनों के कटु संबंधों के लिए जिम्मेदार हैं। कुलदीप नैय्यर के शब्दों में 'विभाजन के लिए आप किसी को भी दोषी ठहराए, वास्तविकता यह है कि इस पागलपन ने दो समुदायों और दो देशों के बीच दो पीढ़ियों से भी अधिक समय तक के लिए संबंधों में कड़वाहट उत्पन्न कर दी। दोनों देशों में हर विषय और हर कदम पर मतभेद बढ़ता गया और छोटी-छोटी बात ने बड़े विवाद का रूप धारण कर लिया।'[2]

माइकल ब्रेशर के अनुसार, 'भारत और पाकिस्तान हमेशा अघोषित युद्ध की स्थिति में रहेंगें।'[3]

कुलदीप नैय्यर एवं माइकल ब्रेशर के कहे शब्द वर्तमान भारत-पाकिस्तान संबंधों के विषय में बिल्कुल सटीक बैठते हैं। दोनों देशों के मध्य आज छोटी-छोटी बातों में विवाद उत्पन्न हो रहा है, जो बाद में विकराल रूप धारण कर लेता है। भारत-पाकिस्तान संबंधों में विभाजन के समय उत्पन्न हुई समस्याएं वर्तमान में भी सुलझ नहीं पाई हैं। जिनमें से महत्वपूर्ण है—सिंधु नदी जल विवाद मुद्दा, जम्मू-कश्मीर मुद्दा, सीमा निर्धारण विवाद, आतंकवाद आदि। इन विवादों ने आज अपना स्वरूप बदल लिया है और विकराल रूप धारण कर लिया है। इन विवादों का समाधान वर्तमान में भी शायद ही हो पाए। भारत-पाकिस्तान संबंधों को इस शोध-पत्र से ऐतिहासिक पृष्ठभूमि एवं वर्तमान परिप्रेक्ष्य में विस्तार से वर्णन करेंगे। इन दोनों देशों के संबंधों को प्रभावित करने वाली समस्याएं एवं वर्तमान में दोनों के संबंधों का विश्लेषणात्मक अध्ययन शोध पत्र में किया जाएगा। भारत-पाकिस्तान संबंधों का विश्लेषण वर्तमान परिप्रेक्ष्य में करने से पहले विभाजन से उत्पन्न होने वाली समस्याओं का गहन अध्ययन जरूरी है।

विभाजन से उत्पन्न होने वाली समस्याएं : भारतीय नेताओं को आशा थी कि

देश के विभाजन से शांति और आपसी मेल जोल को बढ़ावा मिलेगा और दोनों देश शांति सद्भावना के वातावरण में आर्थिक विकास के लंबे और कठिन कार्यों में जुट जाएंगे लेकिन पाकिस्तान के जन्म के साथ ही कुछ ऐसी समस्याएं उत्पन्न हो गईं जिसके कारण दोनों देशों मे कटुता आ गई ये समस्याएं निम्नलिखित थी–

1. हैदराबाद विवाद 2. जूनागढ विवाद 3. ऋण अदायगी का प्रश्न
4. शरणार्थियों की समस्या 5. नदी पानी विवाद 6. कश्मीर समस्या आदि।

विभाजन से उत्पन्न इन विवादों में से कुछ को तो सुलझा लिया गया, किंतु कुछ विवाद वर्तमान में भी भारत के लिए बड़ी समस्या बने हुए हैं। शरणार्थियों की समस्या एवं नहर पानी विवाद आज भी समय-समय पर दोनों देशों के बीच झगड़े का विषय बना रहता है, परंतु कश्मीर समस्या विभाजन से लेकर आज तक भारत-पाक संबंधों के लिए चुनौती बनी हुई है जिसका निपटारा अभी तक नहीं हुआ है।

कश्मीर विवाद

कश्मीर की समस्या दोनों देशों के बीच एक ऐसे ज्वालामुखी की तरह है जो समय-समय पर लावा उगलती रहती है।

अलाप माइकल के शब्दों में 'कश्मीर समस्या अनिवार्यतः भूमि या पानी की समस्या नहीं, यह लोगों और प्रतिष्ठा की समस्या है।'[4]

भारत के विभाजन के बाद कश्मीर देशी रियासत का भारत में विलय हो गया, परंतु पाकिस्तान के द्वारा इसे स्वीकार नहीं किया गया तथा सामरिक और सैन्य दृष्टिकोण से कश्मीर के महत्व को देखते हुए पाकिस्तान इसे अपना भाग बनाने का प्रयास करता रहा, जबकि भारत शुरू से ही कश्मीर को अपना महत्वपूर्ण अंग मानता आया है। इस संदर्भ में 1994 में भारतीय संसद के द्वारा प्रस्ताव भी लाया गया। जिसमें उल्लिखित है पाक अधिकृत कश्मीर भारतीय कश्मीर का भाग है। वर्तमान में भारतीय संविधान द्वारा 1954 में जम्मू-कश्मीर को दिया गया विशेष राज्य का दर्जा समाप्त कर दिया है।

जम्मू-कश्मीर में नए युग का प्रारंभ-अनुच्छेद 370 समाप्त

वर्तमान में भारत ने अपनी विदेशी नीति में बहुत बदलाव किए हैं। इसका महत्वपूर्ण उदाहरण है अनुच्छेद 370 व 35ए की समाप्ति। जो जम्मू-कश्मीर को विशेष राज्य का दर्जा दिलाता है। अगस्त 2019 में मोदी सरकार ने एक दृढ़, साहसी एवं

दूरदर्शितापूर्ण कदम उठाते हुए, जम्मू-कश्मीर को स्वायत्तता जैसा विशेष दर्जा दिलाने वाले अनु. 370 व 35ए को न केवल समाप्त कर दिया बल्कि जम्मू-कश्मीर को जम्मू-कश्मीर एवं लद्दाख नाम के दो अलग-अलग केंद्र शासित क्षेत्रों में विभाजित भी कर दिया। इसमें जम्मू-कश्मीर विधान सभा वाला केंद्रशासित क्षेत्र रहेगा, जबकि लद्दाख विधानसभा रहित केंद्रशासीत क्षेत्र बनाया गया है। अन्य केंद्रशासित क्षेत्रों की तरह इन दोनों के लिए भी उपराज्यपाल की नियुक्ति राष्ट्रपति द्वारा की जाएगी। 31 अक्टूबर, 2019 को जम्मू-कश्मीर का पुनर्गठन कर दो नए केंद्रशासित क्षेत्रों जम्मू-कश्मीर व लद्दाख भारत के मानचित्र में उभर आए।[5] भारत द्वारा जम्मू-कश्मीर मामले में उठाए गए इस कदम का पाकिस्तान द्वारा विरोध किया गया और इसे मानवाधिकार का उल्लंघन बताया गया, परंतु भारत ने इसे अपनी संप्रभुता का मामला बताकर पाकिस्तान को इसमें हस्तक्षेप न करने की हिदायत दी। भारत के इस साहसिक कदम से भारत-पाक संबंधों में एक बार फिर खट्टास आ गई क्योंकि पाकिस्तान द्वारा जम्मू-कश्मीर में आतंकवादी गतिविधियों को अंजाम देना मुश्किल हो जाएगा।

उरी आतंकी हमला और उसके परिणाम

18 सितंबर 2016 को जम्मू-कश्मीर के उरी सेक्टर में एलओसी के पास स्थित भारतीय सेना के स्थानीय मुख्यालय पर एक बड़ा आतंकी हमला हुआ, जिसमें भारत के 18 जवान शहीद हो गए। सैन्य बलों की कार्रवाई में सभी चार आतंकी मारे गए। यह भारतीय सेना पर लगभग 20 सालों में किया गया सबसे बड़ा हमला था। भारत सरकार ने इस आतंकी हमले को बहुत गंभीरता से लिया। पहले हुई कई हमलों (पठानकोट आदि) की तरह इस हमले में भी आतंकवादियों के पाकिस्तान से संबंध होने के प्रमाण मिले, जिसके कारण भारत भर में रोश प्रकट हुआ और भारत सरकार ने कई अप्रत्याशित कदम उठाए जिनसे भारत-पाकिस्तान संबंध प्रभावित हुए। भारत द्वारा उठाए गए कदम इस प्रकार हैं—

1. भारत सरकार के कूटनीतिक स्तर पर विश्वभर में पाकिस्तान को अलग थलग करने की मुहिम छेड़ दी।
2. संयुक्त राष्ट्र में भारत की विदेशी मंत्री ने आतंक का पोषण करने वाले देशों की निंदा की। पाकिस्तान को स्पष्ट शब्दों में कहा कि कश्मीर छीनने का सपना पूरा नहीं होगा।

3. प्रधानमंत्री नरेंद्र मोदी के बयान 'खून और पानी साथ-साथ नहीं बह सकते' के साथ ही भारत ने सिंधु जल संधि की समीक्षा शुरू कर दी। पाकिस्तान ने इसे युद्ध की कार्रवाई बताया और भारत के खिलाफ परमाणु हथियारों के उपयोग की धमकी दी। संधि रद्द होने के डर से पाकिस्तान ने विश्व बैंक का दरवाजा खटखटाया।
4. भारत ने नवंबर 2016 में इस्लामाबाद में होने वाले सार्क शिखर सम्मेलन का बहिष्कार करने की घोषणा की। बांग्लादेश, भूटान व अफगानिस्तान ने भी भारत का समर्थन करते हुए बहिष्कार की घोषणा की।
5. भारत ने पाकिस्तान को दिए गए मोस्ट फेवर्ड नेशन के दर्जे पर पुनर्विचार की घोषणा की।
6. 29 सितंबर, 2016 को भारत के डी जी एम ओ ने प्रेस कॉफ्रेंस में बताया कि भारतीय सेना ने आतंकियों के ठिकानों पर सर्जिकल हमले करके उन्हें मार गिराया और उनके ठिकानों को नष्ट कर दिया गया है।[6]

भारत द्वारा उरी हमले के पश्चात् उठाए गए ये कदम वर्तमान में भारत की बदली विदेश नीति का ही परिणाम हैं। भारत ने पूर्व में की गई अपनी गलतियों से सीख लेते हुए समय के साथ अपनी विदेश नीति में बदलाव को आवश्यक समझा। अगर भारत ने पूर्व में ही अपनी विदेश नीति में बदलाव किए होते और पाकिस्तान के खिलाफ कड़े कदम उठाए होते तो भारत-पाक युद्ध, 1965 व भारत-पाक युद्ध 1971 कभी होता ही नहीं और पाकिस्तान कभी भारत को आंखें दिखाने की कोशिश नहीं करता। भारत के नरम रुख वाली विदेश नीति का पाकिस्तान फायदा उठाता रहा है जिसका परिणाम कारगिल संघर्ष, पाक का नियंत्रण रेखा का बार-बार उल्लंघन करना, आतंकी गतिविधियों को अंजाम देना है।

सिंधु नदी जल विवाद

1960 में सिंधु नदी समझौते के अंतर्गत सिंधु, झेलम और चिनाब को पाकिस्तान की नदियों के रूप में जबकि सतलुज, रावी एवं व्यास पर भारत के नियंत्रण को स्वीकार किया गया। इस समझौते के द्वारा भारत को पाकिस्तान की नदियों पर जल की सीमित प्रयोग का अधिकार दिया गया।

पाकिस्तान की आपत्ति : पाकिस्तान द्वारा यह आरोप लगाया जाता है कि

भारत, पाकिस्तान के हिस्से के पानी का प्रयोग कर रहा है।

भारत का तर्क : भारत के अनुसार ग्लेशियर कम होने से और बरसात कम होने के कारण सिंधु नदी में पानी का प्रवाह कम हो रहा है तथा सिंधु नदी के पानी का मुद्दा उठाकर पाक सीमा पार आतंकवाद से ध्यान भटकाना चाहता है।

सियाचिन विवाद : सियाचिन, पाकिस्तान नियंत्रित गिलगिल और बालटिस्तान के समान अत्यधिक ऊंचाई पर होने के साथ ही काराकोरम दर्रे के निकट है जो भारत के जम्मू व कश्मीर राज्य को तिब्बत या चीन से जोड़ता है, इसलिए यह भारत व पाकिस्तान दोनों के लिए सामरिक महत्व रखता है। पाकिस्तान द्वारा 1984 में इस पर नियंत्रण करने का प्रयत्न किया गया, जिसके जवाब में भारत द्वारा 'ऑपरेशन मेघदूत' प्रारंभ किया गया और उसके बाद से यह क्षेत्र भारत के कब्जे में है।

सरक्रीक विवाद : सरक्रीक गुजरात में कच्छ की खाड़ी और पाक में सिंध की सीमा पर स्थित 60 किमी0. का एक ज्वारीय नदी चैनल है। सरक्रीक की विशेषता यह है यह ठीक भारत-पाक सीमा के बीच स्थित है और यह किस देश की सीमा में आता है, अभी तक निर्धारित नहीं हो पाया है। इस विवाद का मुख्य कारण दोनों पक्षों द्वारा सरक्रीक को अपनी सीमा में बताना बताया जाता है। भारत का तर्क है कि सरक्रीक पर सीमा निर्धारण दो बराबर भागों अर्थात् भूखंड के मध्य से होना चाहिए। पाकिस्तान का तर्क है कि पूर्वी भाग से सीमा का निर्धारण किया जाना चाहिए। अर्थात् सरक्रीक का विभाजन 24^0 समानांतर होना चाहिए।

आतंकवाद का मुद्दा : पाकिस्तान द्वारा कश्मीर में आतंकवादी, अलगाववादी व उग्रवादी संगठनों को बढ़ावा देने के साथ-साथ भारत के विरुद्ध छद्म युद्ध भी चलाया जा रहा है। जिसमें 24 दिसंबर 1999 का आई सी 814 का अपहरण, 2001 में भारतीय संसद पर हमला, 2008 का मुंबई हमला, पठानकोठ आतंकी हमला तथा 2016 का उरी हमला, पुलवामा का हमला प्रमुख है। पाकिस्तान द्वारा उन आतंकी संगठनों (जैसे- जैश-ए-मुहम्मद, लश्कर-ए-तैयबा) को प्रशिक्षण व वित्तीय सहायता उपलब्ध कराता है जो कश्मीर के साथ-साथ भारत के विरुद्ध हिंसात्मक घटनाओं में शामिल होते हैं। भारत द्वारा संयुक्त राष्ट्र, सुरक्षा परिषद से लेकर सभी बड़े मंचों पर आतंकवाद के मुद्दे को उठाया गया है। आज पूरी दुनिया में कहीं भी आतंकवादी घटना होती है तो इसका तार कहीं न कहीं से पाकिस्तान से जुड़े होते हैं। चाहे अमेरिका, पेरिस हो या फिर भारत में उरी व पुलवामा। हर आतंकी घटना में पाकिस्तान का हाथ दिखाई देता है। पाक के मंत्री इस बात को कबूल भी कर चुके

हैं कि उनके यहां आतंकी संगठन सक्रिय हैं। ऐसे में भारत व अन्य देश पाकिस्तान की पनाह में पल रहे आतंकवाद के खिलाफ आवाज उठा रहे हैं। भारत ने नैम, दक्षेस, जी-7, SCO व अन्य मंचों पर इस मामले को हमेशा उठाया है और इसे रोकने के लिए अपना पूर्ण सहयोग देना स्वीकार किया है। पाकिस्तान द्वारा भारत की शांति एवं सुरक्षा को हानि पहुंचाने के लिए आतंकी घुसपैठ कराने की कोशिश सदैव की जाती रही है, परंतु भारत द्वारा इन कोशिशों को नाकाम किया जाता रहा है। साथ ही, पाकिस्तान की सरजमीं में घुसकर आतंकी ठिकानों को सर्जिकल स्ट्राइक द्वारा नष्ट किया गया है। भारत व पाकिस्तान के बीच पाकिस्तान में आतंकवाद एक महत्वपूर्ण मुद्दा है। जिसके खिलाफ पाकिस्तान के साथ विवाद हमेशा चलता रहता है। जो कभी भी भारत-पाक संबंधों को मधुर नहीं होने देगा। भारत का हमेशा एक ही प्रश्न है पाकिस्तान कब तक अपनी जमीन पर आतंकवादियों को पनाह देगा।

वर्तमान में भारत-पाक संबंधों का उतार चढ़ाव : वर्तमान में भारत-पाक संबंधों में बहुत उतार-चढ़ाव आए हैं। शांति के नए अध्याय की शुरुआत करने के लिए दिसंबर 2015 में भारत की विदेशमंत्री सुषमा स्वराज ने 'हार्ट ऑफ एशिया' सम्मेलन में भाग लेने हेतु पाकिस्तान की यात्रा की और पाक के प्रधानमंत्री नवाज शरीफ एवं उनके सलाहाकार सरताज से भेंट की। इस भेंट के बाद दोनों देशों के बीच वार्ता के द्वार खुले और लगा शायद अब दोनों देशों के संबंधों में मधुरता आएगी तथा हालात सुधरेंगे, परंतु 2 जनवरी, 2016 को पठानकोट वायु सेना के अड्डे पर आतंकी हमला और 18 सितंबर 2016 को उरी के सैनिक कैंप पर आतंकी हमला करके पाकिस्तान ने भारत के साथ पुनः विश्वासघात किया। एक ओर पाकिस्तान शांति की बात करता रहा और दूसरी ओर भारत में आतंकी हमले कराकर उसको घाव देता रहा है। पठानकोट व उरी हमले के घाव अभी भरे नहीं थे कि पाकिस्तान ने 14 जनवरी, 2019 को पुनः जम्मू-कश्मीर के पुलवामा में सेना की गाड़ी में आत्मघाती हमला कराके नापाक इरादे जगजाहिर कर दिए। पुलवामा आतंकी हमले ने देश को झकझोर कर रख दिया था। इस हमले में सीआरपीएफ के 40 जवान शहीद हो गए थे। पुलवामा हमले की सभी देशों द्वारा निंदा की गई।[8] इसके पश्चात् भारत-पाक रिश्ते और बिगड़ गए। भारत सरकार ने पाक से सभी शांति-वार्ता को रोक दिया और कहा जब तक पाक इन आतंकी गतिविधियों को नहीं रोकता तब तक कोई वार्ता नहीं होगी। इन तीनों आतंकी हमले के कारण भारत-पाक संबंध टूट गए, जो वर्तमान सितंबर 2019 तक काफी हद तक अनसुलझा रहा। यह सभी हमले भारत

और पाकिस्तान के बीच बिगड़ते संबंधों को स्थिर करने के लिए एक नाजुक शांति प्रक्रिया को पटरी से उतारने का प्रयास था।

भारत तथा पाकिस्तान के संबंधों को बिगाड़ने का एक कारण चीन-पाक आर्थिक गलियारा भी है। यह आर्थिक कोरीडोर चीन के शिनजियांग क्षेत्र के काशगर क्षेत्र को पाक के ग्वादर बंदरगाह से जोड़ता है। यह कोरीडोर पाकिस्तान अधिकृत कश्मीर से गुजर रहा है जो वैधानिक रूप से भारत का भाग है और भारतीय सुरक्षा के लिए बड़ी चुनौती है। जिसके कारण भारत इसका विरोध कर रहा है।

दोनों पड़ोसियों के बीच लगातार तनाव के बावजूद, विशेष रूप से भारतीय संविधान के अनुच्छेद 370 को निरस्त करने को भारत के अचानक निर्णय के बाद, भारत और पाक दोनों ने पाकिस्तान में दरबार साहिब का दौरा करने के लिए भारतीय सिखों को अनुमति देने के लिए गलियारे के संचालन के लिए समझौते पर हस्ताक्षर किए। भारत करतारपुर पर पाकिस्तान की पेशकश का विरोध करने की स्थिति में नहीं था, क्योंकि भारत सरकार सिख समुदाय की धार्मिक भावनाओं को ठेस नहीं पहुंचा सकती है। करतारपुर गलियारे का उद्घाटन प्रधानमंत्री मोदी जी ने किया। इसे गलियारे के खुलने को आशावादियों द्वारा सकारात्मक विकास के रूप में देखा जा रहा है। गौर करने वाली बात यह है कि ये करतारपुर गलियारा भारत व पाकिस्तान के रिश्ते को सौहार्दपूर्ण बनाता है या भविष्य में विवाद को जन्म देता है।[9]

भारत व पाकिस्तान के संबंध विगत कुछ वर्षों में काफी उतार-चढ़ाव के रहे हैं कभी आतंकी हमले ने माहौल को बिगाड़ा तो कभी करतारपुर गलियारे ने सौहार्द की शुरूआत की। पाकिस्तान द्वारा अपनी नापाक हरकतों द्वारा भारत से अपने संबंध स्वयं बिगाड़ता रहा है। जैसे - भारत की पहली वर्षगांठ की पूर्व संध्या पर जम्मू-कश्मीर की विशेष स्थिति को बदलने के लिए पाकिस्तान ने एक नया राजनीतिक मानचित्र जारी किया, जिससे जम्मू-कश्मीर के साथ-साथ गुजरात के कुछ हिस्सों को शामिल किया। प्रधानमंत्री इमरान खान ने कहा—'राजनीतिक मानचित्र हमारी राष्ट्रीय आकांक्षा को दर्शाता है और कश्मीर विवाद पर हमारे राजसी रुख का समर्थन करता है।' इस कथन को भारत द्वारा अस्वीकार करते हुए 'न तो कानूनी वैधता' और न ही अंतर्राष्ट्रीय विश्वसनीयता के साथ 'हास्यास्पद' कहा गया। इसी प्रकार कुलभूषण जाधव का मामला भी दोनों देशों के मध्य विवाद का कारण है जहां पाकिस्तान कुलभूषण जाधव को भारतीय जासूस बताकर कैद किए हुए है वहीं भारत इस बात से इनकार कर रहा है और जाधव को सामान्य नागरिक बताकर उसकी

रिहाई की मांग कर रहा। इस मुद्दे के लिए दोनों देशों के मध्य विवाद अंतर्राष्ट्रीय न्यायालय में भी पहुंच चुका है, परंतु इसका अभी कोई समाधान नहीं निकला है।

इसके अतिरिक्त भी बहुत से ऐसे मामले हैं, जो भारत-पाकिस्तान संबंधों को बिगाड़े हुए हैं उनमें मुख्य है पाकिस्तान के भीतर के हालात जो स्वयं चिंताजनक हैं। देश में कमजोर सरकार है, जिसके नेता अनुभवहीन और जबान पलटने वाले हैं। हमारे इस महत्वपूर्ण पड़ोस में लोकतंत्र की नींव कभी ठीक से जम नहीं पाई है। वहां की सेना में 80 प्रतिशत पंजाबी रहते हैं। यही हाल आई.एस.आई. का है, जो अक्सर अमेरिका की सीआईए की तर्ज पर काम करने लगती है। ब्लूचिस्तान के लोग बहुत नाराज हैं तो सिंध में बेचैनी है, उत्तर-पश्चिम सीमांत उबल रहा है। आज पाक अंतर्राष्ट्रीय मंचों से खुद के आतंकवाद से त्रस्त होने का रोना रोता है। जबकि वास्तविकता यह है कि भारत को हजार घाव देने के इरादे से उसने जिन जिहादियों को तैयार किया था वही आज उसके लिए भस्मासुर साबित हो रहे हैं। पाकिस्तान वर्तमान में एक ऐसा मोहरा बन चुका है। जिसे सभी अपने लाभ के लिए इस्तेमाल करना चाहते हैं और पाकिस्तान उन्हें सिर्फ भारत के खिलाफ इस्तेमाल करना चाहता है। भारत-पाक संबंधों में भले ही बातचीत को महत्वपूर्ण बताया जाता हो पर इस बातचीत से आजतक कुछ ठोस बाहर निकलकर नहीं आया है। बातचीत द्वारा ही निकले शिमला और लाहौर समझौतों को दोनों देशों में से कोई नहीं मानता है जब तक दोनों देशों में धर्म और कट्टरता कम नहीं होती बातचीत से कुछ खास हासिल नहीं होगा। साथ ही, पाकिस्तान में चल रही समानांतर सरकारें (सेना, आईएसआई, कट्टरपंथी) इस राह में बड़ी अवरोधक रही है।[10]

वही अगर भारत-पाकिस्तान के आर्थिक संबंधों की बात करें तो वह भी ज्यादा कुछ अच्छे नहीं है। भारत-पाकिस्तान ट्रेड आर्गेनाइजेशन के मुताबिक 2018-19 में भारत-पाकिस्तान के बीच कुल 2.05 बिलियन अमेरिकी डॉलर का व्यापार हुआ। भारत से पाकिस्तान को निर्यात की जाने वाली वस्तुओं में चीनी, कपास, रसायन प्रमुख है। भारत चाय का अग्रणी निर्यातक है और पाकिस्तान सबसे बड़ा आयातक। दोनों के पड़ोसी होने के बावजूद पाकिस्तान अपनी जरूरत की 6 प्रतिशत मात्रा की ही चाय भारत से आयात करता है। पाकिस्तान अपनी गेहूं की जरूरतों को ऑस्ट्रेलिया, अर्जेंटीना से आयात कर पूरी करता है जबकि भारत में गेहूं का भंडार भरे पड़े हैं और वह अपने गेहूं के लिए विश्व भर में बाजार ढूंढ़ रहा है यदि पाकिस्तान, पंजाब व हरियाणा से गेहूं मंगाए तो उसे कम खर्च में गेहूं मिल जाएगा। इसी प्रकार

बेहतर गुणवत्ता और कम कीमत के चलते भारत का कपास पाकिस्तान में स्थान बना सकता है। फिर पंजाब से सड़क मार्ग खुलने से पाकिस्तान के रास्ते अफगानिस्तान और रूस को भेजे जाने उत्पाद 12 से 14 दिनों में पहुंच जाएंगे, जो अभी 30 से 40 दिनों में पहुंचते हैं परंतु ये तभी संभव है जब दोनों देशों के मध्य आर्थिक संबंध समझें। वर्तमान में बहुत से कारण हैं जो दोनों देशों के संबंधों के लिए जिम्मेदार हैं जिसके समाधान के बिना भारत-पाक संबंध हमेशा कटु ही रहेंगे।

उपरोक्त बिंदु और कारणों को देखते हुए हम कह सकते हैं कि भारत-पाक के बीच सहयोग की बजाए विवाद के मुद्दे अधिक हैं जिससे समूचा दक्षिण एशिया प्रभावित है।

निष्कर्ष

भारत और पाकिस्तान के संबंधों की पृष्ठभूमि भावनात्मक लगाव एवं अप्रत्यक्ष घटनाओं का इतिहास है। निकटतम पड़ोसी होने के बावजूद पाकिस्तान अपनी भारत-विरोधी एवं विघटनकारी नीतियों के कारण भारत से लगातार दूर होता गया। वर्तमान में आतंकवाद एवं कश्मीर विवाद से दोनों देशों के संबंध कड़वाहट से भर गए। भारत ने पाकिस्तान के साथ शांति, मित्रता एवं सहयोगपूर्ण संबंध स्थापित करने के लिए सदैव गंभीर प्रयास किए हैं, किंतु पाकिस्तान द्वारा सदैव नकारात्मक प्रत्युत्तर दिया गया। वाजपेयी द्वारा की गई लाहौर बस यात्रा तथा लाहौर घोषणा का जवाब कारगिल घुसपैठ के रूप में दिया गया। कारगिल प्रकरण से भारत की एक जिम्मेदार राश्ट्र की अंतर्राष्ट्रीय छवि को और अधिक मजबूती प्राप्त हुई। कारगिल संघर्ष के बाद पाकिस्तान द्वारा भारत विरोधी दुष्प्रचार करना तथा सीमापार आतंकवाद को समर्थन देना जारी है। समझौता एक्सप्रेस, दिल्ली-लाहौर बस सेवा के जारी रहने, तीर्थ यात्रियों तथा सांस्कृतिक कर्मियों के आवागमन से जनता के स्तर पर परस्पर संपर्क कायम हुआ है। पाकिस्तान के प्रति अपनाई गई नरम नीति से सैन्य मनोबल में कमी, आतंकी गतिविधियों को प्रोत्साहन तथा भारतीय जन-सामान्य में निराशावाद जैसे नकारात्मक परिणाम भी सामने आए हैं, किंतु इस नरम प्रकार की कूटनीति ने पाकिस्तान के वास्तविक मंसूबों को अंतर्राष्ट्रीय समुदाय के सामने पूरी तरह उजागर कर दिया है। डॉ. मनमोहन सिंह के नेतृत्व में नई सरकार ने भी पाकिस्तान के साथ संबंधों को सुधारने पर जोर दिया। इसी संदर्भ में 24 सितंबर, 2004 को न्यूयॉर्क में भारत के प्रधानमंत्री डॉ. मनमोहन सिंह और पाकिस्तान के राष्ट्रपति परवेज

मुशर्रफ के मध्य शिखर वार्ता हुई। 26 नवंबर, 2008 को मुंबई पर आतंकवादी हमलों और इस हमले में पाकिस्तान के तत्वों की संलिप्तता के कारण द्विपक्षीय वार्ता प्रक्रिया को रोका दिया गया। 26/11 के आतंकी हमले के पश्चात् भारत-पाक संबंध अपने निम्नतर स्तर पर पहुंच चुके थे। इस संबंध में भारत ने पाकिस्तान को स्पष्ट शब्दों में बता दिया है कि हमले में साजिश रचने वाले आतंकी समूहों के विरुद्ध कड़ी कार्रवाई करे अन्यथा उससे कोई वार्ता नहीं की जाएगी।

गौरतलब है कि विश्व समुदाय इस समय भारत के रूख से सहमत है एवं पाकिस्तान पर आतंकियों के विरूद्ध कड़े कदम उठाने का दबाव पड़ रहा है। अमेरिका, ब्रिटेन, रूस एवं फ्रांस जैसे देशों ने भारतीय संयम की सराहना करते हुए उन्हें यह आश्वासन दिया है कि वे भारत की हर संभव मदद के लिए तैयार हैं। विगत वर्षों में मोदी सरकार की आक्रामक विदेशी नीति के समक्ष पाकिस्तान घुटने टेकने पर मजबूर हो रहा है। भारत-पाकिस्तान के संबंधों के सुधरने के आसार वैसे तो बहुत कम हैं क्योंकि कश्मीर मुद्दा दोनों के लिए नासूर बना हुआ है। दोनों ही इस मुद्दे को विभाजन से लेकर वर्तमान तक उलझाते रहे हैं। पाकिस्तान भारत अधिकृत कश्मीर में आतंकवाद को बढ़ावा देता रहा है और साथ ही शान्ति वार्ता की बात भी करता रहा है। वर्तमान में भारत सरकार ने स्पष्ट कह दिया है कश्मीर भारत का अभिन्न अंग है जिससे पाकिस्तान अपने नापाक इरादों द्वारा कभी हासिल नहीं कर सकता है। मोदी सरकार द्वारा जम्मू-कश्मीर से अनुच्छेद 370 खत्म करने के पश्चात् यह बात स्पष्ट हो गई है। पाकिस्तान में इमरान सरकार के आने से भारत-पाकिस्तान संबंध सुधरने के बजाय और बिगड़ गए। उपरोक्त सभी बातों को देखते हुए ये कहना गलत नहीं होगा कि भारत और पाकिस्तान के मध्य संबंध मधुर और सामान्य होना एक स्वप्न सा प्रतीत होता है। वर्तमान हालातों पर नजर डालें तो यही स्पष्ट दिखाई देता है कि विगत 10 वर्षों में पाकिस्तान द्वारा भारत में आतंकी गतिविधियों को अंजाम देने और विश्व मंच पर भारत के खिलाफ जहर उगलने के कारण जहां पाकिस्तान की विश्व भर में निंदा ही हुई है वहीं भारत के संयम की प्रशंसा हुई। भारत ने सदैव पाकिस्तान के साथ एक शांतिपूर्ण संबंध चाहे हैं, किंतु पाकिस्तान ने इसके विपरीत भारत को सांप्रदायिकता के आधार पर बांटने के लिए धार्मिक प्रचार प्रसार किया। विभाजन से लेकर वर्तमान तक पाक यही करता रहा है, परंतु अब समय बदल गया। भारत अब एशिया में सबसे बड़ी अर्थव्यवस्था के रूप में उभर रहा है। उसके संबंध हर देश से बेहतर हो गए हैं। आज वह संयुक्त

राष्ट्र संघ की सुरक्षा परिषद में स्थायी सदस्यता का प्रबल दावेदार है। इन सभी बातों को देखते हुए हम कह यह सकते हैं कि वर्तमान वैश्विक परिदृश्य में भारतीय विदेश नीति में विरोधाभासी बदलाव अवश्य हुए हैं। जिसका कारण वर्तमान परिस्थिति है और भारत-पाक संबंधों पर भी इसका गहरा प्रभाव पड़ा है।

संदर्भ ग्रंथ सूची

1. दत्त, वी.पी., *इंडियन फॉरेन पॉलिसी*, विकास पब्लिशिंग हाउस, नई दिल्ली, 1984।
2. जे.एन., दीक्षित, *भारतीय विदेश नीति*, प्रभात प्रकाशन, नई दिल्ली, 2020।
3. दत्त वी.पी., *बदलती दुनिया में भारत की विदेशी नीति*, हिंदी माध्यम कार्यान्वय निदेशालय, दिल्ली वि.वि., 2003।
4. *प्रतियोगिता दर्पण*, साहित्य भवन पब्लिकेशन, आगरा, अक्टूबर व दिसंबर, 2019।
5. https:\\mea.gov.in\foreign-relation.htm
6. Singh Uday Veer, Indo-Pak Relation: Beyond Pulwama and Balakot, Pentagon Press, New Delhi,2018
7. https:\\idsa.in\taxonomy\term\195
8. https:\\thediplamat.com\tag\india-pakistan-relations\
9. जे.एन.दीक्षित, भारत-पाक संबंधः युद्ध और शांति में, प्रभात प्रकाशन, नई दिल्ली, 2018।
10. खन्ना, वी.एन., अरोड़ा लिपाक्षी, कुमार लैस्ली, *भारत की विदेश नीति*, विकास पब्लिशिंग हाउस, नई दिल्ली, 2019।

20

वैश्विक राजनीति में भारत और सॉफ्ट पावर

अविनाश जाटव

सारांश

भारत के लिए सॉफ्ट पावर कोई नया सिद्धांत नहीं है। ऐतिहासिक रूप से भारतीय सॉफ्ट पावर की जड़ें अहिंसा की दर्शनिक अवधारणाओं, हिंदू धर्म की सार्वभौमिकता, भारतीय सभ्यता, भारतीय संस्कृति, बौद्ध धर्म, शास्त्रीय संगीत व नृत्य, योग और आयुर्वेद में सन्निहित है। जो विश्व को सदियों से अपने प्रति आकर्षित करती है, इन्हीं कारणों से भारत को सॉफ्ट पावर के रूप में पहचाना जाता है। सॉफ्ट पावर हार्ड पावर का विकल्प न हो कर पूरक है, एक व्यापक बाहरी रणनीति में दोनों का प्रभावी सम्मेलन ही देश को एक स्मार्ट पावर बना सकता है। उत्तर शीत युद्ध के बाद आए वैश्वीकरण से देशों में आपसी निर्भरता के बढ़ाव के कारण फौज और अन्य बल प्रयोगों का प्रभाव कम हो गया है जिसके कारण सॉफ्ट पावर की राष्ट्र हित के लिए उपयोगिता बढ गई है। प्रस्तुत शोध पत्र में एक विदेश नीति उपकरण के रूप में और अन्य देशों के साथ संबंध स्थापित करने के लिए सॉफ्ट पावर के अध्ययन का प्रयास किया गया है, साथ ही, भारत की सॉफ्ट पावर के कारकों और स्रोतों का अध्ययन भी किया है।

संकेत शब्द : सॉफ्ट पावर, हार्ड पावर, विदेश नीति, सभ्यता एवं संस्कृति, डायस्पोरा, योग, आयुर्वेद , हिंदू धर्म , बौद्ध धर्म, बॉलीवुड।

प्रस्तावना

अंतरर्राष्ट्रीय संबंधों के संदर्भ में, सहयोग तथा किसी प्रकार के आकर्षण के तथा देश की किसी दबाव या बल का प्रयोग किए बिना अन्य देशों को अपने अनुसार कार्य करने हेतु सहमत करने की क्षमता सौम्य शक्ति या मृदु शक्ति (Soft power)

कहलाती है। सॉफ्ट पावर संस्कृति, विचारधारा, प्रतिष्ठा और संस्थानों जैसे अमूर्त शक्ति संसाधनों से संबद्ध होती है। इसके विपरीत 'कठोर शक्ति' (hard power) उस क्षमता को कहते हैं जो बल (सैन्य बल) द्वारा या धन देकर इच्छित परिणाम प्राप्त करती है।

अमेरिकी राजनीति विज्ञानी जोसेफ न्ये ने 1990 में जब इस धारणा को लोकप्रिय बनाया था, उससे पहले से ही भारत की सॉफ्ट पावर बहुत मजबूत है और उसे दुनिया के विभिन्न हिस्सों में शताब्दियों पूर्व से ही स्वीकृति मिलती रही है। विश्व ने दुनिया की प्रचानीतम सभ्यताओं में शामिल इस देश की कला और संस्कृति के बारे में जाना समझा है। लेकिन पिछले दो दशक के दौरान भारत ने अपनी खास तौर पर पावर का ज्यादा व्यवस्थित तरीके से उपयोग करना शुरू किया है। भारत को अंतर्राष्ट्रीय समुदाय के सामने पेश करने के लिए कई कदम उठाए गए हैं। इनमें 2006 में विदेश मंत्रालय के अधीन एक पब्लिक डिप्लोमेसी डिवीजन शुरू करना। भारतीय सांस्कृतिक संबंध परिषद (आईसीसीआर) का दुनिया भर में विस्तार, पर्यटन मंत्रालय का 'अतुल्य भारत अभियान' और प्रवासी कार्य मंत्रालय के काम काज भी शामिल है। इन प्रयासों ने न सिर्फ भारत के सामाजिक और सांस्कृतिक पहलू को विदेशों में प्रदर्शित करने में मदद की है, बल्कि देश की अहम विदेश नीति से जुड़े प्रयासों में भी मदद की है। इनमें अफ्रीका में की गई सामरिक मदद और व्यापारिक साझेदारी भी शामिल हैं। अब व्यापार और कारोबार का संवर्धन और उसके साथ रोजगार के अवसरों का विकास प्रधानमंत्री नरेंद्र मोदी के कूटनीतिक प्रयासों का अहम तत्व है। संयुक्त राष्ट्र द्वारा मसूद अजहर को वैश्विक आतंकवादी के रूप में घोषित किए जाने को भारत की महत्वपूर्ण कूटनीतिक सफलता के रूप में देखा जाता है जो भारत की बढ़ती हुई सॉफ्ट पावर क्षमता का एक सर्वश्रेष्ठ उदाहरण सिद्ध के रूप में देखा जा सकता है।

इंटरनेशनल रिलेशंस थ्योरी में, सॉफ्ट पावर को संस्कृति या वैचारिक माध्यमों से परोक्ष रूप से दूसरों के व्यवहार या आचरण को प्रभावित करने की क्षमता के रूप में परिभाषित किया गया है। यह तर्क दिया जा सकता है कि हार्डपावर एक महत्वपूर्ण शक्ति स्रोत है जिसे विभिन्न राज्यों द्वारा प्रभुत्व प्राप्त करने के लिए अधिग्रहीत या उपयोग किया जाता है, लेकिन इसकी दोष रेखाएं हैं। उदाहरण के लिए, वियतनाम, अफगानिस्तान, इराक और फिलिस्तीन ने कठोर शक्ति की विफलता साबित की है।

जब हम दूसरों को हमारे मूल्यों और आदर्शों की प्रशंसा करने के लिए प्राप्त कर सकते हैं, तो हमें उन्हें अपनी दिशा या पक्ष में ले जाने के लिए लाठी और बल पर भरोसा करने की ज़रूरत नहीं है। जैसा कि न्ये का तर्क है, "जबरदस्ती की तुलना में प्रलोभन हमेशा अधिक प्रभावी होता है और लोकतंत्र, मानवाधिकार, और व्यक्तिगत अवसर जैसे कई मूल्य गहरे मोहक होते है।"

एक व्यापक स्पेक्ट्रम का गठन करते हुए, सॉफ्ट पावर के प्रमुख घटक आर्थिक से लेकर सामाजिक सांस्कृतिक और यहां तक किए सभ्यता तक होते हैं; मैसेजिंग, इसका वास्तविक मूल है जो आधिकारिक संवादों में रणनीतिक संचार के माध्यम से और हमारे सूचना संतृप्ति के युग में उपलब्ध विविध मीडिया प्लेटफार्मों का उपयोग करके व्यापक लक्षित सार्वजनिक आउटरीच के माध्यम से किया जाता है।

विदेश मंत्रालय अन्य सरकारी संगठनों के साथ व्यापक द्विपक्षीय और बहुपक्षीय आर्थिक कार्यक्रमों का संचालन और समन्वय करता है। सहयोग, विकास परियोजनाएं, कौशल का उन्नयन, छात्र आदान-प्रदान और छात्रवृत्ति, लोगों से लोगों के संबंध, प्रशिक्षण कार्यक्रम, थिंक टैंक गतिविधि और सांस्कृतिक आदान प्रदान जिसमें रचनात्मक और प्रदर्शन कलाए पुरातत्व, अध्ययन शैक्षणिक सम्मेलन आदि शामिल हैं। यह मीडिया एक्सचेंजों को बढ़ावा देने और विदेशों में भारत की छवि पेश करने में भूमिका निभाता है जिससे भारत की सॉफ्ट पावर में बढ़ोतरी होती है।

आजकल, सॉफ्ट पावर किसी देश की छवि को प्रोजेक्ट करने के लिए शक्ति का मुख्य स्रोत है और नकारात्मक छवि को कम करने के लिए कूटनीति का एक महत्वपूर्ण उपकरण भी है। यह अनिवार्य रूप से एक शून्य योग खेल और नकारात्मक राशि के खेल के रूप में नहीं देखा जाता है, लेकिन आमतौर पर इसे सकारात्मक राशि के खेल के रूप में देखा जाता है और सॉफ्ट पावर की उपयोग के परस्पर क्रिया के कारण जीत की स्थिति होती है। यहां जबरदस्ती की शक्ति के लिए कोई जगह नहीं है। सॉफ्ट पावर की बढ़ती महत्ता का कारण अंतर्राष्ट्रीय संबंधों में वैश्वीकरण, तकनीकी क्रांति और नवउदारवादी सिद्धांत में वृद्धि है।

भारत की सॉफ्ट पावर

एक देश की सॉफ्ट पावर अनिवार्य रूप से देश की अपनी संस्कृति, विदेश नीति और राजनीतिक मूल्यों के माध्यम से आकर्षित करने की क्षमता को संदर्भित करती है। इसने देशों के लिए सार्वजनिक कूटनीति को आगे बढ़ाने और राज्य और गैर राज्य

अभिकर्ताओं दोनों के साथ अपने सांस्कृतिक जुड़ाव को बढ़ाने के लिए आधार के रूप में कार्य किया है।

भारत, जिसकी सॉफ्ट पावर अपनी सभ्यतागत विरासत और सांस्कृतिक कौशल पर टिकी है। भारत की विविध और सुसंगत संस्कृति पूरे देश में तो फैली है ही, साथ ही अन्य देशों में इसका प्रभाव है। इसके अलावा, हाल के दशकों में विभिन्न बहुपक्षीय मंचों पर भारत के वैश्विक कद में वृद्धि, योग और आयुर्वेद की बढ़ती लोकप्रियता और चल रही कोविड 19 महामारी के दौरान नमस्ते के रूप में अभिवादन को अपनाने वाला विश्व समुदाय भारतीय सॉफ्ट पावर के कुछ सबसे स्पष्ट उदाहरण हैं। एक सभ्यतागत राज्य के रूप में, भारत की सॉफ्ट पावर अपनी सहस्राब्दी पुरानी परंपराओं और ज्ञान में प्रकट होती है जो आज भी प्रासंगिक है। भारतीय ज्ञान प्रणाली (आईकेएस) न केवल अत्यंत वैज्ञानिक है, बल्कि सौंदर्यशास्त्र और भाषाविज्ञान के साथ गहन रूप से जुड़ी हुई हैं। स्विट्जरलैंड में यूरोपीय परमाणु अनुसंधान संगठन (सीईआरएन) के परिसर को सुशोभित करने वाली नटराज (नृत्य शिव) की मूर्ति मानव और ब्रह्मांड के बीच सार्वभौमिक संबंध को व्यक्त करती है। भारतीय महाकाव्य *रामायण* और *महाभारत* साथ ही बौद्ध धर्म ने दूर-दूर तक यात्रा की और आज भी, विशेष रूप से दक्षिण पूर्व एशियाई देशों में फल-फूल रहा है। उदाहरण के लिए थाईलैंड का राष्ट्रीय साहित्य *रामाकेन* और इंडोनेशिया में *काकाविन, रामायण* के स्थानीय संस्करण हैं जिन्हें इन देशों में रंगमंच, नृत्य-रूपों और अन्य शिल्पों के लिए अनुकूलित किया गया है, जो उनकी सांस्कृतिक और रचनात्मक अर्थव्यवस्था में अत्यधिक योगदान करते हैं।

भारत का सभ्यतागत जुड़ाव कभी भी युद्ध या उपनिवेश का परिणाम नहीं था, बल्कि विचारों, परंपराओं और संस्कृति के आदान-प्रदान का परिणाम था, जो विभिन्न वस्तुओं के व्यापार के साथ था। 'गैर-आक्रामक देश' के रूप में भारत की वैश्विक मान्यता है जिसकी दृष्टि समावेशी है और विश्वदृष्टि वसुधैव कुटुम्बकम के विचार में टिकी हुई है—दुनिया एक परिवार है। भारतीय सभ्यता का विचार प्रकृति को जीतने के बजाय उसके साथ सह-अस्तित्व के आदर्श में निहित है। इस अर्थ में, "सॉफ्ट पावर का अभ्यास भारत की मूल पहचान में अलंकृत है जो कि सहस्राब्दी से पहले की है, भले ही यह शब्द विदेश नीति और सांस्कृतिक प्रवचन में तुलनात्मक रूप से नया है।"

सांस्कृतिक और सभ्यतागत विरासत से परे, भारत को वैश्विक चुनौतियों का

समाधान करने और विभिन्न विकास संबंधी पहलों में सबसे आगे रहने में अपनी भूमिका के लिए पहचाना गया है। यद्यपि भारत की अंतर्राष्ट्रीय भागीदारी इसकी सुरक्षा और सामरिक हितों द्वारा निर्देशित है, यह सभी के लिए समावेशिता, बहुलता और कल्याण के मूल्यों पर भी टिकी हुई है। उदाहरण के लिए, अंतर्राष्ट्रीय सौर गठबंधन की स्थापना ने बहुपक्षीय सहयोग के माध्यम से पर्यावरणीय जोखिमों को कम करने की दिशा में भारत की प्रतिबद्धता को प्रदर्शित किया। इसी तरह, भारत ने आपदा के समय अन्य देशों को आर्थिक और मानवीय सहायता प्रदान की है। संयुक्त राष्ट्र शांति सेना में भारत का योगदान दुनिया में सबसे अधिक है। दुनिया को हाइड्रो क्लोरोक्वीन की आपूर्ति के माध्यम से COVID–19 से लड़ने के लिए द्विपक्षीय और बहुपक्षीय मंचों पर देश के सहयोग के साथ-साथ वैक्सीन विकास की दिशा में अनुसंधान एवं विकास प्रयासों को निर्देशित करना, वैश्विक दवा और कल्याण क्षेत्र में भारत के योगदान को उजागर करता है।

1959 में दलाई लामा ने भारत में शरण मांगी, और भारत में तिब्बती आध्यात्मिक नेता और उनके अनुयायियों की उपस्थिति दुनिया भर से आगंतुकों और समर्थकों को आकर्षित करती रही।

भारत में अपेक्षाकृत बहुलवादी सरकार, अहिंसक, और उदारवादी गैर, खतरनाक वैश्विक नेतृत्व की आशावादी दृष्टि है। महात्मा गांधी, रवींद्रनाथ टैगोर, साहित्य, संगीत, नृत्य, सॉफ्टवेयर उद्योग तथा प्रतिष्ठित व्यक्ति, सॉफ्ट पावर परिसंपत्तियों की एक असाधारण श्रृंखला का उत्पादन करते हैं जो विदेशी आबादी के लिए भारत के आकर्षण को चित्रित करते हैं।

सम्मान सद्भाव और बंधुत्व का महत्व ऐसे तत्व हैं जिनके लिए भारतीयों को पहचाना जाता है, अशोक, बुद्ध और गांधी प्रमुख प्रतिनिधि के रूप में खड़े हैं। *महाभारत* और *रामायण* जैसे पौराणिक महाकाव्यों की तुलना *ओडिसी* और *इलियड* जैसे महान यूनानी लेखकों के लेखों से की जाती है। भारत को उसके सकल घरेलू उत्पाद के लिए 1 और 1000 ईस्वी के बीच 'गोल्डन बर्ड' के रूप में सराहा गया, सदियों से, भारत ने यहूदियों, ईसाइयों, मुसलमानों और कई अन्य धर्मों को आश्रय, धार्मिक और सांस्कृतिक स्वतंत्रता प्रदान की है। भारत का इतिहास और संस्कृति दुनिया के लिए उसकी विरासत है जो भारत के इतिहास के कायापलट को प्रदर्शित करता है कि कैसे भारत ने विभिन्न धर्मों को सामंजस्यपूर्ण रूप से आत्मसात किया, फिर भी अपनी संस्कृति और इतिहास से कभी नहीं चूका। प्रख्यात प्राचीन भारतीय

दार्शनिक, चाणक्य की समझौता नीति और गैर आक्रामकता व्यवस्था और अनुदान द्वारा आसन्न शक्तियों को हासिल करने के लिए, प्राचीन भारतीय राज्य कला में महत्व को प्रदर्शित करता है।

भारत के प्राचीन विश्वविद्यालय शिक्षा के सबसे प्रख्यात केंद्र थे जिसने दुनिया के विभिन्न हिस्सों से बड़ी संख्या में विद्वानों और शिक्षार्थियों को आकर्षित किया। भारत एक रहस्यवादी सभ्यता के रूप में दुनिया के विभिन्न हिस्सों से भारत में शिक्षाविदों, विद्वानों और विभिन्न क्षेत्रों के लोगों की दिलचस्पी रखता है, जिसके कारण विभिन्न इंडोलॉजिस्टों का उदय हुआ।

नेहरू की पंचशील (शांतिपूर्ण सह-अस्तित्व) की पांच अवधारणाएं और शीत युद्ध के दौरान विश्व स्तर पर समर्थित गुटनिरपेक्ष आंदोलन (एनएएम) ने वैश्विक संघों में एक महत्वपूर्ण अभिनेता बना दिया।

भारतीय अंतरिक्ष अनुसंधान संगठन (इसरो) जैसे भारतीय संस्थानों की बाहरी अंतरिक्ष अन्वेषणों और अन्य देशों के लिए उपग्रहों को लॉन्च करने में सफलता ने भारत की क्षेत्रीय और वैश्विक छवि को प्रभावित किया है।

मोदी 1.0 में हमारे प्रधान मंत्री ने सॉफ्ट पावर के नए तत्वों को मिलाकर भारतीय कूटनीति को नया रूप दिया। सामरिक अर्थों में उपयोग की जाने वाली इस सॉफ्ट पावर के पांच स्तंभ सम्मान, संवाद, समृद्धि (साझा समृद्धि), सुरक्षा (क्षेत्रीय और वैश्विक सुरक्षा), और संस्कृति एवं सभ्यता (सांस्कृतिक और सभ्यतागत) हैं। ये भारत के देश के व्यापक राजनीतिक और आर्थिक लक्ष्यों से जुड़े हुए हैं। अब अपने दूसरे कार्यकाल में, पीएम मोदी ने भारत के राजनीतिक मूल्यों को एक बड़े भू-राजनीतिक संदर्भ में लागू करने पर जोर दिया है और इस विचार पर विशेष जोर दिया है कि भारत 'विश्वगुरु' या विश्व शिक्षक हो सकता है। इसका उद्देश्य 'विकासवाद' के आधार पर एक एशियाई सदी का निर्माण करना है जो शांति और स्थिरता लाएगा। जैसा कि भारत और चीन के बीच 'चेन्नई कनेक्ट' प्रदर्शित करता है, एशिया, दुनिया का सबसे बड़ा महाद्वीप, दुनिया के बाकी हिस्सों में शांति, भाईचारे, सह-अस्तित्व और समृद्धि का संदेश ला रहा है।

सांस्कृतिक बंधन संघर्ष को रोकने और शांति को बढ़ावा देने के तरीकों में से एक हो सकता है। भारत में सांस्कृतिक कूटनीति और सॉफ्ट पावर की खोज MEA की प्रतिष्ठित संस्थागत संरचना, भारतीय सांस्कृतिक संबंध परिषद (ICCR) द्वारा की गई है, जिसे 1950 में शेष दुनिया के साथ भारत के सांस्कृतिक संबंधों को पुनर्जीवित

करने और मजबूत करने के उद्देश्य से स्थापित किया गया था। हमारी विदेश नीति का यह पुनर्विन्यास वास्तव में न केवल हमारे पड़ोस में बल्कि अफ्रीका और लैटिन अमेरिका में हमारे रणनीतिक भागीदारों और नए संवाद भागीदारों के साथ एक सफल विदेश नीति पहल के लिए समय पर और अंतर्निहित था।

सदियों से भारतीय आध्यात्मिकता की वैश्विक उपस्थिति रही है। आज की दुनिया में इसकी एक महत्वपूर्ण अभिव्यक्ति दुनिया भर में फैले बड़ी संख्या में योग केंद्र हैं। 2014 में उनके चुनाव के तुरंत बाद पीएम मोदी की व्यक्तिगत पहल पर, संयुक्त राष्ट्र महासभा ने 21 जून को अंतर्राष्ट्रीय योग दिवस के रूप में मान्यता दी। 21 जून, 2015 से पूरे विश्व में उस दिन को मनाया जा रहा है।

प्रधानमंत्री ने 27 सितंबर, 2014 को संयुक्त राष्ट्र महासभा में योग से संबंधित एक शक्तिशाली प्रस्तुति में यह प्रस्ताव रखा जिसे 11 दिसंबर, 2014 को यूएनजीए के 193 सदस्यों द्वारा अनुमोदित किया गया। उन्होंने कहा, ''योग भारत की प्राचीन परंपरा का एक अमूल्य उपहार है। इसमें शामिल है। मन और शरीर की एकताय विचार और क्रिया, संयम और पूर्ति; मनुष्य और प्रकृति के बीच सामंजस्य; स्वास्थ्य और कल्याण के लिए एक समग्र दृष्टिकोण। यह व्यायाम के बारे में नहीं है, बल्कि अपने आप को, दुनिया और प्रकृति के साथ एकता की भावना की खोज करने के लिए है हमारी जीवनशैली में बदलाव और जागरूकता पैदा करके, यह हमें जलवायु परिवर्तन से निपटने में मदद कर सकता है। आइए हम एक अंतर्राष्ट्रीय योग दिवस को अपनाने की दिशा में काम करें।''

धार्मिक पर्यटन 'बौद्ध सर्किट' सहित भारत की सीमाओं पर इस सॉफ्ट पावर को फैलाने का एक और तरीका है। यह विशुद्ध रूप से आंतरिक शांति के लिए एक यात्रा है। यह पवित्र बौद्ध मंत्रों के रहस्यमय मंत्रों के साथ गूंजते हुए कठोर स्तूपों और प्राचीन मठों के माध्यम से एक यात्रा है। बौद्ध सर्किट के हर बिंदु का इतिहास मिथक और अर्थ में डूबा हुआ है; हर स्मारक वास्तविकता में जुड़े विश्वास की गवाही देता है। संस्कृत में, 'बोध' शब्द का अर्थ है ज्ञान; इस प्रकार बुद्ध का अर्थ होगा 'वह जिसने सभी ज्ञान प्राप्त कर लिया है' या 'वह जिसमें कोई संघर्ष नहीं है, कोई पीड़ा नहीं है', संक्षेप में, जिसने खुद को महारत हासिल कर लिया है। चीनी उसे ज़ेन मास्टर कहते हैं।

एक अन्य उदाहरण 'रामायण सर्किट' है। मई 2018 में, प्रधानमंत्री नरेंद्र मोदी और उनके नेपाली समकक्ष केपी शर्मा ओली ने संयुक्त रूप से जनकपुर (नेपाल)

और अयोध्या (भारत) के बीच सीधी बस सेवा का उद्घाटन किया। स्वदेश दर्शन योजना के तहत 'रामायण सर्किट' थीम के तहत विकास के लिए 15 गंतव्यों की पहचान की गई है। वे अयोध्या, नंदीग्राम, शृंगवेरपुर और चित्रकूट (उत्तर प्रदेश), सीतामढ़ी, बक्सर और दरभंगा (बिहार), चित्रकूट (मध्य प्रदेश), जगदलपुर (छ.ग.), महेंद्रगिरि (ओडिशा), नासिक और नागपुर (महाराष्ट्र), भद्राचलम (तेलंगाना), हंपी (कर्नाटक) और रामेश्वरम (तमिलनाडु) है।

कुछ उदाहरण भारत और बांग्लादेश द्वारा गुरुदेव रवींद्रनाथ टैगोर की 150वीं जयंती और नजरुल की 100वीं जयंती का संयुक्त स्मरणोत्सव हैं। यह अद्वितीय है कि भारतीय और बांग्लादेशी राष्ट्रगान दोनों की रचना रवींद्रनाथ टैगोर ने की है। भारत ने अपने व्यापक पड़ोस में नेपाल, श्रीलंका, भूटान और अन्य राज्यों के साथ जोड़ने के लिए पुराने बौद्ध पर्यटन सर्किट को पुनर्जीवित किया है, जहां बुद्ध के पदचिह्न थे। इस प्रकार, भारत की संस्कृति और सॉफ्ट पावर इस बात का उदाहरण है कि कैसे दोनों राज्यों को आपसी अविश्वास के वर्षों को दूर करने और क्षेत्रीय एकीकरण की प्रक्रिया को आगे बढ़ाने में मदद करते हैं।

अंतर्राष्ट्रीय अनुबंधित श्रम मार्ग परियोजना को यूनेस्को के कार्यकारी बोर्ड द्वारा स्लेव रूट के समान 'मेमोरी ऑफ द वर्ल्ड रजिस्टर' में एक महत्वपूर्ण योगदान के रूप में मान्यता दी गई है। यह दुनिया भर में फैले अपने डायस्पोरा की सांस्कृतिक विविधता में भारत के योगदान पर भी प्रकाश डालता है, जिसमें हमारी मौखिक परंपराएं शामिल हैं, जैसे कि भोजपुरी भाषा और गीत जो अब भी मॉरीशस, गुयाना और सूरीनाम और पूरे कैरिबिय में गाए जाते हैं। वे अपनी महान मातृभूमि भारत की यादों को याद करते हैं और 150 साल पहले इन देशों में लाई गई सांस्कृतिक परंपराओं को जीवित रखते हैं।

भारत की पहचान और उसकी सॉफ्ट पावर के निर्माण में संस्कृत ने महत्वपूर्ण भूमिका निभाई। भारतीय विद्वानों ने लंबे समय से संस्कृत में लगभग 1,60,000 ग्रंथ जमा किए थे। जबकि संस्कृत अपने इतिहास के महत्वपूर्ण हिस्से के लिए परिदृश्य पर हावी थी, अन्य भाषाएं और धर्म धीरे-धीरे भारतीय संस्कृति और परंपरा का एक अविभाज्य हिस्सा बन गए। विशेष रूप से, दुनिया के तीन प्रमुख धर्म हिंदू धर्म, बौद्ध धर्म और सिख धर्म की उत्पत्ति भारत में हुई थी। दुनिया के कई अन्य हिस्सों की तुलना में ईसाई धर्म भारत में बहुत पहले (पहली शताब्दी ईस्वी में) आ गई थी। वेद और वेदांत जैसे शास्त्रों में निहित भारतीय संस्कृति और आध्यात्मिकता ने इस

विविधता को उपयुक्त रूप से समाहित किया है। छांदोग्य उपनिषद में लिखा है, ''एकं सतए विप्र बहुधा वदंती'' सत्य एक है, लेकिन बुद्धिमान इसे अलग-अलग तरीके से बोलते हैं। इसी तरह, ''सर्वे भवन्तु सुखिना सर्वे संतु निरामय। सर्वे भद्राणी पश्यंतु, मां कश्चित दुखभाग भावेतष्''–''सभी सुखी होवें, सभी रोगमुक्त रहें, सभी मंगलमय घटनाओं के साक्षी बनें और किसी को भी दुःख का भागी न बनना पड़े।'' मुंडक उपनिषद कहता हैं, सत्यमेव जयते (भारतीय राष्ट्रीय प्रतीक में भी प्रयुक्त)–''सत्य की ही जीत होती है''। भारतीय परंपरा व्यक्तिगत मूल्यों को सार्वभौमिक मूल्यों के साथ पहचानती है, और धर्म, भाषा, नस्ल या रंग के आधार पर व्यक्तियों को अलग नहीं करती है।

भारत के प्रमुख सॉफ्ट पावर आइकन में से एक स्वामी विवेकानंद थे। 1893 में शिकागो धर्म संसद में अपने संबोधन के बाद 30 वर्ष के युवा स्वामी अचानक प्रसिद्धि के लिए उठे। उन्होंने हिंदू धर्म के प्रतिनिधि के रूप में एक स्थान हासिल किया। जबकि अन्य वक्ताओं ने पारंपरिक शब्दों 'देवियों और सज्जनों' के साथ दर्शकों को संबोधित किया, स्वामी विवेकानंद के शुरुआती शब्द 'अमेरिका के भाइयो और बहनों' ने दर्शकों को प्रभावित किया। स्वामी ने दुनिया भर में हजारों भारतीयों और गैर-भारतीयों को प्रेरित किया। उनके बाद श्री अरबिंदो आए, जिन्होंने ब्रिटेन में शिक्षा प्राप्त की, लेकिन बड़ौदा राज्य में संक्षिप्त सेवा के बाद स्वतंत्रता संग्राम में शामिल होने का फैसला किया। जब 15 अगस्त, 1947 को भारत को स्वतंत्रता मिली, तो श्री अरबिंदो ने अपने रेडियो संदेश में भारत के लिए पांच सपनों की कल्पना की। चौथा, 'दुनिया को भारत का आध्यात्मिक उपहार', जहां 'भारत की आध्यात्मिकता यूरोप और अमेरिका में प्रवेश कर रही है' प्रधानमंत्री मोदी ने 15 अगस्त 2014 को दिल्ली में लाल किले की प्राचीर से अपने पहले स्वतंत्रता दिवस भाषण के दौरान श्री अरबिंदो के इस सपने को याद दिलाया। उन्होंने कहा, ''... आज, 15 अगस्त को, हमारे महर्षि अरबिंदो की जयंती भी है...भारत के भाग्य के संबंध में, उन्होंने टिप्पणी की, 'मुझे विश्वास है कि दिव्य शक्ति और आध्यात्मिक विरासत भारत विश्व के कल्याण की दिशा में एक महत्वपूर्ण भूमिका निभाएगा...मैं किंवदंतियों के शब्दों में दृढ़ता से विश्वास करता हूं।''

निस्संदेह, भारत की सॉफ्ट पावर के सबसे प्रसिद्ध राजदूतों में से एक महात्मा गांधी थे। 21 साल (1893-1914) के लिए दक्षिण अफ्रीका में एक अनिवासी भारतीय, ब्रिटेन के शिक्षित वकील, गांधी ने दक्षिण अफ्रीका में अन्याय के खिलाफ

लड़ते हुए प्रसिद्धि हासिल की। गांधी ने दक्षिण अफ्रीका में अपने संघर्ष के दौरान सत्य और अहिंसा के सिद्धांतों को प्रसिद्ध किया और ब्रिटिश शासन के खिलाफ भारत में उनका अभ्यास किया। उन्होंने दुनिया भर के हजारों स्वतंत्रता सेनानियों को प्रेरित किया, और अप्रैल 1947 में नई दिल्ली में एशियाई संबंध सम्मेलन के दौरान 'एशियाई मार्ग' का आह्वान किया, जब उन्होंने कहा,...पूर्व का संदेश, एशिया का संदेश, यूरोपीय चश्मे से, पश्चिमी चश्मे के माध्यम से नहीं सीखा जाना चाहिए... यदि आप पश्चिम को फिर से संदेश देना चाहते हैं, तो यह ' 'प्रेम' का संदेश होना चाहिए, यह 'सत्य' का संदेश होना चाहिए। मार्टिन लूथर किंग जूनियर ने महात्मा गांधी को ''अहिंसक सामाजिक परिवर्तन की हमारी तकनीक का मार्गदर्शक प्रकाश'' के रूप में संदर्भित किया, और 1959 में अपनी भारत यात्रा के दौरान, एक रेडियो संबोधन में कहा, 'एक वास्तविक अर्थ में, महात्मा गांधी ने अवतार लिया। उनके जीवन में कुछ सार्वभौमिक सिद्धांत हैं जो ब्रह्मांड की नैतिक संरचना में निहित हैं, और ये सिद्धांत गुरुत्वाकर्षण के नियम के समान अपरिहार्य हैं।''

आयुर्वेद (जिसका अनुवाद 'जीवन का विज्ञान' के रूप में किया जा सकता है), एक प्राचीन प्रथा, एक अन्य भारतीय सॉफ्ट पावर उपकरण है। 'आयुर्वेद वेदों की शाखाओं में से एक है। चरक, जिनकी *चरक संहिता* को आयुर्वेद के प्रमुख ग्रंथों में से एक माना जाता है। आयुर्वेद विकसित दुनिया में तेजी से लोकप्रिय हो गया है, और इसे योग के संयोजन के रूप में देखा जाता है। वर्तमान में, दुनिया भर में लगभग 2,000 आयुर्वेदिक रिट्रीट केंद्र हैं, जिनमें से लगभग 100 केंद्र संयुक्त राज्य अमेरिका में स्थित हैं। एसोसिएशन ऑफ आयुर्वेदिक प्रोफेशनल्स ऑफ नॉर्थ अमेरिका (AAPNA) (2016) का उद्देश्य 'आयुर्वेद के उपचार विज्ञान और इसके तौर तरीकों को पश्चिम में एकीकृत चिकित्सा में सबसे आगे लाना' है। नवंबर 2014 में भारत सरकार ने नवंबर 2003 में स्थापित आयुर्वेद, योग और प्राकृतिक चिकित्सा, यूनानी, सिद्ध और होम्योपैथी विभाग को एक पूर्ण मंत्रालय में अपग्रेड किया।

भारत का फिल्म उद्योग, बॉलीवुड, दुनिया में सबसे अधिक फिल्मों का निर्माता है और अफगानिस्तान, पाकिस्तान, मध्य एशिया, मध्य पूर्व, दक्षिण-पूर्व एशिया और दुनिया के कई अन्य हिस्सों में लोकप्रिय है। शशि थरूर एक उदाहरण का हवाला देते हुए बताते है कि सीरिया में हाफ़िज़ अल असद के शासन के दौरान, तत्कालीन बॉलीवुड सुपरस्टार अमिताभ बच्चन का आदमकद चित्र अल असद जितना बड़ा था। अक्टूबर 2008, इंडोनेशिया में जाकार्ता के बटाविया क्षेत्र में घूमते हुए, एक

स्थानीय ने लेखक के साथ बातचीत शुरू की और यह जानते हुए कि लेखक भारत से है, उन्होंने भारतीय फिल्म सितारों मिथुन चक्रवर्ती और अमिताभ बच्चन के नामों का उल्लेख किया, जिनके वे प्रशंसक थे। शीत युद्ध के दौर में राज कपूर जैसे फिल्मी सितारों ने भारत और अन्य देशों के बीच सेतु का काम किया। राज कपूर और उनकी *आवारा* और *मेरा नाम जोकर* जैसी फिल्में सोवियत संघ में बेहद लोकप्रिय थीं। मध्य पूर्व में, भारतीय फिल्में दिनों तक चलती हैं, और प्रवासी फिल्मों को लोकप्रिय बनाने में सक्रिय भूमिका निभाते हैं। संयुक्त राज्य अमेरिका जैसे देशों में, भारतीय प्रवासी की बढ़ती मांगों को पूरा करने के लिए मल्टीप्लेक्स में हिंदी फिल्मों का चलन बढ़ रहा है। बॉलीवुड के साथ-साथ भारतीय संगीत और सांस्कृतिक तत्वों जैसे नृत्य और नाटक ने भी भारत की छवि को एक सॉफ्ट पावर के रूप में बढ़ाने में भूमिका निभाई है। उदाहरण के लिए, यूएसए स्थित बॉलीवुड अमेरिका, सालाना नृत्य और अन्य सांस्कृतिक कार्यक्रमों का आयोजन करता है। संगठन का उद्देश्य दुनिया में 'दक्षिण एशियाई संस्कृति की विविधता और परंपरा में रुचि का जश्न मनाना और फैलाना' है। लोकप्रिय स्मृति भारतीय सितार वादक रविशंकर और योगी योगानंद के साथ बीटल्स की दोस्ती को संजोती है। और, जोड़ने के लिए, कई भारतीय अभिनेता हॉलीवुड फिल्मों के साथ साथ टेलीविजन शो का भी हिस्सा बन रहे हैं।

भारतीय भोजन, सॉफ्ट पावर का एक अन्य तत्व, दुनिया के विभिन्न हिस्सों में तेजी से लोकप्रिय हो रहा है। ज्यादातर जगहों पर भारतीय रेस्टोरेंट आसानी से मिल जाता है। उल्लेखनीय है कि अन्य दक्षिण एशियाई देशों के कई रेस्तरां मालिक अपने भोजनालयों का नाम भारतीय रखते हैं। भारतीय मसाले भी दुनिया भर के कई गैर भारतीय घरों में पहुंच चुके हैं। समोसा, चाट, चिकन टिक्का, मसाला, मसाला डोसा, करी और ऐसे कई भारतीय व्यंजनों ने दुनिया भर में पैठ बना ली है।

भारतीय मसालों ने *मिस्ट्रेस ऑफ़ स्पाइसेस* और *टुडेज़ स्पेशल* जैसी फ़िल्मों में और उदाहरण के लिए आउटसोर्स्ड और *द बिग बैंग* थ्योरी जैसे टेलीविज़न शो की पूरी मेजबानी करके लोकप्रिय कल्पना पर कब्जा कर लिया है। कबाब, चिकन टिक्का मसाला, बिरयानी, करी सहित भारतीय भोजन, मसाला डोसा और यहां तक कि नान भी यूके, कनाडा, मध्य-पूर्व, अमेरिका और यहां तक कि चीन जैसे स्थानों में बेहद लोकप्रिय और उपलब्ध हैं यह भारत के विदेश में अपने भोजन के माध्यम से सॉफ्ट पावर को दर्शाता है। 2003 की एक रिपोर्ट के अनुसार, यूनाइटेड किंगडम में लगभग 1,000 भारतीय करी हाउस हैं, जिनमें लगभग 7,0000 कर्मचारी कार्यरत हैं।

यूनाइटेड किंगडम में भारतीय खाद्य उद्योग 3.2 बिलियन पाउंड का है और कुल खाने का दो-तिहाई हिस्सा है। लंदन में, मुंबई और दिल्ली की तुलना में अधिक भारतीय रेस्तरां हैं और ब्रिटेन में भारतीय रेस्तरां हर हफ्ते लगभग 2.5 मिलियन ग्राहकों को सेवा प्रदान करते हैं।

ऐतिहासिक दृष्टि से भारत की सॉफ्ट पावर पश्चिम की ओर नहीं बल्कि शेष विश्व की ओर निर्देशित थी। भारत और शेष एशिया के बीच सदियों पुराने संबंधों का एक मजबूत सांस्कृतिक और संचार आयाम है और बौद्ध धर्म इस बातचीत के केंद्र में था : बौद्ध धर्म भारतीय विचारों के प्रसार की सबसे बड़ी परियोजना थी। नौवीं शताब्दी में प्रकाशित संस्कृत पाठ *वज्रछेदिका प्रज्ञापारमिता सूत्र* (डायमंड सूत्र), कागज पर दुनिया की पहली मुद्रित पुस्तक का चीनी में अनुवाद एक बौद्ध पाठ था। प्रतिष्ठित भारत आधारित चीनी विद्वान के रूप में, तान चुंग ने सुझाव दिया है : "बौद्ध धर्म ने महायान का कार्य किया, जो कि 'महान वाहक' (चीन में सर्वोत्कृष्ट भारतीय सभ्यता को ले जाने वाला) है," जिसके परिणामस्वरूप 'ऐतिहासिक चिंदियन प्रतिमान' हुआ। उन्होंने नोट किया कि 'चीन में भारतीय सभ्यता का आगमन निमंत्रण से हुआ था," जबकि "व्यापार एक अभूतपूर्व अंतर-सांस्कृतिक संयुक्त उद्यम था, यानी संस्कृत चीनी अनुवाद उद्यम"। बौद्ध दर्शन में रुचि वृद्ध चीनी विद्वानों, विशेष रूप से ह्वेन त्सांग को कानून, दर्शन और राजनीति पर विचारों का आदान-प्रदान करने के लिए नालंदा (5 वीं और 12 वीं शताब्दी के बीच पूवी भारत में स्थित एक अंतर्राष्ट्रीय बौद्ध विश्वविद्यालय) जाने के लिए प्रोत्साहित करती है। "वास्तव में भारतीय बौद्धिक जीवन का केंद्र" के रूप में वर्णित, विश्वविद्यालय ने "पूरे बौद्ध एशिया में" भारतीय संस्कृति को प्रसारित किया। भारतीय भिक्षुओं ने भी नियमित रूप से चीन का दौरा किया और ये बौद्धिक आदान-प्रदान सदियों तक जारी रहे, और आज भी बौद्ध धर्म दो सभ्यताओं के बीच एक शक्तिशाली कड़ी बना हुआ है।

भारत सरकार भी देश की सॉफ्ट पावर को बढ़ावा देने में सीधी भूमिका निभाती है। भारतीय सांस्कृतिक संबंध परिषद (ICCR) के मिस्त्र, जर्मनी सहित लगभग 37 देशों में केंद्र हैं। रूस, चीन और मैक्सिको, सबसे प्रमुख लंदन में लंबे समय तक चलने वाला नेहरू केंद्र है। ये केंद्र उन कार्यक्रमों के आयोजन पर ध्यान केंद्रित करते हैं जिनका उद्देश्य भारत के लोगों के सांस्कृतिक ज्ञान को बढ़ाना है। आने वाले महीनों में 'अंडरस्टैंडिंग इंडिया' और 'डेस्टिनेशन इंडिया' जैसी और पहलें भी शुरू

होने वाली हैं। भारत के लिए प्रशंसा बटोरने के लिए सार्वजनिक ज्ञान का उपयोग करने के अलावा, सरकार अपने डायस्पोरा को एक मान्यता प्राप्त सॉफ्ट पावर संसाधन से भी जोड़ती है। प्रवासी भारतीय दिवस (पीबीडी) जैसे सम्मेलन, जो 2003 से प्रतिवर्ष मनाया जाता है। ये सम्मेलन प्रवासी भारतीय समुदाय के साथ जुड़ने के लिए गतिविधियों और संवाद का उपयोग करते हैं, यह सुनिश्चित करते हुए कि वे देश के विशाल सॉफ्ट पावर संसाधनों की याद दिलाते हुए एक साथ शामिल महसूस करते हैं। भारत में हो रहे ऐसे सम्मेलनों के अलावा, प्रवासी भारतीय दिवस एक क्षेत्रीय स्तर पर भी आयोजित किए जाते हैं। अतीत में, प्रवासी भारतीयों के लिए एक आउटरीच के रूप में कार्य करते हुए, कनाडा, दक्षिण अफ्रीका और संयुक्त राज्य अमेरिका जैसे देशों में पीबीडी आयोजित किए गए हैं। विशेष रूप से, इन आयोजनों में अक्सर मेजबान देश के संसद सदस्य भी शामिल होते हैं। विश्व स्तर पर भारतीय संस्कृति को बढ़ावा देने के अलावा, भारत सरकार की विदेश नीति भी स्वाभाविक रूप से अपने पड़ोस को बहुत महत्व देती है। एक्ट ईस्ट पॉलिसी जैसी नीतियां। नेबरहुड फर्स्ट पॉलिसी और कनेक्ट सेंट्रल एशिया पॉलिसी, सभी में एक महत्वपूर्ण सॉफ्ट पावर घटक है। विदेश मंत्रालय के पास एक सार्वजनिक कूटनीति प्रभाग है जिसके पास सॉफ्ट पावर तत्वों के लिए विशिष्ट जिम्मेदारी है।

अपनी लोकतांत्रिक ताकत के समान, तकनीकी मामलों और अंतरिक्ष कूटनीति में भारत की प्रमुखता एक अन्य मुख्य रूप से राज्य द्वारा संचालित सॉफ्ट पावर संसाधन है जिसमें अपार संभावनाएं हैं। 2013 में अपने मंगलयान मिशन और 2017 में पीएसएलवी-सी37 (एक राकेट में 104 उपग्रह) के प्रक्षेपण के साथ, भारत की अंतरिक्ष पहल ने दुनिया भर में सराहना प्राप्त की है—विशेष रूप से, दक्षिण एशियाई उपग्रह (जिसे पहले सार्क उपग्रह कहा जाता है) का प्रक्षेपण। भारतीय अंतरिक्ष अनुसंधान संगठन द्वारा, जो है इसका उद्देश्य पाकिस्तान को छोड़कर सभी सार्क देशों के उद्देश्यों की पूर्ति करना है। भारत की असाधारण अंतरिक्ष प्रौद्योगिकी इस प्रकार विकासशील देशों को उपग्रहों को लॉन्च करने के लिए सस्ता और अधिक लागत प्रभावी विकल्प प्रदान करती है, और दक्षिण एशियाई उपग्रह के मामले में, एक सामान्य उपग्रह के लाभों को पुनः प्राप्त करने के लिए। दक्षिण एशियाई उपग्रह के लिए, सदस्य देशों को केवल अपने स्वतंत्र ऑपरेटिंग ग्राउंड सिस्टम की लागत वहन करनी पड़ती है, जबकि उपग्रह के प्रबंधन के लिए एक अंतर-सरकारी टीम का हिस्सा बनने के लिए प्रतिनिधियों को भेजने का अवसर होता है। यह सभी सदस्य

देशों के लिए फायदेमंद है, विशेष रूप से भूटान और मालदीव जैसे जिनके पास अपने स्वयं के अंतरिक्ष कार्यक्रम नहीं हैं और भारत के उदाहरण का अनुकरण करने का लक्ष्य रखते हैं। यदि प्रभावी ढंग से उपयोग किया जाता है, तो भारत की अंतरिक्ष कूटनीति दक्षिण एशिया के भीतर और अंतर्राष्ट्रीय स्तर पर वैश्विक दक्षिण में अपने हितों को आगे बढ़ाने और द्विपक्षीय और बहुपक्षीय संबंधों को मजबूत करने में मदद कर सकती है। इसके अलावा, इसके उपग्रह आपदा प्रबंधन से निपटने में भी मदद कर सकते हैं, एक ऐसा गुण जो जलवायु परिवर्तन जैसे शक्तिशाली मुद्दों के लिए आवश्यक है। इसका एक उदाहरण उपग्रह सक्षम चक्रवात चेतावनी केंद्र और अन्य रिमोट सेंसिंग सुविधाएं हो सकती हैं, जिन्होंने प्राकृतिक आपदाओं को रोकने में मदद की है और इस प्रकार पर्याप्त कार्रवाई करने की अनुमति दी है। नई दिल्ली की पड़ोस की पहली विदेश नीति पहल के अनुरूप, ये सुविधाएं भारत के पड़ोसियों को शामिल करने के लिए अपना दायरा बढ़ा सकती हैं। इस तरह के उपायों से न केवल इस क्षेत्र को पर्यावरणीय स्तर पर लाभ होगा, बल्कि इस क्षेत्र के भीतर भारत की भूमिका को मजबूत करने में भी मदद मिलेगी। इस प्रकार अंतरिक्ष कूटनीति में काफी संभावनाएं हैं; यह भारत का एक पहलू है जिसका उपयोग दुनिया में इसे आगे बढ़ाने के लिए किया जा सकता है।

भारत का विभिन्न एशियाई देशों के साथ एक सभ्यतागत जुड़ाव है जिसका उपयोग वह दुनिया में अपनी स्थिति बढ़ाने के लिए कर सकता है। बौद्ध धर्म—जिसकी उत्पत्ति भारत में हुई—जापान, अधिकांश दक्षिण-पूर्व एशिया और नेपाल में व्यापक रूप से लोकप्रिय है। इन देशों में बौद्ध धर्म का विशाल प्रभाव उन्हें भारत के साथ एक आध्यात्मिक संबंध प्रदान करता है, जिसकी संस्कृति ऐतिहासिक रूप से बौद्ध शिक्षाओं के माध्यम से प्रसारित हुई है। बोधगया, जिसे बुद्ध को ज्ञान की प्राप्ति का स्थान कहा जाता है, सबसे महत्वपूर्ण बौद्ध तीर्थ स्थलों में से एक है। लेकिन यूपी में सारनाथ समेत कई और हैं।

भारतीय डायस्पोरा (हम भारतीय नागरिकों और भारतीय मूल के लोगों को एक साथ इस उद्देश्य के लिए समूहित करते हैं) को विदेशों में भारत की स्थिति को बढ़ाने में एक बड़ी भूमिका है। इसमें सीमाओं को लांघकर बातचीत को सुगम बनाने और सहयोग बढ़ाने की शक्ति है। कॉरपोरेट दिग्गजों के कई सीईओ भारतीय हैं या रहे हैं सूचना प्रौद्योगिकी की दुनिया में, भारतीयों या भारतीय मूल के अधिकारियों के पास Google, Microsoft और Adobe सहित कुछ सबसे बड़े निगमों के

प्रमुख भारतीय हैं। अंग्रेजी भाषी दुनिया में शीर्ष शैक्षणिक संस्थानों और थिंक टैंकों में मात्रा और गुणवत्ता के मामले में भारतीय संकाय और छात्रों की महत्वपूर्ण उपस्थिति है। हार्वर्ड बिजनेस स्कूल के डीनए एमआईटी में अर्थशास्त्र के लिए हाल ही में नोबेल पुरस्कार विजेता, शिकागो में आरबीआई के पूर्व गवर्नर, कुछ साल पहले रसायन विज्ञान के लिए नोबेल पुरस्कार विजेता, सभी प्रकाशकों की इस लंबी सूची में हैं।

निष्कर्ष

सॉफ्ट पावर की अवधारणा को दुनिया के सामने पेश करते समय, न्ये ने तर्क दिया कि ''एजेंडा निर्धारित करना और विश्व राजनीति में स्थितियों की संरचना करना उतना ही महत्वपूर्ण है जितना कि विशेष मामलों में दूसरों को बदलना।'' सॉफ्ट पावर एक राष्ट्र को एजेंडा तय करने में मदद कर सकती है और सौदेबाजी की मेज पर आने से पहले दूसरे राष्ट्र की पसंद को बदल देने की क्षमता रखता है।

भारत के पास महत्वपूर्ण सॉफ्ट पावर संसाधन हैं और वास्तव में, उन कुछ देशों में से एक है जो पश्चिम को वैकल्पिक राजनीतिक, आर्थिक और सांस्कृतिक मॉडल प्रदान करने में सक्षम है। भारत की सॉफ्ट पावर वैश्विक स्तर और आंतरिक सुधारों पर निर्भर करता है जो लगातार विकास, सामाजिक और राजनीतिक कमियों को दूर करने में मदद करेगा। भारत की सॉफ्ट पावर व्यापक स्तर पर के आयाम बदले नहीं है सिर्फ विदेश नीति के संदर्भ में सॉफ्ट पावर के प्रति जागरूकता बढ़ी है। राजनीतिक वर्ग उन संसाधनों का उपयोग विदेश नीति के लक्ष्यों को प्राप्त करने के लिए कर रहा है। यद्यपि सॉफ्ट पावर उपकरण के तौर पर स्वतंत्रता के बाद से ही उपयोग में लाया जाने लगा था परन्तु 1990 के दशक में वैश्वीकरण के आगमन से सॉफ्ट पावर पर ध्यान और विदेश नीति में उपयोग तेजी से दिखाई देने लगा था। भारत की विदेश नीति में सांस्कृतिक संसाधनों के प्रति जागरूकता और उपयोगिता की गति बढ़ रही है। अंतर्राष्ट्रीय राजनीति में, जहां राज्य की यथार्थवादी धारणा से राज्य संबंधों का बोलबाला रहता है, भारत की सॉफ्ट पावर हार्ड पावर के समर्थन के बिना पर्याप्त लाभ प्रदान नहीं कर सकती है। नरम और कठोर शक्ति दोनों का उद्देश्य राष्ट्रीय हितों को साकार करना है। 2000 के दशक के मध्य से, भारत ने सॉफ्ट पावर के निर्माण के द्वारा अपनी सार्वजनिक कूटनीति में सुधार किया है जिसमें ICCR द्वारा आयोजित सांस्कृतिक आदान-प्रदान और नए तरीकों का उपयोग करना, जैसे मीडिया और सोशल मीडिया द्वारा अतुल्य भारत जैसे कार्यक्रमों द्वारा विश्व को

भारत के प्रति आकर्षित करना शामिल है।

सॉफ्ट पावर की अवधारणा भारत की विदेश नीति पर एक अलग प्रकाश डालने में मदद करता है। भारत में कई विशेषताएं हैं जो देश को इक्कीसवीं सदी की भविष्य की सॉफ्ट पावर में से एक के रूप में योग्य बनाती हैं। परंतु क्षेत्रीय और वैश्विक दोनों स्तर पर क्षमताओं और क्षमताओं को देखते हुए तस्वीर मिश्रित हो जाती है क्षेत्रीय और वैश्विक स्तर पर, भारतीय विदेश नीति-निर्माताओं ने हाल के वर्षों में सॉफ्ट पावर के लाभों की खोज की है। भारत रक्षात्मक सॉफ्ट पावर के रूप में कार्य करता है और देश के अंतर्राष्ट्रीय प्रभाव को बढ़ाने के लिए अपनी क्षमताओं को बदलने के लिए अनिच्छुक है। भारत ने सॉफ्ट पावर संसाधनों का उपयोग अपनी छवि बनाने के लिए अधिक करा है। लेकिन इस असाधारण वैश्विक क्षण को समय पर भुनाने के लिए एक महत्वाकांक्षी और सकारात्मक योजना के साथ आने के हमारे सर्वोत्तम प्रयासों के बावजूद, यह स्पष्ट है कि भारत में वर्तमान में अपनी सॉफ्ट पावर के सफल प्रचार के लिए एक सक्षम वातावरण का अभाव है।

इस बात से इनकार नहीं किया जा सकता है कि देश की ताकत बढ़ रही है; लाभकारी मूर्त परिणाम सुनिश्चित करने के लिए भारत को अपनी सॉफ्ट पावर में समान वृद्धि के साथ इसे पूरक करने की आवश्यकता है। वर्तमान स्थिति को उबारने के लिए, भारत को अपनी वैधता खोने से बचने के लिए बहुआयामी दृष्टिकोण का उपयोग करना होगा—शायद अपनी हार्ड और सॉफ्ट पावर को एक स्मार्ट पावर पहल में संयोजित करने पर ध्यान केंद्रित करके। उदाहरण के लिए, यह दुनिया भर में अपने आर्थिक प्रभाव का विस्तार करना जारी रख सकता है, जबकि अपने डायस्पोरा के साथ संबंधों को मजबूत करने और राजनयिक पहुंच में सुधार करने पर भी ध्यान केंद्रित कर सकता है। शक्ति का लाभ उठाने के लिए भारत के विशाल बाजार का उपयोग करने से नई संभावनाएं भी मिलती हैं, हालांकि इसके लिए देश को पश्चिमी निवेशकों के लिए अपने अधिनियमों में सुधार करने की आवश्यकता होगी—विशेष रूप से मानव अधिकारों और पर्यावरण संरक्षण के क्षेत्र में। इसी तरह, विदेशों में एफडीआई का उपयोग करना लाभ उठाने के एक बिंदु के रूप में महत्वहीन नहीं है और एक संयुक्त स्मार्ट पावर पहल के एक हिस्से में प्रकट हो सकता है। हालांकि तब तक, भारत के लिए यह अधिक यथार्थवादी है कि वह गैर राज्य अभिनेताओं पर भरोसा करके वर्षों में बनाए गए में सॉफ्ट पावर लाभ को बनाए रखने पर अपना वर्तमान ध्यान केंद्रित करे।

सन्दर्भ ग्रन्थ

1. Pradhan, Ramakrushna & Mohapatra, Atanu. (2020). *India's diaspora policy: evidence of soft power diplomacy under Modi.* South Asian Diaspora.
2. Wagner, Christian. (2010). *India's Soft Power Prospects and Limitations.* India Quarterly, SAGE Publications.
3. Mahapatra, Debidatta Aurobinda. (2016). *From a latent to a 'strong' soft power? The evolution of India's cultural diplomacy.* Palgrave Communications.
4. Hall, Ian. (2012). *India's New Public Diplomacy: Soft Power and the Limits of Government Action.* Asian Survey.
5. HYMANS, ACQUES E. C.(2009). India's Soft Power and Vulnerability. India Review.
6. Gupta, Amit. (2014). *Commentary on India's Soft Power and Diaspora.* International Journal on World Peace.
7. Mazumdar, Arijit. (2018). India's Soft Power Diplomacy Under the Modi Administration: *Buddhism, Diaspora and Yoga.* Asian Affairs.
8. Tharoor, Shashi. (2008). *India as a Soft Power.* India International Centre Quarterly.
9. Khanna, Shrey & Moorthy, P. (2017). *Analysing India's Soft Power Functioning in the Twenty-first Century: Possibilities and Challenges. Indian Council of World Affairs* (ICWA), SAGE Publications.
10. Tufail Ahmad, Peerzada. (2020). *Critical Analysis of India's Soft Power Capability.* Research Review International Journal of Multidisciplinary.
11. Blarel, Nicolas. (2012). *India the next superpower?: India's soft power: from potential to reality.* LSE Research Online.
12. Shetty, Salil & Sahgal, Tara. (2019). *India's Soft Power: Challenges and Opportunities.* Rajiv Gandhi Institute for Contemporary Studies.
13. Kumar, Nabin. (2018). *Understanding of India's Soft Power Dynamics.* Asian Review of Social Sciences.
14. Nye Joseph S, (2004), *Soft Power : The Means to Success in World Politics,* New York, Public Affairs.
15. Thussu Daya Kishan, (2013), *Communicating India's Soft Power: Buddha to Bollywood,* New York, Palgrave Macmillan.
16. Kugiel Patryk, (2017), *India's Soft Power : A New Foreign Policy Strategy,* New York, Routledge.
17. MEA. (2019). *"India's culture Diplomacy and Soft Power."* Ministry of External Affairs.Govt of India.